Cuss 9/03

MARCHING ON WASHINGTON

MARCHING ON WASHINGTON

The Forging of an American Political Tradition

LUCY G. BARBER

UNIVERSITY OF CALIFORNIA PRESS
Berkeley · *Los Angeles* · *London*

University of California Press
Berkeley and Los Angeles, California

University of California Press, Ltd.
London, England

© 2002 by
The Regents of the University of California

Library of Congress Cataloging-in-Publication Data

Barber, Lucy G. (Lucy Grace), 1964–.
   Marching on Washington : the forging of an American
political tradition / Lucy G. Barber.
      p. cm.
   Includes bibliographical references (p.) and index.
   ISBN 0-520-22713-1 (alk. paper)
   1. United States—Politics and government—20th
century. 2. United States—Politics and government—
1865–1900. 3. Demonstrations—Washington (D.C.)—
History—20th century. 4. Civil rights movements—
United States—History—20th century. 5. Social
movements—United States—History—20th century
6. Political participation—United States—History—
20th century. 7. Political culture—United States—
History—20th century. 8. Mall, The (Washington,
D.C.)—History—20th century. 9. Washington (D.C.)—
Politics and government—1878–1967. 10. Washington,
(D.C.)—Politics and government—1967–1995. I. Title.

E743.B338 2002
975.3—dc21   2002011193

Manufactured in the United States of America

10 09 08 07 06 05 04 03

10 9 8 7 6 5 4 3 2 1

The paper used in this publication meets the minimum
requirements of ANSI/NISO Z39.48–1992 (R 1997)
(*Permanence of Paper*). ⊛

To my parents, Putnam Barber and Patricia Holland, who marched for me and with me

CONTENTS

ILLUSTRATIONS

FIGURES

MAPS

PREFACE

It is spring. I am six and half years old. I am in Washington, D.C. I am at my first march on Washington. I do not remember that day in April 1971, though I can relive it by watching the home movies my father shot of our family's participation in this protest against the Vietnam War. I can watch myself stand in the midst of marching people. I see myself holding a sign demanding "Out Now." Marchers notice my father's camera and turn, smile, flash a peace sign. More than 200,000 other people were also in Washington, also marching down Pennsylvania Avenue, also listening with mixed degrees of attention to the speakers on the steps of the Capitol. It may have been my first march on Washington, but for many others in the crowd, this was only the latest in a series of marches in which they had participated. By 1971, the act of protesting in the capital of the United States had become an American tradition.

When I began exploring the history of marches on Washington, I was not really thinking about my father's movies, my experiences that day, or of that specific anti-war protest. I never intended this book to be a personal memoir of protesting in Washington. Rather, I wanted to tell a story that was unfamiliar and unavailable to most: the history of marches on Washington from the first attempt in 1894 to the institutionalization of such protests in the 1960s. Now, after much time poring through files in archives, reading old newspapers and current memoirs, and examining photographs, cartoons, newsreels, and even pulp fiction about marches on Washington, I am still focused on the practical process and political ramifications of that transformation. This focus means that I have emphasized the points of view of three sets of major decision makers whose negotiations shaped these events. By describing the efforts of organizers, the responses of authorities, and the coverage of journalists, I explore how these demonstrations used and challenged notions of American citizenship to make a powerful claim to the public spaces of the capital.

This broader sense of history has helped me reflect on the experiences of ordinary marchers, like myself. Now, I treasure in a new way that home movie and my memories of other demonstrations I attended. Like many other Americans, I have responded to specific marches on Washington with a very personal sense of connection. Millions of Americans have taken part in these protests. Millions more have watched on television or read about them in newspapers. Depending on our political sensibilities, some marches inspire us and others infuriate us. Nonetheless, marching in the capital is a political and personal tactic that people now see as a given in American culture.

Today, when I participate in a march or catch a glimpse of one in the news, I see that protesters use the streets and parks of our nation's capital in ways marked by their predecessors. The pathways created by these earlier activists have also changed our country's political landscape. My hope is that this book will both invoke other people's memories and challenge them to think about what role these demonstrations have had and should have in our country's politics.

INTRODUCTION

When A. Philip Randolph, a lifelong activist for the equality of African Americans, spoke at the March on Washington for Jobs and Freedom in 1963, he asked the quarter of a million marchers who had gathered around the Lincoln Memorial to consider "the meaning of our numbers." His answer reflected his particular political ambitions: "We are the advance guard of a massive moral revolution for jobs and freedom." But his defiant rejection of labels used to marginalize previous protesters in the capital—"pressure group" or "group of organizations" or "mob"—showed his confidence that this group of protesters had political legitimacy. Randolph's question and his confidence are critical to understanding the history of marches on Washington. Today, people living in the United States are so familiar with the tactic that they only occasionally probe the significance of people protesting in the capital. Of course, some gatherings with large turnouts and extensive publicity campaigns—such as the Million Man March or the Promisekeepers' Stand in the Gap—attract media attention, presidential comments, and public debates. In other cases, however, only the participants or those who read Washington newspapers carefully may know a protest has occurred. Whether the protests are noticed or not, that people choose to march on Washington seems unremarkable to most Americans. Less familiar is how the tactic became so entrenched in the American political system.[1]

In 1894, the first "march on Washington" was a mystery for observers.

They did not know what to make of this concerted effort by citizens to claim the capital for national public protest. On May 1, 1894, thousands of Washington, D.C., residents crowded the sidewalks of Pennsylvania Avenue. They watched intently as more than five hundred ragged men did their best to march in precise ranks. As the horse riders, carriages, and marchers filed by, exuding a mixture of respectability and scruffiness, spectators cheered. The roar of applause echoed the vigorous debate surrounding these visitors to the capital. Some residents supported the group's right to march on Washington and even their call for federal action to help the victims of the ongoing economic crisis. Others worried that the group they called Coxey's Army might disrupt the city's peace. Though this tired band of men posed no realistic military challenge to the city's residents or the nation's government, some observers, including members of Congress and President Grover Cleveland, saw the demonstration as a serious threat to the national political order.

Critics of the tactic of marching on Washington feared—correctly, it turned out—that Coxey's Army might inspire many organized protests in the capital of the United States. Before Coxey's Army even reached the District of Columbia, a senator cautioned his colleagues that if they tolerated this march, "it is quite possible . . . that it may become a habit to make pilgrimages annually to Washington and endeavor to dominate Congress by the physical presence of the people." More than a century later, some of what the senator predicted has happened. Since 1894, millions of people have marched on Washington.[2]

When I began exploring the history of marches on Washington, I thought that the story would be relatively easy to tell. By exploring how ambitious, skillful, and daring organizers challenged the government for the right to protest in Washington during the twentieth century, I would counter prevailing assumptions at the end of the twentieth century that ordinary people no longer influence national politics. The story turned out to be more complex but also more interesting. Two intertwined and interrelated themes became the focus of my narrative: the changing spatial politics of the capital and the strategic uses of American citizenship. With these lenses, the history of marching on Washington is a story of spaces lost and spaces won. It is a story about the power of American citizens but also about the shifting terrain of citizenship. It is a story about the possibilities and the limits of the tradition of marching on Washington for changing national politics.

What was seen as outside the political order in 1894 has become, more than a century later, an accepted, even routine, gesture in American political culture. It is this change—from the unheard of to the common—that I narrate in the following chapters. Today, marches are so well accepted that some observers criticize them as meaningless, ineffective, or distracting. I disagree. It is true that marches on Washington do not always result in immediate political victories for the organizers and supporters of protests. The success of the marches, though, has been the creation of what I call "national public spaces" in the American capital, centered on the Mall but including Pennsylvania Avenue and most of the Capitol grounds. Participants in social movements today can use these spaces for large marches on Washington. It has become a place where groups of citizens can project their plans and demands on national government, where they can build support for their causes, and where they can act out their own visions of national politics. The visible public controversies embodied in these demonstrations improve American politics by energizing political debate on terms set by the people and the organizations they support. The events, in turn, spark wider debates over policy, the appropriate ways for citizens to influence politics, and the effectiveness and legitimacy of the federal government. Thus, by creating a tradition of marching on Washington, organizers, authorities, and other observers have won a "place" for American citizens in the nation's capital.

Before 1894, there was no national public space available for popular protest in the American capital. Many European nations had long traditions of protest in their capital cities, traditions that predated the founding of the United States in the late eighteenth century. During the first hundred years after the District of Columbia was created in 1791, however, most Americans imagined the capital as a symbol of representative government and its landscape exclusively as the site for the operating and celebrating of that government. This view and use of the District's streets and parks faced practical obstacles, but few frontal challenges, before the 1890s.

During the imperial crisis that led to the Revolutionary War, colonists demonstrated their displeasure at merchants and government officials much as they or their relatives had done in Europe. Before the outbreak of any clear hostilities between colonists and the English government, dissatisfied residents resorted regularly to the tried method of the "moral crowd," in which a group of aggrieved people would gather, often burn in effigy the person deemed responsible for the problem or seize the goods whose prices caused outrage, and demand satisfaction. Quite often, the demands were met. This moral crowd generally respected the authority of the government, and elected officials sometimes considered such actions an essential gauge of public opinion. Not surprisingly, though, as colonists began to challenge the legitimacy of British authority, official acceptance faded and crowds became a potent political challenge to British imperial power. Actions such as the Boston Tea Party used symbols unique to the colonists, demonstrated clear defiance of the authority of the government, and served as important rituals on the path to revolution.[3] As these protests propelled the crisis toward war, the leading politicians among the colonists constructed elaborate defenses of the right of the people to protest.

When the victorious revolutionaries established national, state, and local governments, their tolerance of public protest diminished. In the early days of the new nation, magistrates often forcibly repressed spontaneous crowds. Many states and cities passed laws regulating the right to assemble. These restrictions did not end such protests but did limit their size and increase the potential risks to participants.[4] This growing disenchantment with popular protest affected the purpose and location of the national capital.

The delegates to the Constitutional Convention determined that Congress was to consist of elected representatives who had the freedom to debate and the power to make policy. Most of the founders of the United States government believed the capital should be an isolated official "district" suited for calm reflection by the elected representatives of the nation. For them, the capital city's location along the Potomac River, far from existing urban centers, reinforced the structure of the new republic. Its relative isolation would free the delegates from the hurly-burly of street politics in more established cities. In addition, the politically disfranchised District residents—unlike the citizens of the alternative cities proposed as capitals, New York or Philadelphia—would have fewer reasons to interfere with the representatives. Those who wanted a more cosmopolitan capital faced an important symbolic defeat in 1783 during the Constitutional Convention in Philadelphia. Pennsylvania's legislature was meeting at the time in the same building where the Constitutional Convention was under way. A group of veterans of the Revolutionary War assembled there, demanding payment for their military service from the Pennsylvania government. Advocates of locating the capital on the Potomac claimed the veterans had disturbed their deliberations and diminished "the dignity and authority of the United States." Though the actual disruption was minimal and separation from the people was only one reason for choosing the District's location, the event became a major justification for the location and political structure of the District of Columbia and a touchstone in future debates about marches on Washington.[5]

The First Amendment to the Constitution, with its guarantee of free speech, recognized the importance of popular debate. It also crucially—for protesters in the twentieth century—guaranteed the "right of the citizens peaceably to assemble and petition the government for the redress of grievances." Today, the language suggests that political leaders expected the people to come to the capital. To the delegates at the end of the eighteenth century, however, the word "assemble" meant to hold an organized meeting of concerned people to deliberate and vote on resolutions. Indeed, after the importuning of petitioners repeatedly interrupted their deliberations, members of Congress quickly rejected the right of individuals or small groups to present personally their petitions to Congress.[6] As the imagined nation became a functioning state, and as the imagined capital became a city, federal legislators continued to expect physical and political distance from the populace.

The planners of the new city wanted a capital—like those of other important nations—that would impress foreign leaders and represent the place of the people in the new nation. One of its principal designers, Pierre L'Enfant, laid out a plan with an eye for ceremonial parades. Pennsylvania Avenue was wide to facilitate the processions between the Capitol and the White House. In turn, the Mall at the base of the Capitol was where the army would perform drills. These ceremonial spaces depended on the presence of spectators to attend the events and confirm the country's status as a nation.[7]

The symbolic power and spatial dignity envisioned by Washington's original designers were frustrated for many decades by practical challenges. Realities of financing, transportation, and politics limited the capital's transformation into a convincing national showplace. In part, the capital fell short of these ambitions because it was a city as well as a capital. As Washington's population grew, election day riots, labor conflicts, and interracial violence intermittently disrupted the calm so central to the founders' imaginations. The flocks of lobbyists also suggested that neither political theory nor location could protect federal representatives from some people's political desires.[8]

The designers' ceremonial ambitions suffered as well. Pennsylvania Avenue as the retail and transportation hub for the city served many functions, which tarnished its ceremonial dignity for national processions. The end of the Avenue near the Capitol became the preferred location for prostitutes and saloonkeepers eager for the business of politicians, lobbyists, and their hangers-on. The Mall began as a swamp and served for a while as a pasture. After the Civil War, an improvement campaign resulted in a park with curving paths for genteel recreation, not a place for national ceremonies.[9]

Yet, politicians, authorities, and many other people still held on to the original idea of a peaceful capital suitable for political deliberation and national ceremonies. Hoping to preserve calm after riots, Congress strengthened the District's police forces repeatedly in the nineteenth century. They modeled laws on local ordinances in many American cities that sharply restricted use of the city streets. One federal act reflected the general thrust of these actions. In 1882, an act "to Regulate the Use of the Capitol Grounds" prohibited the carrying of banners and the making of "any oration or harangue" on the Capitol grounds. A broad clause forbade all actions "designed to bring into public notice any party, organization, or movement."[10]

Other people tried to achieve the ceremonial ambitions of the capital's original designers and later boosters by portraying Washington as an ideal location to learn about the political meaning of the nation. Large parades took place. The enormous review of the Union troops after the Civil War was the most celebrated example; but increasingly other groups also used the capital to give a national flavor to their celebrations and meetings. Two years before Coxey's Army arrived in the capital in 1894, the Grand Army of the Republic attracted thousands of its members to come "on to Washington" for an encampment and a mass parade down Pennsylvania Avenue.[11] The increasing popularity of the city for such gatherings gave hope to authorities and people that the capital was becoming the centerpiece of the nation.

In the meantime, cities across the country and the District itself experienced demonstrations by local residents on every sort of issue. By the nineteenth century, although the riotous crowd remained a potent force, two forms of peaceful public parades emerged. Business leaders sponsored parades that both entertained spectators in elaborate displays and reminded watchers of merchants' power and influence in the city. Workers took to the streets with more spontaneity but no less purpose. They used their processions on holidays to demonstrate community values. During work stoppages, parades through the streets provided visual reminders of the terms of the dispute between the workers and their employers.[12]

While the labor movement was establishing its own traditions on the streets of the United States, political parties, both mainstream and third party, were using the streets of America's cities and towns as well. In the nineteenth century, the main political parties used flamboyant parades and spectacular meetings to entertain spectators and provide strong visual evidence of the strength of their support. Despite being nominally associated with national political parties, these public spectacles were local events that served to connect people directly with politicians and parties. Likewise, third parties, such as the Populists, that emerged during the same time depended on public celebrations to show their legitimacy and to bind their supporters even closer.[13]

When people protested in the streets on national policy, however, they tended to choose local manifestations of their distress rather than focus on national symbols. For example, the New York City Draft Riots of 1863 began with a militant parade to the site of the draft lottery for the United States Army. Soon, though, it became a deadly five-day riot directed at city officials, African American residents, and shopkeepers—not national officials or federal representatives.[14] The rarity of national political demonstrations illustrates that, during most of the nineteenth century, local, organizational, and state issues dominated American politics of the streets.

Nevertheless, some people imagined that collective protests in Washington could challenge the existing national political order, though their ambitions came to little. In January 1877, Henry Watterson, a Democratic representative from Kentucky, called for "a hundred thousand petitioners" to come to Washington in support of Samuel Tilden's claim to the presidency. Disgusted, President Ulysses Grant moved soldiers to protect the capital and Tilden personally intervened to cancel an event he considered insurrectionary. The only protest that did take place was so small and so spontaneously organized that it went almost unnoticed. In 1878, Dennis Kearney, a California leader of the nativist Workingmen's Party, and Carl Browne, a Kearney supporter who would subsequently organize Coxey's Army, impulsively decided to speak against Chinese immigration on the Capitol steps. At first, the Washington police threatened to arrest the men. However, the authorities dropped the threat when the event attracted only a small number of spectators. This small gathering received barely any coverage in most newspapers.[15] Though these few people opposed to the established political system were beginning to imagine protests staged in Washington, the view of the capital as the preserve of elected representatives and admiring citizens still dominated.

In 1894, the arrival of Coxey's Army in the capital challenged this view. Over the course of the twentieth century, a series of demonstrations transformed such perceptions entirely. Close studies of exemplary marches on Washington spread over this period explain the causes and the significance of this transformation. In each case, three sets of people interacted, often dramatically, to shape events. The ambitious organizers of these demonstrations and their participants were often center stage. The politicians and officials, sometimes supporting, sometimes restricting, sometimes opposing marches, played roles deserving special attention. Finally, the journalists and the American people, who influenced the events and interpreted their meanings, complete the cast of characters. Bringing these intersecting groups together in a study of protest illustrates how their interactions were as important as the strategies of organizers. Repeatedly, these three sets of characters debated the meaning and the usefulness of national political demonstrations. These debates uncovered fissures in views about who had power in the United States, whose voices deserved to be heard, and how federal officials should answer the protests of the excluded.[16]

Without any precedent to draw upon, however, the first marchers on Washington in 1894 faced many uncertainties. Did ordinary citizens even have a right to use the physical spaces of the capital? Doing so challenged the assumption that the capital was the official space for representative, not direct, democracy. Members of Coxey's Army claimed they needed access to Washington's spaces to influence the course of national politics. This claim, reiterated by subsequent protesters, helped transform parts of the capital city from ceremonial and official spaces into what I call national public spaces. Protesters redrew the capital's spaces: first, Pennsylvania Avenue, later, the Mall, and most recently, enshrined locations near the Capitol and White House. The transformation of these spaces both reinforced the idea that citizens deserved an active voice in national politics and provided a forum from which they could present and promote their own positions.

Capital spaces—filled with a potent mixture of actual policy making and national symbolism—are a rich source for understanding how people actually imagine themselves as members of the nation. A park, an empty lot in a suburban neighborhood, the banks of a river, a deserted city street on Sunday morning can be public spaces. People use these spaces for a variety of purposes, but they are not entirely free of constraints. The uses of public spaces evolve through interactions between different groups of users, authorities, and politicians. This evolution is particularly obvious in national public spaces. These are physical locations where the people of a country can gather to address national issues—for example, Trafalgar Square and Hyde Park in London, Tiananmen Square in Beijing, and the Potsdamer Platz in Berlin.[17] In such places, people can hold gatherings at certain times and in certain ways with a reasonable expectation that other people in the country will hear their claims. Yet, they do so under circumstances determined by broader politics, controlled by national authorities, and influenced by the media.

Both the possibilities and limits of marching on Washington also rested on how activists, politicians, and the media transformed and expanded notions of American citizenship. Many demonstrators had difficulty securing recognition as citizens and used protests in Washington as an opportunity to assert their citizenship on this national stage. In this regard, organizers and participants had three related tasks: they had to claim their status as citizens, declare their rights to the existing privileges of citizenship, and, often, forge new rights for citizens as well. The process was a complex mixture of nationalistic, patriotic, and revolutionary performances and rhetoric. Meanwhile, critics of the demonstrations often disputed these claims to and of citizenship. The resulting debates provide a revealing lens on evolving understandings of citizenship in the United States. Gradually, these highly visible events actually helped contribute to the development of a broader and more inclusive view of American citizenship: a citizenship that embraced more rights and more people.

There is a paradox connected with the prevalence and acceptability of marches on Washington today. Since Jacob Coxey's arrest for walking on the grass at the Capitol in 1894, the perception that people have little to do with the political functioning of the United States has increased. Voter participation has decreased, government bureaucracy has expanded, and incumbency of elected officials has lengthened.[18] The organizers and the participants in these marches on Washington suggest by their efforts an alternative view. Their efforts and actions remind the country and the government of the need for active democracy. Marches on Washington have transformed the capital from the exclusive domain of politicians and officials into a national stage for American citizens to participate directly in national politics.

CHAPTER ONE

"WITHOUT PRECEDENT"

Coxey's Army Invades Washington, 1894

In 1944, a ninety-year-old man stood on the eastern steps of the United States Capitol and completed a speech he had begun fifty years earlier. In words that echoed the labor struggles of that earlier time, he spoke of "millions of toilers whose petitions have been buried in committee rooms." He championed those people "whose opportunities for honest, remunerative, productive labor have been taken from them by unjust legislation, which protects idlers, speculators, and gamblers." He described a massive program of public works he had proposed to end the depression of the 1890s.[1] A small crowd of spectators stopped to hear him with polite curiosity, mostly servicemen home from the war, a few journalists. Capitol police officers looked on with benign indifference, for he spoke that day with the formal blessing of the vice president and the Speaker of the House. The speech needed completing because, fifty years earlier, he had hardly begun speaking when the District of Columbia police hauled him off to jail.

In 1894, Jacob Coxey had helped organize the first real march on Washington. Coxey and his co-organizer, Carl Browne, proclaimed that they and half a million distressed American workers would collect at the Capitol on May 1 to petition Congress to enact a sweeping legislative package. They wanted Congress to end permanently the suffering of unemployed workers by building modern roads throughout the United States and funding new community facilities with federally subsidized bonds. Coxey called the marchers the "Commonweal of Christ"; their observers labeled them "Coxey's Army." His expectations were bold; the demands, far-reaching. It was their tactic, however, that caused the most controversy and had the longest legacy. Coxey called it a "petition in boots." Federal politicians and journalists called it an "invasion."

Their group traveled seven hundred miles from Coxey's hometown of Massillon, Ohio, to the border of the District of Columbia. Then, on May 1, 1894, the two organizers and around five hundred Common-wealers paraded down Pennsylvania Avenue to the Capitol. There, Coxey confronted police officers intent on enforcing the law that forbade groups from using the Capitol grounds for political action.[2] Coxey and Browne were to spend twenty days in jail. Their confused and demoralized followers spent the rest of the summer in crude camps waiting in vain for Congress to address their claims. Public reaction was harsh. In Oregon, the editor of the *Portland Telegram* called the protesters a sign of fatal "blood poisoning in the republic." To Republican Senator Joseph Hawley of Connecticut the demonstration in Washington was "extraordinary" and "without precedent."[3]

The unprecedented claim that ordinary Americans had a right to voice their demands in the capital was one that activists and politicians would struggle with for the next century. The organizers' effort would lay the groundwork for a new style of protest and a new form of national public space that would change the relationship between the American people and their government. Coxey claimed the ceremonial spaces of the Capitol Building; it was "the property of people." In 1894, Coxey and Browne were pioneers—and unlikely ones at that. Pulling their demands out of a mishmash of other causes, these two virtually unknown political activists based the national demonstration on established techniques of local protest. Understanding the first national political demonstration in Washington therefore requires suspension of one's modern sense of how demonstrations happen in Washington. And, though the events that took place in the capital on May 1, 1894, were important, the previous months of discussion of the leaders and groups and their tactics did as much to shape the perception of marching on Washington in the future.

"A PETITION IN BOOTS"

The man who gave the march its name was barely a public figure before 1894. Jacob Coxey combined respectability, ambition, and radicalism in his personal and political life. Born in 1854, Coxey spent his first twenty-four years in the shadow of the iron mills of Danville, Pennsylvania. After attending school, he joined his father in the mills at the age of sixteen.

FIGURE 1. Jacob Coxey riding in a carriage driven for him by an aide. Unlike most of the men in the Commonweal of Christ, Coxey did not walk to Washington. This practice drew criticism from his supporters and derision from his detractors. Yet, he strove to maintain his business owner's respectability at the same time that he advocated radical changes in the American political system. (Library of Congress, Prints and Photographs Division, LC-USZ62–9362)

With help from relatives, Coxey left manual labor behind. By 1881, he had moved to Massillon, Ohio, where he purchased a stone quarry. As Coxey moved from ironworker to successful business owner, his politics followed a somewhat surprising path. Beginning as a Democrat, he espoused the Greenback cause in the 1870s and 1880s, and by the 1890s was a confirmed Populist.[4] From the Populists, Coxey learned to doubt the dominant parties and to believe a reformed federal government with the proper policies could cure the nation's problems (fig. 1).

The 1890s were a period of severe economic depression and turbulent politics. As the crisis spread across the country in 1893, most people felt the strain and devastation. Investors and journalists noted with alarm the failures of the Philadelphia and Reading Railroad in February and then the National Cordage Company in May. Soon, the stock market took a dramatic fall, and the monetary supply contracted sharply. By July, many banks had no cash; by September, nearly four hundred banks had closed. Unemployment spread rapidly. Forty-three percent of Michigan workers were unemployed in the fall, and more than a third of New York State workers had no employment by winter.[5]

Working-class activists saw this suffering as confirming the need for new political methods and more protection of workers, while even national politicians and journalists spoke of the need for some economic assistance. Throughout the nineteenth century, but especially after the Civil War, working people in the United States had been challenging the changes accompanying the rise of industrial capitalism. Working people struggled against their employers through strikes; they formed organizations such as the Knights of Labor, the Farmers' Alliance, and trade unions. Increasingly, they sought a voice in government. In the 1890s, these efforts proved more successful than ever before. Representatives of the Populist Party won elections to local, state, and federal offices. Even the major parties began to speak as though the interests of the working people concerned them. And, more and more members of Congress and federal officials acknowledged the federal government's influence over the national economy and became more likely to listen to a broader spectrum of people.[6]

In this political atmosphere, Coxey first proposed a comprehensive national solution to the monetary and employment problems of the United States. In 1891, he drafted the Good Roads Bill to propose a massive program of road building funded by the federal government. Like most of Coxey's ideas, this scheme was a mishmash of other people's political proposals. Many were already lobbying local and national authorities; the League of American Wheelmen, a group of cyclists, entitled their newspaper *Good Roads Bulletin*. But Coxey melded these demands with the concerns of the Greenbacker and Populist parties for more currency. The bill required the treasury secretary to print "five hundred millions of dollars of treasury notes" without any backing in metal or bank loans. The secretary of war was to spend this money, at least $20 million a month, building roads across the country. The roads would be built by an army of labor, guaranteed an eight-hour day and wages of at least $1.50 per day. Considering that the total government expenditure in

1891 was $332 million, the bill represented an increase in federal spending of nearly 75 percent. Likewise, the road builders would earn at least 80 percent above the going hourly rate.[7] In short, Coxey's proposal sought to transform the entire economic system of the United States by expanding the money supply and changing working conditions.

Coxey's plans resonated with the thinking of many reformers about how to help the unemployed. In the United States, working people had often supported the idea that the government should provide work in times of economic difficulty. By the 1890s, authorities in private charities and municipal welfare offices occasionally set up programs for men to build roads, cut wood, or clear trash.[8] The goal of the Good Roads Bill, however, was to employ more than a few workers deemed deserving by local authorities; it aspired to put thousands of men to work for government money on a federal project. Coxey's program moved an arena almost exclusively controlled on a local level to the national.

If his plan was grand, Coxey's first attempts to enact it were modest. He did persuade a Populist congressman to introduce the bill. As with most bills sponsored by third-party legislators, however, the proposal went nowhere. Still optimistic, Coxey turned to the other avenue for reform in the late nineteenth century: the association.[9] He formed the J. S. Coxey Good Roads Association of the United States in 1892 and named himself president of the group.

Though he did not know it in 1892, Coxey's proposal and his national ambitions would depend on a radical agitator, consummate mythmaker, and self-promoter in California named Carl Browne. Browne claimed he was born on the most American of days, the Fourth of July, in 1849 in a log cabin in Illinois. In the 1870s, he moved to California, where he took up the habit of wearing a long leather jacket and a sombrero. Browne was by training a printer and a journalist; by avocation, he was a painter and a dramatist. Along the way, he supported himself by writing freelance articles, occasionally selling patent medicines, and running labor newspapers illustrated with his own cartoons (fig. 2).[10]

The culture of working-class protest in California shaped Browne's view of political action. As a reporter and supporter, he attended the numerous protests and demonstrations organized by the Chinese Exclusion movement. Working-class leaders had seized hold of the sometimes violent and destructive outbursts by workers against Chinese people and business and channeled them into mostly peaceful public demonstrations. For a while, they led a successful—and virulently racist—political movement that transformed California politics. For Browne, the highlight

FIGURE 2. Grand Marshal Carl Browne posing on the horse Jacob Coxey lent him for the march to Washington. Browne's frontier appearance, with worn leather jacket and broad-brimmed hat, stood in contrast to Coxey's disciplined respectability. (Jarvis Stereograph, Library of Congress, Prints and Photographs Division, LC-USZ62–4489)

of these protests came when Dennis Kearney, the most noted leader, and he made a speaking tour in the eastern United States, including a speech from the steps of the Capitol Building.[11] From many experiences with radical causes, Browne learned that dramatic public protests could lead to successful political campaigns and great personal satisfaction.

In the 1890s, Browne embraced a new religious faith that came to infuse his political ideals. His wife fell ill and died on Christmas Day of 1892. As she died, he felt her soul pass into his body. This miracle confirmed his faith in Theosophy and its concept of reincarnation.[12] Because Theosophists believed so fervently in practicing enlightenment through social reform, Browne's religious faith inspired even more enthusiastic endorsement of political causes.

In the summer of 1893, Jacob Coxey, armed with his Good Roads Bill, and Carl Browne, blessed with his religious commitment to political action, met at a Chicago conference on monetary policy. This conference, bringing together party and association activists, like Coxey, and protest organizers and journalists, like Browne, helped transform both activists into figures with even more expansive national visions. The Bimetallic Convention took place during the world's fair known as the Columbian Exposition and attracted more than six hundred delegates. Impressed by Browne's passion during debates, Coxey realized that Browne's skills at self-promotion and political organizing might help the Good Roads Association. Coxey sought out Browne and convinced the westerner to visit him in Massillon.[13]

At first, the two men schemed to expand the reach and efforts of Coxey's Good Roads Association. They printed the first issue of a newspaper describing Coxey's proposal for road building. They sent the paper to acquaintances in the Populist and labor movements across the country. In December, Browne brought the cause of good roads to the annual meeting of the American Federation of Labor in Chicago. He convinced the delegates to endorse the Good Roads Bill and collected their signatures on a petition to Congress urging its passage.[14]

Emboldened by the labor federation's support and shocked by the suffering of workers in Chicago and elsewhere, Browne conceived of the idea of a "petition in boots" to Washington. He rejected the notion of mailing in petitions to Congress, as activists in the United States had done for years. Nor did he think that Coxey and he should merely deliver the petitions to Congress. Instead, Browne declared that a group of unemployed men ought to walk to Washington and present their demands.[15]

The more conservative Coxey hesitated at first to adopt Browne's grander vision. Gradually, Coxey changed his mind. Browne converted the previously agnostic Coxey to Theosophy, flattering him with the idea that both Coxey and he were reincarnations of Christ. With them at the helm, a march to Washington would be like the "Second Coming of Christ." In addition to a religious sanction, Coxey reassured himself that Browne's proposal was an extension of the constitutionally protected right of petition. On January 31, 1894, the Good Roads Association's newspaper consisted of a pictorial petition that portrayed the transformative possibilities of the Good Roads Bill and encouraged people to go "On to Washington."[16]

Since they were inventing a new form of political expression, the two men scrambled to make a "petition of boots" appealing and practical. Browne, ever conscious of symbolism, emphasized the group's Christian roots. To signal that their protest was peaceful and godly, he named the group carrying the petition the "Commonweal of Christ." In keeping with this theme, Coxey and Browne decided to leave Massillon on March 25— Easter Sunday. Like pilgrims of old, the Commonweal of Christ intended to travel the more than seven hundred miles on foot and horseback, succored only by the goodwill of the townspeople they met along the way.[17]

Coxey concentrated on the political and practical side. Though he wanted the effort to be funded by contributions as much as possible, he turned to his local contacts for immediate help and supplies in Massillon and contributed some of his own funds to support the Commonwealers' march to the capital. Aware that "good roads" were mainly a concern of rural residents, he added to his proposals measures that would allow states and cities to deposit "Non-Interest Bearing Bonds" in the federal treasury. In exchange, they would receive treasury notes to finance "public improvements" such as libraries, schools, utility plants, and marketplaces.[18] Such support from the federal government, he hoped, would build support for the "petition" among urban people. And, their journey would end with a "monster mass meeting on the Capitol steps" on May 1. Choosing that date clearly connected their efforts to those workers who claimed it as Labor Day.[19] As for Congress, both Browne and Coxey believed that "our Representatives, who hold their seats by grace of our ballots," would respond to their petition by immediately enacting both the Good Roads Bill and the Non-Interest Bearing Bond Bill.

Despite their high hopes, Coxey and Browne struggled to convince people to join their moving petition. For support, they turned to a network of labor activists. In Los Angeles, one of Browne's acquaintances, Lewis Fry, organized the first of many sympathetic groups who would travel to Washington that spring. Fry named himself the general of what he called the "United States Industrial Army" and demanded that the railroads transport him and his men east. To make arrangements in Washington, Browne contacted A. E. Redstone, a journalist and patent attorney. As his first task, Redstone took the responsibility of finding congressional sponsors for the two bills. If Congress was actually considering the legislation, the demonstration could safely claim to be simply a petition about a matter of political record.[20] He succeeded on March 19. William Peffer, a Populist from Kansas who knew Coxey, introduced the two bills in the Senate.[21]

The political backgrounds of Coxey and Browne, their demands for the "petition in boots," and their method of organizing show that the first march on Washington had its roots in political traditions, however marginal. Both men came to the "petition in boots" from involvement in third-party agitation. Both men shared a sustained concern with solving the problems that they associated with the industrial development of the country. Moreover, to solve these problems, Coxey and Browne wanted to change the way the national government operated and to win more influence over federal policy for ordinary citizens. Browne's involvement with public demonstrations in the United States soon convinced them both that going to the capital itself was within the rights and indeed responsibilities of American citizens. Such claims struck many observers as deeply suspect.

"AN ARMY OF TRAMPS"

Today, the extent of television coverage is the way many people judge the success of marches on Washington. In 1894, national networks of newspapers served by wire services determined the fate of the Commonweal of Christ. The invention of the telegraph in the 1840s and its use during the Civil War had encouraged many newspaper owners to create formal, though mainly regional, organizations. By 1893, some of these groups had consolidated into the Associated Press, serviced by a national "wire service" to share news, creating a more coordinated national press.[22] The Army's march to the capital became a national event only because of the intense interests of journalists connected to these wire services. But, just as television coverage today conveys only part of protesters' behavior and demands, so newspaper journalists in 1894 were selective, and not particularly sympathetic, in their coverage. Most of the journalists were scornful of the participants and their tactics. Their stories portrayed the protest as a folly by marginal men they dubbed tramps rather than a legitimate challenge to an already unbalanced system of national politics by citizens.

Even before Coxey's Army had taken their first steps, newspaper reporters were transforming the Commonweal of Christ and their "petition in boots" into a matter of national concern. A reporter in Massillon, intrigued by Coxey and Browne's plan, began sending out reports on their activities over the newspaper wire services in late February.[23] Editors and reporters for papers across the country picked up these stories. Soon journalists were moving toward Massillon. Among the first was Ray Stannard Baker, then a young reporter for the *Chicago Record*. As his editor sent Baker out of town, he told him of a "queer chap . . .

named Coxey" whose plans were "getting a good deal of support."
Baker arrived in Massillon on March 15 and sent his reports back to
Chicago; the wire services relayed them to other parts of the country.
Baker found Browne, Coxey, and their march "crazy." Nevertheless,
other reporters came to the small town in Ohio, and eventually more
than forty reporters joined the group as it traveled to Washington.[24]

As the first marchers set off for Washington, journalists published their
initial assessments of the Commonweal's plans and hopes. Fry left Los
Angeles with five hundred men on March 16. After two days of marching on foot, they climbed aboard an empty freight train heading over the
mountains to the east. Railroad officials objected, but eventually carried
them as far as St. Louis. In Massillon, a far smaller contingent assembled.
Around a hundred men had trickled into Massillon by March 24. On
Easter Sunday, the Commonweal of Christ departed, as announced, for
Washington. A wire service story adapted by the *Washington Post* set the
tone of public reaction to the protesters: mockery and denigration. The
Post's writer generalized that the nearly 10,000 spectators who turned out
to watch the Commonweal embark "regarded the affair as a huge joke."
The appearance of the participants received doubtful scrutiny: they were
"hard looking citizens" who marched "as pleased their fancy."[25]

Despite this dismissive tone, journalists had good reason to continue
covering the Commonweal's long march. Journalists needed a new way
to cover the ill effects of the economic depression. As the English commentator W. T. Stead observed, by spring 1894, it was becoming difficult
to transform "this grim and worn-out topic" into "good saleable newspaper articles." Moreover, the month-long march from Massillon to
Washington allowed the journalists to fit their coverage into one of the
most popular conventions of the time—the serial story.[26]

Most importantly, Coxey's Army attracted a great deal of interest because the press, like much of society at large, had a serious interest in and
concern with how "mobs" could change governments and what governments should do in response. Though Washington had suffered less
than foreign capitals from violent events occasioned by "mobs," other
American cities had found themselves the centers of widely publicized incidents. To many, these incidents seemed to threaten the whole country
rather than just the single city. For example, the demonstrations in
Chicago at Haymarket Square in 1888 had resulted in deaths of police
officers and years of court battle over the anarchists charged with the disturbances. By 1894, "Haymarket" was shorthand for the tragedy organized protests could bring to the country. One reporter damned

Browne with the charge that he was "a 'Red' of as deep dye as any that ever trod Haymarket."[27]

The events surrounding a group of sympathizers in Montana in late April suggested the risks were serious and even deadly. Under the auspices of the Butte Miners' Union, unemployed workers rallied to the idea of demonstrating in Washington. They spent most of April trying to collect supplies and to persuade the railroad to transport them. Railroad officials had no sympathy. Finally on April 24, the men's impatience overcame their intentions to be lawful and peaceful. They seized a Northern Pacific train and began racing east. Railroad officials were outraged and turned to both the state and the federal government for help in retrieving their property. A confrontation between the men on the train and federal marshals resulted in two deaths, but the men still had the train. Two days later, a division of the U.S. Army successfully stopped the men's desperate trip east. To most journalists covering the protest, these deaths merely confirmed their worst fears about what "an army of tramps" could do. Capturing the prevailing attitudes of reports, the *New York Times* announced, "Blood Flows from Coxeyism."[28] But Coxey and Browne's plans resulted in few such violent incidents.

Because of the extreme fears and relative lack of actual violence, most reporters reconciled these two viewpoints by mocking the protest and its supporters. The reporters who traveled with the Commonwealers were keenly conscious of the lack of organization, Browne's eccentricity, and the grandiose nature of the legislative demands. Before the Commonwealers had even left Massillon, the *Independent* called Coxey a "poor fool" and predicted that if any men did reach Washington they were destined for the jail.[29]

The most enduring expression of this fearful and mocking attitude was the name journalists gave to the march, "Coxey's Army," influenced by California coleader Lewis Fry's use of "Industrial Army." And despite his lack of military service, Coxey became "General Coxey." The use of "army" to refer to organized groups, particularly of workers, was pervasive and not always contemptuous in the nineteenth century.[30] Still, the journalists exploited the term as a double-edged sword. They not only used "Coxey's Army" to imply a violent purpose in their approach to Washington but also judged the protest harshly when the group did not meet standards of military discipline.

This form of attack became clear as the journalists began routinely describing the marchers as "tramps." In a relatively moderate statement, the *New York Times* described the group of men who had assembled in

Massillon on March 24 as "a lot of tramps, cranks, and a few men who would doubtless work if they could find work." The *Commercial Gazette* in Pittsburgh labeled them a "motley aggregation of homeless wanderers." In an oxymoron that revealed the fears generated by the demonstration, the *Philadelphia Ledger* called them "organized tramps." In these descriptions, journalists repeated common tropes that transformed working-class radicals into tramps. According to John McCook, writing in *Charities Review,* a tramp was characterized by "aimless wandering, no visible means of support, capacity to labor along with fixed aversion to labor, begging from door to door, camping on property of others without their consent." Many in the middle class imagined tramps, people who wandered from place to place, as simultaneously outside of and disruptive to the social order.[31]

By accusing the marchers in Coxey's Army of being tramps, journalists struck at the very core of their mission: their right to speak as members of the American polity. These "social scourges" should not expect to affect Congress, their critics concluded. The editors of the *Independent* declared, "It is idle to suppose that an army of tramps, however numerous, can or ought to have any influence whatever on legislation or Congress." The men, the editors arrogantly declared, did "not belong to the bone and sinew of the country."[32]

The characterization of the members of Coxey's Army as tramps influenced how authorities in Washington planned to respond to the demonstration. Because citizenship in the United States rested on allegiance to the social, economic, legal, and political order, tramps were the antithesis of ideal political citizens. The negative view of tramps was powerful enough to convince cities, counties, and even states to pass and enforce harsh vagrancy laws that allowed the police to arrest people without visible means of support. Those arrested had to leave the region or work. In late March 1894, authorities in the District of Columbia— after private urgings from President Cleveland—announced that if the men reached Washington and proved to be tramps, police officers would arrest them under the District's vagrancy law.[33] By categorizing the men as tramps, journalists not only marginalized the Commonweal and its political ambitions; they also helped justify plans to suppress the protest.

Most journalists saw Coxey's Army and its trip to Washington as a challenge to the political order they supported. Consequently, they sought to control the meaning of the protest by attacking the men behind the movement as unworthy. This attack allowed journalists to individualize the marchers' political demands. Tramps wanted handouts of any sort—hence their demands for the Good Roads Bill. The label of tramp

suggested that the men were not the kind of people who could legitimately protest in Washington. In the following decades, this method of
slighting the political purposes of demonstrations by denigrating the protesters as unworthy individuals remained common and effective. For
Coxey and Browne, it required an immediate response.

"WE ARE ALL CITIZENS"

Caught in this hailstorm of negative publicity, Coxey and Browne scrambled to reshape the Commonweal's public image. They recognized that
they had to refute the related charges that the marchers were tramps and
that their mission violated the norms of political behavior. With characteristic gusto, they countered that participants were "citizens." And, as
citizens, they insisted, Americans had an obligation to go to the capital
if that was what it took to improve the country.

Although the *Post* and other newspapers mocked their departure from
Massillon, their parade followed well-established conventions for public
celebrations in the late nineteenth century. The Commonwealers tried to
communicate respectability, patriotism, and adherence to the social order
when they appeared in public. Leading the parade on March 25 was
Jasper Johnson, an African American, carrying the United States flag. Following him was a band to entertain the spectators. Then came Browne on
a grand horse. Next came Coxey riding in a carriage with Mrs. Coxey and
their recently born son with the odd and political name of Legal Tender.
Behind Coxey walked the Commonwealers, trying to march in the disciplined ranks of soldiers. The men maintained this form until they reached
the edge of town, where the serious task of walking the seven hundred
miles required less formal order. In town after town, however, the Commonwealers repeated their performance to signal not revolution but a desire for a social order firmly rooted in the flag, the family, and discipline.[34]

Central to the Army's performance and arguments was that the men
were citizens. To the Commonwealers, resting their demands on their status as citizens had practical and ideological power. As they were aware,
however, citizenship involved much more than a simple legal claim.
Americans tended to define legitimate citizens by their behavior and values as well as their birthplace. So as the Commonwealers struggled
through spring snowstorms, climbed mountains, and rode canal boats to
reach Washington, they worked to prove themselves as citizens (fig. 3).[35]

According to their supporters, these "straightforward, honest Americans" were unemployed men who would work if they could find work.

FIGURE 3. Members of Coxey's Army receiving haircuts at the camp in Washington. Such efforts served to counteract stereotypes about tramps. Supporters often publicized the tendency of the men on the march to wash clothes and bathe at every opportunity. (Underwood, Library of Congress, Prints and Photographs Division, LC-USZ62–4561)

When a reporter told Coxey that the marchers were "bums and black-mailers," Coxey countered that many carried "certificates from labor organizations."[36] In asserting the legitimacy of the men as workers, the Commonwealers made clear they wanted not a revolution in society, but assistance in what they saw as a fundamental need for work.

Browne believed strongly that citizens—as opposed to foreigners—deserved both respect and power in the United States. By excluding certain people from the group, he—like other organizers of political causes—could bolster his claim that his men were politically deserving. While the Commonwealers were camped in Frederick, Maryland, on their way to Washington, some "Hungarians" tried to join. Browne explained that he gave the men "no badges, as I had 'weeded out' all but bona-fide citizens." In pleading the group's cause in the District, Populist activist Annie Diggs claimed that "there is not a man in the ranks of that army but who is either a naturalized citizen or a native born."[37]

The Commonwealers asserted their status as citizens in part by emphasizing their masculinity. Supporters tended to use Coxey and his family to show that families were behind the men's efforts. Coxey's wife and daughter both played prominent roles in parades in Massillon and in Washington. His son accompanied the participants on the long trip to the capital. In other places, the presence of women as enthusiastic supporters of the men's effort was publicized. For her part, Diggs assured her Washington listeners that these men were on the march because their "wives and children . . . are starving." [38]

But organizers carefully kept women as mainly symbolic recipients of the Commonwealers' devotion to their families. Browne's illustration at the top of the original petition portrayed how the Good Roads Bill would restore the order of the family: a man employed on the roads project returns home at the end of the day to a happy baby and a devoted wife cooking dinner. When faced with actual women who wanted to join the march, organizers rejected them.[39] By emphasizing that they were protecting their own families and family unity in general while also preventing women from taking part in this unprecedented political act, the marchers emphasized their status as that most respectable of all citizens: the family man.

These efforts to establish themselves as citizens related closely to the Commonwealers' desire to reform national politics so that it would respond to the demands of deserving Americans. They constantly reiterated arguments about the rights of citizens and the responsibilities of national politicians. To a crowd of spectators along the way to Washington, Coxey asserted that if "the people . . . come in a body like this, peaceably to discuss their grievances and demanding immediate relief, Congress . . . will heed them and do it quickly." Coxey's belief spread to the men marching toward Washington as well. A writer who interviewed some marchers said, "They believe that the congressmen who represent them will not dare to refuse them legislative relief."[40]

This vision grew from more than the idealism of direct democracy; the Commonwealers had faith in personal appeals because of prior experience with working-class agitation at the local level. As Browne's California activities illustrated, working people without other forms of access to the political system often successfully used the streets to support their causes. If the workers were unified, strikes sometimes did win higher wages. If enough people turned out for parades and went to the polls, working-class candidates sometimes won. If the unemployed pushed hard enough, city officials sometimes initiated public works programs. In going to Washington, Coxey and Browne hoped to have the same results.[41]

Central to their argument, however, was that national politics was both corrupt and ineffectual. Members of the Commonweal of Christ detested the power of the dominant political parties. Coxey saw the month-long trip to Washington as part of an educational process through which the American people would learn more about the "money question" than they had "through any one political party in ten years." Likewise, the marchers reportedly believed "the Government has fallen into the hands of persons who are administering it in the interest of the favored few." While these statements clearly show a bitter resentment toward the way the federal government worked, the marchers' willingness to struggle to reach Washington demonstrated their faith that Congress could do better if pushed. By focusing its anger on political parties, the Commonweal was able to maintain its position that passage of the Good Roads and Bond Bills would redeem the government and the country.[42]

The Commonwealers' presentation of themselves as citizens persuaded many. As the men continued their march to Washington, reports acknowledged that the men were indeed mostly workingmen and that they were orderly and honest along the way.[43] Despite the journalists' rhetoric, many of the people who saw the men marching behind their flag did not equate these men with tramps. Many communities provided filling meals, opened public parks and buildings as resting spots, and donated funds. Even in Pittsburgh, where the city authorities deemed the marchers a threat, controlled their route through the city, and ordered them confined to their campground, workers and other sympathizers defied the police to cheer the marchers and rallied to their defense. A sign of the power of the Commonweal campaign came when authorities in Washington backed away from plans to arrest the men as vagrants.[44] Though the authorities continued to disparage the cause and the Army's tactics, the men had won an important recognition of their status as political actors.

"SOCIALISM AND POPULISM AND PATERNALISM RUN RIOT"

Still, the Commonweal's fate depended on what District and federal authorities and politicians thought of the marchers, their goals, and their tactics. The Commonwealers had modeled their protests on local demonstrations in which government officials responded to the claims of the community, but they also made political arguments that challenged the legitimacy of the existing political order. While they found some support among the few Populist and third-party politicians in Washington, most authorities considered the demonstration in Washington an unreasonable assertion of a new role for American citizens in the national government. As much as Coxey's Army tried to wrap their tactics in the First Amendment, they found little support for this constitutional claim. The *New York Tribune* warned, "The very purpose and the method of this organized movement are hostile to the spirit of our Government, and at war with the fundamental principle upon which free institutions rest."

While authorities abandoned the fantasy of mass arrests at the city limits, they still prepared to control the approaching group. By March 15, "one policeman . . . in citizen's clothes" was already stationed in the Capitol to watch for "advance agents of the army." Later in the month, the District of Columbia Militia practiced special drills in anticipation of what they termed an "invasion." With the unconvincing argument that such money-hungry men might invade the treasury, the secretary of the treasury sent Secret Service agents in disguise to Ohio to infiltrate the army. Meanwhile, the superintendent of the Metropolitan Police, William Moore, and attorneys for the District began searching for laws that would permit them to control the demonstration. Superintendent Moore explained that the Capitol grounds in particular were off limits because the 1882 Act to Regulate the Grounds specifically prohibited speeches, parades, and the carrying of banners. Soon the District authorities could assure the White House they had the means to control the march.[45]

As District and federal authorities monitored the Commonwealers, members of Congress debated the meaning of the march. Populist senators brought the issue of demonstrating in Washington off the newspaper pages and onto the floor of the Senate. Senator Peffer, who had sponsored the bills that Coxey and Browne used to justify their trip to Washington, asked on April 19 that the Senate receive the men and their petitions. Horrified that the police might "arrest men as vagrants who come upon a peaceable mission to the capital of their country," he proposed that the Senate establish a new "Committee on Communication" to meet such groups and report to the Senate on their demands. These were not men with violent purposes, Peffer explained, but rather men who simply wished to confer "in person with the chosen representatives of the people." Another Populist senator supported Peffer's resolution publicly. William Allen of Nebraska argued that "any American citizen has a right to come to Washington." He continued by explicitly comparing the Commonwealers to another group welcomed not just in Washington but in the Capitol Building itself: lobbyists. His language rang with scorn and shame as he described how the "great bodies of lobbyists" arrived every day and walked "right into the corridors of this Capitol," where they were greeted by members of Congress with their "hats off." Allen questioned the law, which regulated the Capitol grounds, and asked why lobbyists were allowed on the "sacred" grounds of the Capitol, and under the "dome," while the Commonwealers were "to be stopped at their edge."[46] Peffer's proposed Committee on Communication and Allen's outrage illustrated how some national politicians in 1894 could appreciate the claim of Coxey's Army to use the capital.

These two men did not find support from their colleagues. In a series of speeches in late April, senators from both parties attacked the demands of the Commonweal and their plans to parade to the Capitol on May Day. They defeated Peffer's resolution and a subsequent resolution by Allen that sought to affirm the right of "citizens" to come to Washington and "enter upon the Capitol Grounds." These responses exposed the threats and challenges the senators saw in the tactic of a "petition in boots."[47]

Mainstream politicians united in describing the demand of the Commonweal for the federal government to come to the aid of unemployed men as a call not for justice, but for "paternalism." The year before, in his inaugural speech, President Cleveland, in a classic and blunt statement, had explained, "The lessons of paternalism ought to be unlearned and the better lesson taught that while the people should patriotically and cheerfully support their government its functions do not include the support of the people."[48] Hence, the central premise of Coxey's Army that the national government should provide "support" for unemployed workers countered an essential political tenet of the president.

On April 26, Senator Edward Wolcott, a Republican from Colorado, made this very point in response to Allen's resolution. Wolcott's speech showed how critics feared both the tactics and the demands of Coxey's Army. "I am tired . . . of this talk of a national demonstration," he declared. He asked his fellow senators to have "the courage to stand together against socialism and populism and paternalism run riot, which is agitating and fermenting this country." He warned that inaction risked "the destruction of the blessed liberties which the laws and the Constitution give us."[49]

To further discredit Coxey's Army, senators and others described the Commonwealers as being precisely what the Commonwealers accused Congress of being: unrepresentative. Senator Joseph Hawley of Connecticut declared, "The men who are coming here do not represent the great voice of the American people." Democratic Congressman Bourke Cockran from New York echoed Hawley when he scorned the idea that "the workingmen of the United States have constituted Coxey and his crowd their representatives." According to these critics of Coxey's Army, who did represent the people? The answer was Congress. Hawley asserted that it was senators who, as the result of a "most complex and universal system of selection," knew the "will of the people."[50]

In reality, however, Congress had already begun to recognize that they needed to solicit the advice of particular groups and people as they made decisions. In the aftermath of the Civil War, Congress increasingly heard testimony from experts and representatives of organized groups on legislation. Working people were not entirely excluded from this trend. Congress regularly constituted special committees to investigate strikes that recognized the spokesmen of workers. In a study of legislative methods published in 1898, Lauros G. McConachie praised the increasing "publicity" of Congress brought about by the committee hearing, which meant "the despised secret lobby" was replaced by "the open and fair voice of all who desire to be heard."[51] Because Congress did acknowledge these groups publicly, the Commonweal's critics had to reassure themselves that the Commonwealers were not a legitimate organization.

For these reasons, the senators tried to distinguish between respectable individuals and illegitimate groups as they endorsed plans by the Metropolitan Police to prevent the Commonwealers from entering the Capitol grounds. "No one denies the right of any citizen to visit the capital," Senator Joseph Dolph explained, but he warned that if "they violate the law and commit a crime," by marching as a group or making speeches, they would be arrested. These politicians supported federal and District officials in their decision to use their legal authority to draw a line in the sand that Coxey's Army could not cross. The Commonweal camp would be allowed at the Brightwood Riding Park on the edge of the District, and the Commonwealers would be permitted to march down Pennsylvania Avenue. They would not be allowed to come too near the Capitol itself. By preventing the Commonwealers from using the Capitol to support their cause, Congress and the District authorities effectively signaled that this group did not deserve access to the central space of American politics.[52]

The main problem authorities faced in using the 1882 Act to Regulate the Grounds of the Capitol was that they had almost never before enforced it. The authorities brazenly tried to establish a precedent for denying groups access to the official spaces near the Capitol. A parade by the Odd Fellows fraternal society up Pennsylvania Avenue, which President Cleveland reviewed on April 26, gave them the needed opportunity. When one division, dressed in the elaborate costumes of the group and carrying its banner, tried to cross the Capitol grounds on its way home from the White House, the Capitol police informed them that this was against the law. Obediently, the Odd Fellows walked around the long way.[53] Armed with this weak precedent, the men in control of the nation's capital braced for the arrival of Coxey's Army.

With this debate swirling ahead of them, the men made their way across the mountains of Pennsylvania, through the countryside of Maryland, and arrived just over the border of the District of Columbia on April 29, where they camped at Brightwood Riding Park (see map 1). After their long march through farms and country towns, marchers were struck by Washington's imposing scale and monumental architecture. The weary marchers might not have known that such glories had only recently transformed Washington into a popular destination for tourists. A contemporary guidebook noted that the "much needed improvement" had only begun in 1870. Since then, the writer proudly declared, the city was becoming annually "more worthy of the greatness of the Republic." Visitors could access easily many parts of the nation's city. The grounds of the White House were open to the visitor "with no restriction." For visitors, a trip to the Capitol to admire the statues, observe a congressional debate, or perhaps call at a politician's office was a required part of a Washington tour.[54]

As Coxey's Army entered the District, these sites of patriotic tourism faced competition from those interested in seeing the invading force. Because of their own experiences with economic suffering, many District residents expressed sympathy for the Commonwealers' crusade. Washington had not escaped the vagaries of the economic depression. By the time the Commonweal arrived, a relief committee for the capital had concluded its aid was no longer needed, but unemployment still afflicted many District residents. Some of these may have been among the people who greeted the group on Sunday, April 30. More than a hundred cyclists accompanied the men as they marched into the District. A crowd of at least 3,000 gathered to watch them enter their camping ground. To fill the empty coffers of the group, Browne asked people for donations to enter the grounds of the Riding Park itself and watch the men set up their tents. On Sunday, more than 8,000 people, including congressmen,

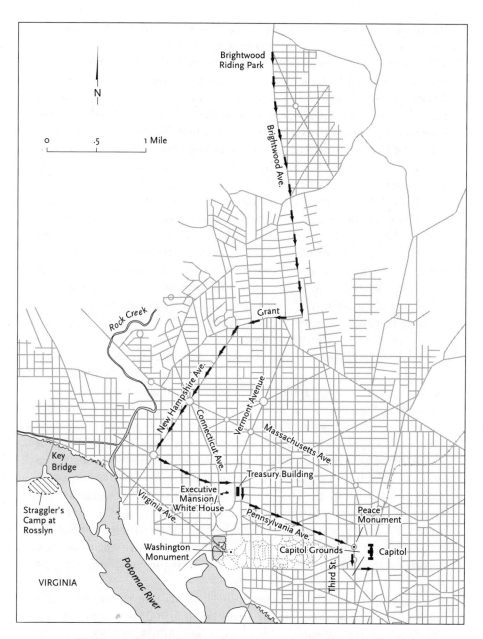

MAP 1. Washington, D.C., at the time of Coxey's Army's arrival. Source: Maps on Office of Coast Survey (http://achor. ncd.noaa.gov/).

foreign dignitaries, and residents, visited the camp, studied the men and their banners, and listened to speeches by Browne and Coxey.[55]

Nonetheless, by the time the marchers arrived in Washington, both their leaders and their critics had muted their expectations. Coxey and Browne's faith that Congress would respond quickly and earnestly to their demands and their march seemed shaken. Speaking in the Riding Camp on April 29, Coxey attempted bravado by claiming that his group was "like Grant before Richmond" and would not turn away until their goal was met. But his doubts about immediate results came through: "It may be in three days or five weeks, but we will stay as long as we are able to subsist." Browne grew disheartened as he realized that the size of the group was nowhere near his ambitious predictions. He was also discouraged because the Washington authorities, warned in advance of the Commonweal's plans to use the public spaces of the city, greeted the men with firm prohibitions and dismissive attitudes. The police sent a small force out to Brightwood Riding Park to keep order, claiming this was what they always did for "circuses, picnics, and other gatherings." The *Washington Post* described the men waiting in Brightwood Riding Park "as properties for a third-rate dime museum."[56]

On the day before the Commonweal was to enter the city, Coxey seemed particularly overwhelmed by his encounters with the authorities in Washington. In a day full of meetings, he talked with the District commissioners, Superintendent Moore from the police, the health commissioners, and the sergeant of arms for the Capitol. Expecting confrontation, Coxey appeared surprised by the officials' cordial tones. They all assured him that the plans for the parade down Pennsylvania Avenue were acceptable, but emphasized that he and his men could not enter the Capitol grounds. By the end of the day, Coxey told a reporter that the Commonwealers would come to the Capitol anyway on May 1, not "as a parade, but as private citizens." While Coxey conceded the issue of the parade on the grounds, he remained defiant about his right to make a speech on the grounds, asserting, "We will test the constitutionality of the law."[57]

Coxey's new focus on his right to speak shows how the experience of the long walk to Washington, the attacks on him and his supporters, and the disparagement of their political goals had shifted his attention from legislative changes to some basic premises about how American citizens could participate in national politics. From the beginning, he had justified his effort as protected by the First Amendment. He referred in speeches to their "right . . . peaceably to assemble, and to petition the

Government for a redress of grievances." Although the District authorities realized that complete repression would violate even the narrowest
interpretation of this first provision of the Bill of Rights, they still did not
believe that the First Amendment gave all citizens the right to claim
spaces they considered official.[58]

"THE PROPERTY OF THE PEOPLE"

May 1 was already a sunny and warm day when the Commonwealers
left their camp heading for the Capitol at 10 A.M. Reports of the number of marchers ranged from 600 to more than 1,000 depending on the
degree of sympathy for the cause. In form, their parade echoed that of
other parades that Washingtonians had seen in their city. At the front of
the procession was the traditional phalanx of police officers to clear the
way and preserve order. A flag bearer led the way with the requisite Stars
and Stripes to mark the parade as patriotic. Behind him came carriages
filled with members of the local committees that had collected supplies
for the demonstrators and had successfully arranged the parade. Next
came a pair of riders, each on fine horses. One was Coxey's daughter,
Mamie. Browne had named her the Goddess of Peace and picked her
subtle, but patriotic, costume of white with red and blue accents. As chief
marshal, he rode by her side. Behind the pair came a carriage carrying
Coxey, his wife, and their infant son. Finally came the Commonwealers,
still attempting to march in even rows like the military parades more typical on Pennsylvania Avenue.[59]

The Commonweal's challenge to traditional politics and conventional
uses of the capital was emphasized as they marched down Pennsylvania
Avenue in the opposite direction of most ceremonial parades. Tradition-
ally, parades in Washington began at the plaza that surrounded the Peace
Monument at the base of Capitol Hill and then proceeded up Pennsylvania Avenue and past the White House; if deemed important enough,
participants received a presidential review. But Coxey's men began near
the White House and marched past it without pausing, heading directly
to the Capitol. The route reflected the reality that political power in 1894
rested firmly with Congress as well as the Commonweal's ideals that
Congress could restore democracy by hearing the people.[60]

The spectators also confirmed that the marchers appealed to a different kind of District resident. Importantly, in a period when crowd size
for spectacles and political events was the main indicator of success, a
huge group gathered to view the march—as large or larger than any

attracted to presidential inaugurations of the era. One estimate reported that 30,000 people had turned out to watch the Commonwealers. Moreover, the crowd's racial and class composition was equally divided between blacks and whites and seemed to consist overwhelmingly of workingmen.[61]

Both the Commonwealers' continued belief in their cause and the apparent support of many observers strengthened the authorities' resolve to control the marchers. One of the most visible differences between the Commonwealers' march on May 1 and other parades in the District was the pervasive presence of the police. More than forty officers accompanied the men on their seven-mile hike to the center of the District. As the Commonwealers proceeded through Washington, they passed more officers. Special guards policed the grounds of the White House and two hundred policemen patrolled the perimeter of the Capitol grounds. Inside the Capitol Building, the Capitol police protected the House of Representatives, which was meeting in regular session that Tuesday. Undercover agents marched in the midst of the men, and a division of the U.S. Army waited in readiness.[62]

As the men approached the Capitol grounds, the crowds of spectators grew denser. Observers stood all over the pathways and grass, and carriages holding viewers filled the great plaza on the east side of the Capitol. Some people climbed part way up the steps of the Capitol, but stopped at a human barricade of police officers. Members of Congress, staff, and privileged visitors stood further up the steps under the portico to the Capitol or crowded into the windows of the building. A few adventurous souls even climbed onto the roof.[63]

The tension grew as the Commonweal halted at the southern edge of the Capitol grounds. Soon, there was excitement. Browne and Coxey defied the previous warnings of the District and federal authorities and the immediate presence of hundreds of policemen and went onto the grounds. Browne and another Commonwealer jumped over a low wall and ran toward the Capitol, a move Browne later described as a purposeful distraction to enable Coxey to make his speech at the Capitol. Police rushed to seize them both, swinging their batons. At 1 P.M., a telegram informed the White House that because Browne "resisted arrest he received a clubbing." Still defiant, Browne reminded the crowd of his central justification for the entire effort: he shouted that he was a "citizen."[64]

Coxey's efforts were both less dramatic and less violently suppressed. He made his way through the crowds on the Capitol grounds unnoticed and went up five steps of the Capitol. There, police stopped him and re-

FIGURE 4. Police officers removing Coxey (in light suit) from the Capitol Building, May 1, 1894. Surrounded by police officers, Coxey calmly walked off the grounds. The police used more force to arrest Browne and to drive off onlookers. (*Harper's Magazine,* Library of Congress, Prints and Photographs Division, LC-USZ62–105022)

minded him that he could not deliver a speech. Coxey tried to read his prepared remarks, but the officers "hustled him off the steps" and escorted him back to his carriage and the waiting Commonwealers. While not surprised at his treatment, Coxey was disgusted at being prevented from exercising his constitutional rights on the steps of a building he considered "the property of the people" (fig. 4).[65]

At first, it seemed that the authorities had succeeded in their goal of tolerating the parade while restricting the use of the Capitol grounds. To

some, the parade and its quick dispersal was such an anticlimax that one
observer commented on "the disappointment" of the spectators who had
hoped for a longer-lasting drama.[66] Browne's flagrant and purposeful violation of the law had resulted in his arrest, while Coxey's more modest
efforts were handled peacefully. The editors of the *Washington Post*
praised the authorities for their "commendable discretion and efficiency." As for Coxey, they suggested he should now lead the men out of
the District and back to their homes.[67]

Coxey did not follow the advice of the *Post*'s editors. Instead, he and
his supporters reiterated their demands for a hearing and a place in the
capital. On the evening of May 1, Browne, bailed out of jail, addressed
their dispirited followers. "I congratulate you upon your splendid action
to-day," Browne said. He described the events of the day as just a "temporary" setback and predicted "the wounds of liberty" would soon heal.
Browne then announced that the Commonweal intended to stay in
Washington "until there is a greater gathering here of men than confronted Lee on the banks of the Potomac." When this group was assembled, Browne declared they would win "the passage of Brother Coxey's
good roads bill."[68] Comparing their effort to the Civil War reinforced the
notion that the men were not so much destroying the nation as trying to
restore the Union to its initial purpose.

District authorities continued to reject the protesters' claims to belong
in the capital and stepped up their efforts to control the marchers. On
May 2, Coxey went to observe the bail hearing for Browne. To his surprise, Coxey was arrested. The warrants cited each of them for the display of banners in violation of part of the statute regulating the Capitol
grounds. The warrants failed to point out that in each case the "banner"
was a lapel pin that measured only "3 inches by 2 inches wide." To bolster the authorities' obviously weak case, a second accusation of walking
on the grass was added to Browne and Coxey's charges.[69] Although
Browne had definitely stepped on the grass, so had the thousands of spectators. Coxey had scrupulously stayed on the paths. In court, the obvious
hostility of the presiding judge soon indicated there was little hope the
men could defeat the charges. Still, Populist congressmen rallied to their
cause, serving as their lawyers. Their defense disputed the constitutionality of the 1882 statute, the singling out of the leaders from the many other
people who had walked on the grass and worn lapel pins, and the contrast between the treatment of the "finely dressed and well fed lobbyist"
and these men. With appeals, it was not until May 21 that the judge was
able to issue their sentences: twenty days in prison and a $5 fine.[70]

The people's right to use national public spaces was simultaneously debated in the Senate. The Populist senators began the argument by challenging this treatment of citizens who claimed the right to go to national spaces. On May 9, Senator Allen introduced a resolution calling for a Senate hearing on the arrests. He saw in their arrests a pernicious effort aimed at preventing them from exercising their rights of assembly and petition. Passionately, the senator argued that Congress had a constitutional and moral obligation to listen to the people. "There was a singular unanimity" among the Republican and Democratic senators, he observed, in support of "driving poor Coxey and his followers from the Capitol Grounds."[71]

Allen's charge inspired senators of the major parties to defend the protection of the Capitol grounds from the likes of Coxey and Browne. They emphasized that Washington and especially the Capitol was foremost for official business by elected representatives, rather than belonging to the people. John Sherman, a Republican from Coxey's home state of Ohio, invoked the commonly accepted myth that the District of Columbia had been established because "our Revolutionary ancestors were driven from their seats in Philadelphia by a mob in the city." The former Confederate general from Georgia, John Gordon, a Democrat, blamed the Commonweal's origins on the much-hated "paternalism" and concluded that Congress should neither listen to these people nor enact their programs. George Hoar, the Republican senator from Massachusetts, joined in, declaring only "the majority of the duly chosen representatives" could find solutions.[72]

The Commonweal's claim to represent others faced strong criticism in these attacks. Inspired in part by Coxey's Army, the House Labor Committee had decided to hear testimony on the causes of the economic depression. This hearing was the sole legislative success of the Commonweal's march to Washington. As part of it, Coxey presented a petition to the committee supporting his two bills. The congressmen showed little interest in his proposals. Instead, they used the hearing to establish that Coxey and his army did not represent any legitimate group. "How are you the representatives of the people?" Speaker Charles Crisp asked. "By what authority do you undertake to represent the 65,000,000 people of this country?" He reminded Coxey that the "people's representatives are the 356 Representatives elected to Congress."[73]

While the court and Congress deliberated the fate of the two leaders, the rest of the Commonwealers, now joined by many more men coming from the West, struggled to maintain themselves and their political message. Competition for limited supplies and attention caused conflicts between the men already in Washington and the groups that arrived later. Splits developed and new camps were set up around the borders of Washington in both Virginia and Maryland. The camp on the bluffs above the Potomac River in Roslyn, Virginia, eventually grew to more than a thousand men. Conditions were rough; some men begged door to door to keep themselves from starving. Once their original leaders were in jail, new leaders tried to organize further parades in Washington, including one on Memorial Day, but they did not attract many spectators or persuade Congress to act in their support.[74]

When Coxey and Browne were released from jail on June 11, they announced plans to revive their cause on July 4. An embittered Coxey explained that the steps of the Capitol seemed to him "the most appropriate place" for a Fourth of July celebration. He announced, however, that he would not be at the celebration since he had decided to run for Congress in Ohio on the Populist ticket. The experience in Washington seems to have convinced him to return to electoral politics.[75]

With Coxey in Ohio, Browne orchestrated the ill-fated Fourth of July parade. This event was beset by difficulties from the outset. For one thing, journalists' attention had drifted away, and Browne went overboard as he tried to revitalize the cause with more outrageous performances. On July 4, three hundred men marched to the District from Maryland. On a wagon, Browne had painted one of his political "panoramas" decrying attempts to prevent "free speech, franchise, and free assemblage" in the capital. Accompanying the parade was a very odd-looking "Goddess" of Liberty. Reporters noted, "Her arms were bare, but browned with exposure to the sun, such as one might find with the man who had followed the fortunes of the army." Led by this Goddess, the men avoided the Capitol grounds, again patrolled by numerous police officers. Instead, they gathered at the Peace Monument on Pennsylvania Avenue. There, the Goddess spoke briefly about how corruption was destroying liberty in the United States. At the end of her speech, she "fell as in a trance" from her horse, was caught by waiting members of the Commonweal, and was placed behind the panorama. And soon "after some rustling," Browne, who had been strangely absent from his own parade, appeared without the beard he had worn since Massillon.[76]

Browne's divine cross-dressing dramatizes the difficulty the Commonwealers faced as they came to realize that their claim to be heard in the capital was being ignored. Critics reported the incident with a sense of fulfilled prophecy; Browne was not a political leader, but an insane and desperate performer. To them, the movement and its leaders had now shown their true colors. Sympathizers remained silent. Browne soon departed, hoping publicity stunts in other cities might raise money for the men in Washington and revive interest in the cause. He faced major competition, however. By this point, the strike at the Pullman Company in Chicago and the accompanying boycott of Pullman cars by the American Railway Union preoccupied both legislators and the press. Relying on reports of interference with the U.S. mail, President Cleveland ordered federal troops to protect the railroads in Chicago. News of the Commonwealers quickly faded from most newspapers beyond Washington. Even in the District, the stories grew briefer and more likely to appear off the front page.[77] In the beginning, the newspapers had brought the Commonweal to public attention; in the end, their inattention hastened its demise.

Soon the authorities' tolerance of the camps near the District ended. Supporters still collected donations of food and money, but supplies were short and the purpose of remaining unclear. Some men began to leave of their own accord, and sympathizers arranged for rides in railroad boxcars for others. Finally, on August 9, the governor of Maryland ordered the arrests of the hundred or so men in the camps in his state and their placement in the workhouse. On the same day, the Virginia militia warned the men in Roslyn that soldiers would close the camps the next day. The soldiers arrived early, drove the men from the camp, and sent them onto the bridge crossing into the District. A standoff ensued as the District police prevented them from entering the capital until definite plans were made to take the men out of the area. By August 14, the last 165 men were either riding trains or walking out of Washington. With this anti-climactic departure, Coxey's Army and their "invasion" of Washington was over.[78]

The Commonweal of Christ did not win its demands or gain the respectful attention of Congress. Congress did not immediately take up, much less approve, either the Good Roads Bill or the Non-Interest Bearing Bond Bill. Nor did the federal government institute a similar program designed to alleviate the problems of workers and farmers with jobs and a looser money supply, although it did gradually shift in this direction. In the 1930s, the federal government became directly engaged in public works programs, hiring thousands of workers to build city halls, dams, and roads.[79] The legacy of the demonstration lies less with policy implementation than with the type of protest Coxey and Brown envisioned, however. The Commonwealers' ambitions for a demonstration in Washington were thwarted in important ways. Local techniques of protest based on moral and personal claims did not translate comfortably into the actual space of Washington. Unlike demonstrators in cities and towns, who sometimes could confront politicians directly, the Commonwealers in Washington faced a battalion of specially hired police officers. With the single exception of Coxey's appearance before the House Labor Committee, they never did force federal officials to listen personally to their demands. Nevertheless, they established the precedent for a new type of national public political protest.

LEGACIES

Less than a month after Jacob Coxey and Carl Browne's march on Washington landed them in jail, as their followers began to scatter and lose focus, their campaign took on a fantastic new life as the theme of the latest installment of a popular series of pulp fiction. By late May, fans of the adventures of Old Cap. Collier—a detective who was a master of disguises, regularly defeated multiple opponents with only his wits and his hands, and always sent true criminals to their appropriate fates—could pick up the latest account at the newsstands for five cents. The fictional Collier always appeared in the midst of events familiar to readers of the newspapers; and the novel, with remarkable precision, focused on the crucial issues at stake in the development of this new style of protest. In *On To Washington or Old Cap. Collier with the Coxey Army,* the intrepid detective is asked by the Secret Service to infiltrate Coxey's Army. But Collier is outraged when the chief of the Secret Service calls the participants "tramps" who he wishes he could "blow . . . into smithereens." A believer in working-class independence, Collier is always inclined to judge right and wrong for himself rather than accept the word of authorities. He challenges the stern bureaucrat by insisting that the demonstrators are "peaceful citizens, petitioning for their rights" who have "a constitutional right to assemble." In the end, he accepts the assignment in order to protect the marchers. He travels to Coxey's home base at Massillon, disguises himself as a farmer, and soon finds plenty to do. He spots "notorious" criminals among the groups, fights them, and ensures their eventual capture. He advises Coxey and even restores a thwarted love affair. Heroic in his efforts, Collier remains ambivalent about the effort. While he respects the unemployed men and their rights, he doubts the tactic of marching on Washington. Indeed, at the conclusion of the story, Collier makes the romantic hero swear that he will involve himself in no similar activities; instead the man will seek improvements for "the laboring people and unemployed" through the traditional method: "the ballot box" (fig. 5).[80]

Both the swift publication of this special number of Old Cap. Collier's

FIGURE 5. The cover of the sensational account *On To Washington or Old Cap. Collier with the Coxey Army.* The story was an early example of how the march to Washington attracted the imagination of people in the late nineteenth century, even as many were deeply concerned about the protest and its implications. (Courtesy of Harry Ransom Humanities Research Center, University of Texas at Austin)

adventures and the ambivalence that ran through it emphasize the importance of the precedent established by Coxey's march on Washington. In a dramatic, new way, the march raised the possibility that Americans and their political causes actually belonged in the capital and evoked visions as extreme as they were contrasting. Coxey and Browne never gave up on their fantasy of transforming the American political system with their "petition in boots." Despite the failure of their protest to win their political demands, both men continued to believe that marches on Washington belonged in the political repertoire and were constitutionally protected. They were personally emboldened by the attention paid to them over the course of the protest, and continued to search for ways to win that attention again. Politically, Browne remained a gadfly with a radical stripe, turning more and more to explicitly socialist causes. Browne remained fixated on Washington, returning in 1913 at age sixty-four. According to Arthur Young, who wrote a melancholy portrait of Browne for *The Masses,* Browne was often found on the corner of Tenth Street and Pennsylvania Avenue standing on a soapbox. Young observed that his speeches had not changed much from earlier years; he still "spoke against the capitalists and the money-lenders." Likewise, he still wanted to challenge official control of Washington's spaces. Browne defiantly gave a speech on the Capitol grounds in late December 1913. Despite the lack of audience and national attention, it seemed to be enough for Browne. Three weeks later, on January 16, 1914, Browne died. "He had nothing left to live for," Young remarked. "His life's work was accomplished." In the same year but apparently without any coordination with Browne, Coxey organized another march to Washington. A few men joined him, but again few paid any attention. Without novelty or the obsessive interest of journalists, neither man was able to revive the national debate caused by their earlier efforts. By the time Coxey finally did speak at the Capitol, at age ninety, the man, the speech, and the controversies surrounding his tactics had become historical relics.[81]

For many in the 1890s and later, the efforts of Coxey's Army became both a cautionary tale and a subject of humor. Consider how the phrase "Coxey's Army" became part of American slang. For some, the phrase "looking like Coxey's Army" became an American expression for labeling a ragtag, dirty, disorderly group. In this form, the image of the participants as tramps carried on in American popular images. Another usage simply dismissed the group's political goals and its leaders: "an unorganized gang under the leadership of an agitator."[82] Interestingly, in all such cases, the claim of the group for citizens' right to use national spaces drops out of sight.

In the 1890s, however, citizens routinely claiming the capital seemed like a possible nightmare. Just after the Commonwealers started out from Massillon, the *Washington Post* ran a satirical editorial that declared there should be "no monopoly for Coxey." It entertained the idea that groups of all sorts might also come to the District. The editorial concluded by wondering what else was "Washington here for, anyhow, if not for the use and glory and delectation of the evangels, the reformer, the complainants and the cranks?" Senator Joseph Hawley saw less humor in the situation. As he warned the Senate of the dangers in Coxey's Army, he predicted that if the Senate did not handle the "business gently and firmly . . . it is quite possible . . . that it may become a habit to make pilgrimages annually to Washington and endeavor to dominate Congress by the physical presence of the people."[83]

Hawley's fear that marching on Washington might become habitual was prescient. Coxey's Army had established unquestionably that political protest in Washington was possible under certain conditions and that it would attract considerable attention from both Congress and the press. Even in the midst of virulent attacks on the Commonwealers, authorities did not deny that political groups had the right to parade in some parts of Washington. While the Capitol grounds were firmly and emphatically closed to such demonstrations, the rest of Washington had been established as both a legitimate and potentially powerful place for national protests. But the squelching of Coxey's Army was such that no other groups would successfully use those streets to attract the nation's attention until 1913. In that year, woman suffragists built on the precedent set by Coxey's Army and held a national march in the capital that received praise and federal support. In 1913, different strategies and different alliances would result in a very different spectacle and a more encouraging precedent. In contrast to the Commonwealers of Christ, who laid claim to Washington as the property of citizens, the suffragists conceived of Washington as a powerful stage that citizens could borrow and use to further their own political ends.

A "NATIONAL" DEMONSTRATION

The Woman Suffrage Procession and Pageant,
March 3, 1913

In 1972, Alice Paul was eighty-seven years old and impatient with the nostalgic interviewer sent by *American Heritage.* He seemed interested only in reminiscences about her role in the early struggles of the women's rights movement at the turn of the century, rather than her current efforts to pass the Equal Rights Amendment. Though demurely dressed, with her short gray hair held back by a band and a floral brooch at her neck, Paul was as irascible and future-minded as ever. Pressed to speak about the past, she eventually described an elaborate procession and pageant that she had organized in the nation's capital some sixty years earlier. With pride, Paul explained that she and the National American Woman Suffrage Association had orchestrated the 5,000-woman strong procession to "impress the new President" with the need for a constitutional amendment guaranteeing women the right to vote. Paul had pointedly upstaged President-elect Woodrow Wilson's inauguration by holding the march the day before. The unique and colorful form of the march emphasized the beauty and dignity women could bring to national politics. Reluctant as she was to bask in the comforting glow of past achievements, she felt the 1913 suffrage march proved that dramatic public action in the capital was a critical tactic in the struggle for winning the vote—and set a precedent that decisively shaped the possibilities for other activists seeking to march on Washington.[1]

The suffragists' demonstration, nineteen years after Coxey's Army straggled away from Washington, was a critical turning point for the acceptance of protesting in the capital. Their effort showed that Washington demonstrations could be both dramatic and respectable. Remember that the "petition in boots" by Coxey's Army had seemed radical and unprecedented. In contrast, throughout the planning of the procession in 1913, the suffragists drew on techniques already in use by their movement in other parts of the country. They politely but firmly asserted their entitlement to use the political space of Washington as they saw fit. The protest attracted the attention of Congress, outgoing President William Howard Taft, incoming President Woodrow Wilson, the press, and the nation.[2] Having come to Washington, Paul and other suffragists became a highly visible force in national politics.

The visibility of the procession represents the skill with which Paul and her supporters took advantage of changing currents in American political culture. They recognized that activists could capitalize on the emphasis on exposure in the Progressive Era by using the public streets of the capital to advocate their cause of political equality for women. As they sought to make their cause visible they did not so much challenge the authority of the federal government as co-opt that authority to their own cause. At the same time, the procession and pageant became a public display of how Paul and other suffragists imagined a nation that included women. The demonstration emphasized how the beauty and dignity of the participants could carry over to public life in general. Not surprisingly, the suffrage procession Paul organized generated considerable controversy—but this controversy was mostly about the style of the procession, the behavior of spectators, and the responsibilities of authorities in relation to demonstrations. Few questioned the basic principle of marching on Washington.

The 1913 suffrage procession helped establish Washington as a public national space, open not only to official ceremonies but also to large-scale popular demonstrations. The march Paul organized used the existing ritual of presidential inauguration to interject the cause of woman suffrage into this space and onto the political agenda. The suffragists took physical control of the center of Washington and remade it into a forum for their cause of national suffrage for women.

"THE CENTER OF THE STAGE":
REVEALING THE PLACE OF WOMEN IN THE CAPITAL

After the fact, when Alice Paul and others described the place of the Suffrage Procession and Pageant in the history of the suffrage movement, they emphasized the role of the march in making their cause visible.[3] This retrospective emphasis reflects more than just the obvious facts that the procession took place outdoors, in front of scores of spectators, and that it was widely reported. Rather, visibility represented to the suffragists an essential political achievement. They shared a growing faith in the power of exposing ideas, problems, or people to public scrutiny and consideration. Such visibility was a part of American political culture during the first decades of the twentieth century, known as the "Progressive" period, a time characterized not so much by specific initiatives and accomplishments as by a widespread faith among politicians and activists that progress was possible. In this optimistic vision, the first step toward change was making information about current conditions and future possibilities available and more visible. This emphasis on visibility inspired Progressive reformers to undertake intensive sociological studies of neighborhoods, to photograph slums and publish the results as exposés, and to advocate laws requiring reporting of the ingredients in foods and medicines. Moreover, activists increasingly displayed their vision of progress and their ambitions for an improved society with public demonstrations in the streets.[4]

Alice Paul enthusiastically embraced this new emphasis on political visibility. She came from a family of Quakers, long known for their involvement in political activism, and Paul found irresistible those actions that challenged conventions about women and their place in public life. Like Carl Browne a generation earlier, Paul was shaped by her previous experience with street protest. After receiving a master's degree in sociology from the University of Pennsylvania in 1907 at the age of twenty-three, she went to England to study at the London School of Economics. She soon realized that her strengths were not as a social worker but as a political thinker and activist, and she threw herself into the activities of the most "militant" branch of the English suffrage movement.[5] Through the action-oriented Women's Social and Political Union, Paul learned the value of dramatic, challenging public demonstrations in carefully chosen locations that made the suffrage cause visible. The group's slogan, "Deeds, not Words," epitomized its members' commitment to action rather than the traditional focus of suffragists on education. The range of their dramatic public—and sometimes disruptive—actions was wide. In 1906, the group marked the opening of Parliament with their own small procession; later that year they held a mass outdoor meeting in Trafalgar Square, the traditional site of such protests in central London. The activists also began to break the law. They argued that only such actions could show how intensely they believed in the need for political equality. Activists, including Paul, purposely sought arrest by disturbing public meetings and breaking shop windows in busy commercial districts. Though explicit victories were few, these actions ensured that suffrage was a constant concern of British politicians and often on the front pages of the newspapers. Even in the United States, journalists eagerly reported on the activities of the "militant suffragettes," including those of Paul herself.[6] For Paul personally, her own drive and her deep commitment to women's equality meshed with the organizational demands and the excitement of these dramatic activities.

When Paul returned to the United States in 1909, she found the American suffrage movement in comparison weak, timid, and invisible. Since 1880, woman suffragists in the National American Woman Suffrage Association had used gentility to make their cause both more public and more respectable. To do so, though, they had relied almost exclusively on discreet conferences with legislators, quiet conventions in rented halls, and small gatherings in private homes. They deliberately reduced public controversy about woman suffrage by marginalizing advocates with unconventional views, like Elizabeth Cady Stanton, who criticized traditional Christianity. They also compromised with racist supporters who demanded the exclusion of African American women from the movement. These efforts allowed the association's membership to grow and for its cause to be regularly debated among respectable women.[7] But others, especially politicians, ignored their demands. To Paul, ambitious and autocratic, the weaknesses and failures of the suffrage movement were opportunities to refocus the movement on winning a federal amendment enabling all women to vote and to increase the public visibility of the suffrage movement.

Though Paul often talked as if she alone brought parades and spectacles to the United States movement, other suffragists had already begun using these methods to increase the visibility of their cause. It helped that in the time since Coxey's Army, American intellectuals were thinking about crowds and lobbying in more positive terms. At the turn of the century, Gustave Le Bon's influential study *The Crowd* (it appeared in English in 1896) sparked a discussion of the appropriate place of collective action in the United States. Le Bon viewed crowds as essentially evil, transforming individuals into lunatics. Most commentators in the United States recognized that some crowds did indeed get out of control, but asserted that with proper attention to individuality, people could act together responsibly and indeed usefully.[8] Often these thinkers incorporated a sense of the power of visibility, of watching and being watched, in disciplining the behavior of people in an increasingly complex society. By 1913, leading American social psychologists regularly considered how to control and direct groups and crowds toward positive ends.[9] A related change was a more positive view of lobbying. The negative view of lobbying that Coxey and Browne had carried with them in 1894 still had much power. A popular understanding was that lobbying constituted "the use of secret and personal influence" for the private gain of industries and their owners. To control this influence, many states passed laws requiring that lobbyists reveal their efforts to the public by registering and disclosing who paid them. Such reforms helped some to believe visible lobbying could be educational and thereby improve the quality of legislation.[10]

Still, the long-standing association between women in the streets and prostitutes made these suffragists reluctant to move from the more moderate methods of education to actual marching in the streets. For many, however, the new Progressive celebration of visibility helped convince the most conservative of women activists that suffragists needed to enter public space if they wanted to achieve political recognition. One of the first American suffrage parades was in New York City in 1907: two dozen mainly working-class women marched to publicize the state campaign. By 1909, even Anna Howard Shaw, the cautious president of the American association, who remained horrified by the British Women's Union's illegal and violent acts, conceded the American effort could use "a little more gusto and display." She observed that "street parades with banners and speeches by curbstone orators would throw the life needed into our efforts." The following year, middle- and upper-class suffragists in New York City joined the working-class activists in large parades organized by Harriot Stanton Blatch, the founder of New York State's Women's Political Union. In 1910, at the annual convention of the Suffrage Association in Washington, D.C., where Paul praised the British tactics, Blatch led a session on "open-air meetings." She and three other panelists explained how to speak in public and then took a group of women down to Pennsylvania Avenue to practice.[11]

Some of these women took what they learned to the state campaign in California. There, they combined parades and mass rallies with a sophisticated mixture of slide shows, movies, and political pamphlets. They won the vote in 1911. Similar campaigns led to victories in Washington, Oregon, Kansas, and Arizona between 1910 and 1912. Alice Paul introduced such street protests to Pennsylvania when she moved to

FIGURE 6. Alice Paul wearing her academic robes. This picture was taken just before she moved to Washington to organize the Suffrage Procession and Pageant. In Philadelphia, she organized rallies near Independence Hall. In Washington, she sought to use the capital to make visible the need for a federal amendment granting woman suffrage. (Library of Congress, Prints and Photographs Division, LC-USZ62–48792)

Philadelphia to pursue a Ph.D. in sociology. Pushing local suffragists into new activities, she instigated a series of outdoor meetings. In the culminating rally in September 1911, some 2,000 supporters took possession of a national symbol of political liberty: Philadelphia's Independence Square (fig. 6).[12]

Such local and state efforts convinced Paul that what the movement really needed was an even bolder national campaign. Frustrated by compromises necessary in the local and state campaigns, she sought to focus instead on a single, sweeping change: a federal amendment granting women the vote. Having finished her studies at the University of Pennsylvania, she looked for a way to work for woman suffrage at the national level. She succeeded in 1912 when she successfully lobbied the National American Woman Suffrage Association's leadership to let her lead its congressional committee. Paul knew that the congressional committee was supposed to serve as the main national political base for woman suffrage. In actuality, this committee had tended to do little. The chairwoman whom Paul replaced reported that the highlights of 1912 were the annual testimony in favor of the woman suffrage amendment and a "suffrage tea for the wives of Senators and Representatives."[13] In contrast, Paul hoped to use her position as chairwoman of the committee to spark a considerably more militant and visible campaign for a federal amendment.

Long committed to the importance of visibility, Paul believed that a stronger physical presence in Washington would improve chances for passage of the federal amendment, especially if the suffragists used the British Women's Union's tactics. Although the delegates of the American suffrage group refused to endorse all her ideas, Paul did convince them to allow her to organize a suffrage demonstration in the capital. For Paul personally and the suffrage movement generally, the planned procession came to symbolize the switch from the state-level campaigns of the past to a highly visible national campaign.[14]

Paul eagerly began planning how to use the capital. Within days of her appointment to the congressional committee, Paul left for Washington to begin organizing the approved demonstration. Once there, she met with the previous chairwoman and recruited experienced fellow organizers. Soon, her single-mindedness and compelling belief in her methods convinced some local suffragists in the District to join the effort. Intent on attracting attention to her plans, she rented headquarters for the committee in a storefront on F Street in the midst of the shopping district and put up a large sign. Then, with the help of the local suffragists, she started contacting the District and federal officials who could authorize the procession that she hoped to hold on March 3, 1913.[15]

With her characteristic flair for drama, Paul wanted the demonstration to proceed up Pennsylvania Avenue on the day before President-elect Woodrow Wilson's inaugural parade would follow the same route. Aware of the potential for both huge numbers of immediate spectators and considerable press coverage, one suffragist congratulated Paul that having the march in the midst of this important political transition and celebration "was a master stroke." Unlike Coxey's Army, which took a combative stance against the government, Paul's strategy was to co-opt the symbolic grandeur of the increasingly monumental capital and to use the inaugural procession to dramatize her own cause. She declared that the women's procession and pageant should "occupy the center of the stage" in Washington. She would juxtapose the patriotism and nationalism of the inaugural rituals with the conspicuous marginalization of women from public life and political power. In order to fulfill this plan, however, she personally had to tread a careful political path as she negotiated with a series of executive, congressional, and District officials. This path, like the march she was planning, was a useful analogy for the suffragists' political goals. Just as they argued that women deserved the vote because they were like men, so they asserted that the women's processions, like those of men, had a right to march in the capital because women were like "other law-abiding citizens."[16]

Alice Paul planned this national suffrage parade in a mixed climate of tolerance for some sorts of public demonstrations and severe repression of others. In 1897, the Supreme Court had firmly established the right of authorities to control the use of streets and parks, but city officials did not bar all political demonstrations. Authorities sometimes suppressed religious appeals and parades by Jehovah's Witnesses or the Salvation Army, even arresting proselytizers who defied official orders. Likewise, demonstrations by members of the Industrial Workers of the World to end the oppression of workers resulted in regular violence against the speakers, arrests, and far-reaching bans on such activities. Yet, most cities continued to permit large political gatherings of groups they deemed respectable.[17]

Paul's juxtaposition of the suffrage procession with Wilson's inauguration on March 4 revealed how she sought to take advantage of this ambivalence, especially in the context of the nation's capital. In particular, Paul understood that the presidential inauguration served as a moment of symbolic political definition and nation building. By the beginning of the twentieth century, inaugural parades had become elaborate ceremonies illustrating the growing power of the presidency, the national government, and the United States. At the same time, these ceremonies also made particularly visible the reality that men controlled political power. In 1906, Theodore Roosevelt displayed his masculine bravado when he rode up the avenue as a band played "There'll Be a Hot Time in the Old Town Tonight." Wilson—hardly a Rough Rider—delegated all the planning to an inaugural committee, which began designing an elaborate event to include many delegations from all-male civic and military groups. Wilson's inaugural committee refused to allow women to march in the actual inaugural parade. Paul wanted to highlight this exclusion of women from public life. She explained her choice of date by saying it would show that "one-half of the people have not participated in choosing the ruler who is being installed." Paul recognized that the timing of her parade would bring considerable attention to the cause of woman suffrage. Everyone—the inaugural committee, the long-term District residents, and Paul—knew that thousands of out-of-town supporters of the incoming president and his political party and watching journalists came to Washington for the inauguration. She had picked the date of March 3 precisely because "most of the crowds are here by that time and they are not yet tired out by the inauguration."[18]

Already schooled in the art of appropriating political sites for demonstrations, Paul also recognized the potential of the capital as her stage. The city's character had changed since 1894, when Coxey's Army arrived. Between 1894 and 1913, Washington combined general civic improvement with the aggrandizement of the federal image. In 1902, federal and District leaders announced the ambition to make Washington into the "most beautiful city." Improving Pennsylvania Avenue was at the core of the plan. District leaders of the City Beautiful movement convinced the Baltimore and Ohio and Pennsylvania Railroads to remove their tracks from Pennsylvania Avenue and move into the grand Union Station by 1908. Installing electrified track for streetcars on the avenue removed the mess of the old horse-drawn system. Simultaneously, the physical presence of the federal government grew. The Capitol campus expanded with the erection of the House and Senate Office Buildings. The White House's West Wing was completed in 1903. The completion of a new building for the National Museum on the Mall ensured a majestic home for the memory and treasures of the nation.[19] These changes in the center of Washington helped make the capital more impressive and more symbolically powerful for someone like Paul, who wanted to use it for gaining national attention.

To use this increasingly monumental space, though, suffragists needed to obtain permission from various authorities. With Paul as their strategist and respectable Washington women as the negotiators, the suffragists won extraordinary, unprecedented access to official spaces. District officials quickly acquiesced to the concept of a suffrage procession. The District commissioners also approved a series of related open-air meetings; Paul crowed that this was "the first time . . . that this permission has ever been granted to any organization as far as we know; not even the Salvation Army have ever received this privilege." Soon after, federal authorities approved access to other areas. The suffragists wanted to use the south steps of the Treasury Building for a pageant about the virtues women would bring to politics with the vote. Despite the lack of a precedent, on January 2, the secretary of the treasury, Franklin MacVeagh, granted permission.[20]

More difficult, Paul found, was securing the cooperation, or at least acquiescence, of the chief of the Metropolitan Police, Richard Sylvester. Having held the office of police chief for fifteen years, Sylvester was secure in his position and confident that he knew the capital and its streets better than Paul did. He had developed a national reputation by pursuing policies designed to improve the efficiency of the force, the treatment of its officers, and its files on criminals. His success in encouraging tourism in the city by reducing pickpocketing, swindling, and most other forms of crime brought him to leadership within the International Police Association and praise from local newspapers.[21] In the District, his approval was needed for a public procession on Pennsylvania Avenue—and he was not inclined to give it.

Sylvester viewed Pennsylvania Avenue as an inappropriate venue for women citizens. Sylvester's argument against Pennsylvania Avenue and in favor of Sixteenth Street rested on spoken and unspoken assumptions about the capital, middle-class women, and how they should use the capital's spaces. For "a dignified parade such as should take place in Washington," he favored a parade along Sixteenth Street because it went through a respectable, mainly residential, upper-class neighborhood, before ending in front of the White House. That street was certainly important in the political and social geography of Washington in the 1910s. A contemporary guidebook for Washington mentioned that Sixteenth Street was often called Executive Avenue and esteemed it for the large mansions of the leading politicians and "other equally famous people." This route, Sylvester assured the suffragists, would give them "just as much by way of an audience" as Pennsylvania Avenue. Pennsylvania Avenue, he emphasized, was far from respectable. While the City Beautiful movement had succeeded in cleaning up parts of Washington, its success at eliminating vice from the center of the city was not complete. He told Alice Paul that "the lower part of the avenue was the bowery district."[22] If the police chief was motivated partly by a sense of propriety, he was also anxious to safeguard his reputation from the public embarrassment that might attend a procession of well-connected ladies through an area tainted by drinking, gambling, and prostitution.

The suffragists shared none of the police chief's concerns and flatly refused to consider the proposed alternative. Despite their own concern for respectability, they were not interested in being protected from disagreeable encounters or associations. Rather, they embraced the potential to confront the bowery and refused to abandon their claim to Pennsylvania Avenue. In part, their determination came from their sense of what made for an effective procession. Paul and her supporters knew the combination of commercial and governmental establishments—and indeed even the disreputable conditions of Pennsylvania Avenue—would draw a much more diverse crowd. They saw this attempt to move the procession to Sixteenth Street as a serious challenge to their plans to use the central and most potent national spaces of the nation. To one outraged supporter, Sylvester's suggestion was an attempt to move them to a "side street," albeit "a fashionable one." A parade down such a street might attract their supporters, but, as another suffragist explained, only on Pennsylvania Avenue could the marchers hope to "present our claims for the ballot to the people who are not . . . interested in suffrage."[23]

In order to win their point, the organizers used their own respectability and their skill with publicity to pressure other city and federal officials. The suffragists won the battle for Pennsylvania Avenue by combining private lobbying with publicity in the newspapers. As soon as Sylvester raised his objections, there were "delegations of influential women here calling upon one official after another." They soon won endorsements from the Chamber of Commerce and the powerful Washington Board of Trade. Still, this support was insufficient, and Paul mobilized wives of members of Congress, who lobbied the Senate District Committee and the Inaugural Committee. Meanwhile, she and her assistants fed the Washington newspapers a steady stream of press releases about all aspects of the planning process, including this controversy. Paul soon reported that "all of the Washington papers" supported their "claim . . . at length." An editorial in the *Washington Times,* Paul reported, declared "there is no reason why we should not have that particular street, since men's processions have always marched there," and the *Washington Post* equated the suffragists to "any other body of law-abiding citizens." Even President Taft put some pressure on the police chief. The combination of influence, publicity, and persistence generated the desired permission. In early January, the chief of police grudgingly gave his assent.[24]

As the power of and attention paid to the federal government increased and the efforts to improve the appearance of the capital bore fruit, Washington physically became a space to which citizens felt entitled. The women and their supporters in the press and government saw Sylvester's effort to exclude them from Pennsylvania Avenue in the gendered terms of their struggle for the vote. And, they saw his assent as a victory in that struggle because it implied the same equalities that were fundamental to their argument for the vote. The victories that allowed the women their demonstration on March 3 were significant not just for that day's event; they were also proof of the power of making their cause both national and public.

"THE MOST BEAUTIFUL AND DIGNIFIED THING"

In 1913, March 3 fell on a Monday, a cool but sunny day. Early in the day, the marchers gathered to begin their procession from "the doors of the National Congress" to those of "the National Executive." Around noon, the horsewomen ready to lead the procession waited at the foot of Capitol Hill, and the lines of marchers behind them virtually surrounded the Capitol. Meanwhile, fifteen blocks away at the Treasury Building, more than a hundred suffragists in elaborate costumes, accompanied by a small orchestra, prepared for the beginning of the pageant. After walking up the historic Pennsylvania Avenue through the commercial center of the city, the marchers planned to meet these performers, proceed south of the White House, and conclude their day's activities at Continental Hall, part of the newly completed headquarters of the Daughters of the American Revolution. This journey through the nation's capital attracted the attention of hundreds of thousands of spectators. The procession even overshadowed the newly elected president's arrival in the city for his own inauguration, delighting suffragists still smarting from his refusal to endorse their cause. By 3:30, when Wilson pulled into Union Station, the procession was just beginning, and Wilson was surprised by the sparse crowds greeting him. He asked companions where all the people were. They replied, "Watching the Suffrage parade."[25]

Having consciously juxtaposed themselves with the presidential inauguration, the suffragists worked to present their most compelling face to the public eye. Like the members of Coxey's Army, who strove to avoid being labeled as "tramps" and instead asserted themselves as reliable workingmen, the organizers had to decide how to present themselves as citizens. And, just as beliefs about the relationship between masculinity and citizenship shaped the style of the march of Coxey's Army in the capital, so specific views of femininity shaped the suffragists' portrayal of themselves as citizens. They designed the form and style of the demonstration to communicate simultaneously the beauty and dignity on which they based their claim to full citizenship. They repeatedly focused on these paired qualities. To one active organizer, the demonstration was "the most beautiful and dignified thing that had been attempted in America or any place else."[26]

The suffragists did not find either beauty or dignity simple qualities to represent or control symbolically. Beauty was a central component of the presentation for the suffragists because the organizers wanted to convey that women with full citizenship would bring to public life a refinement and beauty they believed necessary for a better world. Paul explained to a prospective marcher that they were not "trying to compete with the Inaugural procession as far as numbers" but hoped instead that "the procession may even excel the Inaugural one in point of beauty."[27] Beauty, for the suffrage organizers, had multiple meanings on March 3. It meant the quality of something arresting to the eye, a procession and pageant worth watching. It also meant something most associated with women in the early twentieth century: a feminine attention to appearance, color, and harmony. Beauty was, in the rhetoric and design of the events on March 3, something that improved society by showing an alternative to the grubby, disorderly world epitomized by the bowery conditions surrounding Pennsylvania Avenue.

In the minds of the organizers, an essential complement to beauty was dignity. Marshals at the procession instructed participants "to march steadily in a dignified manner, and not to talk or wave to anyone in the crowd." Dignified participants in the suffrage demonstration showed the individual worth of the participants and of women in general. If beauty could improve society, the women's dignity could convince society of the worth of women in public life. If women marching in public could still possess dignity, then suffrage, a private individual act, would not pose any significant danger. An image of dignity could help counteract the notions of immorality and frivolity that critics associated with woman suffragists. In speeches, cartoons, and even movies that attacked woman suffrage, woman suffragists' undignified, frantic entries into public life led to the home breaking and loss of femininity that proved women were harmed by even asking for the right to vote. In contrast, the women in the suffrage procession in Washington displayed self-control and self-worth. Showing such qualities was so important to suffragists that they could overcome doubts about the use of the demonstration. When the president of the National American Woman Suffrage Association, Anna Howard Shaw, wrote Alice Paul expressing doubts about the cost of the procession, she reassured herself by emphasizing dignity: "Let the women march, if that is their desire, but let us march in a dignified way and let our presence sympolise [sic] the thing we seek."[28] In the context of the suffrage procession, marchers who presented themselves as dignified embodied the argument that women would make reliable independent political actors, capable of controlling themselves.

The pageant on the treasury steps was an essential part of the attempt to bring this dual political vision to life. Around 3:30 P.M., at the Treasury Building, a massive crowd had gathered in anticipation. In addition to the hundreds of people who had paid or been invited to sit in the grandstand, nearly 20,000 spectators crowded into the vicinity to watch the performance. According to the elaborate "Official Program," avail-

FIGURE 7. Originally printed in full color, the program illustrates the emphasis the organizers put on beauty as part of their politics. At the same time, the word "Official" on the cover and the detailed descriptions of the planned events inside the program suggest how organizers hoped to use their dignity to win their demand. ("Votes for Women," Library of Congress, Prints and Photographs Division, LC-USZ62–20185)

able to participants and spectators, the pageant, titled simply "Allegory," illustrated the "ideals toward which both men and women have been struggling through the ages and toward which, in co-operation and equality, they will continue to strive."[29] The supplied synopsis was helpful, since the performance itself was wordless, depending on symbolism and aptly chosen music to tell its story. The southern steps of the classically inspired Treasury Building provided a dramatic stage for the performance that argued for suffrage by looking ahead to an ideal nation (fig. 7).

The figure of Columbia, dressed in a flowing gown of red, white, and blue, appeared first and alone at the top of the steps. The strains of the "Star-Spangled Banner" accompanied the descent of this national symbol to the broad plaza, its space an appropriate metaphor for the huge country she represented. Columbia then called for another woman to help improve her rule over this expanse. Wearing a blue robe, blinded by a hood, and carrying scales, came Justice. Next appeared Charity, sheltering young girls in her cloak. Liberty, the third figure and crucial to the cause of women's rights, appeared without any call. She joined Columbia after a moment of hesitation, as if to signal her concern about the state of freedom in a country that denied political rights to women. But neither the country nor the performance was complete. Columbia still needed companions, just as American male voters did. After a moment of silence, Peace appeared and released a dove. The most hesitant and last of the virtues to lend their strength to Columbia was Hope, "bearing the promise of the future." By the end of the pageant, a rainbow of nearly a hundred performers filled the treasury steps, embodying the potential beautiful nation.[30]

The use of women to play all the virtues as well as to embody the nation reinforced the idea that woman—in that singular, universal sense—held the key to the salvation of the country. Indeed, the allegory suggested to one supporter that women not only had the "intrinsic right to possess" suffrage but also the "power to transform it to public uses more civilized than men thus far have put in practice."[31] With the combination of goddess-like women, dancing young girls, and colorful costumes, the pageant communicated a message of beautiful patriotism that gently rebuked those who would exclude women from political action (fig. 8).

Feminine beauty pervaded the march, from the cover of the official program, which portrayed in the foreground a beautiful young woman beckoning everyone to Washington, to the style of the women who marched up the avenue toward the pageant performers. On March 3, a group of women on horseback, led by grand marshal Mrs. Richard Burleson, started the march. A huge banner with the blunt declaration "We demand an amendment to the Constitution of the United States enfranchising the women of this country" came next. The next figure was a very familiar one to American pageantry of this era: the solitary beauty. In this case, it was Inez Milholland, as a herald riding a white horse. The suffragists used this device just as Coxey's Army had used Mamie Coxey as a goddess of peace on a white horse on May 1, 1894. To observers, Milholland was "beautiful," or in one case of hyperbole, she was a "grand ecstasy in white."[32] The highly sexualized figure of the solitary woman beauty was a mainstay of male demonstrations. Using this woman at the forefront of a parade dominated by women partici-

FIGURE 8. Liberty and other performers in the suffrage pageant posing on the steps of the Treasury Building. This all-woman tableau, accompanied by an orchestra, represented the beauty and dignity that women would experience and then bestow on their fellow citizens if they won the vote. (Library of Congress, Prints and Photographs Division, LC-USZ62–53227)

pants reassuringly suggested that women would continue to embody beauty even if they gained political rights.

At the same time, organizers also wanted to convey another side of beauty: something collective and arresting in its harmony. This came across in the plan to use all the colors of the rainbow in both the pageant and the procession. Organizers assigned colors to groups in the order of the rainbow. Women artists—actresses, musicians, and writers—wore shades of red. The hues of professional women ranged from dark blue for social workers to librarians in pale blue.[33] The color scheme united the procession and the pageant and emphasized the harmonious element that was so important to the suffragists' view of beauty. This harmony suggested that allowing women to be full citizens in the United States would reduce the contentiousness that so many reformers bemoaned in the Progressive Era.

Here was where the suffragists saw beauty and dignity as such useful political complements. Women together and individually could bring beauty and harmony into public life, but they would do so in a way that would continue to celebrate dignity, long seen as an essential component of effective citizenship. One way the procession emphasized harmony and dignity was through dividing the marchers into seven sections, each with a specific theme, designed to draw attention to the great diversity of the women who were unified behind the demand for enfranchisement. Beginning with floats illustrating "the world-wide movement for woman suffrage" and ending with the "Delegation from States Working for Equal Suffrage," the sectioning of the procession illustrated the diversity of the women participating. By marching in groups as farmers, home-makers, actresses, and "wage-earners," the marchers showed that they—like men—contributed to society in many recognizable ways. Small groups of women voters from the western states, marching behind a ban-ner that proclaimed "Nine States of Light Among Thirty-Nine of Dark-ness," dramatized the claim that women who could vote remained re-spectable members of society. Delegations from suffrage organizations in the "dark" states followed their blessed sisters in the last section. By ar-ranging the women in divisions, the organizers appropriated a tradi-tional scheme for demonstrations by men and made a subtle argument about how women would behave if given the vote. Divisions by occu-pations and regions were a standard method of arranging public demon-strations. Indeed, the parade celebrating the completion of the U.S. Con-stitution in Philadelphia in 1787 included men arranged by their occupations.[34] Thus, in setting up divisions for women to march in, the organizers made clear that women had recognizable public identities. Denied the choices given voters in elections, women lining up in the demonstration proclaimed their ability to choose individually and col-lectively how to appear before the public with dignity.

The orderly procession also dramatized the discipline of which women citizens were capable. Mobs, picket lines, and riots consisted of undisciplined swirling masses, whereas this kind of respectable, peaceful demonstration modeled itself on the military parade. Within their cho-sen divisions, women lined up in even rows and columns. A newspaper story illustrated the procession with a picture of marchers assembling on the plaza in similar clothes, four to a row. Even a political cartoon that poked fun at the parade showed the marchers lined up in rows. The marchers themselves practiced their marching beforehand and struggled to stay in the rows when spectators interfered.[35] The even rows of marchers signaled controlled, disciplined citizens who could bring dig-nity to public life.

The pageant also drew on forms of performance that communicated dignity. Pageants were favorites of middle- and upper-class reformers.

Like the classes in painting at settlement houses, which aspired to bring beauty to lives suffering from poverty, pageants interjected art into a public world seen as lacking grace. Primarily community celebrations, pageants often told a stylized history of progress: Europeans conquered Indians for the benefit of both groups; immigrants happily and easily joined the communities they entered; inventions and industries improved the quality of life. Using the familiar form of a pageant implicitly made the cause of suffrage part of history and crucial to further progress.[36] In the context of the Progressive Era's concern with visible improvements to society, presenting oneself in public with both beauty and dignity was not just a good tactic but also a political vision of the society that would emerge when women received the vote.

Some participants, however, feared that organizers would create an apolitical "spectacle." A discussion over the use of floats and costumes for marchers raised these concerns concretely. Color-coordinated costumes were an important part of the attempt to make the procession beautiful. But, to some, costumes seemed undignified. During the planning stages of the national procession, Elizabeth Hyde, a local suffragist, warned that if she had to wear the "purple cap and cape," she might watch rather than march. Her concern was that the use of beautiful costumes would obscure "the individuality of the personnel of the procession" and make the entire effort "artistic, but meaningless." The debate over the use of floats spoke to similar concerns about balancing individuality with group display. For some, floats represented crass "spectacle." A Philadelphia supporter wrote Alice Paul on New Year's Day of 1913 that she hoped for "just a plain walk—a line of marching women—no floats no spectacular arrangements." Even active organizers of the events questioned the use of floats because "we want our story to be told as fully as possible by *women* instead of things."[37] For their critics, floats threatened to replace independent, persuasive political women with silent beautiful objects.

For journalists assessing the procession and pageant, too, the attempt to use dignity and beauty as part of a public political argument brought a mixture of praise and derision. Many journalists complimented the women for their marching style and acknowledged it as dignified and suggestive of women's ability to be disciplined individuals. But their aspirations for beauty were—as their internal critics warned—easier to mock. One headline read, "Female Sense of Color Beauty Will Charm Inaugural Crowds." In the coverage of the actual event, many journalists, including the Associated Press's wire service report, recounted verbatim the suffragists' own descriptions of the beauty of the pageant and procession. Nevertheless, some reporters could not resist mocking the beauty because they recognized that beauty could be subjective and divisive. For example, it could be used to divide women. The *Washington Post* reported that suffragists were trying to hire "pretty girls" for $2 to march in the procession and that anti-suffragists were "counter-offering" with $3 to stay home. Other reporters also stressed what they saw as the absurdity of performers dressed in light gauze dresses "flitting" about on a cool March day. J. A. Lynd's cartoon in the *New York Herald* caricatured the performers as awkward middle-aged women and highlighted their "bare feet" on "cold hard stone."[38] Such reports showed the particular difficulty of emphasizing beauty in an arena in which its political worth was uncertain.

The tensions between beauty and dignity, between pleasing spectacle and realistic politics, were most pronounced in the controversy surrounding the presence of black women in the march. Was it possible for a dignified and beautiful march to include black women? some implicitly asked. Others wondered explicitly, was it reasonable for a movement arguing for the equality of women with men to exclude certain women? Such questions of inclusion and exclusion were central to debates about citizenship and public life in the early twentieth century.[39] Because the concept of marching in public in Washington required the suffragists to assert themselves as citizens, some organizers, including Paul, believed the presence of black women could weaken their claims to political legitimacy. In part, these white organizers believed that because black women were excluded from citizenship on racial grounds, they were not true suffragists. In part, the organizers feared that because black women were commonly stereotyped as not beautiful and not respectable, their presence would weaken the visual argument of the procession.

In the weeks before the march, a group of Howard University women raised the question by asking to march in the procession. Paul's initial response went so far as to claim that "we must have a white procession, or a negro procession, or no procession at all." Though Paul backed down from this stark position, she and other organizers still hesitated to include African American women in the procession. They tried to justify their position by explaining that the "color question" would result in the withdrawal of white marchers from the procession. In the midst of cajoling white women from across the country to join the demonstration, the organizers were reluctant to offend the white supremacist beliefs of some suffragists. They also claimed that Washington as "primarily a southern city" was a particularly risky place for an interracial march. In any case, to some organizers, the woman citizen was essentially white. Paul explained, "We are not making any effort to organize the colored women as such, any more than we are endeavoring to organize the Indian women or the women of any other race." Ultimately, Paul appeared to conclude that black women could take part as long as they were "scattered among some of the northern delegations where the other members will feel no objection to walking beside them."[40]

Some black women did march on March 3, most as members of divisions ranging from state delegations to housewives. Only the Howard students marched in a large group. By scattering African Americans throughout the procession, the organizers subordinated an identity based on race. In the April issue of *Crisis,* the journal for the National Association for the Advancement of Colored People, Mrs. Carrie Clifford of the Washington, D.C., branch reported that forty-two African American women participated, the largest group consisting of thirty-two women from Howard University. She concluded her report with praise for the marchers, who demonstrated the "courage of their convictions" and "made such an admirable showing in the first great national parade."[41]

In contrast, W. E. B. Du Bois, the noted founder of the NAACP and featured speaker at the Suffrage Association's previous annual meeting, did not let the suffragists sidestep the issue so easily. As editor of *Crisis,* Du Bois included, in the same issue that carried Clifford's report on the parade, an acerbic commentary in his regular listing of racist incidents. "The Woman's Suffrage party had a hard time settling the status of Negroes in the Washington parade," he began. Du Bois went on to describe how requests to participate were met with stalling and discomfort. He concluded, "Finally an order went out to segregate them in the parade, but telegrams and protest poured in and eventually the colored women marched according to their state and occupation without let or hindrance."[42]

Perhaps because he sought to emphasize the efficacy of such protests against racist exclusion, Du Bois exaggerated the extent to which white organizers accommodated women of color. At least one black woman experienced hindrance when she tried to claim her place in the march. Ida Wells Barnett, the noted crusader against lynching and the founder of a suffrage group for black women in Chicago, planned to march with her fellow suffragists from Illinois. But other marchers, southern in affiliation, objected a few days before the march to Barnett's plans because they did not want to see a black woman marching in a "white" delegation.

The march organizers supported this policy of segregation. Humiliated and enraged to the point of tears, Barnett argued that "if the Illinois women do not take a stand now in this great democratic parade then the colored women are lost." Barnett was even abandoned by most of her peers in the Illinois delegation, who declined to protest her exclusion. Rather than confronting that question directly, Barnett sidestepped open conflict by avoiding the staging area near the Capitol. She and two of her supporters instead moved down Pennsylvania Avenue and joined the Illinois delegation in the midst of the procession. At that point, no one objected. It was a shrewd move: for them to have attempted to exclude her at that point would have been a disruptive and conspicuous embarrassment. The *Chicago Tribune* published a picture of Barnett marching with dignity, surrounded by other Illinois women, wearing similar clothes, and waving a suffrage banner.[43] However humiliating the experience, and however misleading the photograph was about the racial politics of organizers and her fellow Illinois delegates, Barnett had outmaneuvered her opponents. A firm believer in the power of the print media, she captured the power of the image to project the ideal of interracial harmony and respectability she wished to establish.

These ongoing struggles over the place of black women in the procession reveal how public demonstrations called attention to the question of who belonged in political movements. As the care taken with the form of pageant, the costumes, and the divisions also made clear, presenting one's cause in public required special attention to appearance. The sense of privilege and white supremacy that most of the white suffragists embraced grew more intense at moments of public presentations. Even Mary Ware Dennett, who wholeheartedly defended the right of "colored women" to march since the "suffrage movement stands for enfranchising every single woman in the United States," still needed to reassure herself that the "delegation in any event would not be a large one."[44]

Since the suffrage procession was an attempt to inspire political action by the federal government, Paul and the other organizers were reluctant to challenge what they perceived as entrenched social norms, to criticize the national government, or to ignore the broader political culture. As the suffragists sought the right to participate in the political system in Washington, their tactics and assumptions embraced and exploited prevailing political conventions. Their successful campaign for Pennsylvania Avenue depended on skillful lobbying of both local and federal authorities. Likewise, they idealized a model of female citizenship that rested on qualities like respectability, discipline, beauty, and dignity. These qualities incorporated significant aspects of the class and racial biases of male citizens and embraced common stereotypes about what women could bring to the political system. Yet, using these biases and stereotypes helped the organizers stage a widely observed event in support of women's political equality.

"THE CROWD WAS IN WITH US"

As the procession moved up Pennsylvania Avenue, the suffragists' plan went awry. The marchers discovered that they could not control the performance they had so carefully planned. At first, spectators stood calmly behind ropes on either side of the avenue, applauding the women and waving yellow flags that demanded "votes for women." Only four blocks into the route, however, the crowd began to ignore the ropes strung along the edges of the sidewalk and soon filled in the avenue up to the edges of the trolley tracks that ran down its center. The avenue appeared a "solid mass of people."[45] Some of the spectators, moreover, actively taunted the marchers, harassing them about being out in public or mocking their appearance. One marcher reported hearing someone laughingly call out, "Who will go home and cook the supper?" She also noted that once a remark was made, "the shouts and the jeers and the guffaws . . . would go up in the crowd" generally. Others went beyond verbal assaults and grabbed at the women as they marched by (fig. 9).[46]

The disruption ruined what was supposed to be the climax of the day, when the marchers were to conclude their parade in front of the performers in the pageant. After waiting more than an hour beyond the scheduled arrival, the shivering actresses retreated inside the Treasury Building. By the end of the day, thirteen men were in police custody, charged with being "disorderly" and "annoying paraders." The crush of people in general resulted in more than a hundred people going to first aid stations and hospitals. The crowding of the avenue, the disruption of the procession, and the verbal and physical assaults blurred the boundaries between the spectacle and the spectators. As one participant reported, the sense of orderly division disappeared as she went further up the avenue and "the crowd came closer and closer and closer." Another marcher complained that during most of her march on the avenue, "the crowd was in with us."[47]

This transformation of the demonstration resulted in a sustained debate among suffragists, observers, and politicians about the responsibility of

FIGURE 9. Spectators filling Pennsylvania Avenue and beginning to interfere with the progress of the marchers. A truck carrying the sign demanding passage of a federal amendment was near the front of the line of 8,000 marchers. The buildings were already decorated with bunting in anticipation of Woodrow Wilson's inauguration the following day. (Underwood Stereograph, Library of Congress, Prints and Photographs Division, LC-USZ62–090463)

authorities for protecting marchers in the capital. This debate was irresolvable because each group described the nature of the crowd, the actions of the police, and the responsibility of the suffragists in such different and contradictory terms. At the heart of the debate were questions about spectators, spectacle, and public protest in the Progressive Era. Yet, these contradictions revealed the fissures in perceptions about the nature of public politics and the responsibility of authorities for order, especially when women were using the streets of the capital. In the immediate aftermath of the parade and through the summer of 1913, suffragists, police officers, residents of the District, and senators considered what had happened on March 3 in light of their own attempts to understand what it meant for the capital to be a public site.

All agreed the presence of police officers on the avenue was not sufficient to control the crowding. More than seven hundred regular and special policemen, including around fifty men on horseback, were on duty, a larger force than that used for any previous public occasion in Washington. The men in this force had regularly dealt with the large crowds associated with inaugurals and other special events. Indeed, a phalanx of police vehicles led off the procession. These cars tried to clear the way for the leaders of the march. Neither the cars nor the police could keep the crowd back, however, nor for that matter could the United States cavalry. When Major Sylvester learned that attempts to move the crowds back to the sidewalks were proving fruitless, he called upon the United States Army's cavalry. A division soon left from Arlington, Virginia, at "a fast trot," and arrived south of the Treasury Building around 4:30 P.M. With limited success, the mounted men began assisting the police "in forcing back the crowd." [48]

For the suffragists, the large crowd was their triumph, though obviously it also entailed problems. Paul and her fellow organizers knew they needed a large number of spectators to make their demonstration meaningful. Spectators gave public political action the complicated mixture of legitimacy and publicity that the organizers desired. In fact, it was more important to have large numbers of spectators than it was to have many marchers, in order to prove that the suffragists' cause was central and compelling. Accordingly, they worked hard and concertedly to ensure a sizable audience. They took advantage of the visitors attending the inauguration. In addition, the organizers worked to ensure that District residents would attend. Suffragist speakers visited local clubs explaining plans for the demonstration. Other women spoke in the streets, collecting money and publicizing the procession. Their efforts bore fruit. A police inspector observed that local residents flocked to the women's procession because it was "something that was new to us." The excitement carried over into the media, with newsreel companies recording the events and newspapers across the country giving the story front-page coverage. Many stories used the size of the audience to confirm the importance of the march. The *New York Herald* emphasized the presence of 225,000 spectators in headlines and concluded that the demonstration "attracted a greater crowd than any inaugural ever did." [49]

The suffragists had also anticipated, however, that a large number of spectators might interfere with their plans and had sought assurances from District and federal authorities that they would prevent this from happening. Organizers were very concerned that authorities accept that it was their responsibility to control the audience. To some extent, suffragists knew they needed to take precautions because spectators had disrupted earlier suffrage demonstrations in other cities, intrigued by the novelty of women parading through the streets. In addition, police chief Sylvester had warned the organizers in Washington that members of the state militias tended to spend the time before the inaugural parade drinking and carousing and might find particular fun in mocking the suffrage parade.[50] Such fears and cautions, however, only accentuated the political reasons for demanding that the authorities guarantee protection.

Such demands were a metaphor for their larger demand that the government recognize women as full citizens. The organizers insisted that the authorities, local and especially national, could and must control the spectators. As the actual date of the parade approached, the organizers focused on the need for United States military troops to supplement the District police officers. The organizers insisted that because their demonstration was national in scope the federal authorities should recognize their responsibility to the marchers. On the very morning of the march, outgoing Secretary of War Henry Stimson yielded to the numerous demands from suffragists and arranged for a troop of cavalry to be "on call" at Fort Myer.[51]

When the crowd intermingled with the marchers on March 3, the leaders of the suffragists intensely reiterated these arguments about national responsibility. After struggling through the crowd, many of the suffragists assembled at the recently built Continental Hall. Starting two hours late, the speakers condemned the loss of order during the procession. The president of the Suffrage Association, Anna Howard Shaw, praised the "greater dignity" of the suffragists "under trying conditions," but lamented that she "never was so ashamed of our National Capital as I am tonight."[52] The meeting as a whole approved a resolution that made clear the organizers' belief that the police bore total responsibility for the loss of order. Because of their political connections, the suffragists succeeded in convincing a committee of the Senate that it ought to investigate the affair and determine if the suffragists' accusations were true.

During these hearings, it became clear that many participants saw the problem of the crowd as the problem of men. To them, the spectators were lewd, dangerous, and male. The police not only failed to control this crowd; they joined in and encouraged the misbehavior and abuse of the suffragists. One New Hampshire suffragist marching with her daughter described in horror how "the crowd did hoot and jeer and make the most insulting remarks." This indignity horrified the mother, but even worse was that "there were two policemen standing together that were egging the crowds on to jeer, and they themselves were making remarks to us and jeering." Similarly, a woman who helped plan the procession and was in a car on the avenue was shocked when she asked a policeman to protect a marcher from a drunken man and he told her, "There would be nothing like this happen if you would stay at home."[53] In their testimony, these suffragists stressed the sexual or sexist remarks of the crowd, the attempted assaults, and the complicity of the policemen. For these women, the crowd confirmed a view of the political order as deeply flawed by the immorality of men. "The women's procession at the National Capital was broken up and the participants insulted," Blatch declared, "because the State taught lack of respect for the opinion of women, for the affairs of women, and the unthinking element, the rough element in great crowds, reflected the State's opinion of its women citizens."[54] This emphasis on the violation of women by men resonated with many women's sense that the streets were spaces of sexual and physical danger to women. Such dangers, they concluded, could change only if male domination of these spaces was limited.

Leading suffrage organizers, however, were reluctant to adopt this argument. They feared that such arguments might make women appear so vulnerable that they did not deserve access to politics. Instead, they emphasized that their three months of planning, their permits, and their earnest efforts to obtain protection should have allowed their group not only access to the streets but also a right to access in a form that would preserve their plans for a beautiful and dignified display of their cause. These organizers, led by Alice Paul, described the crowd as "good-natured" and blamed the police for the problems. Later one suffragist testified that "allowing the crowd, even a good-natured crowd, to become so dense was dangerous." For these suffragists, blaming the police made the problem of the disruption an explicitly governmental and political issue. Alice Paul told a journalist the disruption proved "that women should not only be allowed to vote, but to run things."[55]

The police, however, adamantly countered their arguments and instead blamed women for the problems on March 3. First, they disputed the testimony of both camps of the suffragists. Major Sylvester argued that there was a sufficient force of men on the street—indeed more men than at the inaugural parade the next day. Not only that, but he presented evidence that policemen did try to control the crowd. He introduced affidavits from those who saw the officers working hard and conducting themselves like gentlemen. Some officers also denied that spectators verbally or physically abused the marchers. Instead, Sylvester and his officers asserted that the most pressing problem on March 3 was the presence of women and children among both the marchers and the spectators. Captain Henry Schneider commanded a group of policemen in the midst of the worst crowding by the Treasury Building. Schneider described how the "crowd, which was composed mostly of women, some with baby carriages and babies in their arms, became unmanageable, and swept the officers who were deployed off their feet." He added that his efforts to control the crowd failed because the female presence prevented the use of "violent means, such as using our batons, etc." A prominent Washingtonian said the spectators were "a mob of irresponsible people, . . . that is women and children," who had "an inordinate curiosity to see this parade." Such comments revealed that the police blamed the suffragists' gender for attracting women as spectators who could not control themselves or be controlled in crowds.[56] Though the officers and their supporters tried to deny any hostility to suffrage itself, they strongly implied that by leaving the protection of their homes, the women in the procession and in the crowd had proven themselves irresponsible citizens.

The final report of the Senate Committee on the Suffrage Parade did not support the argument of the police that women in public were dangerously volatile. But, neither did it adopt the argument of the organizers of the procession and condemn the police. It accepted that the police's arguments about the nature of the crowd were distorted. The crowd did include women, but men dominated it. The senators included in their reports pictures brought to the hearing by suffragists that showed that men made up the bulk of the crowd. One suffragist told the senators: "I really think we do not need to say much, unless the women all wear derby hats." Another suffragist noted the prevalence of men in suits in the crowds and commented that "unless the spring styles have changed extraordinarily, those are all men in that crowd."[57] The senators' acceptance of the composition of the crowd, however, was only a limited victory for the suffragists. They preferred to emphasize the variety of the crowd: "all classes of people, good, bad, reckless and frolicsome were present." The elected officials rejected the accompanying arguments that men needed to be controlled in public so that women's rights would be respected or that the government had failed women citizens.

The senators did agree that something had gone wrong. As the report concluded, "It is unfortunate that a quiet, dignified parade, composed mostly of women, could not be held upon the best known avenue in the Nation's capital without interference or insult." To the committee, the problem was essentially the crowd in all its diversity, and the solution was simple: the District government needed more control over the streets. The senators suggested new legislation giving the commissioners the ability to shut down traffic during parades. For the Senate committee, the problem with the parade was inadequate traffic control, not suffragists, men or women in public, or governmental neglect.[58] Their decision, though sympathetic to the stances of both those suffragists who criticized the police and those who criticized the men in the crowd, ultimately declared that the best way to ensure order at a procession was to ensure that the authorities had as much power as possible to determine the form and timing of a demonstration.

The results of the debates over the disruption of the suffrage parade reflected an endorsement of orderly parades. Emerging from the testimony and press interviews was a sense that demonstrators who had permits in Washington had inalienable rights to march with protection. The responsibility of the marchers was to be organized, legal, and dramatic. The police and government were responsible for controlling the crowd. The spectators, for their part, should simply watch rather than interact with the marchers extensively. The *New York Times* expressed this view emphatically in an editorial. Though they disliked the women's cause, the editors declared that the parade "was in the exercise of right the legality and legitimacy of which, as an expression of sentiment and desire, are beyond question." Because of this apparently unquestionable right, the editors declared that the suffragists like "other American citizens . . . were entitled to protection."[59] This guarantee of protection, however, carried with it the assumption of governmental control.

LEGACIES

On March 4, the inaugural parade for Woodrow Wilson took place without serious incident. Spectators stood behind cables strung along the avenue; the militiamen marched; the police reported few problems. The contrast with the events of the previous day was clear to the suffragists.

Less clear was the suffragists' next move. There had been immediate, if mixed, political gains for the suffrage movement. President Wilson granted them a meeting and the Senate voted on the federal amendment. But President Wilson declined to endorse the cause and the majority of the senators voted against suffrage.[60] Alice Paul, like Jacob Coxey and Carl Browne, found the experience of staging a demonstration in Washington inspirational—but ultimately frustrating. She remained in Washington and continued to stage demonstrations—including large, peaceful, national marches following the 1913 precedent. Yet, gradually, Paul lost faith in this kind of march and shifted her attention to a new, more combative style of protest—picketing—which challenged some of the very compromises she had accepted while organizing the 1913 suffrage procession.

Paul's frustration with respectable, peaceful demonstrations grew as she saw that the more women marched in the capital, the less significant each protest became. In this realization, she seemed to understand a dilemma that would bedevil organizers of marches on Washington for years in the future. The more respectable and more familiar the protest, the less likely it was to bring widespread attention, even if it still might serve to bring supporters together and illustrate their status as citizens. Eventually, Paul's experiments and frustrations meant that she would break with the National American Woman Suffrage Association and form her own competing organization, the National Woman's Party.[61] In 1917, Paul committed her group to the tactic of picketing the White House and other national buildings. On January 10, twelve women left the headquarters of the party and walked to the front of the White House, where they stood silently. For the next three years, these silent picketers carried banners justifying the vote for women to every national political site in Washington. At first, the picketers drew only minimal attention, but in time the suffragists' banners, with their harsh criticisms of Wilson, generated violent reactions from onlookers and eventually arrest and jailing by the District authorities.[62]

The choice to picket rather than to march was a reaction to the limits encountered during the Suffrage Procession and Pageant in 1913. Picketing did not represent a rejection of all aspects of the experience in 1913. Just as the procession took advantage of the national space surrounding both Congress and the White House, so picketing allowed the suffragists to associate their cause with national symbols. Whether lined up at the gates of the White House or outside the Senate Office Buildings, the silent pickets both asserted their right to these centers of power and illustrated their exclusion. Most importantly, picketing had some of the same benefits that the disruption by the crowd had brought to the suffrage procession. Paul explained that she considered picketing "more useful at this stage than processions, because it has continuous publicity, at least at Washington, while the publicity of a procession is over in a day." And, she noted, "processions have become so common now that they are no longer quite as valuable to us as in the early days."[63] Paul's careful assessment indicated that the value of this new form of protest was that it resulted in sustained "attention" to the cause, just as the disruption by the spectators had extended the power of the earlier protest.

Still, through picketing, Paul tried to move beyond the tense combination of protesting government policy while asking for and receiving government tolerance of the protest. She shifted from polite display toward political confrontation. Such steps were very controversial, especially for women, and especially during wartime. For observers, including ardent supporters of suffrage, the picketing of the White House was unacceptable because it meant that the picketers were not acting like proper citizens: they were violating the government rather than respecting it. The National American Woman Suffrage Association repeatedly blamed the picketing for continued Senate opposition to the amendment; the women were acting undignified, these critics asserted, thus undermining the cause. At the time, as the Senate failed repeatedly to approve the amendment and President Wilson hesitated to endorse it, this analysis seemed insightful.[64]

The debate over picketing raised major questions for the suffragists— about the importance of national politics to their cause, the basis of women's right to protest, and the form that protest should take. After the procession, Paul and her supporters who continued to work in Washington remained committed to directly engaging the federal government and asserting their rights as citizens, even without the vote, to change national policy. Other suffragists, reluctant to make confrontation such a constant part of their political strategy, preferred to stage peaceful parades as spectacles to complement their intensive lobbying of influential leaders.

It was not only the suffragists who struggled with the issue of how to use the capital for political purposes in the 1910s. Other groups also used the streets of Washington to advocate their political goals, though most chose to stay with the legal demonstration. Just eight months after the suffragists paraded for the first time in Washington, more than a thousand members of temperance associations marched on the Capitol. Though less elaborate than the March 3 procession, its organizers hoped to "rival the performance of the women suffragists." The event drew respectful coverage from Washington newspapers.[65] After the war, in 1922, African Americans held a silent parade in the capital to protest lynching that was similar to a much larger one held in New York City in 1917. Although the parade attracted only a few lines of press in the white newspapers, the march of 1,500 represented a strong showing by the beleaguered black community of Washington and the surrounding area. With considerable more fanfare in 1925 and 1926, the Ku Klux Klan illustrated their annual national conventions with a parade down Pennsylvania Avenue. In their robes, but denied their hoods by a decision of the District commissioners, the 25,000 Klansmen and women used their parade and meeting to assert the strength behind their nativist, racist cause.[66]

However, in general the 1910s and 1920s did not represent a period of support for public demonstrations. In Washington, as in other cities across the country, "race riots" illustrated the potential for violence and death in the street. In early August 1919, black and white Washingtonians engaged in a violent series of counterattacks in the wake of an alleged assault on a white woman by a black man.[67] These events in Washington spurred District and federal authorities to prepare elaborate plans to control all sorts of demonstrations. Simultaneously, the Progressive emphasis on visibility that permeated the suffrage procession in 1913 grew quieter as most reformers retreated from ambitious plans and turned to the language of planning and bureaucracy.[68]

The Woman Suffrage Procession and Pageant attempted to make protest in America acceptable. Paul and her supporters used the familiar form of the inauguration and cooperated with the authorities even as they asserted their right to use the public space of Washington. They concentrated on designing a protest that would be tolerated by authorities and middle-class respectable Americans. The apparent failure of the demonstration to convince the Senate to support their cause, however, led Paul to give up on orderly, legal techniques; making protest tolerable, it seemed, did not necessarily make protest effective with legislators. Subsequent protesters in Washington continued to struggle to find the proper balance between spectacle and disruption. Likewise, authorities and the media tried to develop the appropriate response to these national demonstrations. These issues of decorum and challenge all appeared in new ways in the crucial Bonus March of 1932, which was another important turning point in the development of this genre of protest as powerful, pervasive, and constrained.

CHAPTER THREE

"A NEW TYPE OF LOBBYING"

The Veterans' Bonus March of 1932

In February 1992, an eighty-six-year-old widow told her story of the Bonus March of 1932 to a reporter from the *Wenatchee World,* a newspaper in central Washington State. Wilma Waters described a time sixty years earlier when her husband, Walter, set off with three hundred of his fellow veterans from Portland, Oregon, on a 3,000-mile journey to Washington, D.C. The men hoped they could persuade Congress to issue a payment—often called a bonus—promised to them for their service during the First World War. The payment was not due until 1945. But the veterans, out of work amid rampant unemployment, argued that they, as good citizens, deserved the money immediately.

Waters's group inspired thousands of others to join them in Washington, where they became known as the Bonus marchers. For nearly three months, they camped in parks and abandoned buildings. They paraded, lobbied, and waited as Congress debated, voted, and ultimately rejected their demands. As Mrs. Waters flipped through the 288 pages of her husband's book, *B.E.F.: The Whole Story of the Bonus Army,* she recalled the successes of their efforts. But she knew most people's memories of the event were dominated by its conclusion. On July 28, army troops under General Douglas MacArthur drove the Bonus marchers out of the capital city. Even decades later, she mourned that the "eviction" of the Bonus marchers "was so terrible that my husband was afraid that people wouldn't accept the truth."[1]

For Mrs. and Mr. Walter Waters, the Bonus March involved far more than just its draconian end. The protests lasted for nearly eight weeks during the summer of 1932 and required much of participants, authorities, and observers. To understand the Bonus March today requires a detailed look at how these groups—the protesters, the various District and federal authorities, Congress, the army, and the media—planned, acted, and reacted.

One of the most remarkable things about this demonstration was its duration. Since they were unemployed, some of the veterans were able and willing to stay in Washington for months if necessary to win their demands. The length of their stay strained the group's organizational capacities but also put unprecedented pressures on the authorities. Ironically, the long duration of the protest also meant that protesters and observers had more time to experiment with this political tactic. The result was constant negotiation and discussion by marchers and observers alike about the significance of such protests for American political culture. Moreover, such debates meant this event shaped the distinctive form of the march on Washington.

Protesters justified their use of public spaces with a range of arguments. At first, the group legitimized its presence and demands largely by invoking their status as former soldiers, the epitome of good citizenship. They also closely associated their method with the already routine tactic of lobbying Congress. As organizers staged public events in the city and settled in for a long stay, they introduced broader and more innovative reasons for their political legitimacy. Emboldened by praise from some quarters and some successes, they used the public spaces of the capital with a vigor that disturbed some onlookers.

Authorities and politicians responded to the protest with a mixture of tolerance and apprehension. By 1932, authorities were very familiar with demonstrations in the streets of Washington. At first, District and federal authorities responded to the Bonus Army with a new policy of accommodation. At the same time, many feared Communists and Fascists were lurking among the veterans, and these fears shaped their planning. The authorities' use of force and strong public condemnations did for a time make the protest appear both a failure and an inappropriate political tactic. Indeed, in 1992 Mrs. Waters still feared they had succeeded, believing that most copies of her husband's book had been "bought up" to prevent the true story of the veterans' efforts from coming out. Ultimately, though, the use of military force to suppress the demonstration raised new questions about how political officials should respond to such long-term claims to the capital's public spaces. In the end, many people deplored the military suppression of the Bonus March and it became a formative moment in national political protest in the United States.[2]

"ON TO WASHINGTON"

On May 11, 1932, nearly three hundred men climbed aboard boxcars in Portland, Oregon. They shared a common destination: the United States capital. But they—and the thousands of other veterans who would soon join their march on Washington—differed widely about what they would do in the capital and how their presence there might persuade politicians to act on their request. Some saw the trip as part of the democratic process. "All we can hope to do is make them statesmen in Washington vote on the Bonus and go on record," one of them explained. "Then we can the lick the guys that voted against it in November."[3] Others thought they could save their cause from legislative defeat. Some, out of work, did not know what else to do. The social and economic crisis made these veterans desperate enough to leave their homes. At the same time, it is important to note that protests in the nation's capital were something that these people could imagine. The men's confidence in the rightness of their journey showed in their banner: "On to Washington."[4]

If their reasons for going to Washington varied, their methods of reaching the capital were often unconventional and sometimes illegal. The group of men leaving Portland won free transportation on freight trains from Union Pacific Railroad officials by presenting themselves at the yard and refusing to leave until their demand was honored.[5] This victory was lucky. These veterans had none of the systematic political experience that previous organizers like Jacob Coxey, Carl Browne, and Alice Paul had brought to their efforts. Only over the course of the journey did leaders and something resembling a strategy emerge.

Some of the men on the train did have some personal experience with the technique of protesting in the capital. There had been significant public attention when, on January 21, 1931, 1,000 veterans—including some on the train leaving Portland—paraded to the Capitol. They bore a petition with millions of signatures asking for full and immediate payment of their Adjusted Service Certificates, which almost everyone, supporter and opponent alike, called their bonus. Congress had issued veterans of the First World War these certificates—good for a payment based on time served—because, unlike earlier American soldiers, they had received few cash benefits. Rather than pay the veterans directly, however, Congress reduced the immediate cost of the program by creating an insurance policy due upon the death of the veteran or in 1945. But 1945 seemed far away as the economic depression spread in the early 1930s. Supporters of immediate payment—including, by then in his seventies, Jacob Coxey—emphasized the benefit of introducing more money into the economy, the millions who signed petitions in support, and the deserving nature of the veterans (fig. 10). In the aftermath of the January parade, Congress voted to allow veterans to borrow against the certificates. President Herbert Hoover vetoed the measure because of the threat he saw to the "self-reliance" of the American people and because it would increase the federal budget when he believed in retrenchment. Congress overrode the veto. Over the course of the following year, 2.5 million veterans filed for loans on their certificates.[6] Loans, however, did not satisfy everyone.

Many veterans still wanted to receive their full bonus. In a later analysis of the claims of veterans who participated in the Bonus March, the Veterans' Administration found that about two-thirds were entitled to around $1,000, the rest to less than that. The possibility of such payments fueled the idea of returning to the capital in even larger numbers. It took the Oregon veterans less than two weeks to recruit three hundred out-of-work men for the journey to Washington. There was something audacious—or desperate—about this plan. In 1932, most of the unemployed were not inclined to see their situation as political, but rather blamed their bad habits or miserable luck for their situation. When the unemployed did protest, they tended to focus on local improvements: more cash relief or public works jobs.[7]

In contrast, the veterans traveling across the country pinned their hopes on Congress. In February 1932, Wright Patman, a Democratic congressman from Texas, had reintroduced the bill calling for immediate payments against the certificates. The House Committee on Ways and Means held hearings on the so-called Bonus Bill. President Hoover again objected to the measure because of its cost and threats to individualism. Representative Fiorello La Guardia, the progressive Republican from New York, also attacked the bill because he wanted federal aid for all people in need—not just the veterans. With opposition coming from both sides, the committee rejected the measure. Patman, however, quickly turned to another method to win a direct vote. He began collecting signatures from individual representatives to support bringing the measure to a vote. The veterans hoped that their presence in the capital might result in more signatures and eventually a positive vote.[8]

FIGURE 10. Bonus Army commander Walter Waters standing with Jacob Coxey. Coxey's visit to Washington demonstrated his belief that the Bonus marchers were following his precedents, both in traveling to the capital and in demanding more aid for the unemployed. (Collection of Wilma Waters, copy supplied to the author)

But, the veterans were only loosely organized and did not even have trustworthy leadership. The group's initial "Commander-in-Chief" lost his position when his comrades discovered he was pocketing the funds donated for food and supplies.[9] A young man emerged to fill the leadership gap in the group: Walter W. Waters. Just over thirty, he had little background in political organizing, but a fine military record. Called up from the Idaho National Guard in March 1917 to go overseas, he served as a medic and rose to the rank of sergeant. After his discharge in 1919, he returned to the West, where he shifted from job to job. Eventually, he moved with his wife to Portland in 1931. For the next year, the couple apparently lived on savings, the proceeds from selling their belongings, and their earnings at odd jobs. Depressed by this struggle, Waters pinned his personal and political hopes on immediate payment of his bonus. At a meeting in Portland to discuss the Bonus Bill, Waters immediately supported the proposal to go to Washington. Once he came to lead the group, he emphasized the need for military-style discipline.[10]

Though the men's journey began in obscurity, it eventually became a matter of national concern. In contrast to previous marches on Washington, they initiated no concerted publicity campaign. They did not invite reporters to join them on their journey to Washington, as Browne and Coxey had in 1894. Unlike Alice Paul in 1913, they released little information to explain their tactics. The men's push to reach the capital nevertheless drew the attention of journalists because of repeated confrontations with railroad officials. Across the country, newsreels showed the veterans' determination and papers began to report on the veterans' journey to the nation's capital.[11]

As a result of this publicity, frustrated city and state officials decided it would be easier to move the men toward their destination than to confront them. In St. Louis, local veterans joined with the sheriff in arranging transportation to Indiana. From there, the governor ordered the National Guard to move the veterans to Ohio. The trend continued as the veterans moved through Ohio, Pennsylvania, and into Maryland. By May 28, the three hundred men were on the outskirts of Washington.[12]

Press coverage of the men's confrontations transformed the effort into a national event with a defiant strategy and inspired other unemployed veterans around the country. Many hopped trains, while others patched together convoys of trucks and cars. On May 28, Waters concluded there were more veterans already in the District than in his own group; he predicted that 20,000 veterans would appear "within the next two weeks." The increasing attention also inspired Waters to make new claims about the men's intentions. When asked by reporters, he said that the veterans intended to stay in the capital "until the Bonus bill is passed if it takes until 1945."[13] From its haphazard beginnings, the veterans' protest was becoming a genuine threat to the normal humid somnolence of a Washington summer.

"FORCEFUL COURTESY"

Around 5:30 P.M. on Sunday, May 29, 1932, Washington police officer James E. Bennett, a veteran, greeted the Portland veterans at the District border. He assured the men of their welcome, but cautioned, "The minute you start mixing with Reds and Socialists, out you go." By 1932, Washington's various officials had become experienced, if reluctant, hosts to demonstrators. They continued to debate the proper techniques with which to accommodate national protests. The District's Police Superintendent, Pelham Glassford, and President Hoover developed a policy of public toleration that allowed demonstrators considerable access to the capital. Simultaneously, the police chief and military intelligence officials emphasized the potential for disorder and repeatedly invoked the threat of a Communist-led insurrection. A local journalist aptly dubbed this mixed response "Forceful Courtesy."[14]

District authorities' response to the veterans evolved as even more of them poured into the city from nearly every state. Newspaper reports and the Military Intelligence Division suggested that by the end of the first week of June somewhere between 3,000 and 5,000 veterans had come to Washington. Arriving veterans joined the others squatting in abandoned buildings and parks. Many concentrated in a camp of makeshift shacks across the Anacostia River. Waters, now called commander-in-chief, and the other leaders set up a headquarters in a building about halfway between Camp Anacostia and the Capitol.[15]

The District's new chief of police, himself a veteran of the World War, critically influenced the organization of these camps and much of the protest's first weeks. Pelham Glassford had combined a distinguished military career with a bohemian lifestyle, joining the circus, riding motorcycles, and serving as a newspaper reporter. Given Glassford's reputation as an incorruptible military man, it was hoped he could redeem the District police force from Prohibition-related scandals (fig. 11).[16]

After his appointment in 1931, he was willing to help the demonstrators, presenting a sharp contrast to the previous police chief. In 1930, when a group of about one hundred Communists paraded in front of the White House and violated a law governing conduct in that area, the police quickly suppressed the entire protest using tear gas and arrests. Just over a year later, on December 7, 1931, Glassford supervised the "National Hunger March" from astride his motorcycle. Federal military commanders put local troops on alert, and both the White House and the Capitol were under "war-time guard." The officers and soldiers,

FIGURE 11. Pelham Glassford, superintendent of the District of Columbia Police and secretary-treasurer for the Bonus Army visiting Camp Anacostia. Some men were clapping; others appeared less enthusiastic about his presence. The multiracial composition of the veterans who came to Washington is also apparent. (Library of Congress, Prints and Photographs Division, LC-USZ62–19645)

however, did little more than observe as the 1,500 marchers paraded to the Capitol and on to the White House. Glassford's policy of "forceful courtesy" won praise.[17]

President Hoover played a critical role in shaping this tolerant policy. During the Hunger March, Hoover had privately supported Glassford's efforts. A month later, Hoover recognized a group of 10,000 men who marched to the Capitol seeking federal relief for the unemployed. In so doing, he became the first president to reveal publicly that, although he disagreed with protesters' demands, he supported their right to march on Washington.[18]

With presidential backing, Glassford supported the veterans as they settled in the capital. Because of Waters's announcement that the group intended to stay in Washington as long as necessary, Glassford began a "campaign of discouragement," telling veterans they could only stay for two days and trying to arrange for their transportation back home. But Glassford's sympathy showed in other actions as he met with federal officials, and with the help of Hoover's aides, secured materials to set up camps and kitchens.[19]

His most important and unprecedented contribution was his personal leadership. On May 26, alongside five hundred Bonus marchers, Glassford attended an outdoor meeting in the center of Washington. Asked to speak, he expressed his sympathy for the veterans "and all others who are unemployed." He also went so far as to give the group a name. Invoking the label for the U.S. armed forces in 1917, he proposed they call themselves the "Bonus Expeditionary Forces." The veterans agreed to this new formal name, though most participants and observers used the short label of the Bonus Army. Heartened by the general's words and suggestions, the men asked Glassford to serve as secretary-treasurer for the force. He accepted.[20] Suddenly, the nascent demonstration in Washington had as a named officer the metropolitan superintendent of police!

With dual authority, as both chief of police and as secretary-treasurer of the Bonus Expeditionary Forces, Glassford expanded his efforts to find accommodation and food for the marchers. Securing the permission of federal officials, he put veterans in abandoned buildings on federal property. He went to work collecting donations from local merchants, sweetening the pot with $100 of his own money. Such support from a ranking District official gave the first month of the protest an unprecedented feeling of cooperation. The Bonus marchers grew devoted to the police chief. Waters praised him as "friendly, courteous and above all humanely considerate."[21]

Yet, Glassford and others still feared the possibility that the marchers might violently disrupt the capital and they prepared accordingly. The Workers' Ex-Servicemen League, a Communist-sponsored organization, also included the cash payment on its own political agenda and sent members to join the Bonus Army. League members regularly used rhetoric that suggested they were willing to use violence to achieve their goals. Their presence convinced some observers that Communists dominated the Bonus March. Although Glassford thought otherwise, he still prepared for the possibility of serious disruptions. In doing so, he relied on tactics that had been developed since 1913, when officers had struggled to control the spectators at the suffrage parade. One simple strategy was to direct most veterans to Camp Anacostia. If trouble should arise, Glassford could raise a drawbridge, preventing access to the District's center. In addition, he prepared his officers to use tear gas, an increasingly popular

ntrolling demonstrations after its introduction during the
.r.[22]

dition, Glassford explored suppressing the protest with federal
.e cautioned the District commissioners that they might have to
in. .e the "White Plan." The United States Army developed this outline
for "handling a civil disturbance" in the early 1920s in response to the
Bolshevik revolution in Russia and the labor and racial unrest in the
states after the end of the World War.[23] Though the "White Plan" was
mostly ignored in the later 1920s, Glassford's awareness of its terms was
important because its use was soon advocated by another Washington
official: the recently appointed Chief of Staff of the U.S. Army General
Douglas MacArthur.

Separate from but always aware of Glassford's effort, MacArthur ensured that the U.S. Army kept close tabs on the Bonus Army. He was virulently anti-Communist and convinced early that the Bonus Army was
a front for "reds." The protest provided a test case for MacArthur's
scheme to reinvigorate the Military Intelligence Division. Under his direct order, the small intelligence staff in Washington began collecting information on "The General Subversive Situation," which soon came to
include the Bonus March. The officers, under the command of Colonel
Alfred T. Smith, prepared daily reports for MacArthur on the Bonus
March from May 25 until August 3, 1932. From the beginning, they believed that the Communists planned to "create disorder such as would
necessitate drastic action by the authorities." Accordingly, members of
the military planned how to control the Bonus marchers with force. On
June 4, two experimental vehicles, "a T-4 armored car and a 75 mm self-
propelled gun," were moved to nearby Fort Myer; army staff believed
their maneuverability could be useful in case of a riot. On the same day,
the commander of the army troops responsible for the Washington area,
Brigadier General Perry Miles, submitted to MacArthur a revised "White
Plan" that reflected the specific circumstances of the veterans' presence
in Washington. Miles concentrated on how the army should handle the
threat of Communists among the veterans.[24]

The contradictions in official responses to the arrival of the Bonus
marchers show that authorities were struggling to come to terms with the
demands of citizens to use the capital to present political arguments. On
the one hand, Glassford, with the help of the Hoover administration,
gave the veterans active assistance, indeed personal leadership. On the
other hand, unable to interpret the demonstration without reference to
Communists, he and, to a much greater extent, MacArthur planned for

what they saw as an almost inevitable need to use force against the protest. While Glassford closely involved himself with the Bonus marchers, the military officers always kept a suspicious distance from the veterans. By simultaneously helping the Bonus March and planning for its forceful suppression, these authorities displayed their increasing expertise in responding to these demonstrations.

"WE ARE AMERICANS ALL"

On Tuesday, June 7, the people of Washington had their first opportunity to see the veterans as a unified group when the Bonus Army sponsored a parade down Pennsylvania Avenue to the Capitol. In the late afternoon, the men trudged from Anacostia and the other camps to gather on the western side of the White House. The parade took place with the knowledge that the House of Representatives had scheduled a vote on the bonus for the next week. Nearly 5,000 or 8,000 veterans (depending on who counted) marched down Pennsylvania Avenue to the Capitol Building. One hundred thousand spectators lined the route. The parade provided the veterans with the opportunity to make clear what kind of citizens they were.[25] In contrast to participants in Coxey's Army and to the suffragists, the veterans' obvious status as legitimate citizens permitted them to speak of entitlement. Yet, they did not rely on this justification alone. They also emphasized a form of collective American citizenship that built upon the heterogeneity of the marchers. This parade and the subsequent weeks of peaceful lobbying combined to give the Bonus marchers significant early victories and to encourage more and more veterans to join them. As in earlier marches, presenting themselves as veterans and hence deserving citizens helped reinforce their argument that they belonged in the capital's public spaces. What was new was the extent to which the parade was followed by a prolonged period of lobbying, which resulted in positive action from the House of Representatives. For everyone—organizers and participants, authorities and politicians, journalists and concerned observers—the Bonus March became, as Coxey's Army and the Suffrage Procession and Pageant had become, a moment to consider how people should take part in politics, what was acceptable, and how participants could justify their presence in the capital.

Their parade took place in a capital that was more than ever an essential symbol of the nation's importance. In 1925, a railroad company dubbed the destination "Washington: The Place of Pilgrimage for Patriotic Americans." Patriotic pilgrims could make their devotions at new sites completed since the suffrage parade in 1913, including the Tomb of the Unknown Soldier and the Lincoln Memorial. Official buildings for both the legislative and executive branches also became grander during the period. The largest part of this visual transformation was still in progress: the massive Federal Triangle complex of the offices for executive departments and commissions bounded by Pennsylvania Avenue, the Mall, the Capitol grounds, and the White House. Hired to alleviate unemployment, crews had already torn down buildings on much of the site, but new construction was not yet completed. Indeed, rubble lined parts of Pennsylvania Avenue as the veterans marched that evening. Nevertheless, the coming changes were to a contemporary observer "a visual symbol of the triumph of the Federal idea."[26]

The veterans knew they needed to use their time in the federal capital to convince politicians and the public of their political legitimacy. Their parade took the model of the military parade. At the front were the commanders of the Bonus Army. Then came the men in careful rows. Given places of prominence were "14 heroes of the World War" who had received medals for their service. In addition, scattered throughout the various companies were trucks carrying disabled veterans, showing how the war continued to influence the men's lives.[27] These displays of discipline, valor, and suffering provided visual support for the veterans' argument that they were entitled to immediate payment.

For some, however, the sight of veterans marching through the streets of the capital and their claims of entitlement suggested the quasi-military groups that supported Fascist regimes. In Italy and Germany, former soldiers from the World War had supported Benito Mussolini and Adolph Hitler. These parallels gave added weight to arguments that demonstrations in Washington were an inappropriate way to convince Congress. Republican Senator William Borah of Idaho echoed critics of Coxey's Army when he said, "I will not vote one penny for the veterans as long as they are in the Capital exerting pressure on Congress by their physical presence."[28]

In response to such fears, the June parade also presented the veterans as ordinary citizens trying to bring the faces of a diverse and suffering America to Washington. One observer poetically noted the "grease-stained overalls of the jobless factory workers," the "frayed straw hats of unemployed farm hands," and the "shoddy elbow-patched garments of idle clerks." The parade highlighted the racial diversity of the marchers by including among the heroes a "colored" man, William Butler, a District resident who had received both a Distinguished Service Cross and the Croix de Guerre. In fact, around four hundred African Americans marched in the parade, as much as 8 percent of the total on the Avenue. Roy Wilkins, assistant secretary of the National Association for the Advancement of Colored People, was impressed that, with a few exceptions, black and white Bonus marchers lived, slept, and demonstrated together, in striking contrast to the highly segregated conditions of the rest of the District. An editorial cartoon by a supporter conveyed the diversity of the veterans by labeling men marching to the capital as everything from taxpayer to dentist and "local merchant," and by showing them carrying signs proclaiming, "We are Americans All."[29]

The emphasis on the heterogeneity of the demonstrators reflected emerging ideas that the strength of the American nation depended on the diversity of its citizens. Part of the origin reached back to World War I. In 1917, proponents of conscription celebrated that it would "jumble the boys of America all together, shoulder to shoulder, . . . prompting a brand of real democracy." In reality, the United States Army remained racially and ethnically segregated. Still, laws regulating citizenship became slightly more flexible and the background of citizens became more diverse during the 1920s. Concurrently, some political theorists and activists began to embrace "cultural pluralism" and to encourage wide political participation. In 1932, thus, a "polyglot" mixture of citizens— as one observer labeled the Bonus Army—could be an effective political tool.[30]

The June 7 parade served the Bonus Army well. The press, authorities, and politicians in Washington grew more supportive. On June 5, the editors of the *Washington Post* had decried "the descent of thousands of penniless men upon Washington for the purposes of browbeating Congress." On the Thursday morning after the parade, they called for the veterans to go home, but they now supported paying for their transportation and noted that "those who marched are true Americans." In the Senate, John Blaine, a Wisconsin Republican, urged his fellow senators to aid the veterans because "the men, in that march, . . . demonstrated a self-control, which . . . entitled" them to consideration. Many residents of the District also reacted to the veterans' patriotic and peaceful parade with generosity and curiosity. Some visited the main camp in Anacostia, and there were boxes and jars in many Washington stores for customers to donate spare change to the veterans. The parade strengthened the internal organization of the Bonus Army as well. Pleased and encouraged by the response to the parade, Waters abandoned plans to resign from his leadership position because he felt "the sympathy of a nation seemed to be with us."[31]

This sympathy led the veterans to follow the parade with a sustained campaign of lobbying. Waters called it a "new type of lobbying," a claim that was part propaganda and part an honest appraisal.[32] It combined public demonstrations with an energetic and persistent presence in the halls and galleries of the Capitol. Unlike earlier groups who faced the challenge of convincing politicians that their issue belonged at the federal level, the veterans had the advantage and the challenge of the fact that the destiny of the Bonus Bill was unarguably in the hands of Congress. In June, the veterans put as much pressure on Congress as they could.

The majority of the veterans concentrated on appeals to Congress. A sign of their increasingly sophisticated tactics was their legislative committee, which coordinated these efforts. At its head was Harold Foulkrod, who brought to the Bonus Army needed experience in political agitation and protest. In Washington, Foulkrod soon molded the veterans into an omnipresent lobbying force on Capitol Hill. For a number of weeks, one could usually find veterans sitting on the steps of the Capitol and filling the galleries of both chambers. Further, all veterans were encouraged to take the more conventional tactic of personally visiting with legislators from their home state. Looking back, Waters wrote that the Bonus marchers "frankly, made a nuisance of themselves."[33]

In all these ways, the Bonus marchers sought to turn to their advantage the prevailing customs and perceptions of lobbying. As veterans, they were probably all aware of the methods of the American Legion, though that group opposed the current Bonus Bill as fiscally unwise. The legion employed a well-paid and effective lobbyist, John Thomas Taylor. If his private lunches with important politicians and public testimony failed to achieve the Legion's goals, he turned to the membership. He could generate thousands of letters and telegrams to Washington from individual constituents. Because of this ability, the veterans of the World War and their organizations were routinely acknowledged as one of the most powerful and successful "voters' blocs" of the 1920s. Though the label of "bloc" illustrated a continuing uneasiness, such methods were increasingly common and considered quite different from the lobbying done by representatives of corporations. While the veterans' organizations were perhaps the most effective at such mobilization, many other groups, such as farm organizations, temperance societies, and motorists' clubs, used similar techniques and even came to mark the geography of the city as they erected visible headquarters in Washington. Such a commitment of space and money to lobbying reflected how much the air of outrage over lobbying present at the time of Coxey's Army had dissipated by the time of the Bonus Army. A leading political scientist, E. Pendleton Herring, praised the strength of these groups because they gave individual citizens an alternative to political parties, allowing them to express their convictions and to help elected officials weigh policy options.[34]

By emphasizing both their distinctive status as veterans and their universality as heterogeneous Americans, the marchers were able to pressure politicians to respond to their demands. On June 15, the House approved the Bonus Bill, sending it on to the Senate.[35] If they had shared with the woman suffragists who marched the same avenue in 1913 a desire for a symbolic foray into Washington, the Bonus marchers might have gone home at this point. But the veterans, wanting definitive results, stayed in the capital, raising new questions about their tactics and their rights in the capital.

During their parades and lobbying, the marchers left ambiguous whether they were demanding only just compensation for their service or relief for all suffering citizens. In many ways, this ambiguity reflected widespread ambivalence. Americans in the 1930s were simultaneously attracted by the kind of strong, repressive government associated with Fascism, committed to using their democratic structures to demand federal and state relief, and full of praise for individualism. The veterans, like many others in the United States, were trying to develop a language for group protection in a country still enmeshed in the "rugged individualism" that Hoover espoused.[36]

"DIGGING IN"

On June 17, the Bonus marchers, especially Walter Waters, were in the spotlight as they waited for senators to vote on the Bonus Bill. During the day, the veterans had gathered at the Capitol, filling the east plaza. As the numbers grew into the thousands, the authorities became nervous enough that they actually pulled up the drawbridge over the Anacostia River to prevent more veterans from joining the vigil. Just after eight o'clock, a Bonus marcher approached Waters with the bad news: the Senate had defeated the bill sixty-two to eighteen. In words also meant for the nearby reporters, Waters told his compatriots that the vote simply illustrated "the men who are supposed to represent the common man are not fit for their great duty."[37]

Waters then turned to address the crowd. When he expressed his "disappointment," an angry murmur spread through the crowd. Waters quickly cautioned them the senators would "be justified and excused if you riot" and asked them to prove "the Nation's faith" by marching back to camp "in line." Before the group left, however, a bugle sounded, the veterans removed their hats, and together they sang the popular anthem "America."[38] This show of control and patriotism reassured viewers who feared riots, but it still left hanging the question of what the veterans would do next.

Instead of leaving the capital after this legislative defeat, the Bonus marchers hunkered down for an indefinite stay. Veterans continued to arrive in the city. Two days before the Senate vote, the army's Military Intelligence Division had counted more than 18,000 veterans, with 14,800 encamped in Anacostia alone (see map 2). After the vote against the Bonus Bill, on June 21, there were nearly 20,000 Bonus marchers in the city.[39] Over the next month and a half, the Bonus marchers awkwardly tried to shift from a focus on Congress to an appeal to the American people. They redefined the objectives by adding demands for general relief, by emphasizing the presence of women and children in the demonstration, and by working to shape the response of the media to their demonstration. Such a shift showed how marches on Washington were increasingly becoming moments for groups not just to try to win specific political demands from elected officials but also to move public opinion. Authorities were not entirely comfortable with this new objective, especially in the context of a demonstration that was now stretching on and on. They began to attack the veterans' personal and political legitimacy. Authorities also began to limit with new vigor the Bonus marchers' use of the capital's public spaces.

The options of both participants and authorities were shaped by the practical realities of protesters living in abandoned buildings and the enormous Anacostia shantytown. For marchers, such conditions were difficult and tedious. Pictures of the Anacostia camp depicted an array of makeshift shacks and lean-tos that provided little protection from the summer heat and thunderstorms. There were inadequate sanitary facilities in all camps. Food grew scarcer as donations from Washington residents dried up. In early July, the situation was "so acute" that Waters flew to New York City, desperate to raise cash or collect food.[40]

These practical difficulties accentuated struggles among the demonstrators. When some of the participants questioned Waters's authority, he abruptly resigned as commander. He returned to the post five days

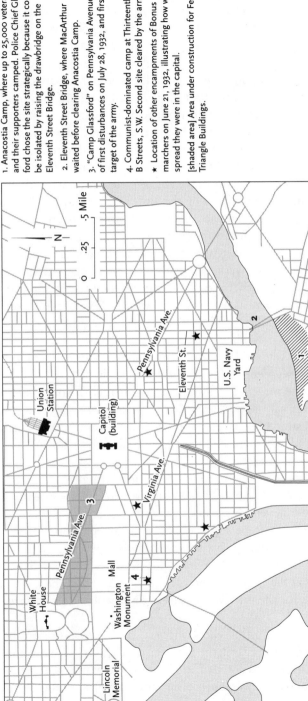

1. Anacostia Camp, where up to 25,000 veterans and their supporters camped. Police Chief Glassford chose the site strategically because it could be isolated by raising the drawbridge on the Eleventh Street Bridge.

2. Eleventh Street Bridge, where MacArthur waited before clearing Anacostia Camp.

3. "Camp Glassford" on Pennsylvania Avenue, site of first disturbances on July 28, 1932, and first target of the army.

4. Communist-dominated camp at Thirteenth and B Streets, S.W. Second site cleared by the army.

★ Location of other encampments of Bonus marchers on June 21, 1932, illustrating how widespread they were in the capital.

[shaded area] Area under construction for Federal Triangle Buildings.

MAP 2. The camps of the Bonus Army in Washington, D.C., 1932. Source: *The New International Encyclopedia*, 2d ed. (New York: Dodd, Mead), s.v. Washington.

later on the condition that he had "complete dictatorial powers." Still, Waters found maintaining control a continuing struggle. He evicted one of his critics from Anacostia and imposed "Hard-Boiled discipline," including daily marching drills, on his supporters.[41] Clearly, the extended stay was straining the abilities of both leaders and participants.

Despite these challenges, the group tried to shift tactics by appealing to the American public, the abstract but widely accepted arbiter of legitimate political action. They used both personal publicity and appeals to national journalists. The Bonus Army put considerable resources into publishing their own newspaper. Ten days after the Senate vote, on June 25, they released their first issue of the B.E.F. News, complete with views of life in the camps and editorials on the aims of the group.[42] The Bonus marchers also struggled to attract more attention from the national media. Though newspapers across the country gave the protest regular coverage, radio broadcasts and newsreels mostly ignored them. Since 60 to 75 million movie tickets were sold each week to theaters that opened with newsreels, and nearly every American listened to the radio daily, such coverage was seen as essential. Frustrated Bonus marchers suspected conspiracy. Waters claimed he was kept off a national radio network show because a "higher up" canceled the show. In a similar vein, a newspaper story reported that only two national newsreel companies had carried short segments. At least once, police chief Glassford prohibited filming of the marchers on the Capitol grounds. Both radio and newsreels avoided the subject, probably because their styles of news reporting were ill suited for covering an extended protest in Washington. Radio news broadcasts were very brief. Newsreels rarely devoted any attention to events in progress.[43]

So the veterans struggled to keep the nation's attention. To prevent negative publicity, Waters purged Communist veterans from leadership positions. Individual veterans also staged publicity stunts, such as burying themselves alive (a pipe supplied necessary air and food). This emphasis on national publicity became even more apparent on the long weekend of July 4. Although Congress was in recess, the marchers held demonstrations at the Capitol. Waters acknowledged that the legislators would be absent for the protest, but said, "They will learn of it through newspapers."[44]

Meanwhile, the Bonus marchers offered a new justification for being in Washington by emphasizing the need for a federal response to the depression. John Dos Passos noted in late June that veterans speaking in the camps often slipped unconsciously from discussing the Bonus to "talking about the general economic situation of the country." By mid-July, the Bonus marchers had extended their agenda to include "all suffering Americans."[45] This change in self-description of the Bonus Army implied that granting the veterans payment of the bonus was equivalent to granting relief to the broader population.

As they broadened their goals to include the needs of all Americans, they emphasized their membership in families as a sign of their political legitimacy and pointed to the presence of women and children among them. In truth that presence was minuscule; accepting the largest exaggeration, women and children amounted to 5 percent of the protesters in the capital.[46] In a well-publicized move, Waters used donations to bring his wife, Wilma, to Washington. Likewise, the marchers made a big fuss at the end of June when the first "Bonus baby" was born to a Bonus couple. They also established a special "family section" in Anacostia.[47] The dependence of these family members served to reinforce for spectators the genuine need of these veterans for some kind of relief (fig. 12).

Most importantly, this emphasis on family roles rather than past military service suggested a different kind of claim to citizenship. Under the pressure of the depression, the American family became an increasingly compelling symbol to justify political action. Men remained at the center of this politics as the most forceful protectors of their family's interest, but the demonstrated needs of women and children were also essential. For the Bonus marchers, their protest was becoming a family affair.[48]

Such efforts to attract broader attention and to portray themselves as family members only went so far toward convincing observers that veterans ought to continue to stay in Washington. Glassford, pulling away from the marchers after their legislative goals were defeated, resigned his official position and began advocating the protesters' departure. He was not alone. Hoover also successfully pressured Congress to authorize transportation home in early July. General Frank T. Hines, the efficient director of the Veterans' Administration, quickly sent trucks out to the camps to transport the veterans to the railroad station. The authorities, however, were disappointed; only hundreds rather than thousands of veterans took advantage of the offer each day. And, during the first week of the program, it appeared that for each veteran who left, another arrived to replace him. The authorities' effort did not dampen the continuing appeal of the protest for many veterans. According to Waters, there were still more than 14,000 veterans in the District on July 20, though the Military Intelligence Division counted only 6,000.[49]

Having made a good-faith effort to help the veterans leave, politi-

FIGURE 12. A veteran putting the final touches on his family's cottage in Camp
Anacostia. The Bonus marchers' efforts to provide for their families helped communicate
their Americanism, and their respectability countered criticism of their long stay in the
capital. (Underwood, Library of Congress, Prints and Photographs Division, LC-
USZ62–35304)

cians, authorities, and representatives of the press began to attack the
character of the veterans remaining in Washington. No longer did they
praise the men as determined veterans with a legitimate if misguided
political goal. Rather they tried to dismiss them as desperate men without any real purpose. They were, in the words of one journalist, "the

most intransigent, the disinherited, the diehards."[50] Such views helped justify more control over the group's action in the District.

As the protest stretched on, authorities began to restrict the veterans' use of the capital's public spaces. On Tuesday, July 12, a group of California veterans arrived at the Capitol grounds, where their leader, Royal Robertson, said they intended to "sleep . . . until Congress either grants the bonus or adjourns." Authorities tried to halt this effort by invoking the 1882 regulations about the use of the Capitol grounds, though these regulations had been ignored during the previous six weeks. Around 10 P.M., the police ordered the veterans to leave. Instead, Robertson's group began to circle the Capitol and continued for three more days. This action, which became known as the Death March, attracted considerable attention from journalists and photographers, who were struck by the veterans' desperation and determination (fig. 13).[51]

On the morning of the final day of the 72nd Congress' first session, July 16, officers watched as 5,000 veterans came to the Capitol. District police and federal officials again tried to invoke the regulations. They barred the Bonus marchers from congregating on the east plaza of the Capitol. For the first time, Waters disobeyed a police order and led his supporters onto the forbidden part of the plaza. Though Glassford twice arrested Waters, each time he released him when the remaining veterans grew unruly. Eventually, the group left peacefully.[52] After weeks during which large, though technically illegal, gatherings at the Capitol had been tolerated, these incidents showed that authorities, disturbed by the marchers' tenacity, were ready to curtail the veterans' use of the capital's ceremonial spaces.

Such conflicts grew particularly intense when Communist veterans tried to expand the protest to the White House. Though most Bonus marchers were hostile to the Communists' efforts, authorities increasingly viewed the Communists' actions and rhetoric as though they characterized the entire group. Officials' fears received added impetus when leaders of the Communist group spoke of the need to "replace the hat-in-hand lobbying policy with an organized fight of masses of veterans in Washington."[53] When Communist veterans began protesting at the White House, their actions resulted in the most preemptive repression of a protest in District history. Though earlier activists had demonstrated at the White House, the Bonus marchers, aware of Hoover's hostility to their cause, had avoided the location until faced with legislative defeat. And then, it was only the Communist Workers' Ex-Servicemen League

FIGURE 13. In the days before Congress ended its session in July 1932, a contingent of veterans holding a vigil around the clock. This picture was taken before members of Congress pressured Superintendent Glassford to enforce the regulations against such behaviors on the Capitol grounds. (Library of Congress, Prints and Photographs Division, LC-USZ62–115566)

who planned protests there. At an already tense moment, the prominence of Communists and their selection of the White House resulted in
sharp measures. Twice, federal authorities ordered Glassford to cordon
off not only the White House grounds but also all neighboring streets.
Officers in cars and on motorcycles circled the area, turning away all
pedestrians and motorists alike. The officers arrested members of the
league when they arrived, though they had violated no specific statutes.[54]

As the Bonus marchers camped on through June and July, they succeeded in making their protest a symbol of the broader social, economic,
and political crisis of the depression. Simultaneously, the continued duration of the protest led to attempts by authorities to discredit the veterans and to prevent unrestricted use of the capital. Such efforts soon intensified as authorities determined to end the protest.

THE "BATTLE OF WASHINGTON": JULY 28, 1932

By dusk on July 28, parts of the capital looked like a battlefield, albeit a
rather subdued one. More than five hundred soldiers near the bridge
across the Anacostia River awaited orders to empty the last and largest
camp of the Bonus marchers. Under the command of General MacArthur
and with the ambivalent support of President Hoover, the men had spent
the previous three hours using tanks, cavalry, and bayonets to drive the
veterans out of the center of Washington. For the most part, the soldiers
had encountered limited resistance. Those veterans who were tempted to
defy the armed soldiers moved on when assaulted with tear gas. The soldiers fired no regular bullets and wounded no one, though a few protesters ended up in the hospital from the tear gas. The soldiers paused
now for two reasons: to eat dinner and to allow the women and children
in the camp time to find transportation out of the District. Despite urgings from Hoover to wait, MacArthur ordered the soldiers to drive the
remaining Bonus marchers out of the camp with warnings and tear gas.
By midnight, journalists were snapping pictures of the shanties burning
with the lighted Capitol Building as a background (fig. 14).[55]

After eight weeks, the authorities had concluded that the only way to
end the protest was to remove the veterans' means of staying in the capital: the camps. Local and national officials cooperated in issuing a series
of eviction orders. Authorities justified their use of force by pointing to the
end of the congressional session and to the failure of the transportation of-
fers to entice enough veterans to leave voluntarily. They also argued that
some of the camps were holding up construction projects. Clearly, though,

FIGURE 14. Camp Anacostia burning. This scene of flaming huts in the shadow of the Capitol became a visible symbol of the defeat of the Bonus Army, but also of the seeming indifference of official Washington to the veterans' pleas for help. (Still Pictures Branch, RG 111, SC-97532. Courtesy of National Archives)

the main issue was ending the growing tension over the veterans' claim to occupy several areas in the capital city. Though authorities hoped—and Glassford believed—the veterans would obey these orders, some resistance and disruption by veterans gave authorities the pretense for a rapid and forceful expulsion of the veterans. The protesters certainly seemed defeated at the "battle of Washington." Their successful portrayal of themselves as deserving, needy citizens ultimately made this use of force a disturbing symbol of the state's repression of a demonstration in the capital.

Glassford initially resisted the use of force. On July 21, the District commissioners overruled him. Ironically, they specified that he should begin with Camp Glassford, an abandoned building owned by the federal government on the north side of Pennsylvania Avenue. Further, he was to clear the rest of the camps, including the biggest one at Anacostia, by August 4. He challenged the commissioners' orders, explaining he feared "riot and bloodshed." He also disputed his officers' legal authority to drive people from federal property. Glassford's reluctance to use force against the Bonus marchers resulted in a four-day delay of the eviction.[56]

General MacArthur, however, harbored no such doubts. Primed by weeks of reports of Communist influence on the effort, he was intent on suppressing the Bonus marchers with a vigorous show of force. Throughout June and July, troops at nearby forts were on alert and practiced regular riot drills.[57] Meanwhile the Military Intelligence Division continued to exaggerate the risk of violence from the Communist-led groups. Though any involvement of his troops would require both the District commissioners' requesting help from the federal authorities and Hoover's support for the request, MacArthur was prepared.

In the interim, Waters responded to the plans for eviction with a confusing mix of acquiescence and defiance. Initially, Waters told the commissioners that the Bonus marchers would "co-operate" in the "evacuation" of the first camp. Meanwhile, he tried to negotiate with federal officials to convince them to delay the eviction, invoking the presence of women and children. He also warned that the officials were risking a takeover of the entire group by Communists if they evicted people from the camps. By the end of some last-minute negotiations on July 27, he thought—incorrectly—he had won some time. Yet, Waters also encouraged veterans to interfere with the authorities' plans. He told veterans to "visit" the camps along Pennsylvania Avenue, making the evictions more difficult when they took place.[58] The result of Waters's mixed messages was that both authorities and Bonus marchers were uncertain of how the veterans might respond when the District and federal authorities definitively agreed to clear the camps in the center of the city on July 28.

Nevertheless, the eviction of the Pennsylvania Avenue camps began peacefully on the sunny morning of July 28. Around 10:00 A.M., police officers and federal agents gathered at Camp Glassford near Pennsylvania Avenue to clear the largest building. Though the Bonus marchers did not leave the building on command, Glassford ensured that police officers patiently escorted out each veteran. By noon, the building was empty.[59]

Waters, however, felt betrayed: he thought he had won agreement to a delay. He told men in the Anacostia camp to rush to the central camps to prevent further evictions. The Communist-dominated group also headed toward Pennsylvania Avenue. As they arrived, the men pressed up against a rope fence surrounding the emptied buildings. Some were disgusted by the involvement of Glassford, their ally for the last two months. One man ripped Glassford's badge off his shirt. Others began to throw rocks. In minutes, the police arrested the angriest men, other veterans intervened, and almost as quickly as the violence began, the crowd grew subdued.[60]

But the momentary outbreak accelerated fears that the protesters might increase their resistance. Although Glassford maintained confidence that he could control the veterans, other police officers informed the District commissioners they needed more help. For the next hour, the officers and the District commissioners debated whether the army needed to be involved. Glassford suggested delaying everything for a day. But most of his deputies wanted to complete the evictions immediately with the help of the army.[61]

The death of a Bonus marcher tipped the balance. After the noon break, two veterans began to quarrel and police officers rushed inside a building to halt the conflict. This "invasion" infuriated onlookers, and a crowd followed the officers, shouting threats. Once inside, Bonus marchers cornered some officers and began to punch them. In reaction, one officer fired his gun at William Huska, who was approaching with a brick. After shooting Huska, the officer fired again, wounding three other marchers, one seriously. Moments later, everyone was stunned into a tense peace.[62]

This violence was the last straw. The commissioners called President Hoover and asked him to send the troops. Hoover, hesitant to use federal troops to repress the protest, insisted that the commissioners give him their request in writing and obtain Glassford's approval. By this point, however, the commissioners were so convinced of the need for the troops that they dispatched a letter that falsely claimed the police chief was convinced that the "situation" was "a dangerous one." Reassured, Hoover authorized the use of the army. But he refused requests from MacArthur that he impose martial law; instead the army was to assist the District officials.[63] MacArthur, however, did not agree with Hoover's decision and soon was acting as if he had full authority to proceed independently.

Several hours passed before the army was ready to intervene. This slow start became emblematic of the army's suppression of the protest, which methodically and mechanically overwhelmed the veterans. With his characteristic intensity, MacArthur insisted on leading the operation even though this meant breaking the normal chain of command. As called for in the "White Plan," six hundred troops, including members of the cavalry and the tank regiment, assembled south of the White House. From there, they moved east to Pennsylvania Avenue.[64] The troops were able to proceed on mostly open roads, lined with Bonus marchers and other spectators, some cheering, some booing. When the troops reached the area where the trouble had begun, they found that Glassford had calmed the veterans down.

Nevertheless, MacArthur now proceeded to clear the camps. His soldiers began with one building that was still full of veterans. Though most fled, a few veterans resisted by throwing rocks. Tear gas and prodding by bayonets persuaded them to move along with the others—marchers and spectators alike—east toward Anacostia. By 6:45 P.M., an intelligence officer wrote a succinct report, "4½ Penna. Ave. cleared out—driving BEF towards river."[65] After finishing with the Pennsylvania Avenue area, MacArthur turned his attention to the camp that housed the Communist group on the south side of the Mall. To the soldiers' surprise, the buildings were virtually empty and easily secured (fig. 15).[66]

Ignoring President Hoover's commands, MacArthur moved on toward the Anacostia camp. The general did send Glassford ahead to warn the residents that they must depart or be driven out. Meanwhile, he halted his troops near the Anacostia Bridge for a last rest. Around 10:00 P.M., the troops entered the Anacostia camp and systematically drove out the remaining veterans and destroyed the shantytown. The vast majority of the Bonus marchers had already left, walking dejectedly to the northeast. Army troops pushed on the laggards. A few veterans challenged the soldiers, but a steady barrage of tear gas convinced them of the futility of such action. As the troops moved through the camp that had once housed more than 15,000 people, they set fire to the huts to ensure that no one would return. News of the eviction spread quickly. At 11:00 P.M., just as the extremely popular *Amos 'n' Andy* show was about to start, one of NBC's radio networks broadcast live reports from Washington. In addition, MacArthur had facilitated extensive coverage by print journalists and newsreel camera operators.[67]

MacArthur aggressively tried to justify this use of force to the public. In a press conference held outside the White House early in the morning on July 29, MacArthur declared he believed the veterans on July 28 had been "animated by the essence of revolution." He emphatically claimed that "not more than one out of ten of those cleared from the camp yesterday were genuine veterans." He also criticized Glassford's tolerant policy by explaining that "the gentleness and consideration with which the men had been treated was mistaken for weakness." These attacks helped MacArthur to characterize the eviction as a battle. Instead of handling the final stage of a drawn-out if tense ending for the demonstration, MacArthur, in his own mind, had led a dramatic charge against a mob that was "about to take over . . . the Government."[68]

FIGURE 15. Soldiers and marchers milling about in a haze of tear gas.
The contrast between the well-protected and armed soldiers and the Bonus
marchers was symbolic of the weakness of the veterans when faced with
General Douglas MacArthur's determination to drive them from the
capital. (Library of Congress, Prints and Photographs Division, LC-
USZ62-115565)

President Hoover, angry at his general's insubordination, nonetheless
publicly echoed MacArthur's characterization of the eviction as a necessary response to radical subversives intent on overthrowing the nation's lawful government. Hoover was well informed throughout the expulsion and knew that the Bonus marchers had offered little resistance
to the soldiers' efforts. He reproached the general for ignoring the limits of his authority in an early morning meeting on July 29. In a public

letter to the District commissioners, however, the president supported MacArthur's characterization of the marchers as "subversive" and criticized the "civil authorities" for their "lax enforcement of city ordinances and laws." He concluded by firmly repudiating the Bonus marchers and their demonstration: "There is no group, no matter what its origins, that can be allowed either to violate the laws of this city or to intimidate the government."[69]

The president and his administration repeatedly reiterated this claim. Within days, Hoover's attorney general met with representatives of the chief security and intelligence divisions of the federal government, including J. Edgar Hoover of the Bureau of Investigation and officials from the Veterans' Administration and the immigration service. He ordered them to secure evidence to prove that the Bonus marchers were under the control of the Communists. In the meantime, the secretary of war lashed out at people who criticized the evictions by accusing them of "making common cause with reds who are trying to promote unrest and violence."[70]

Their efforts to shape public opinion succeeded for a time. In the immediate aftermath of the evacuation, most journalists, kept unaware of Glassford's success at calming the veterans and of MacArthur's flouting of Hoover's directives, explained the use of troops as an appropriate reaction to the "riots" on Pennsylvania Avenue. They praised the army for its restraint, noting there were no serious injuries while MacArthur was in command. This journalistic support appeared to carry over to the broader public. Using a metaphor drawn from boxing, the *New York Times* declared, "Press opinion, accurately reflecting public opinion, has been almost unanimous in holding up the hands of Mr. Hoover."[71]

This approval depended on ignoring important elements of the Bonus marchers' long stay in the capital that also could have justified the eviction. In MacArthur and Hoover's explanations, they did not remind the country that Congress had considered and rejected the marchers' demand; they did not point out the problems resulting from Bonus marchers' camping and begging in the city; nor did they explain the complicated and genuinely threatening events of July 28.[72] Rather, they emphasized that the main reason was the purported predominance of Communists.

Public support for the army's heavy-handed suppression of the protest proved temporary, perhaps because of the overly simplistic justification. Extensive investigations by federal agents failed to support MacArth~ and Hoover's statements that marchers were not really veter~

Communists had substantially influenced the course of the protest before or on July 28. Equally damaging were Glassford's vehement assertions that the Bonus marchers were not out of his control on July 28, that he had not asked for the help of the army, and that the marchers were not under the direction of the Communists. As this evidence became public, attacks on the Hoover administration for its use of armed forces against the veterans became more frequent, with most criticism noting the peacefulness of the veterans and their family members. The ardently progressive *New Republic* predicted Hoover's defeat in the fall election because of "the strong-arm methods he employed on Anacostia flats." In eight states, legislators passed resolutions condemning his use of the army. In their summary of events, the American Civil Liberties Union called the incident the "most conspicuous of all instances of repression of the last year." Much of the criticism focused on the treatment of the women and children forced from Washington, which suggests that the Bonus marchers' self-presentation as citizens and family men had made an impression on the public. An editorial cartoon in the *Chicago Herald and Examiner* featured a white-robed woman halting an armed soldier with one arm while protectively sheltering the diminutive family of a "jobless veteran" with the other.[73]

The eviction of the Bonus Army from Washington graphically illustrated the strains brought about by the demonstration. The eviction was supposed to be a gradual process orchestrated by Glassford. Instead, because of poor planning, the miscommunications between Glassford and Waters, the spark of violence, and MacArthur's views of the protesters, all of the Bonus marchers were driven not just from the camps, but from Washington itself. The result was as the authorities had hoped, but the means, as it turned out, did not hold up well to public scrutiny. And, the Hoover administration's defense of the eviction backfired. Rather than address the marchers' claims directly, the administration tried to delegitimate those claims by characterizing the demonstration as a violent threat to the nation masterminded by alien Communists. When the administration's account proved false, public sympathy for the Bonus Army increased.

LEGACIES

By the fall of 1932, Americans were beginning to hear the plight of the Bonus marchers mournfully dramatized in Yip Harburg's hit song "Brother, Can You Spare a Dime?" The song's narrator was both a veteran of World War I and the quintessential victim of the depression. He once wore a "khaki suit" and a pair of the "half a million boots [which] went sloggin' thru hell." Now, standing on a breadline, he asks, "Say, don't you remember/I'm your pal/Buddy, can you spare a dime?" The song was the most prominent way that the Bonus marchers were portrayed in popular culture. They also appeared as sympathetic figures in two motion pictures: *Washington Merry-Go-Round,* released in the fall of 1932, and *Gabriel over the White House,* which opened just after Franklin D. Roosevelt's inauguration in 1933. Around the same time, Walter Waters, with the help of an experienced journalist, published his own book about the march, *B.E.F.: The Whole Story of the Bonus Army.* Other participants, including Glassford, also released personal accounts in books or magazine articles.[74] These portrayals, in such a wide range of mediums—combined with the months of national coverage and a subsequent flurry of protests—helped transform demonstrations in the capital into a distinctive part of American political culture. In the aftermath of the Bonus March, such protests were no longer seen as a variation of political tactics such as rioting, lobbying, or celebratory parading, but as a technique in and of themselves.

Back in Washington, District authorities attempted to quell enthusiasm for marching on Washington by abandoning their policy of forceful courtesy. District commissioners convinced Police Chief Glassford to leave his post and then appointed Major Ernest W. Brown, a career police officer, to command the District police—in part, because he believed in tight control of protests. He manifested this attitude when another Communist-influenced Hunger March came to the capital in December 1932. Brown surrounded the marchers in an isolated part of the city with an armed guard, and, at first, refused even to let them leave the camp. Only after the American Civil Liberties Union helped the marchers file a suit in the district court and members of Congress intervened were they allowed to parade to the center of the capital. Still, they were so completely surrounded by policemen that, one reporter commented, "spectators . . . must have thought it was a police and firemen's parade on the way to a ball." Immediately afterward, the police hurried the marchers out of the city. The local newspapers praised Major Brown for his "Excellent Police Work."[75]

But such restrictive policies were short-lived. The enduring legacy of the Bonus March was an increase in federal tolerance and even assistance to political demonstrations. This shift in view first showed when another contingent of veterans came to the capital in May 1933, again seeking their bonus.[76] When 3,000 men arrived over the first twelve days of the month, the Roosevelt administration took an approach that exceeded even Glassford's courtesy. The administration put up the veterans at an army post in Virginia, supplying the men with tents, food, and sanitary facilities. They arranged transportation for veterans wanting to "peaceably assemble and petition" in the capital. Roosevelt politely received a delegation, to which he explained his continued opposition to immediate payment. The administration even helped the veterans to appeal for support on a national radio show and sent Eleanor Roosevelt on a "spontaneous" visit to the camp covered by newsreel cameras. Then Roosevelt signed a special order giving the marchers' priority to enroll in the recently established Civilian Conservation Corps. When still more marchers came in 1934 and 1935, the same methods were used: generous accommodations in Washington and help through New Deal programs. Eventually, the years of agitation had their effect, and in January 1936, the veterans finally won their bonus. In the meantime, however, the new approach to protest showed that Roosevelt and other authorities were reluctant to suppress demonstrations; instead they tended to take an approach that meant the protesters were all but "killed by kindness."[77]

Another sign of an increased acceptance of what we now call "marches on Washington" as a distinctive form of political action came when observers and participants began to compare the Bonus March to the Indian Independence movement led by Mahatma Gandhi. The *New Republic* considered one protest by Bonus marchers to be in the "manner of Gandhi's followers." An article in the *B.E.F. News* declared similarly that "as Gandhi by his invincible courage confounds the high command of England, so have the peaceful men and women of the Washington camps, by their quiet fortitude, compelled American Tories to face the national crisis." In 1933 the editors of the *Nation* commented on a flurry of calls to march on Washington by speculating that such demonstrations were becoming "a successful American technique for direct action."[78]

In addition, during and after the Bonus March, there was a better sense of the history of the technique. Journalists compared the current effort to Coxey's Army, nearly forty years before. Such consciousness of precedents first surfaced at the time of the 1931 Hunger March, which prompted a newspaper retrospective on Coxey's Army and mocking editorial cartoons. References increased when Jacob Coxey traveled to Washington to greet the marchers in their camps.[79] Of course, not all such historical references were positive. When George Sokolsky, a Russian immigrant and well-known journalist, was asked during the summer of 1932 about the possibility of revolution in the United States, he observed ominously that the veterans had "already begun a Coxey's army march on Washington." In the aftermath of the Bonus March, the War Department reviewed the government's treatment of Coxey's Army to help the Hoover administration plan for the future.[80] In these recurrent references to historical precedents, we see the emergence of a new consciousness of marching on Washington as an American tradition.

From the obscure beginnings of the Bonus March in Portland to its tear-gas-clouded conclusion in Washington, the event both built on old traditions of national protest and established new ones. The protesters had tried to balance their claims of entitlement and universal citizenship through a mixture of public display, lobbying, and public relations. They had won some victories that clearly suggested the power of national political demonstrations. While the end of the protest was decisively shaped by the army's fears of Communist subversion and their well-developed plans for control of the demonstration, for two months federal and District officials had experimented with a policy of tolerance. Nine years later, when President Roosevelt confronted the planned March on Washington by African Americans protesting their exclusion from defense jobs and their segregation in the military, his treatment of the organizers and their plans would reflect his memories of the Bonus marchers.

CHAPTER FOUR

"PRESSURE, MORE PRESSURE, AND STILL MORE PRESSURE"

The Negro March on Washington and Its Cancellation, 1941

In June 1968, Eugene Davidson reminisced about his long history of activism in the District of Columbia. With nearly fifty years of fighting for opportunity and equality for African Americans, Davidson had many stories to tell, but he attached special urgency to his memories of the Negro March on Washington in 1941. After serving as the assistant director for the march, he penned a brief account entitled "The Birth of Executive Order 8802." This executive order against racial discrimination in military contracting during World War II was one of the only tangible changes in federal policy directly attributable to any march on Washington—the first protest to fulfill the original hopes of Carl Browne and Jacob Coxey for their "petition in boots": immediate federal action.[1] This result is particularly striking because the Negro March of 1941 never actually happened. At the last minute, the march's organizers decided to call it off. And this is largely why, for a generation of activists like Davidson, the threatened Negro March on Washington represented the potential for political demonstrations in the capital to generate new policies and build political movements.[2]

The Negro March was conceived of by A. Philip Randolph, a prominent labor and civil rights activist. In the early 1940s, as employment opportunities for most Americans increased with defense preparations and sales of materials to the Allied countries, blacks were excluded from many positions in industry, and they were segregated and given secondary status in the military. Randolph decided that only a mass protest

demonstration in Washington would persuade the Roosevelt administration to act. An effective coalition of African American leaders backed
the plans for the protest. This coalition and the support of many African
Americans who planned to march on July 1 did in fact make the president and his aides pay attention. President Roosevelt, Eleanor Roosevelt,
and members of the administration were so concerned by the image of
black Americans exposing the racial inequality in the United States to a
warring and watching world that they tried everything to convince the
leaders to cancel. In the end, there was a private bargain. The president
issued Executive Order 8802, restricting discrimination and, in exchange, the leaders canceled the march. This quid pro quo was obscured
by mainstream journalists who reported the order without any mention
of the threatened march, which might have embarrassed a president and
a nation on the brink of war. In contrast, the power politics behind the
order were celebrated in black newspapers claiming the order as a significant victory: one exulted that the executive order proved that "only
mass action can pry open the iron doors that have been erected against
America's black minority."[3]

Planned, but canceled, the Negro March on Washington will always
remain somewhat mysterious. How many marchers would actually have
come to Washington? How would District residents, authorities, and the
police have reacted? Was Roosevelt right to consider it an intolerable
threat? Such questions remain unanswerable. But the political strategies,
the posturing, and the negotiations that first created a sense of threat and
then defused it also make more explicit than usual the process by which
marches on Washington grew to have increasing power—especially
when they were well timed and well organized. Indeed, the march Randolph planned was conceived with a creativity and boldness that established a precedent for increasing the power and influence of marching on
Washington for decades to come. Though following the tradition of earlier demonstrations in Washington, Randolph tied his protest to new
views of American politics and the rights of American citizens, views that
sanctioned both political protest and the complaints about discrimination. To give the protest political credibility, Randolph organized a
coalition of national African American leaders with extensive organizational and political resources. This coalition attracted an enthusiastic
response from many African Americans, apparently ready to appear in
large numbers in Washington. There, the exclusively black marchers
would use the nation's public spaces to highlight the hypocrisy the organizers saw in the policies of the national government. As Randolph

and Davidson laid out these plans, the president grew increasingly concerned. Although it did not happen, the Negro March on Washington showed the power of the emerging political practice, not just because it won concrete action, but also because its organizers so skillfully sensed the importance of coalitions, of explicit confrontation, and of large numbers for marches on Washington.

"NOTHING COUNTS BUT PRESSURE"

"I suggest that TEN THOUSAND (10,000) Negroes march on Washington, D.C., the capital of the Nation," proposed A. Philip Randolph in a press release dated January 16, 1941, "with the slogan, WE LOYAL NEGRO AMERICAN CITIZENS DEMAND THE RIGHT TO WORK AND FIGHT FOR OUR COUNTRY."[4] His background and choice of method were similar in many respects to those of previous march organizers. Like some of them, Randolph was an experienced political leader. Like them, he decided to hold a large public protest in Washington only after a series of other attempts to influence national policy had failed. Unlike his predecessors, Randolph could take advantage of dramatic changes in national policy and political culture that made his political protest far easier to justify. Randolph connected his protest to new support for the rights of citizens to economic security. He also tied the Negro March to the emerging support for what he called "power politics," more familiarly labeled "interest group politics." He also drew on his own experience with and the national practice of "mass action."

Randolph developed his interest in power politics through extensive experience in politics; by 1941, at age fifty-one, he was a national leader of African Americans. He started his career as a militant socialist in New York City in the 1910s on the fringes of the African American community. Subsequently, he transformed the Brotherhood of Sleeping Car Porters from a small, local organization to one included in the American Federation of Labor, recognized by the federal government and contracting with the Pullman Company. In 1935, Randolph helped found the National Negro Congress to build "the widest possible cooperation of Negro leaders and Negro organizations in an effort to win real economic and social gains for the Negro population in America." While Randolph's involvement in the National Negro Congress was short-lived, his role as its first president consolidated valuable connections with leaders of black organizations and federal officials. The National Association for the Advancement

FIGURE 16. Photograph of A. Philip Randolph by Gordon Parks. By 1941, when he began advocating the Negro March on Washington, Randolph had already had thirty years of experience working for the rights of African Americans. He was an expert at bringing people together and negotiating compromises, skills that were invaluable for making the threat of the Negro March palpable to President Roosevelt. (Library of Congress, Prints and Photographs Division, LC-USW3–11696-C)

of Colored People (NAACP) recognized his growing importance by electing him to its national board of directors early in 1940 (fig. 16).[5]

These experiences in both labor organizations and civil rights groups helped Randolph recognize the potential for protesting the poor treatment of blacks in the burgeoning war effort. The "Call to Negro America" announcing the march declared, "Negroes can kill the deadly serpent of race hatred in the Army, Navy, Air and Marine Corps." The "serpent" was insidious. Every branch of the military discriminated against African Americans systematically, segregating whites and blacks and restricting black people's opportunities. The marines refused to accept black volunteers or draftees. The army accepted blacks but did not allow many black officers, and the treatment of black troops was grossly inferior to that of white soldiers.[6] Defense contractors provided similarly restricted opportunities for African Americans. By the end of 1940, the federal government had signed defense contracts worth over $10 billion. This infusion of money into the economy began to crack the high rates of unemployment, but not for African Americans. As the "Call" described, black workers were "turned away from the gates of factories, mines and mills—being flatly told, 'Nothing Doing.'"[7]

Randolph was not alone in thinking the federal government should act. In the previous years, both President Roosevelt and Congress had taken limited steps to prohibit "discrimination on account of race, creed, or color." In 1939, Congress funded a training program for Negro pilots. The following year, activists won language in the Selective Service Act that allowed "any person, regardless of race or color," to volunteer for military service and that prohibited discrimination against drafted men. African Americans also won some political victories against defense industry discrimination. In New York, Governor Herbert Lehman appointed a "Committee on Discrimination in National Defense" to scrutinize hiring practices. In other states, legislators passed bills prohibiting racial discrimination by military contractors. These orders and statutes were not consistently enforced. But they set a precedent that African Americans leaders began using in the late 1930s to win some changes.[8]

These political victories resulted in little practical change. The War Department stalled by allowing each branch to develop its own procedures. Throughout 1940 and 1941, newspapers and magazines serving African Americans juxtaposed stories about valiant black men going off to serve the country with reports of the ill treatment and segregation they experienced on their arrival (see fig. 17). Employment opportunities remained limited. In 1940 Rayford Logan, a historian who led one group trying to change policies, warned a Senate committee, "The morale of Negro citizens regarding national defense is probably at the lowest ebb in the history of the country."[9]

Meanwhile, like the veterans in 1932, Randolph and his supporters began to lose faith in the power of lobbying and meetings. Compounding the problem was their mistrust of Roosevelt. Since 1938, black leaders had met with Roosevelt to discuss the defense program, with few concrete results. A meeting in September 1940 was cordial enough, but resulted in no action. NAACP director Walter White, Randolph, and T. Arnold Hill of the Urban League met with Roosevelt, who promised to "look into possible methods of lessening, if not destroying," prejudicial treatment. Nothing happened. Then, the army issued a press release announcing that they intended to continue segregating soldiers racially and implying that this policy had been endorsed by Randolph and the other participants in the meeting. What the black leaders had hoped would be a useful step toward improving conditions—the meeting with the president—turned out to be ineffectual and humiliating. Frustrated, Randolph conceived his plan for public protest in the capital. In late December

The CRISIS July, 1940 • Fifteen Cents

WARPLANES—Negro Americans may not build them, repair them, or fly them, but they must help pay for them—See page 199

FIGURE 17. Cover of the NAACP's *Crisis* magazine. Printed well before Randolph began organizing the Negro March, this issue and others illustrated the widespread concern among African Americans about their exclusion from much of the United States defense effort. (*Crisis* [July 1940]. The University of California Press wishes to thank the Crisis Publishing Co., Inc., the publisher of the magazine of the National Association for the Advancement of Colored People, for the use of this work.)

1940, he told his colleague Milton Webster that he believed he could convince 10,000 blacks to "protest against the discriminatory practices in this rapidly expanding economy."[10] Randolph's shift in tactics followed a pattern that was becoming increasingly typical. He had a deep involvement with a widely debated national issue and a sense of having failed with other political tactics.

Randolph skillfully framed the proposed march in terms that resonated with three emerging facets of America's national political culture. First, Randolph tied the march to a new recognition of the economic rights of citizens. During the New Deal, partly in response to the political disorder resulting from the Bonus March, hunger marches, and labor and rent strikes, the federal government had taken on new responsibility for ensuring the economic security of American citizens. New Dealers repeatedly spoke of the need for American to move beyond the "era of the pioneer and the rugged individualist"—which had molded the ways in which the Bonus marchers presented themselves—and toward a new era in which the government guarded the security of individuals. In January 1941, President Roosevelt named the "four freedoms" to which all people were entitled; besides freedom of speech and worship and freedom from fear, the president declared that all people deserved "freedom from want." Randolph used the new support for economic security to justify the march. The "Call" concluded by noting that the "challenge" facing African Americans was to secure "the right to participate in the economic, political and social institutions and life of America upon a basis of absolute equality."[11]

Second, Randolph recognized that American intellectuals and politicians had adopted new views on politics during the course of the 1930s. The "Call" explained, "in this period of power politics, nothing counts but pressure, more pressure, and still more pressure." In making this argument, Randolph echoed the increasing trend among political scientists in the United States, like V. O. Key, to see "the essential character of political behavior . . . in power relations." With war raging in Europe, intellectuals and politicians defended the American political system for permitting interest groups, politicians, and bureaucrats to hammer out workable solutions. Rather than seeing democracy as a system that fostered ideal solutions as a result of careful deliberation, these theorists and practitioners saw democracy as the best system for allowing the competitive forces of "power politics" to reach the most acceptable policy.[12]

Within a system of "power politics," Randolph recognized that protest was more acceptable to Americans. He told Lester Granger of the

National Urban League that "mass pressure . . . is one of the most challenging methods that a minority can wield today in defense of its rights." Like Carl Browne and Alice Paul, Randolph had organized public protests in other cities before turning to the capital. Meanwhile, all across America white and black people had taken to the streets during the depression. The Bonus March was one model. People also conducted many local protests for relief. Increasingly, workers protested publicly as part of labor unions, where they participated in massive and sustained strikes, punctuated by huge outdoor rallies to publicize their demands.[13]

In these same years, the legitimacy of political protests received increased legal sanction. One important case originated with the New Negro Alliance, a black organization in the capital that Eugene Davidson helped found. This group, like others across the country, instigated a "Don't Buy Where You Can't Work" campaign. When negotiations with storeowners fell apart, Davidson and others picketed the offending businesses, whose white owners refused to hire black employees. Eventually, one business secured an injunction to prohibit the picketing. The New Negro Alliance's appeal went to the Supreme Court and was successful in 1938. The following year, in a different case the Court established that the streets and parks of cities were a "public forum" whose use by groups could be regulated but not completely restricted.[14] These decisions, following years of ambivalent rulings, provided growing legal protections for public political actions such as mass demonstrations.

By this time, a collective "history" of protest in Washington was developing—a sense of historical memory that Randolph was also eager to exploit. In 1941, Negro March organizers and observers repeatedly drew attention to the precedents established by Coxey's Army and the Bonus March. Journalists, politicians, and activists were aware that many groups during the 1930s had imitated the Bonus marchers and their expedition to Washington. From pacifists to war hawks, anti-New Dealers to disgruntled relief workers, angry housewives to fearful Jewish leaders, all these groups brought their demands to the streets of Washington.[15] African American political activists had also used the Washington streets and public spaces. Communist-sponsored groups led interracial marches to the Supreme Court in support of the black men accused of rape in the Scottsboro case in 1932 and 1933. The most important precedent was an Easter Sunday concert in 1939 by Marian Anderson. Anderson refused to perform before a segregated audience at the hall of the Daughters of the American Revolution. The NAACP and other civil rights organizations arranged for her to sing—before a crowd estimated at over

75,000—at the Lincoln Memorial instead. The result was national and international attention to segregation in the United States capital. By 1941, the *Baltimore Afro-American* could confidently write in support of the Negro March that "the effectiveness of the orderly mass demonstration and the picket line has been thoroughly demonstrated as a means of creating favorable public opinion."[16]

In calling for the Negro March on Washington, Randolph displayed his keen understanding of American political culture and his strategic savvy. Randolph had more years of experience in political agitation and participation at the national level than any previous march organizer. He also brought new, more strategic, and more intellectually sophisticated arguments to the national protest in Washington, arguments that resonated powerfully with important new currents in American political culture. In first six months of 1941, Randolph drew on his understanding of these currents as he organized the proposed march.

PLANNING A "MASS ACTION" IN AN AGE OF "POWER POLITICS"

Early on, Randolph called on participants to "swarm from every hamlet, village, and town; . . . out of the churches, lodges, homes, schools, mills, mines, factories, and fields." He declared, however, "We shall not call upon our white friends to march with us." The protest was an action that "Negroes must do alone." This decision was an essential part of his strategy of using this protest to illustrate the disjuncture between a national rhetoric of equality and a daily reality of white supremacy, especially as the country came closer every day to war.[17] Randolph also stressed the importance of big numbers. The Negro March was the first march that set a specific goal for a certain number of participants. The spectacle of huge numbers of demonstrators, Randolph reasoned, would be key to the power of the march.

The decision to make this a "Negro" march, and the explicit effort to make it massive, was part of a strategy Randolph and his supports formed to control the meaning and increase the political power of the demonstration. The organizers were determined to emphasize the political power and independence of the prospective marchers. This was particularly necessary because African Americans were widely viewed as incapable of the rights and privileges of citizenship—or even of coherent political action. Randolph knew that African Americans were commonly "supposed to be just scared and unorganizable."[18] In order to get federal policy to change, he believed, he also had to overcome this prejudice and convince the country and the world that African Americans could organize with dignity, harmony, and in huge numbers. This belief lay behind the strategy of pulling together a coalition of African American leaders. The goal was to convince the Roosevelt administration of the unity of African Americans and to encourage many individuals to participate. Randolph was also careful to think strategically about how his march would use the public spaces of the rapidly changing federal capital. As he and his supporters designed the actual protest, they again asserted control over the success of the march by specifying a style and destination for the march that would allow black citizens to highlight the hypocrisy of the nation's racial policies.

The decision to restrict the race of the marchers, for example, reflected how Randolph combined practical politics with a keen appreciation of black sentiment. Anti-Communism constrained all activists in 1941. In Randolph's own experience, most notably with the National Negro Congress, white Communists had come to dominate groups that were designed for African Americans. Once that happened, mainstream politicians, with their virulent anti-Communism, could dismiss both the organizations and the demands for racial equality. To justify an all-black march, Randolph laid out the dual challenge to the NAACP's Walter White: "If we have white persons in the March, we are certain to have trouble with the Communists and it may not be viewed as a true expression of the Negro's protest."[19] But making the march exclusively for black people was also an astute appeal to many African Americans' belief in the importance of working for their own interests. Personally, Randolph had long advocated all-black organizations. In 1939, a commentator noted that Randolph "believes that the mainspring of the Negro lies within itself." In 1940, Randolph explained that he left the leadership of the National Negro Congress, noting that "of some 1200 or more delegates, over 300 were white, which made the congress look like a joke."[20] The Negro March on Washington was to be a chance for African Americans to show themselves as independent political actors who did not need whites to organize or to demand political change (fig. 18).

This ambition was possible only if blacks could be convinced to support the protest. Randolph's years of experience in political organizing and his national reputation gave him many resources for building support for the march. Initially, Randolph began promoting the protest as he traveled around the country on Pullman union business, and he turned to his trusted aides Frank Crosswaith and Owen Chandler for help in

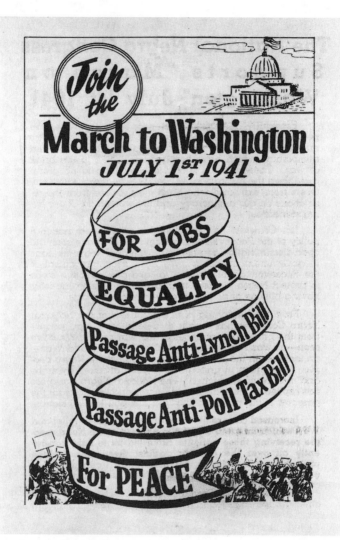

FIGURE 18. A pamphlet advertising the 1941 march on Washington. The National Negro Congress produced this pamphlet in support of Randolph's call for the July 1 protest, but without his approval. The Congress, a group dominated by Communists, omitted the word "Negro" from the title of the march and added demands for specific bills and, most importantly, peace. Committed to keeping Communists out of the proposed march, the Negro March leaders specifically rejected such support. (Printed from "March on Washington Committee, 1941" folder, series 6, box 13, records of the National Urban League, Manuscript Division, Library of Congress)

organizing. By March 1941, Randolph was ready to share the leadership of the march. Because of the NAACP's preeminent role, he first went after the support of that organization's director, Walter White. White, already aware of Randolph's efforts, quickly agreed "that only a mass demonstration is going to have any effect on the situation at Washington."[21]

He then created a coalition with other African American leaders. Forming a coalition to lead the march represented a new step in the organizing of political demonstrations in Washington. In previous protests, coalitions tended to be limited or unstable. But Randolph recognized that coalitions were essential both for interest group politicking and for mass action. He recruited leaders of African American political, economic, fraternal, and religious groups. The coalition's leadership committee included eleven individuals who brought with them crucial experience in lobbying, mass action, or organization building. Randolph, White, Granger (of the Urban League), and Crosswaith filled four slots. Adam Clayton Powell Jr., the politically active minister of the Abyssinian Baptist Church, and the Presbyterian minister William Lloyd Imes also joined. In addition, Rayford Logan of the small but persistent National Committee for the Participation of Negroes in National Defense was recruited. Other leaders came from the Harlem YMCA and the American Federation of Teachers. One member, Richard Parrish, was an activist with student groups in New York City. J. Finley Wilson, the grand exalted ruler of the Improved Benevolent Protective Order of Elks of the World, a black fraternal organization, also signed on. All the leaders had already spoken out against discrimination in the defense program. Some had led public protests on civil rights issues. As it happened, Wilson, years before, had joined a contingent heading toward Washington to join Coxey's Army. The march leaders approved the name "Negro March on Washington for Jobs and Equal Participation in National Defense" as reflecting their goals. They scheduled it for July 1.[22]

While the Negro March committee retained the power to approve particular plans, they delegated organizers to handle daily details and arranged local committees to recruit marchers across the country. This structure emerged, in part, because none of the leaders could devote a major part of his or her time to planning the march. A critical early appointment was Eugene Davidson as assistant director. Davidson's qualifications for the position were extensive. With his years of experience as a journalist and a leader of both local and national civil rights protests in the District, Davidson brought a variety of practical skills to the Washington office, which was to be the "center of planning, publicity, coordination, etc." To assist Davidson, the leaders gathered together contributions and recruited volunteers.[23] By May, the organizational structure of the march was solid.

Because the leaders represented most of the major black organizations in 1941, the organizers could tap a large number of potential marchers. As Randolph explained later, members of his union, the Brotherhood of Sleeping Car Porters, "became couriers, carrying the word to Negro communities throughout the country." The march organizers could also take advantage of the memberships of the Elks, the NAACP, and the Urban League. There were thousands of members of the Elks; the NAACP counted over 100,000 members in 1940, while the Urban League boasted forty-six branches and 26,000 members. Both White and Granger sent special letters to the leaders of their branches informing them of their endorsement of the march and asking them to support the protest. Early in the planning, the organizers recognized that to "carry out something so vast as the Negro March on Washington," they needed to develop such groups "in every city of a sizable Negro population." Local committees came together in at least nineteen different cities, including Los Angeles, Trenton, Washington, Richmond, Atlanta, Savannah, Jacksonville, St. Paul, St. Louis, Cleveland, Milwaukee, and Chicago.[24]

To supplement the work of local committees, organizers publicized their efforts in black newspapers, the only media sources easily available to African Americans in 1941. Media outlets controlled by whites—including the major daily papers—rarely provided detailed stories about the concerns of African Americans. Only one daily paper reported on the planning of the protest: the labor-oriented New York City paper *PM*. So complete was the silence that Randolph described "the white press" as engaging in "a dreadful conspiracy." In contrast, the black weekly newspapers provided invaluable aid by publicizing and, for the most part, endorsing the plans for the demonstration. The nearly 150 black newspapers reached over 1 million readers by 1940. Five newspapers—the *Chicago Defender,* the *Pittsburgh Courier,* the *Norfolk Journal and Guide,* the *New York Amsterdam News,* and the *Baltimore Afro-American*—had national editions. Smaller papers drew their reports from the Associated Negro Press, the largest of the national wire service agencies that served black newspapers.[25]

Some editors were cautious about the march, but others applauded the effort. The editors of the *Pittsburgh Courier,* the most conservative of all the papers, wondered whether "the carfare of 10,000 people might be more wisely expended," but still conceded "this will be a gesture not without value." Many endorsements were wholehearted. J. A. Rogers, whose weekly column was syndicated in a number of black papers, declared the "March on Washington an Effective Means of Forging Democracy." The editors of the Baltimore *Afro-American* labeled the protest an expression of "patriotism" and announced their intention to march down Pennsylvania Avenue to "only one refrain: 'We are Americans, too.'" The *Chicago Defender* labeled the march the "greatest crusade for democracy ever staged by America's black minority." Emphatically, they affirmed, "this is the time, the place, the issue and the method."[26]

By late May, various African American commentators indicated that recruiting efforts were bearing fruit. A number of organizations had fallen in line with the Negro Committee's plans. The NAACP changed the schedule of its annual convention so delegates could attend the protest. In addition, Mary McLeod Bethune, an influential black leader and member of the Roosevelt administration, endorsed the march to the National Council of Negro Women. A wide range of New York City groups contributed to the cause, including the Mt. Olivet Baptist Church, the Supreme Liberty Life Insurance Company, the Musicians' Local 802, and the Manhattan Central Medical Society.[27]

Individual African Americans also expressed their support for the march. Between the monthly fights necessary to defend his heavyweight boxing title, Joe Louis found time to contribute $50. In mid-May, the president of the NAACP branch in St. Louis wrote to Walter White asking for "full details" on the march because "every day I am getting requests for information." By mid-June, the headquarters for the march was "receiving scores of letters from people who wish to register to go to Washington." Reinforcing the impression of enthusiasm, people bought over 10,000 buttons, priced at ten cents each, with the slogan "NEGROES MARCH for JOBS in NATIONAL DEFENSE." As they gauged this enthusiasm, organizers developed new ambitions for the turnout: Randolph had originally called for 10,000 marchers; in May, Davidson claimed 50,000, and by June, leaders routinely used the number 100,000.[28] These increasing numbers indicated the organizers' faith that they had convinced African Americans of the need to unite behind this cause.

As they grew convinced of support, the organizers turned to designing the event. Like organizers of earlier demonstrations in Washington, the planners of the Negro March were keenly aware that the style of the demonstration could do much to communicate their purpose, determination, and power. In designing the march, they strategized how to negotiate the white supremacy that shaped the atmosphere of the nation and the capital.

They planned the event to make the most of the rebuilt and renovated center of Washington. In the 1930s, a major landscaping project on the Mall had cleared away the trees and removed the winding paths that Victorian park designers had built in the 1880s. On Pennsylvania Avenue, the massive array of Federal Triangle buildings was complete, creating a nearly smooth facade of edifices between the Capitol and the White House. In 1941, as Washington bustled with new workers hired to staff the new defense departments, the capital was the "fastest growing metropolis in the land." Washington also had become one of the most popular tourist destinations in the country. This popularity increased the symbolic power of the capital as the site for the education of citizens and attainment of citizenship. One contemporaneous commentator called the center of the city "the axis of democracy."[29]

In this symbolic seat of democracy, the place of African Americans was politically and geographically marginal. By 1940, blacks composed about 30 percent of the population of the District, yet they faced both informal and legal segregation. Most African Americans lived in all-black neighborhoods. Three-quarters of District blacks were laborers or service workers; only one-eighth of District whites worked in these occupations. Deeply ingrained local customs meant that blacks were refused service in most stores and restaurants in the downtown area, and District laws required that public schools and recreation be segregated (see fig. 19).[30] By marching through these renovated but still racially restricted areas, the Negro March on Washington could both claim these spaces for African Americans and dramatically suggest that black exclusion from economic opportunity was a flaw in the democracy of the United States.

Since the rights of African Americans as citizens were central to the march, the organizers strategized about how make their protest a compelling argument for the place of African Americans in the polity. To do so required organizers to think hard about the kind of citizens the African American marchers should represent. The march would include no "hoodlums and ruffians," Randolph assured the press, but rather only "the finest citizens of the nation, sincere in their desire to have justice." The organizers hoped to emphasize the participation of entire families by having separate delegations of men, women, boys, and girls. This decision seemed to reflect the growing importance of the family model of citizenship. Like the Bonus marchers, they wanted to capitalize on the

FIGURE 19. A drawing illustrating customs of segregation in Washington during the 1940s. A national committee that investigated the treatment of African Americans in the capital produced this picture to summarize the mistreatment. With their dignified "March of Mourning," the Negro March participants would have publicly countered such customs. (National Committee on Segregation in the Nation's Capital, *Segregation in Washington* [Chicago, 1948], 16)

sense that had developed during the 1930s that the best citizens were safely ensconced in families. In an atmosphere where black men and women were popularly vilified as disorderly and disruptive to the national order, this claim to citizenship as respectable family members was itself a challenge. To reinforce the point, these respectable citizens would present a unified message. The leaders resolved that all slogans and banners brought to Washington would have to be "approved by the national committee."[31]

Like earlier organizers, the Negro March leaders hoped the military model of a parade would give their protest the unity they saw as so essential, but they added a special twist to make the march a potent reminder of the mistreatment of African Americans. Rather than a triumphal parade, the organizers described the demonstration as a "March of Mourning." Participants would march silently up Pennsylvania Avenue accompanied by only the "beat of a muffled drum," the traditional accompaniment to military funerals.[32] Its rhythm would signal the marchers' political dissatisfaction.

Organizers keenly took advantage of the public spaces of the capital to highlight the marchers' citizenship and their demands. Their route showcased these orderly black citizens and their exclusion from full rights. First, the group would proceed up Pennsylvania Avenue, past the White House to insert themselves into the center of the ceremonial city from which blacks were so often excluded. The march would then end at the Lincoln Memorial. In part, the use of the Lincoln Memorial was a tribute to the powerful Marian Anderson concert two years before. Davidson emphasized the connection when he described the destination of the parade as "the famous Lincoln Memorial, where Marian Anderson sang at the feet of the great emancipator." Further, of course, they campaigned hard for the Lincoln Memorial as the endpoint for the march because locating the march at the Memorial was an effective way of contrasting Lincoln's exalted position as the "freer of the slaves" to the continuing problems of African Americans.[33]

For the Negro March, this shift away from the actual sites of decision making to the Lincoln Memorial was a strategic move for the organizers and represented a significant departure from tradition. Previous protests had focused on the White House, the Capitol, or administrative offices of the relevant departments, whose occupants held the political power to meet the demands of the protesters. Organizers hoped that the novel location would force the president and his aides to come to the marchers, rather than make it seem as if African Americans were once again appealing for help. In the atmosphere of power politics, Randolph and his supporters appreciated the force of making one's opponent move. In May, Davidson told reporters that the organizers intended to invite the president to the march because "we don't want any private meetings with committees." Instead, he declared, "We want the president to speak forthrightly to the problem and tell the world what the administration will and can do on behalf of the underprivileged minority groups." On June 3, Randolph fulfilled the organizers' initial plans and sent invitations to the president, Eleanor Roosevelt, and most of the administration officials.[34]

As these plans gradually became more complete in early June, the Negro March became a serious enough proposition to generate controversy. Some attacked the decision to exclude white people. Advocates of integration noted the irony of attacking "segregation . . . with a segregated march." The black columnist Charley Cherokee observed in May that the organizing committee "had its feverish activities temporarily interrupted by controversy" over the question of white participation. The most outspoken objections to the plan came from the branch of the NAACP in the District of Columbia. The branch, with an interracial leadership, eventually decided not to endorse the effort because of "the policy of excluding other than Negroes from the organization of the proposed March on Washington."[35]

The most sustained attack on the plans came from conservative African American leaders, who suggested the tactic itself was wrong. On June 13, Arthur Mitchell, the only black congressman, a Democrat from Chicago, delivered the commencement speech at Howard University. He labeled Randolph the "most dangerous Negro in America" and spent "much time in condemning the march." The *Pittsburgh Courier* also had a change of heart about the Negro March. While they had given a grudging endorsement to the march in May, the editors came out in mid-June with a scathing critique. The *Courier* editors doubted the march's effectiveness. They argued that "marches on Washington have always failed . . . because Congress has regarded them merely as nuisances organized by publicity hounds, job-hunters, and addlepates, and consisting of the mob-minded and misguided." The *Courier* suggested that African Americans should return to the traditional means of "influencing Congress and the Administration by personal letters and telegrams, . . . by memorials and resolutions sent to both Houses, and by intelligent personal representatives."[36]

The organizers of the Negro March on Washington rejected these criticisms, asserting that their protest in Washington was a confrontation.

Earlier organizers had responded to challenges to their tactics by claiming their protests were like traditional political behavior. The organizers of Coxey's Army claimed they were just a "petition in boots." The woman suffragists in 1913 staged a mock inauguration. Even the leaders of the Bonus Army had wrapped their invasion of Washington in the convention of lobbying. But the Negro March organizers were prepared to make their march into a "fight," to speak of the possibility that the protest might "shake up" both "white America" and "official Washington."[37] Indeed, they designed their protest to emphasize their anger and their despair and as a challenge to the Roosevelt administration. Because the march did not, in the end, happen, there is no way to know how many of the button purchasers and rally attendees would have ridden trains and buses to Washington on July 1. But, the increasingly worried reactions of the Roosevelt administration to these plans soon illustrated that the mere possibility of the march had enormous power.

"GET IT STOPPED"

In the frantic White House, already careening from crisis to crisis associated with the war overseas and defense preparations at home, these plans for the Negro March caused serious consternation. Both the Federal Bureau of Investigation and the Military Intelligence Division scrutinized the planning, speculating that it represented an effort to sabotage American defense efforts. In addition, black administration officials like Mary McLeod Bethune kept the president and Mrs. Roosevelt informed. The arrival of the letters inviting the president to address the marchers at the Lincoln Memorial deepened the concern. On June 7, President Roosevelt described himself as "much upset" about the march and declared he and his aides needed to "get it stopped."[38]

Such strong emotions and declarations suggested the power attributed the possibility of the Negro March, especially considering the other events that concerned the president during this period. In the first six months of 1941, Roosevelt and his staff shepherded the controversial Lend-Lease Bill through Congress, supervised the construction of dozens of new army camps to house thousands of draftees, and positioned American defensive forces as far east as Greenland. In April and May, they charted Germany's invasion of Yugoslavia, the takeover of Greece, and the drive into North Africa. At home, they struggled to stop strikes at critical plants and to manage complaints that defense contractors were taking excessive profits. On May 27, Roosevelt warned the American people that an attack against the United States could come at any time and declared an "unlimited national emergency." Negro March leaders appreciated how this context gave them power; one noted astutely, "at the back of the attitude of the Administration is . . . what effect this march will have on international affairs." The Associated Negro Press commented in mid-June that "the cabinet and White House will have to resign themselves to this particular spectacle which will show to the world . . . that all is not so well in the great United States."[39]

Roosevelt was clearly in a bind. The Roosevelt administration wanted to avoid making substantive changes to racial policies in the country, and they also wanted to avoid the public exposure of the march. His options were limited by his custom of treating protests in the capital with tolerance: he could not simply suppress the march. He clearly saw this march as a very difficult proposition that might publicly embarrass him in the tense atmosphere of the defense effort. This combination of fears meant that he was willing to go extreme lengths to convince the Negro March leaders that they should not use the nation's capital for their protest. But, the Negro March leaders were committed to the notion that their efforts were going to win some concrete results. It would be a difficult negotiation.

The president could not simply forbid the march because he had publicly tolerated previous political protests in the capital. His kind treatment of the returning Bonus marchers in the first years of his presidency set a pattern. In 1940, the president addressed from the back porch of the White House more than 4,000 marchers from the American Youth Congress, who wanted the administration to support the Soviet Union and its invasion of Finland. He rejected their pleas, cautioning them that under the more Soviet-like form of government that the Youth Congress endorsed, "this kind of meeting on the White House lawn could not take place." Likewise, his aides intervened in May 1941 to protect the American Peace Mobilization, a pacifist group with close ties to the Communist Party, who held a small, but continuous, picket at the White House.[40] Yet, these demonstrators were far less politically risky compared to a large number of African Americans threatening to expose the thinness of American democracy.

The president wanted to avoid the domestic political conflict that such a march might inspire. At a meeting with black leaders in the fall 1940, the president told them he could not act against discrimination because the "South would rise up in protest." Eleanor Roosevelt warned Randolph that the protest could "create in Congress even more solid opposition from certain groups than we have had in the past." Trying to avoid antagonizing either the rabid segregationists in the South or his supporters in the shaky alliance of labor activists, liberals, and African Americans, the Roosevelt administration had a great interest in minimizing public racial conflict.[41]

With fear of domestic and international criticism shaping their every move, the president and his aides tried hard to persuade the leaders to cancel. On the evening of June 12, President Roosevelt summoned Aubrey Williams of the National Youth Administration to the White House. Williams recalled the president as "tired and irritable" but also determined. He ordered Williams to leave the following day for New York City. Williams's task was clear: "talk Randolph and White out of this march." Williams did gather together White and Randolph with Eleanor Roosevelt and Mayor Fiorello La Guardia in the City Hall for a serious negotiation over the Negro March on Washington. Roosevelt's allies tried to persuade the leaders of the Negro March that the march was both dangerous and unnecessary. The leaders firmly dismissed these arguments and refused to call off the protest. Back in Washington, the president learned that his advisors were convinced that he would have to meet personally with the leaders and "thresh it out right then and there." Such a meeting was scheduled for June 18.[42]

Intent on taking advantage of Roosevelt's worries, the Negro March committee pressed their advantage by continuing to organize and publicize the march. Some moderate members of the committee suggested cancellation. But, the others refused to compromise. "Don't kid yourself," White told them, "the president's promises are not more than water, and soon forgotten because it is politically expedient." Rather, the committee resolved "to intensify the drive" for the march.[43] When Randolph acknowledged the president's invitation to the meeting on June 18, he reiterated that the march was still taking place. "The hearts of Negroes are greatly disturbed," he wired the president, "and their eyes and hopes are centered on the march, and the committee must remain true to them." The editors of the *Baltimore Afro-American* declared, "Let the New Coxey's Army March."[44]

Though they publicly proclaimed their commitment to mass action, the march leaders, meeting behind closed doors, began laying out the actions the president could take to convince them to cancel. On June 14, the group developed a "minimum of terms" to present to the president. They highlighted the demand for an executive order prohibiting the granting of contracts to business that practiced racial discrimination.

```
                    PROPOSALS OF THE
          NEGRO MARCH-ON-WASHINGTON COMMITTEE
                          TO
                  PRESIDENT ROOSEVELT
                         FOR
                  URGENT CONSIDERATION


POINT 1.    An executive order forbidding the awarding of contracts
            to any concern, Navy Yard or Army Arsenal which refuses
            employment to qualified persons on account of race,
            creed or color.  In the event that such discrimination
            continues to exist, the Government shall take over the
            plant for continuous operation, by virtue of the author-
            ity vested in the President of the United States, as
            Commander-in-Chief of the armed forces and as expressed
            in the Proclamation declaring a state of unlimited
            national emergency, May 27, 1941.

POINT 2.    An executive order abolishing discrimination and segre-
            gation on account of race, creed or color in all depart-
            ments of the Federal Government.

POINT 3.    An executive order abolishing discrimination in voca-
            tional and defense training courses for workers in
            National Defense whether financed in whole or in part
            by the Federal Government.

POINT 4.    An executive order abolishing discrimination in the
            Army, Navy, Marine, Air-Corps, Medical Corps and
            all other branches of the armed services.

POINT 5.    That the President ask the Congress to pass a law for-
            bidding the benefits of the National Labor Relations
            Act to Labor Unions denying Negroes membership through
            Constitutional provisions, ritualistic practices or
            otherwise.

POINT 6.    That the President issue instructions to the United
            States Employment Services that available workers be
            supplied in order of their registration without regard
            to race, creed or color.
```

FIGURE 20. Demands handed to President Roosevelt on June 18, 1941. This list of demands reflected the ambitions of the Negro March leaders when they began to appreciate how much Roosevelt was willing to bargain for the cancellation of the march. Over the course of the negotiations, they did not get all the specifics. An important loss was any provision addressing discrimination by holders of defense contracts already issued. ("March on Washington Movement: Principles and Structures" folder, container 26, A. Philip Randolph Papers, Library of Congress)

The leaders also wanted the president to ban discrimination and segregation within the federal government, especially in vocational training programs and in the armed services. Notably missing from this proposal were explicit statements about ending segregation in the military.[45] In drafting these demands, the leaders saw the strength of their threat, but appreciated the limits of their power (fig. 20).

It was these demands that the Negro March committee presented to the president in a tense meeting at the Oval Office four days later. Roosevelt had gathered together an amazing number of high-ranking administration officials to meet with the march leaders. Present at the meeting were both the directors of the Office of Production Management and the secretaries of the war and the navy. In addition, Roosevelt had invited the administration officials who had met with Randolph and White in New York City. The first lady was missing, since she had already left on vacation. In contrast, the president's aides allowed only Randolph and White to attend the meeting. To the *Pittsburgh Courier,* the meeting was "destined to go down in history as epochal." The march leaders labeled the meeting "the largest conference we had ever been successful in getting on the question of the Negro in national defense."[46]

Throughout the meeting with the president, Randolph and White sought to convince the president to discuss the demands rather than whether the Negro March was an appropriate tactic. In his typical manner, the president began the meeting by telling stories and jokes, but Randolph could take only so much before he reminded the president, "You are quite busy, I know. But what we want to talk with you about is the problem of jobs for Negroes in defense industries." When pushed in this way, the president emphasized his "firm and positive and definite opposition to the march." He began to rattle off all the reasons that the march was a problem. He told Randolph and White that if the Negro March were held, the Irish and Jewish people might also be inspired to march on Washington.[47] He said that the march "would give the impression to the American people that Negroes are seeking to exercise force to compel the government to do certain things." In making these arguments, the president used complaints against previous protests in Washington: that they might encourage everybody to protest in Washington and that they were an inappropriate use of pressure.

He also turned to another familiar argument: the potential for violence. In this case, the fear was not of general chaos, but of white supremacist violence. In the City Hall meeting, Randolph remembered La Guardia exclaiming: "You are going to get Negroes slaughtered!" Some of this fear came from the capital's violent race riots of 1919, begun when white soldiers attacked black residents. As the march drew near, a local army officer began running special drills because he didn't "feel justified in taking any chances on the repetition of the race riots." It also came from the knowledge that Washington police were known to brutalize black residents and had responded coldly to the permit requests of the march organizers.[48] By expressing fears of violent attacks on the marchers, Roosevelt was implicitly acknowledging how intense prejudice was against African Americans, yet using this prejudice as an argument against protests by African Americans.

Neither of the march leaders was willing to accept such a syllogism. Because of their keen appreciation that what Roosevelt most feared was the public exposure of white supremacy in the nation's capital, they rejected Roosevelt's arguments. Randolph suggested that violence would be unlikely if the president himself spoke at the Lincoln Memorial. Disconcerted, the president falsely replied that he did "not speak to any groups who come to Washington." Walter White broke in to remind the president of his address to the American Youth Congress. According to newspaper accounts, the president was "a little nonplussed." Randolph went on to rebut Roosevelt's insinuations about his organizational abilities. "The march-on-Washington movement was not planned . . . by irresponsible, wild-eyed crackpots," he assured the president, but rather by "a national committee composed of sane, sober and responsible Negro citizens." He dismissed the problem of other groups marching on Washington by emphasizing the rightness of the demand for equal treatment: "The public knows that the Negroes have justification for bringing their grievances to the president and to present them to the American people."[49]

Faced with this intransigence, Roosevelt tried to assess whether the organizers really could pull off the massive, dignified protest they were threatening. Significantly, he adopted the same criterion used by the march leaders: the number of marchers. He asked Randolph, "How many people do you plan to bring?" Randolph told him, "One hundred thousand, Mr. President." The president then turned to Walter White and asked, "Walter, how many people will really march?" White replied that he expected "no less than one hundred thousand." Roosevelt stared at White in what the NAACP leader considered an attempt to "find out if I were bluffing or exaggerating." Apparently, White's confidence convinced the president.[50]

Soon after, the president finally shifted the topic from the technique to the demands for action. In the newspaper accounts, he reportedly assured Randolph and White of his commitment to put the "force and weight of the office of the president behind efforts to secure jobs for qualified Negroes." Randolph and White wanted specifics. Befitting the president's dual concern to prevent the march in the short run and, more generally, to stop further complaints about the defense program, he soon threw out a solution: the formation of a committee. He observed that "one of the difficulties Negroes had was that they had nowhere to present their grievances and complaints when they were victims of discrimination." He suggested the possibility of a "board" to investigate such "complaints by Negroes or any one else." Walter White asked whether the board would actually have "power" to act against companies that discriminated. Roosevelt suggested that it would.

The president's suggestion was the important turning point, but it did not result in the march leaders immediately agreeing to anything. In part, they had good reason to doubt the president. Soon after he made the suggestion of a committee, the president left the meeting. Once the president left, it became clear that administration officials disagreed among themselves about the advisability of such a committee and its scope and power. Because of these disagreements, the delegation from the march committee left the meeting with "definite dissatisfaction with the results." And they defiantly declared to reporters that the "march will go on."[51]

In the face of this intransigence, the Roosevelt administration persisted in negotiating with the march leaders. Williams, La Guardia, and other aides began drafting an executive order that would establish a committee to supervise the employment policies of defense contractors. By the following day, White believed the president might immediately issue an executive order. In fact, it took another five days for the administration and the march leaders to agree on an acceptable order. Joseph Rauh, a lawyer who helped draft the appropriate language, remembered his amazement at Randolph's ability to insist on revisions. At one point, discouraged, Williams telegraphed for help from Mrs. Roosevelt, still at the vacation camp. With no phone in the house, the first lady walked to the country store, placed a call to Randolph in New York, and urged him to accept the current offer.[52]

As Roosevelt's aides negotiated, both they and their security forces felt an increased sense of pressure from the international situation. On June 21, Germany invaded the Soviet Union. Suddenly, the United States was the only major power not at war; Roosevelt was in the process of deciding whether to aid the Russians. The head of the Secret Service consulted with army officers over the impending march, and they decided to implement again the "White plan for the domestic security of Washington." The same cavalry units that had been called out for the Bonus March were to be on alert on July 1. The officers thought it advisable, though, to add "one battery of 75 mm. guns" in the hands of a "Military Police Battalion." The concerns of the security forces demonstrated how the tense international situation had increased their vigilance, especially on issues that raised questions about the armed services. Rauh remembered being told that the president did not want the march, because "it'll hurt our image; it'll help Germany."[53]

By June 23, the two sides had agreed on the main components. The march leaders approved an order with three provisions. First, the order fulfilled the demand of the Negro March committee for an end to discrimination in vocational training programs. Second, the order required that future defense contracts contain a clause "obligating the contractor not to discriminate against any worker because of race, creed, color, or national origin." Finally, the order adopted the president's suggestion for a complaint board. Named the "Committee on Fair Employment Practice," the board had the power to review "complaints of discrimination" that violated the executive order.[54]

Even as they came close to an agreement with the president's staff, members of the Negro March committee made a final effort to address discrimination within the federal government, particularly that practiced by the armed services. On June 24, Randolph, Davidson, and Rayford Logan held a final meeting with La Guardia and Williams to try to stretch the draft's provisions to cover the government generally. During the daylong meeting in Washington, the five men wrangled over this last demand and the possibility of canceling the march. According to Davidson, Williams and La Guardia resisted any specific reference to the government, because they said "the forces in opposition"—by implication southern politicians—were already mobilizing against the executive order. Finally, the men in Washington hammered out a rhetorical compromise. The specifics of the executive order remained the same, but they inserted a clause into the preamble saying that the order expressed the president's opposition to discrimination in the defense industry and in the government. It was a minor change with no enforcement mechanism, but the representatives of the march committee clearly felt they had won all they could. They approved the draft, but refused to begin canceling the march until the president actually signed it.[55] Williams rushed to the White House; Roosevelt approved the order and told his aides to "fix it up. . . . Quick." The following day, June 25, the president signed the final text of the order, assigned the number 8802.[56]

In the immediate aftermath of these negotiations, some celebrated. In a letter to Eleanor Roosevelt, Mary McLeod Bethune described Executive Order 8802 as the "most far reaching" presidential action since Lincoln signed the Emancipation Proclamation in 1893. The editors of the *Chicago Defender* called it "one of the most significant pronouncements that has been made in the interests of the Negro for more than a century." In a speech just after the order was issued, Randolph told the delegates of the NAACP annual convention that the order was a "bread and butter victory" that "will mean hundreds of dollars in wages for Negroes."[57]

From the Roosevelt administration's point of view, the terms of the executive order and the negotiations with the leaders represented another kind of victory: a victory over the risks of mass action. For those members of the Roosevelt administration involved with the Negro March and its cancellation, the order came as a genuine relief. During the meetings with the Negro March leaders, the president and his staff seemed most concerned with minimizing political change, with responding to the coalition of leaders of organizations behind the march, and with avoiding unfavorable publicity. The most significant piece of the order was the creation of the committee on Fair Employment Practices, which, on the surface, was a public acknowledgment of the federal government's responsibility to prevent racial discrimination. This committee, however, like the National Labor Relations Board, was intended to channel public protest into hearings and investigations. Critically, the negotiations received such minimal publicity that most white Americans heard nothing about the order's origins in the threat of the Negro March. On Thursday, June 26, the daily press announced the president had issued Executive Order 8802. Only the liberal daily *PM* mentioned the cancellation of the march. The other dailies simply attributed the order to the president's responsiveness to reports of "cases of discrimination against Negroes in some defense industries and labor unions." Mark Ethridge, the first chairman of the Fair Employment Practices Committee, wrote a self-congratulatory memorandum a few months later that made Roosevelt's goals during these negotiations explicit: "Clearly we have accomplished what the president wanted: we paralyzed any idea of a march on Washington."[58]

LEGACIES

The Negro March of 1941 did not simply die with issuance of the executive order; in the aftermath of its cancellation, the march was discussed in a vigorous and illuminating debate about the potential of political demonstrations that shaped the character of future marches on Washington. In 1942, this debate even penetrated the business-minded columns of *Fortune* magazine. Perhaps because of a sympathetic editor, the magazine devoted a lavish spread, illustrated with pictures by Romare Bearden, to how the exigencies for black Americans were being shaped—or not—by the war. The story astutely noted that Roosevelt's anti-discriminatory executive order had been issued when the president had "only a few days left for preventing an international embarrassment." The article noted that, not surprisingly, the order turned out to have had disappointingly limited effects. Strikingly, the *Fortune* essay placed blame not on Roosevelt or defense contractors, but on the process by which the executive order had been negotiated. Randolph's decision to compromise and halt the march was not just a tactical but an ideological mistake: what "could have been an inspiring demonstration of democracy at work came about as a compromise between hardboiled pressure groups."[59] This essay was not alone in criticizing the cancellation of the Negro March. Perhaps *because* political observers had no actual march to evaluate, their discussions of the proposed Negro March provoked an influential examination that laid bare disputed assumptions and differing fantasies about the benefits, limits, and potential of marching on Washington. This debate was the enduring legacy of Randolph's savvy mobilization of mass action in an age of "power politics."

Despite attempts to emphasize their victory, many African Americans, including Randolph himself, recognized that the executive order was weak. The most common word to describe the order was a "step." Randolph used the phrase with the most optimism, calling the order a "signal and profound step of a democratic progress!" But the delegates at the NAACP annual convention could only declare it was "a step in the right direction." Anyone who compared the original demands of the Negro March committee with the executive order could understand the ambivalence. The order said nothing about employers already holding defense contracts; the order offered no specifics about penalties for companies. The NAACP delegates expressed the most pressing concern: "Above all, we point out to the president and to all our fellow citizens that the decree fails completely to touch the matter of discrimination in the Armed Forces." Randolph tried to account for this weakness by reemphasizing that the main priority of the march was "the economic improvement of the Negro people." Yet even he expressed the hope that another executive order might address the inequities in the military. Such concerns dominated the substitute "Victory Meeting," held in Washington on July 1. Davidson secured permission to hold the rally at the Watergate, an outdoor amphitheater to the west of the Lincoln Memorial along the Potomac River. There, La Guardia, Randolph, and White, among others, addressed about 1,000 people. All three honestly admitted that the order was "not a complete victory." Soberly, La Guardia explained he was "too practical to feel that . . . there will be great change over night."[60] They were right.

In the ensuing months, these fears about the limits of the order were realized. The Fair Employment Practices Committee did hold a series of well-publicized hearings into the practices of discrimination and then issued a number of recommendations to reduce discrimination, including directives to specific industries. Once the United States declared war, however, federal officials mostly avoided the issue altogether. For example, in 1943 a ranking administration official simply ordered the committee to halt hearings on discrimination by railroads because the industry was too important to the war effort to face interference. In such an atmosphere, major companies and industries responded to committee directives with outright defiance.[61]

The fate of Executive Order 8802 clarified the limits on the right to economic security and on the techniques of power politics that Randolph had used to rationalize the protest. It was far easier to assert the right of African Americans to have jobs than actually to force reluctant companies to hire them, especially in the midst of a war. While it seemed feasible to expect the state to intervene, the reality was that few in the government had the stomach for the challenge. In the postwar period, too, attempts to strengthen the right to economic security foundered. Likewise, further attempts to increase racial equality faced vigorous rebuffs from southern politicians. Randolph and other believers in power politics correctly asserted the rising power of the interest groups, but elected representatives still had control.

For many of those involved, the most powerful legacy of the march was the realization that mass protest in the capital had great potential. These observers and activists echoed *Fortune*'s criticism about the cancellation of the protest. The most articulate proponents of this view were young student activists in New York City. They were coordinated by march committee member Richard Parrish and were clearly influenced by Bayard Rustin, who was emerging as a key organizer for pacifist and civil rights groups. The student activists dismissed the importance of the "partial victory" of the executive order. Instead, they asserted that the planned protest had been "the hope of a new day" because it was going to allow black people to publicly show their power and their displeasure. Similarly, a black newspaper columnist predicted that because of the cancellation, "it will be most difficult to get Negroes interested in a similar mass movement another time." Astutely, he noted, "Those who would keep Negroes down appreciate this only too well."[62] For these critics, marches on Washington could politicize participants and result in sustained social movements. The cancellation, they complained, short-circuited this potential.

Defensively, Randolph tried to dismiss these objections by reiterating his view that the Negro March was a tactic of power politics. The students, he said, saw "the March as an end in itself." To him, however, the Negro March was simply "a means to an end." He compared the march to "the strategy of a proposed strike." Like union leaders who used a vote in favor of a strike to convince the employers to bargain, the Negro March committee had used the call for the march to convince the Roosevelt administration to discuss their demands. When the president responded, they called off the protest.[63] Though in part a squabble between two different factions and two different generations, this debate went to the heart of the question about the purpose of marching on Washington. Since Coxey's Army, march organizers had emphasized the goal of winning concrete change. Yet, only in 1941 did the winning of a concession require organizers to consider openly the view that Randolph rejected: that perhaps a march was an "end in itself," that marching was an act that, on its own, had value.

Gradually, however, Randolph and his closest aides began to take to heart the criticism that canceling the march itself was a strategic error. Breaking away from most of the other leaders of the Negro March, Randolph formed an independent organization whose name suggested his continued faith in protest in the capital: the March on Washington Movement. The MOWM, as it was known, never became a large group, but it did articulate an influential vision of protest for African Americans. The organizers, including Randolph and Rustin, began imagining an intense challenge to white supremacy in the United States. Recognizing that racism was a problem not just in workplaces but also in American society in general, they encouraged MOWM supporters to use civil disobedience to challenge segregation.[64]

As they broadened the scope of their challenges and their tactics, Randolph and other supporters of the MOWM rethought the role of an actual march on Washington. They acknowledged that such protests had their place as part of a larger organizing effort. But, they cautioned that these demonstrations should have "limited objectives" and "not be considered the ultimate goal of the March on Washington Movement." Such cautions reflected their experience in 1941. Though powerful, such protests could not be expected to change conditions broadly. Instead, they emphasized the importance of using such protests in the capital "to win the widest possible public sympathy and support."[65] Though such sentiments had inspired the Negro March's organizers in 1941, they had ultimately put political concessions ahead of using large national protests to change public opinion. The MOWM activists resolved not to make this mistake again.

One sign of the potential power of this change in strategy came in the virulently negative reaction of southerners to such plans. Just shy of a year after the cancellation of the march, Congressman John Rankin of Mississippi took to the floor of the House to complain about "Communists . . . who are trying to stir up race trouble throughout the Nation" by forcing a vote on a bill to abolish poll taxes and who are "trying to incite the Negroes to march on Washington." Virginus Dabney, a southern journalist, likewise deplored the MOWM and its continued calls for "colored people [to] converge on the national capital from all directions for the purpose of forcing concession." He saw this effort and others as posing serious risks of racial disturbances, not only in the United States, but also among "the colored peoples of China, India, and the Middle East."[66] Such hyperbole was predictable from these die-hard segregationists, but their focus on the tactics of the group suggested the power of MOWM's political vision.

During and after the war, other groups continued to come to the capital to protest, but none in the large numbers that the organizers of the Negro March had found so important in confirming their power with the president. In November 1941, seven members of women's pacifist groups picketed the White House without incident. Between 1943 and 1945, members of the People's Peace Now committee also protested. After the end of the war, the pace of protest increased. Pacifists returned to sidewalks in front of the White House and the Justice Department to demand amnesty for draft resisters who were still imprisoned. In 1946 alone, groups of housewives concerned over plans to end price controls also took to the streets of the capital; Jewish GIs marched on Constitution Avenue, asking for the British government to increase the number of people allowed to immigrate to Israel; and members of various African American organizations paraded to the Department of Justice and the White House after the murder of blacks who tried to vote in a Georgia primary. In 1947, trade unionists held rallies and car parades to protest the Taft-Hartley Act.[67] Combined with the Negro March and the MOWM, these protests established the "march on Washington" as part of the vocabulary and repertoire of American politics.

Not surprisingly, Randolph remained an ardent believer in this form of political engagement. In 1946, he called for marches to support efforts to transform the wartime Fair Employment Practices Committee into a permanent agency, though he could not find funds to back up his call. Two years later, Randolph turned again to the protest in Washington as part of a concerted campaign to win full access to military service for African Americans. With six others, he picketed the White House on May 7, 1948. His picket sign declared, "If we must die for our country let us die as free men—not as Jim Crow slaves." When nothing changed, Randolph threatened to lead a march on Washington in August and called for a nationwide civil disobedience campaign against the draft. Again, the threats bore fruit. On July 26, President Truman used his executive power to guarantee "equality of treatment and opportunity for all persons in the armed services without regard to race, color, religion, or national origin." When assured that these orders would end segregation in the army, Randolph canceled another march on Washington.[68]

Other black organizations, however, considered a large-scale march on Washington too radical. In 1947, the NAACP held its annual convention in Washington. Its finale was a rousing session at the Lincoln Memorial—much like what had been planned for 1941. In this less tense atmosphere, President Truman spoke. White convinced all the three major radio networks to cover the meeting, and the State Department broadcast it on shortwave radio around the world.[69] Such rallies in Washington continued to be a mainstay of the NAACP's political repertoire, a way to appropriate the capital's public space without the confrontation of a declared "march" on the capital.

A generation of activists took from the Negro March crucial lessons. They appreciated the power of the Negro March's initial organizing methods and political analysis, but they realized that a march on Washington would not necessarily win substantive federal action. Black leaders continued to attempt to focus international attention on the treatment of African Americans. Throughout the 1940s and 1950s, fear of international condemnation drove the Roosevelt, Truman, and Eisenhower administrations to enact new policies for African Americans and to treat their political protests cautiously and respectfully.[70] In 1941, African Americans had also discovered the importance of building strong coalitions to back marches on Washington, and they developed some effective techniques for building support for such protest. They had found that the president seemed particularly responsive to such tactics. Most importantly, for future marches, was the lesson learned by some key organizers as a result of the debate over cancellation. Such men as Randolph and Rustin put much of their faith in direct action and civil disobedience, but they continued to support marches on Washington as means to mobilize supporters and achieve publicity—in other words, to build social movements. Over the next twenty years, the various organizers would apply these lessons in a sustained movement against white supremacy in the United States. In 1963, some of them returned to Washington, this time for a protest that did take place: the March on Washington for Jobs and Freedom.

CHAPTER FIVE

"IN THE GREAT TRADITION"

The March on Washington for Jobs and Freedom,
August 28, 1963

On August 28, 1963, more than 200,000 protesters converged on the nation's capital for the March on Washington for Jobs and Freedom. Not long after, Tom Kahn, an organizer for the protest, tried to assess the day's significance. As Kahn emphasized, the marchers had come to Washington as the result of hard-won agreement among leaders of civil rights, religious, and labor groups to sponsor a massive, peaceful demonstration in Washington. The participants had heard of the march because of its effective and unprecedented mass marketing. They also had the unprecedented blessing of President John F. Kennedy. Assembling on the hill around the Washington Monument, the participants marched to the Lincoln Memorial, where they listened to speeches from the protest's leaders. In his assessment, Kahn was unsure whether the march would achieve its stated goals: a strong civil rights bill and measures to reduce unemployment. About one thing, however, he was sure: "The success of the March on Washington is now a part of American history."[1]

Kahn was right about the historic nature of the March on Washington. It is both the most familiar and most remembered protest in the United States. Pictures of the marchers gathered at the Lincoln Memorial cover history textbooks. Clips from Martin Luther King Jr.'s "I have a dream" speech are featured in television commercials.[2] And the march often served as the explicit model for subsequent demonstrations. The pervasiveness of this march in popular memory emerged from the conscious effort by organizers and government officials to ensure that the demonstration would be acceptable to the general public. In the process, the protest helped legitimate a new kind of march on Washington in American political culture.[3]

In 1963, however, the March on Washington was but one aspect of a national explosion of actions against racial discrimination that many criticized as being outside traditional politics. These actions built on traditions of protest by African Americans reaching back to the Civil War, but far surpassed them in scope. In the South after 1960, the widespread adoption of direct action—purposeful defiance of segregation laws and injunctions against demonstrations—inspired activists and attracted new attention from the media, the federal government, and white segregationists. At a local level in the South, activists combined the rhetoric of Christian expectations and American democracy with the tactics of Gandhi's nonviolent direct action. In the North, marches and picket lines expressed sympathy for southern struggles and then expanded to include protests against local discrimination. In May of 1963, while the March on Washington was being considered, the *New York Times* estimated that in just one month more than 75,000 Americans had taken part in demonstrations in support of African American equality.[4] Still, organizers struggled to determine ways to focus the attention of a large and diverse nation on the problems of African Americans, who were only a tenth of the population. Perhaps most challenging of all, they had to form a coalition that included such varied leaders as Roy Wilkins, the somewhat staid director of the NAACP; Walter Reuther, the labor leader and confidant of President Kennedy; the young people who headed the not yet three-year-old Student Nonviolent Coordinating Committee (SNCC); and the fiery James Farmer from the Congress of Racial Equality. Fortunately, pulling together this coalition were A. Philip Randolph, with his years of experience in activism, and Bayard Rustin, one of the most inspired organizers of protests in American history. As they came together to plan the march, these diverse people had to rethink the role of public protest and collective action in American politics.

American political rhetoric proclaimed the centrality of equality under the law, but American practice continued to tolerate grievous discrimination against African Americans. The increase in protests and political activity had, of course, resulted in victories at the national level since 1941. President Harry Truman's executive order to desegregate the armed services in 1948 and its implementation during the Korean War; the Supreme Court's decision in *Brown v. Board of Education* in 1954; and the hard-won passage by Congress of the Civil Rights Act of 1957 all suggested that the various branches of the federal government might be persuaded to do more. The election of President John F. Kennedy in 1960 gave a new tone to national politics. In contrast to Eisenhower's conservative stance on national government, Kennedy spoke as if the federal government really could solve the challenges facing the country: unemployment, juvenile delinquency, rural and urban poverty, and even racial discrimination. But there were still serious obstacles. At the local level, many white southerners showed a fierce determination to halt these changes. At the national level, their representatives in Congress still held enormous power. Elected by a narrow margin, and dependent on the support of white supremacist Democrats, Kennedy hesitated to push for stronger civil rights legislation, issue substantive executive orders, or provide genuine protection for civil rights activists.[5] In this atmosphere of both political possibility and stasis, the demonstration itself balanced challenge and encouragement.

In this delicate position, the organizers put at the center of their plans for the march a notion basic to modern society and democracy: numbers count. Mass politics and mass culture permeated the march.[6] Political organizations of all sorts increasingly tailored their appeals to reach as many people as possible and in turn used high levels of support to justify their political actions. In borrowing these techniques, the organizers increasingly focused their attention less on immediate political goals and more on ensuring that their march would attract huge numbers of participants and that observers, especially the media, would consider it worthy political action.

The convergence of these diverse political forces meant that the success of the March on Washington for Jobs and Freedom would depend on both extensive effort and significant compromise. Creating the coalition of civil rights leaders needed to back the march required these African American leaders with very different politics to agree on a strategy for the march. The organizers and the Kennedy administration dealt with both practical details and important political symbolism in planning and designing the march. Such close cooperation between organizers and authorities transformed the demonstration. Recruiting the hundreds of thousands of participants so crucial to its success was a task of immense organization that depended on effective mass marketing of the protest. Both cooperation with authorities and mass marketing resulted in significant compromises in the style and the political demands of the march. Such compromises need to serve as a cautionary backdrop to more familiar memories of the march. The pictures of the crowds surrounding the Lincoln Memorial and Martin Luther King's visionary speech emerged as the iconic symbols of this protest, despite the ways such symbols obscured the complicated path that created them and blurred the march's consequences.

"A PERFECT COMPROMISE"

In December 1962, A. Philip Randolph and Bayard Rustin combined forces to plan another march on Washington. Once again, Randolph's focus was on employment. Randolph noted that African Americans, though only "11 percent of the workforce," were "22 percent of the jobless." A march, Randolph concluded, could "shake the public conscience out of its complacency about the tragedy of Negro joblessness." To cure these problems, Randolph imagined a massive federal public works program, not unlike the one proposed by Jacob Coxey. Rustin poured his considerable skills as an organizer into a plan for a demonstration that would combine elements of the many forms of political protest occurring in the country at the time. His plans called for two days of activities beginning with lobbying and sit-ins at the Capitol and culminating with a large rally at the Lincoln Memorial. With the support of the Negro American Labor Council that Randolph had founded, in the early months of 1963 the two men began publicizing what Randolph declared would be "a massive March on Washington for jobs."[7]

Despite his early certainties, Randolph's vision of this march evolved in the subsequent months as he and Rustin negotiated with Martin Luther King Jr. King had also announced plans for a protest in Washington, focused on civil rights legislation. In addition, the three men had to come to terms with Roy Wilkins, the cautious leader who had succeeded Walter White as executive director of the NAACP. These four civil rights leaders had significantly different ideas about how American citizens ought to demand rights for black people.

How they approached the various ideas for marches in 1963 was shaped by their views of the effects of earlier marches on Washington. In the previous several years, all four of these men had observed or participated in three major demonstrations in the capital. In 1957, King and the Southern Christian Leadership Conference (SCLC) sponsored the "Prayer Pilgrimage to Washington." This rally at the Lincoln Memorial publicized the lack of national action on school desegregation and civil rights. Wilkins, executive secretary of the NAACP, and Randolph, president of the Brotherhood of Sleeping Car Porters, agreed to serve as co-sponsors of the march with King. Then, Randolph and Rustin arranged two Youth Marches for Integrated Schools with the blessings of King and the reluctant support of Wilkins. The first, in October 1958, attracted 8,000 college and high school students to Washington; the second, in April 1959, drew more than 20,000.[8] Though they worked together on these three events, Randolph, Rustin, King, and Wilkins developed very different views of their significance.

Randolph and Rustin's experiences convinced them that another similar demonstration in Washington could build a stronger social movement for civil rights. An element of personal struggle also contributed to their enthusiasm, as both men felt on the margins of the civil rights movement. Though widely respected, Randolph was less active than other leaders because of his age and his commitments to the labor movement. Many civil rights leaders had doubts based on Rustin's homosexuality and his former membership in the Communist Party. Sustaining both leaders, however, was a deep belief in the importance of nonviolent protest. Of course, Randolph's support for marches on Washington reached back to the canceled Negro March; his enthusiasm for the technique never flagged. Rustin added a theoretical framework to this enthusiasm. He convinced Randolph of the value of Gandhi's arguments about nonviolent action. To him, protests were rarely methods of winning immediate governmental action but rather essential tactics for organizing and inspiring people to fight for political change.[9]

What King took from the Prayer Pilgrimage and the later youth marches was that such demonstrations brought national media attention to his efforts. His effectiveness as a speaker at two of the events led to the label "the No. 1 Negro Leader of men." The three national protests did more to ensure him a national reputation than the hundreds of speeches King gave in the South. As a result, he grew increasingly attracted to protests in Washington as an effective method for reaching national politicians and convincing more of the American people of the evils of white supremacy.[10]

Roy Wilkins, however, doubted the value of the three efforts in the 1950s. As the diligent executive secretary of the NAACP since 1955, Wilkins combined anti-Communism and fervent devotion to the NAACP's reputation with doubts about the practical outcome of protest. His doubts reached back to his own observation of the 1932 Bonus March and the canceled 1941 Negro March on Washington, neither of which, Wilkins believed, had won concrete change. The three protests in the 1950s did little to alter his view. African American journalists blamed Wilkins and the NAACP for the lower-than-expected turnout at the Prayer Pilgrimage because they believed the group's leaders "dragged their feet" in mobilizing for the demonstration. Better than marches on Washington, Wilkins told Randolph, was "analysis, understanding and countermaneuvers."[11]

Randolph and Rustin disagreed with Wilkins in 1963. But they knew a coalition of the major civil rights groups was essential to give the protest credibility among participants and with the federal government. In late March, Randolph wrote to the other leaders asking them to join him in sponsoring the march. He addressed letters not only to Wilkins and King, but also to Whitney Young of the National Urban League, James Farmer of the Congress of Racial Equality (CORE), Charles McDew of the SNCC, Dorothy Height of the National Council of Negro Women, and Rosa L. Gragg of the Association of Colored Women's Clubs. To Rustin and Randolph, these seven leaders and their organizations represented the most important powers in African American politics. The initial response to Randolph's letter was lukewarm. Only a few organizations sent representatives to a planning meeting, and of them, only CORE representatives immediately endorsed the proposal.[12]

In the meantime, Martin Luther King's own ideas about using the capital for protests began to surface. At first, caught up in protests in Birmingham, Alabama, King and his staff neglected Randolph's call. Then in late May, with a settlement from Birmingham officials in place, King went west, where he presided over a series of successful mass rallies and fund-raising events. He found particular support in Los Angeles, a city whose diverse population and involvement in the entertainment industry symbolized the mass society of the United States. The city was also full of people actively backing the southern civil rights movement and challenging racial discrimination in California as well. Generous donations from movie actors and high turnouts in open stadiums for his speeches gave King a sense that both the common people and the new cultural elite supported the cause of civil rights. In the midst of these events, King spoke by telephone on June 1 with Stanley Levison and Clarence Jones, two of his key advisors in New York City. Exuberantly, he told them that the time had come for a "mass protest" of over 100,000 people in Washington to win a strong civil rights bill.[13]

Ever conscious of the power of television and other media to build enthusiasm, King and his aides quickly announced his ideas. In a television interview on June 9, King mentioned the possibility of a march combined with "sit-ins in Congress." Two days later, New York representatives of the SCLC made the plans more concrete. They warned of "massive, militant sit-ins on Congress" and reminded reporters that the "Negro question was 'no longer just a Southern thing.' " Like Coxey's Army and the Bonus marchers, King's marchers would come to Washington with a specific legislative goal: passage of Kennedy's proposed civil rights bill. Yet, unlike those earlier leaders, King spoke as if he and his supporters truly intended to disrupt Congress with sit-ins, rather than just impress them by their presence. Randolph and Rustin soon agreed in principle to combine their announced march with King's protest.[14]

All three men, however, had to adjust their plans to the president's decision the same week to send a civil rights bill to Congress. Southern senators instantly threatened a filibuster to halt any such legislation. In a late-night conversation on June 10, King and his associates agreed that a "march on Washington" could "dramatize this thing and put a kind of pressure on Congress, so that the Civil Rights bill . . . offered by the President will get through." When King came to New York City on June 18, he met with Rustin and representatives from SNCC and CORE to plan for their march in this new political atmosphere. Despite King's preference for a "spontaneous" protest to counter the expected filibuster, they agreed that a large march needed careful planning and a specific date. They chose Wednesday, August 28.[15]

But they still needed the support of Wilkins. His attitude toward protests appeared to be softening. June was a turning point. First, Wilkins took part in a direct action protest and was arrested. Then, the murder of Medgar Evers, one of the NAACP's most valued field secretaries, brought home the risks facing all activists. On June 19, Wilkins firmly rejected the suggestion that demonstrators should take a break during the debate over the civil rights bill, describing such protests as part of American tradition.[16]

A meeting at the White House during which Randolph and King showed their determination to hold the protest finally convinced Wilkins. On June 22, the president met with African American leaders, primarily to discuss the challenges of passing the civil rights bill. The proposed march, however, soon changed the direction of discussion. Like Wilkins, Whitney Young, executive director of the National Urban League, was also doubtful and asked the president his opinion. Unconsciously echoing words spoken in 1894, Kennedy answered that "a big show at the Capitol" could create "an atmosphere of intimidation." Randolph responded quickly to Kennedy's suggestion that lobbying was preferable. He emphasized that this protest was going to happen, re-gardless of the administration's views. King added that the march could complement lobbying by "mobilizing support." Throughout the discussion of the march, Wilkins remained ambivalent and avoided comment.[17] Yet, later that day, he agreed to support the march—if Randolph and King forswore all civil disobedience and kept the march entirely law abiding. Convinced that the protest was going to happen with or without him, Wilkins conceded that this kind of peaceful march was the "perfect compromise." Once Wilkins signed on, Young also lent his name to the effort.[18]

On July 2, the leaders announced their revised plans to the press. The leaders of the march—dubbed informally the Big Six—were Randolph, Wilkins, King, Young, John Lewis (the new president of SNCC), and Farmer. Rustin was named the deputy director. CORE and SNCC had agreed to endorse the protest, still expecting it would include the use of civil disobedience against the Kennedy administration, especially its Justice Department, which remained notoriously slow to respond to obvious violations of federal laws. King and Randolph rebuffed these ideas for the protest in order to honor the compromise struck with Wilkins. Indeed, King assured reporters that "no acts [of] civil disobedience will occur," and Wilkins confirmed there would be no "wild and woolly acts."[19]

The Big Six named the protest the "March on Washington for Jobs and Freedom." The new name emphasized the combined purposes of the march. As the "Call to Action" signed by the leaders explained, the legislative demands of the protest were for a strong civil rights bill and for a "massive works program." They named as their enemies the "Southern Democrats and reactionary Republicans" who "fight against the rights of all workers and minority groups." Despite naming these specific demands and enemies, the call still emphasized that the broader purpose of the march was "to accelerate the dynamic, non-violent thrust of the civil rights revolution" and "to offer a great witness to the basic moral principle of human equality and brotherhood."[20] The leaders combined the specific demand-oriented approach of King with the broad agenda-setting and movement-building approach of Rustin and Randolph. Inspiring both approaches was the goal of convincing the nation, as they had Roy Wilkins, that the protests of the civil rights movement were an acceptable part of the American tradition.

A sign of the march's broad appeal was its strong endorsement during the annual convention of the NAACP, held July 4–6 in Chicago. When a handful of voices criticized the march as too confrontational, the speakers were literally shouted down. The NAACP delegates overwhelmingly resolved to back the march in the capital. In a rousing speech reminiscent of Carl Browne's, Wilkins urged everyone to join in challenging the "clique" in Washington by participating in a "living petition."[21]

"COOPERATION": ORGANIZERS AND AUTHORITIES PREPARE FOR THE MARCH

On July 17, just returned from a three-week trip to Europe, President Kennedy held a televised press conference. When asked about the upcoming March on Washington, Kennedy praised the plans for what he labeled a "peaceful assembly." In particular, he noted the "cooperation" of the organizers "with the police," and he described the march as part of a "great tradition" in the United States. Kennedy's willingness to describe the march as acceptable and traditional reflected a calculated cooperation with the organizers of the march. Such cooperation had been a part of earlier Washington demonstrations—most notably during the Bonus March. Over time, it had become harder for presidents to ignore well-planned and well-publicized marches. In 1963, Kennedy was aware of the international scrutiny of white supremacy in America and hopeful that a peaceful march would reflect well on his administration. As federal officials and organizers worked together to plan the march, Washington authorities became simultaneously its regulators and supporters, even as they remained, to some extent, its target.[22]

In the 1950s and early 1960s, protesting in the capital had become commonplace. Among the most active protesters were local residents seeking an end to segregation in the District. Other demonstrations addressed national issues, such as the execution of Ethel and Julius Rosenberg. Even Eisenhower, who tried to remain above the civil rights fray, found it necessary to acknowledge the three civil rights marches in the 1950s. By 1962, protests in front of the White House were so frequent that a police officer labeled the practice "a national habit."[23]

Although the Kennedy administration had voiced support for civil rights demonstrations in the past, a leading reason to work closely with the march organizers was to prevent violence in the capital. Officials had no choice but to deal with this question forthrightly: commentators constantly mentioned it. When the *New York Times* reported on the announced protest, the newspaper cautioned that "the capital is already beset with racial troubles of its own." More cataclysmically, Representative

James Haley, a Democrat from Florida, speculated that the march "could be the spark which would touch off an ugly, blood-letting riot, accompanied perhaps by killings." This hyperbolic prediction had an edge of plausibility as violence and disorder had often accompanied civil rights demonstrations. Although white citizens or police officers were responsible for the vast majority of destructive violence, on rare occasions frustrated blacks had fought back. In the District itself, in 1962, fighting broke out after a Thanksgiving Day football game between a predominantly white Catholic school and an all-black team from a public school. Hundreds of people, mostly whites, reported injuries. Such a fight revealed how despite the removal of the most blatant forms of segregation, the capital still split along racial lines.[24]

To quell their own fears and those of their critics, officials and organizers planned how to prevent violence and disorder. In coordination with the Kennedy administration, the police department proposed to keep on duty all police officers on August 28 and to commission firefighters and the police reserve as temporary officers. In addition, they decided to mobilize 2,000 National Guardsmen preemptively. Likewise, the Kennedy administration planned to turn out every Capitol, White House, and Park Police officer and arranged to supplement the 1,000 soldiers in the area with 3,000 additional men. The organizers countered with measures to ensure that they would also get credit for a peaceful protest by recruiting their own marshals to maintain order.[25] The extensive nature of these preparations reflected the joint decision of the Kennedy administration and the organizers that a march subject to public control would best convey the marchers' commitment to legal change.

The shared investment in designing an acceptable march showed as the Kennedy administration's assistance went beyond just security planning to actively assisting the organizers to ensure that the marchers were comfortable and the march went as planned. By the middle of July, an assistant attorney general in the Justice Department was working nearly full time on the protest. The aide, with the help of other staff members, drew up long lists of possible problems, met regularly with organizers, and intervened with federal and District officials. These efforts mostly took place behind the scenes, but Kennedy gave a more public blessing when he agreed to meet with the march leaders at the conclusion of the day.[26]

The Kennedy administration cooperated extensively in the protest for national and international reasons. There was a practical component: organizers claimed that more than 100,00 people—many more than the usual number for such demonstrations—would arrive in Washington on August 28, and officials appreciated that traffic, sanitation, and policing problems would multiply. More importantly, Kennedy closely associated the march with the success or failure of his civil rights bill. Like Roosevelt in 1941, Kennedy was also keenly aware of international scrutiny of the treatment of African Americans in the country. Accordingly, the administration tried to make the march an expression of American values, not a symbol of the flaws in the country. The United States Information Agency arranged for Bayard Rustin to address a group of foreign correspondents. A filmmaker in the agency received permission to make a movie about the march for distribution to U.S. embassies. The Voice of America also planned to broadcast reports in thirty-six languages. To keep the pressure on Kennedy, supporters of the civil rights movement living outside the United States solicited support for the march. Groups of expatriates arranged for petitions expressing sympathy for the march to appear in the international editions of the *New York Herald-Tribune* and the *New York Times* and asked the signers to turn the slips in to United States embassies.[27] This promotion of the march outside of the United States both took advantage of Kennedy's sensitivity about international views of the civil rights movement and emphasized that the protest had not just national but worldwide significance.

The cooperation between the organizers and authorities transformed the political symbolism of the demonstration, most concretely by shifting its route. Rustin's original plan for Randolph's march had been designed to take full advantage of the political space of Washington, with protests near both the Capitol and the White House. This design changed radically during the negotiations in July. In the end all that remained of Rustin's original march was its destination: the Mall and the Lincoln Memorial. As they discussed the practicalities of having more than 100,000 protesters gather in Washington, both organizers and officials agreed that the marchers would assemble at the Washington Monument, march into two streams down Constitution and Independence Avenues, and regroup in front of the Lincoln Memorial (see map 3).

The new route reflected the political goals of the organizers, the political fears of the Kennedy administration, and the practical concerns raised by the expected turnout of more than 100,000. Though later some would blame the Kennedy administration for what they saw as a protest "confined" to the Mall, many of the decisions were made jointly. For example, the Kennedy administration did not want the participants to march near the Capitol, but Wilkins also objected to such plans as too

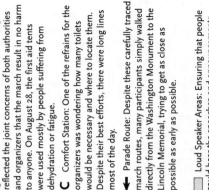

✚ First Aid: The numerous first aid locations reflected the joint concerns of both authorities and organizers that the march result in no harm to anyone. On August 28, the first aid tents were used mostly by people suffering from dehydration or fatigue.

C Comfort Station: One of the refrains for the organizers was wondering how many toilets would be necessary and where to locate them. Despite their best efforts, there were long lines most of the day.

➤ Parade Route: Despite these carefully traced march routes, many participants simply walked directly from the Washington Monument to the Lincoln Memorial, trying to get as close as possible as early as possible.

▦ Loud Speaker Areas: Ensuring that people could hear the speeches and announcements reflected the change in emphasis from demonstrations focused on moving through Washington to ones focused on speeches to huge crowds.

MAP 3. Plan for the March on Washington for Jobs and Freedom, 1963. Source: "Lincoln Memorial Program," fiche 005, 966-1, "March on Washington" folder, Schomburg Clipping Collection.

much pressure. A parade before the White House and down Pennsylvania Avenue was abandoned because organizers accepted that the expected size of the crowd made a route in front of the White House unfeasible, while the Kennedy administration clearly wished to avoid any impression that the protest was directed at the president.[28]

In addition, as both sides appreciated for different reasons, the new location would put the marchers in the most familiar part of the capital, its ceremonial center. During the 1940s and 1950s, the importance of and appearance of Pennsylvania Avenue had declined. Its south side was lined with government buildings; its north side was a bedraggled, fading shopping area. In contrast, the museum-studded Mall—where the march would take place—was becoming the cultural and tourist center of the city. For authorities, a protest centered on the Mall posed fewer security challenges and less general disruption to the city or the federal government. Most important, organizers used the central location on the Mall and at the Lincoln Memorial to symbolize their movement as a force independent of the president and of Congress. "We do not come to beg or plead for rights denied for centuries," prospective marchers were told. Rather they should expect "every single Congressman and Senator *to come to us*—to hear our demands for jobs and freedom, NOW."[29]

This extensive cooperation between organizers and the authorities did not please everyone. Segregationists and black nationalists launched scathing criticisms at the Kennedy administration for its support. For rabid segregationist Representative W. J. Bryan Dorn, a Democrat from South Carolina, the absurdity was that the government wanted to cooperate. He was astonished that for "the first time in the history of our Nation . . . the Federal Government itself has encouraged a 'march on Washington.'" Malcolm X, convinced that only radical actions could change the situation of African Americans, objected to the idea that civil rights activists might want presidential support. "When he joins you," he warned the leaders, "you're not going in the same direction you started in."[30] Such criticisms captured the way in which the cooperation between the organizers and the Kennedy administration transformed this march. It encouraged the organizers to focus the protest on influencing members of Congress and the American people. Earlier protesters had made similar choices at times, but without so much private, let alone public, assistance from the president. The cooperation also meant that the protest that had earlier threatened most of the official symbols of federal authority would now challenge that authority from their own distinct space on the Mall.

"ALL AMERICANS OF GOOD WILL"

On August 2, after only four weeks of intensive organizing, march organizers had distributed 42,000 buttons. The design was simple: just an image of a black and a white hand clasped together and surrounded by the words "March on Washington for Jobs and Freedom" with the protest's date. Sale and distribution of buttons were crucial parts of funding and advertising the march. Another 82,000 were on order, and organizers estimated they could well need another 200,000 before the march. Such high numbers seemed reasonable in light of the fact that march supporters had already passed out 385,000 flyers and were going through them "at a rate of from 70,000 to 110,000 per day."[31] These figures reveal how the march in 1963 operated on a scale unprecedented in the history of marching on Washington.

The August 28 march became the first mass-marketed protest in the history of demonstrations in Washington. Skilled organizers and leaders used all available forums—buttons, flyers, newspapers, radio, television, rallies, and concerts—to promote the march and recruit participants. This focus on numbers led organizers to widen their coalition, thus welcoming "all Americans" and persuading many in the process that this kind of protest was a traditional part of American politics. Yet this focus on large numbers necessitated compromises. Organizers struggled to highlight the participation of women, purposefully and publicly excluded radicals, and altered their political demands to keep the coalition together.

Critical to marketing efforts was the goal of a turnout of more than 100,000, in order for the march "to be politically impressive and have the massive impact needed." Even President Kennedy expressed his worries to Arthur Schlesinger about turnout, fearing that fewer than 100,000 marchers might indicate that "demand for civil rights legislation was exaggerated." The decision of the organizers to focus on "numbers" also reflected the specific political position of African Americans. As Tom Kahn, an organizer, commented, "for black Americans, lacking decisive economic and political power," only their ability to act together felt like power. He concluded, "Numbers are important to a minority."[32]

At the head of this effort to attract marchers was Bayard Rustin, who had long made planning demonstrations his vocation. In the 1940s, besides working with Randolph on the March on Washington Movement, he had participated in pathbreaking actions against segregation. During the 1950s, he had organized protests of hundreds against civil defense drills in New York City and marches of thousands against the atomic

FIGURE 21. Bayard Rustin discussing plans for the March on Washington for Jobs and Freedom. His title as deputy director of the march was a concession to those who feared that his previous association with the Communist Party and his homosexuality would discredit the demonstration. Yet, everyone acknowledged that without his formidable skill at organizing the march, it never would have come off in such an orderly fashion. (Library of Congress, Prints and Photographs Division, LC-USZ62–118984)

bomb in Britain. Labeled by *Newsweek* "a genius at organization," he was also a master of publicity. Like the suffragists with their storefront office in Washington in 1913, Rustin turned the march headquarters in Harlem into an advertisement, with a huge banner announcing the protest and its date from the second-story window. With drive and experience, Rustin helped ensure a huge number of participants (see fig. 21).[33]

Efforts on this scale clearly required money to spread the word. The three marches in the 1950s left Rustin and the six leaders keenly aware how much large protests in Washington cost. They prepared a budget of $100,000. While each of the sponsoring organizations contributed seed money, Randolph, Rustin, and other supporters also assiduously solicited funds from labor unions, churches, and individuals, collecting over $87,000 in direct contributions and through the sale of merchandise.

The sale of buttons at twenty-five cents apiece alone generated more than $25,000 in revenue, for a net profit topping $15,000. Organizers also used entertainment and celebrities to publicize the march and to raise funds. In Birmingham, New York City, and other locations, supporters of the protest held benefit concerts. Prominent actors like Charlton Heston, authors like James Baldwin, and singers from Bob Dylan and Joan Baez to Marian Anderson and Mahalia Jackson lent their names and talent to the effort.[34]

Simultaneously, organizers worked to make the protest acceptable to the authorities and to the general public. Organizers urged groups to have their communities' elected officials "proclaim August 28 as FREEDOM DAY." They suggested convincing ministers and rabbis to offer prayers, and lobbying employers to close for the day and "grant workers paid vacation" to participate in the march. These campaigns won some notable successes. Both Mayor Richard Daley of Chicago and Mayor Robert Wagner of New York City agreed to give city employees a paid leave of absence. A number of small companies also announced they planned to shut on August 28 in honor of the demonstration.[35]

The organizers brought to the protest a historical self-consciousness in their efforts to cast their demonstration as a legitimate part of American politics. In addition to the attempt to make August 28 into a holiday, organizers and supporters made constant references to past events and past marches. These deliberate associations suggest that organizers were engaged in the "invention of tradition," a process critical to creating and shoring up new political forms. Memories of the Marian Anderson concert at the Lincoln Memorial in 1939 and the threat of the Negro March in 1941 were invoked to support the tactic and location of the event in 1963. Supporters also linked the march to a broader American history, one that included a tradition of marching on Washington. Representative Robert Nix of Pennsylvania, one of five African Americans in the House, spoke in its chambers on August 22, 1963. He detailed the history of protests in Washington, including Coxey's Army, the Suffrage Procession and Pageant, the Bonus marchers, the Negro March, and the three civil rights demonstrations of the 1950s. He emphasized that all these protests were the result of "the failure of the Congress and the President to act positively to remove the evils which produced demonstrations."[36]

As in 1941, the support of the black press was crucial for recruiting marchers. But circulation had dropped considerably since the 1940s, so the coverage of mainstream papers, magazines, and television became even more important to the organizers. The leaders and organizers agreed to hire "an experienced public relations person . . . to handle all press relations for the March on Washington." Members of the Big Six and Rustin held news conferences attended by both print and television reporters and made appearances on major talk shows.[37] In contrast to the virtual news blackout by major newspapers during the planning of the Negro March, the media in 1963 eagerly covered the announced demonstration.

These efforts by the planners in 1963 to legitimate and publicize the march widely also contributed to the remarkable receptivity to support from many different types of individuals. The organizing manual forthrightly answered the question "Who Will March" with the blanket statement, "All Americans of good will who will subscribe to the aims and purposes of the March." The organizers wanted the marchers to include men and women, black and white, from all classes and backgrounds. This inclusive view reflected the continued widening of the definition of "appropriate" citizens begun in the 1910s. During the 1950s, the legal definition of citizenship and notions about legitimate political actors had continued to change. The McCarran Immigration Act of 1952 finally permitted Asian immigrants to become citizens, and the 1957 civil rights act had furthered citizenship protections for all. Equally important, the civil rights movement itself had widened definitions of citizenship. In their strident rejection of southern laws and American customs against the full participation of African Americans, movement activists had themselves discovered the value of including a wide range of people. And though the media focused most of its attention on a few male leaders, men and women, young and old, were in the forefront of daily activism.[38]

The focus on recruiting huge numbers of participants and this new view of citizenship also influenced the conscious interracialism of the march. In early August, Randolph told reporters that the "visible marching" of whites and African Americans side by side would have "moral significance." This marked a significant shift from 1941, when Randolph had argued that a "Negroes-only" march would not only lessen the likelihood of accusations of Communist domination but also best communicate the sense of exclusion and the desire for inclusion of African Americans. By 1963, the involvement of whites in the civil rights movement, the impassioned arguments against segregation, and the growing prominence of black nationalism as espoused by the Nation of Islam made this position less tenable.[39] By making the march publicly interracial, the organizers improved their claim to be speaking for, as well as to, the nation.

Organizers looked to a wide range of established groups to recruit marchers, relying in particular on labor unions and religious organizations. In early August, the leaders agreed to transform the Big Six into the Big Ten by adding four representatives from these groups. To represent labor, the leaders turned to Walter Reuther of the United Auto Workers, who had been advising them since June. The three other additions to the Big Six were religious leaders of organizations that had endorsed the protest: the Reverend Eugene Carson Blake from the Commission on Race Relations of the National Council of Churches, Rabbi Joachim Prinz of the American Jewish Congress, and Mathew Ahmann of the National Catholic Conference for Interracial Justice. All four men were white, which visibly emphasized the interracial nature of the march. Even more important was that these organizations had links to thousands of people whom they promised to recruit as marchers.[40]

Yet, the efforts to portray the march as inclusive and to widen the coalition faced obstacles. Organizers and leaders alike struggled to find a place for women in the leadership of the march. Everyone clearly expected both women and men to participate in the demonstration, and women were staff members. Nevertheless, no woman was among the Big Six or Big Ten. Only one woman, Anna Hedgeman, served as a member of the administrative committee. Hedgeman herself repeatedly complained about the failure of the leaders to include women among their numbers. Finally, the organizers made tentative plans to recognize the role of women by presenting five civil rights activists—Mrs. Rosa Parks, Diane Nash Bevel, Mrs. Medgar Evers, Gloria Richardson, Daisy Bates—during the program at the Lincoln Memorial. They concluded, however, that none of the women should speak because of the "difficulty of finding a single woman to speak without causing serious problems vis-à-vis other women and women's groups." This plan infuriated Hedgeman, who appreciated that such differences in approach had not prevented the men being scheduled to speak. The leadership's inability to respond to such criticism indicated that women continued to be put at the periphery of national efforts, even as they served in the front lines of civil rights protests across the country.[41]

As had been the case since Coxey's Army, fears of appearing too radical also limited the recruiting for the march. Though some of the excesses associated with Joseph McCarthy in the early 1950s had disappeared, numerous laws and practices still sought to exclude Communists from public life. The leaders in 1963 announced, "We expressly reject the aid or participation of totalitarian or subversive groups of all persuasions." In part, the organizers of the march wanted to avoid Communist participation because of accusations by southern politicians. Governor Orval Faubus of Arkansas claimed the demonstration was "inspired by Communists," while Senator Strom Thurmond declared that Rustin was a Communist—as well as a homosexual—on the Senate floor. Under pressure from J. Edgar Hoover, who was convinced that Communists controlled the civil rights movement, Kennedy himself and his aides had warned King to break off most contact with Stanley Levison, whom the FBI considered a Communist agent. To the irritation of the officials in the Justice Department who were working with the organizers, the FBI continued to submit reports that sought to discredit the march by claiming the participation of Communists.[42]

Besides rejecting the support of explicitly radical groups, the organizers sought to ensure a uniform message by excluding radical statements. The planners in 1963, like their predecessors in 1941, informed potential participants that the march organizers would supply all signs, which would communicate only approved messages; indeed the organizing manual emphatically declared, "*No other slogans will be permitted.*"[43] These decisions to reject certain groups and control the messages at the march illustrated how the pressure of creating a large, acceptable march came at the expense of allowing participants to express their particular political views.

The scale of recruiting and the inclusiveness of the coalition also required compromises in political demands. The shift toward a focus on turnout resulted in decreased specificity, especially around the economic inequalities that had initially inspired Randolph. Rustin acknowledged that many people came to believe the march was just about "demonstrating support for the Kennedy Administration's Civil Rights Bill." In the process, some supporters raised concerns about a demand for an increase in the minimum wage to $2.00, complaining that so high a figure was too controversial and incompatible with organizing a "massive witness." As a result of such complaints, the final ten demands asked vaguely for a minimum wage high enough to provide "all Americans a decent standard of living." In addition, a footnote stated that "support of the March does not necessarily indicate endorsement of every demand listed."[44] Such a distancing statement suggested how the concrete demands behind the march were downplayed in the interest of gaining broad support.

FIGURE 22. Buses lined up, waiting for the marchers to return. Some of the hundreds of buses used to transport the marchers to Washington, parked in spaces reserved for them near the Mall. (Library of Congress, Prints and Photographs Division, *U.S. News and World Report* Magazine Collection, LC-U9–10333, no. 11)

Even as authorities and organizers worked together to ensure a peaceful, trouble-free march, a ban on the sale of liquor on the day of the protest betrayed the deep anxieties that the demonstration elicited for some in the District. Such a ban had been unprecedented in the District since the end of Prohibition. Though the District commissioners claimed their decision was not a "reflection upon the organized groups" sponsoring the protest, the ban nevertheless left the unavoidable impression that a group of African Americans was incapable of behaving properly if alcohol was available.[45]

Despite these compromises, differences with potential supporters, and invidious attacks, the mass-marketing techniques used in 1963 worked. By publicizing the march widely, by finding groups and organizations to sponsor it, by sending materials or people to help with the practical details, Rustin and his staff members ensured that transportation to Washington would be available. They estimated that 40,000 marchers from New York City alone had reserved seats on hundreds of buses for the day's journey. Further west, groups in Los Angeles, whose enthusiasm had first inspired King, decided to charter planes to attend the march. By the middle of August, there were reports on the East Coast that no more buses were available to transport marchers on August 28 (fig. 22).[46]

"THE MEANING OF OUR NUMBERS"

On August 28, 1963, marchers traveling to Washington could see the enormity of their effort. Whether they came in single buses from small towns or in the grand caravan of 450 buses that left New York from Harlem, marchers rode to Washington alongside other buses and carloads of marchers. By midmorning, buses were passing through the Baltimore Harbor Tunnel at the rate of 100 an hour. Those arriving on trains also sensed the enormous turnout. Marchers on trains from the North, from cities like Boston and Philadelphia, from the West, such as from Cincinnati and Chicago, and from the South, including from Jacksonville and Birmingham, all emptied into the vast space of Union Station and then moved off toward the Mall. Long before the scheduled 1:30 start, people covered the hill around the Washington Monument. By the end of the day, nearly a quarter of a million people had come to the capital, setting a new record for marches on Washington.[47]

All these marchers combined to take over the core of the capital and made its spaces into their own. Carefully watched by police officers and visually captured on film, they created an indelible image of unity. Yet this aura depended upon the words of the leaders to translate the presence of the marchers into specific demands and hopes. The speeches addressed not only the marchers but also the national and international audience scrutinizing the event. Though the leaders tried to mirror the apparent unity of the crowd, their speeches revealed the tensions in the civil rights movement. Fortunately, Martin Luther King Jr.'s ability to sense the need of his audience for a vision of unity shaped the immediate and lasting meaning of the March on Washington for Jobs and Freedom.

The thousands of marchers entered a city filled with security forces. Little serious need for these forces developed. The day before, the police had blanketed with No Parking signs an area stretching from the Memorial east past the Capitol and for ten blocks north of the Mall to ensure enough space for the buses. On August 28, their most onerous tasks were directing buses and cars to the proper parking areas and helping lost people find their companions. The most risky moment was when the group of fifty or so members of the American Nazi Party showed up to register their belief in white supremacy. This gathering had no permit and the police moved promptly to break it up. The Nazis dispersed quickly, and the day continued peacefully as thousands of marchers filled the Mall.[48]

Representatives from the media had a busier day. According to an NAACP press release, more reporters were in Washington than had ever come for any other event. More than 2,000 press passes were issued to reporters from all over the country and around the world. Organizers designated special press areas at both the Washington Monument and the Lincoln Memorial to allow for interviews. All three of the television networks had cameras there to cover the march in detail. ABC and NBC planned regular reports throughout the day, while CBS committed to live coverage of the formal program, scheduled to begin at 1:30 P.M. Recent technological changes had made such intensive television coverage more feasible. Cameras equipped with videotape allowed reporters to rove more freely. In addition, just a year before the march, the Telstar satellite had gone up, allowing the march to be broadcast live all across Europe. Whether at Union Station, on special stands dotting the Mall, in a crane on Constitution Avenue, or among the crowd with portable cameras on their shoulders, journalists filmed the events from every angle (see fig. 23).[49]

In the morning, the masses of marchers set a tone of joyous determination. Many picked up signs from the enormous pile set up by the information tent. Those who wanted to mark their participation in the event could buy a new button that declared "I Was There." Various groups started spontaneous sing-alongs. Others prayed. When a contingent of entertainers finally arrived, Joan Baez led off with the movement anthem "We Shall Overcome." The stage near the Washington Monument was too small to entertain the massive crowd. Indeed, as they waited, many people grew impatient to start the actual march. A spontaneous departure began just after 11:00 A.M., when one large group headed off toward the Lincoln Memorial. Others followed. One reporter observed that "the plain people" took the lead "as if on common impulse."[50] These early starters were a potent reminder of how important individual participants were to even this massive, carefully planned day.

As the thousands marched toward the Lincoln Memorial, commentators noted the difference from earlier protests and other forms of group activities. A NBC reporter noted, "This is not a regular parade, no bands, people not marching as such." The reporter for *Time* described

FIGURE 23. One of the many television cameras filming the march. Cameras like this one were positioned all over the Mall, for the most extensive coverage of a protest in history. The importance given to television coverage during the march put pressures on organizers and authorities alike to make sure both that the march could be easily filmed and that it communicated a message of democratic protest. (U.S. Agency for Information, RG 306, series SSM, 4C[43]26, National Archives)

the procession as "informal, often formless." Unlike previous protests in Washington, no military metaphors could describe the marchers. Because of the number of marchers and the shortness of the route, organizers never intended to arrange people in the careful rows and special sections that had appealed to earlier planners. Another change was the lack of any spectators. Scared by the numerous press reports about the risks of horrific traffic problems and disorder, few Washingtonians turned out to watch the march.[51] The focus on turnout changed the style of how people marched on Washington. In the past, protests had emphasized individual and collective discipline displayed to an immediate audience and then conveyed by the media. Instead of performing for an audience, these marchers on Washington took their inspiration from the other marchers and the intense attention of the media.

In this new style of demonstration, signs took on a new role, allowing the large crowd to convey a unified message. The marshals did not stringently enforce the prohibition on self-made signs, but most of the marchers used the ones supplied at the Washington Monument. Each sign was colored either red and white or blue and white; massed together they gave the march the colors of American patriotism. At the same time, the signs conveyed the urgency of the protest with their common conclusion of "NOW." These unifying elements still allowed for a diversity of demands. Signs declared, "We demand Jobs for ALL NOW," "We demand integrated schools NOW," and "We march for Equal Rights NOW."[52] For the first time, a march on Washington featured the mass presence of tens of thousands in a public space using signs to convey their political demands through television footage and printed photographs (fig. 24).

Once the marchers reached the Lincoln Memorial, they filled all the areas available. Some lined the long reflecting pool, dangling their feet in the water as the temperature climbed into the low eighties. Others tucked themselves under the trees beside the open areas; the earliest or most persistent marchers leaned against the fence that protected a special area of reserve seating for guests on the plaza below the Memorial. Even as the crowd grew thick, the atmosphere was orderly and enthusiastic. Participants commented on how their fellow marchers moved through the crowd, murmuring "excuse me," "sorry," and "thank you." Soon, the crowd filled the area from the Lincoln Memorial all the way back to the end of the reflecting pool.[53] This space, normally dotted with tourists moving respectfully between the presidential memorials, was now occupied by tens of thousands of protesters demanding change in the nation.

Yet, there was a tension underlying this appropriation, because everyone—participants and observers—had to wait for the leaders to appear and give voice to this collective effort. As much as the huge turnout was critical to the day, the participants' role was in large part to give the ten leaders a forum in which to speak as national political voices. The Big

FIGURE 24. A sea of signs in the hands of marchers moving toward the Lincoln Memorial. The success of the organizers' determination to ensure a unified message for the march shows in the dominance of the signs with common slogans. In addition, each poster was printed in red or blue on a white background, giving a patriotic appearance to the crowd. (Library of Congress, Prints and Photographs Division, *U.S. News and World Report* Magazine Collection, LC-U9–10347, no. 21)

Ten had begun their day at 8:30 that morning. They started on Capitol Hill with a series of pro forma meetings with the Republican and Democratic leadership. The civil rights bill was stuck firmly in committees. In the midst of one of these meetings, the leaders were disturbed to learn the marchers had begun their spontaneous march. Breaking off their meeting, they rushed to Constitution Avenue, already filled with marchers. There, anxious aides cleared a space so the ten leaders could link arms as though they were at the head of the crowd. Then the photographers and filmmakers shot pictures of the leaders "leading the march" (fig. 25).[54] This staged moment symbolized how important it was to both the organizers and the media for this massive crowd to appear to be under the control of the designated leaders.

Once the formal program at the Lincoln Memorial began, though, the leaders and their words dominated the occasion. Speeches had been a component of protests in Washington before, but in 1963, they became central. Before the 1950s, the speeches provided ceremonial conclusions for elaborate parades or were symbolic gestures that challenged the regulations prohibiting them on the Capitol grounds. In 1963, the content of the speeches was the focus. In part, the change was the result of technology: the loudspeakers made the speeches audible to most participants, and the conventions of media coverage dictated a focus on leaders and celebrities. Yet, this focus also reflected the consequences of compromises made by both the organizers and the authorities during the planning of the event. The organizers had abandoned the civil disobedience that would have highlighted the participation of individuals. They agreed to a protest limited to the Mall so that marchers would not directly confront the White House or the Capitol. The Memorial steps could serve as an ideal platform for the leaders as they struggled to find a unified voice for a movement that was divided over tactics, goals, and rhetoric.

The speakers addressed not just the marchers, but a diverse audience around the world. They spoke to the journalists and the people watching on television. They knew that in countries as diverse as Holland, Ghana, Israel, and Germany, people had organized sympathy marches for the same day, and that reporters across the world, by now accustomed to covering the topic of civil rights, were prepared to quote and to comment about their words.[55] Domestically, their audience included civil rights activists in prison and the most ardent critics of integration. It included members of Congress, some seated on the steps of the Memorial, others watching on television in the Capitol building. In the White House, Kennedy kept the coverage on. Never before—and never again—did leaders of a march on Washington address such a large and immediate audience.

Randolph spoke first, intent on translating the significance of this crowd to its participants and observers. He congratulated participants for being part of the "largest demonstration in the history of this nation." He then spoke to the media as much as to the marchers themselves by trying to explain "the meaning of our numbers." He emphatically rejected that the marchers were just a "pressure group" or a "group of organizations" or a "mob." Instead, he declared, "We are the advance guard of a massive moral revolution for jobs and freedom." He emphasized that the march was not just about "passage of civil rights legislation," despite the pervasiveness of that view. Rather, he declared, "we want a free democratic society" with "new forms of social planning" and "full employment." Standing between these goals and the marchers

FIGURE 25. The leaders "leading" the march. Notice the man directing this staged start of the march from the Lincoln Memorial. Creating the picture was necessary because so many of the participants had left before the official start and the leaders needed to be seen as in control of the march. (U.S. Agency for Information, RG 306, series 4C[35]6, National Archives)

was one force, Randolph suggested: "the coalition of Dixiecrats and re-actionary Republicans that seeks to dominate the Congress." To end their power, Randolph announced, "we shall return again and again to Washington in ever growing numbers until total freedom is ours."

None of the ten leaders wanted to suggest that all the potential for change was in Washington. Instead, the leaders made clear that the march would have regional, national, and international importance. Most of the leaders referred to earlier southern demonstrations as the inspiration for this national demonstration. Reverend Blake from the National Council of Churches praised those who "have offered their bodies to arrest and violence, to the hurt and indignity of firehoses and dogs." Though the march was very different from the protests in the South, the speakers did all they could to connect the two styles of demonstrations.

The presence of singers, throughout the program, punctuated this point. As participants and scholars both emphasize, music provided essential ties for civil rights activists. When Marian Anderson, Mahalia Jackson, and a gospel choir sang, the crowd came alive. The marchers responded with more enthusiasm to the singing of Jackson than to any of the speeches. Merging the mournful song "I've Been Abused" with the bold verses of "They Can't Buy Me," Jackson recalled the mixture of suffering, hope, and defiance that marked so many of the southern civil rights protests.[56]

The speakers also contextualized the protest in the tradition of American national politics. They continued to connect it to American history. Half of the leaders referred to what they saw as the unfulfilled promise of the Emancipation Proclamation to end the oppression of African Americans. John Lewis declared the march part of an effort to complete the American "revolution of 1776." Others were more focused on the present situation. Roy Wilkins said the march was designed to allow the "Congress of the United States to hear from us in person what many of us have been telling our public officials back home, and that is, WE WANT FREEDOM NOW." Against the backdrop of the Memorial and the view of Capitol at the other end of the Mall, such references made clear that the marchers expected national change.

To achieve this change, all the leaders stressed the international implications of the protests and the civil rights movement. Whitney Young of the National Urban League noted that "the rumble of the drums of discontent . . . are heard in all parts of the world." Walter Reuther, the labor leader, criticized the hypocrisy of the United States by referring to Kennedy's recent trip to Germany: "We cannot defend freedom in Berlin so long as we offend freedom in Birmingham." Lewis reminded the listeners of the struggles against colonial rule in African countries, by saying, " 'One Man, one vote,' is the African cry" and "It is ours too." Such references were a potent warning to Congress and the Kennedy administration that both their supporters and enemies abroad were scrutinizing their response to the civil rights movement.

Despite some common strategies in the speeches, there were significant differences between some of the leaders about the significance of the protest and its political emphasis. The disparities came through most explicitly and publicly in the controversy surrounding John Lewis's speech. When Randolph introduced Lewis as the second speaker, there was a noticeably mixed reaction. The crowd cheered this representative of the SNCC activists who had awed many supporters of the movement with their commitment to the struggle. But, those on the platform looked nervous. And the television audience knew that the speech was already controversial. Roger Mudd, anchoring CBS's live coverage, gave a brief overview of the problem.[57]

Many people, including the other leaders, had seen a draft of Lewis's speech the night before and some objected to its radical and critical tone. A joint effort of several SNCC activists, the draft speech took a dim view of the pending civil rights bill, declaring it "too little, and too late." The authors charged that the bill lacked effective provisions for police brutality, voting rights, and employment discrimination. The text also pointed to the hypocrisy of American politics, claiming that most American politicians "build their careers on immoral compromises." The SNCC activists noted that each party contained ardent opponents of racial equality and asked, "Where is *our* party?"

The writers' vision of what should happen was also deeply challenging to the status quo. Echoing the slogans of the march, they wrote, "We want our freedom and we want it now." However, they distanced themselves from the march and its emphasis on leaders by arguing that only the "masses" could cause "radical social, political and economic changes." And unlike Randolph, they saw marching in Washington as an act of moderation, rather than as part of the revolution. They wrote, "The time will come when we will not confine our marching to Washington." Instead, they threatened to re-create General Sherman's march through the South and swore that "we shall pursue our own 'scorched earth' policy and burn Jim Crow to the ground—non-violently."

As the other leaders, press, and members of the administration read this draft, the careful compromises that had brought the marchers to Washington threatened to fall apart. An earnest effort to convince Lewis to change its tone began the night before the march and continued backstage at the Lincoln Memorial. For some, the reference to Sherman's march would be too inflammatory to the South. Members of the Kennedy administration objected to the pointed attack on the civil rights bill and wrote an alternative draft. The leaders huddled at the Memorial ignored it. Finally, Randolph and King used their standing with Lewis to persuade him to cut the reference to Sherman's march and to express a little more enthusiasm for the civil rights bill.

Despite these changes, the speech still contained the bitter critiques of the original. Lewis, however, was not a dynamic speaker, and it took a while for the crowd to appreciate the power of his challenge. When delivered, the speech clearly conveyed Lewis's sense of distance from many of the marchers and the other leaders. Unlike Randolph, he called for protests everywhere. He told the marchers to "get in and stay in the streets of every city, every village and hamlet of this nation until true freedom comes." He ended with a challenge: "Wake up America, wake up, for we cannot stop and we will not and cannot be patient." As he walked back to his seat, accompanied by enthusiastic applause, none of the white leaders smiled. The controversy over the speech, its actual content, and the response revealed the divisions developing within the civil rights movement and the country.[58]

Yet, these differences faded, temporarily at least, under the glory of the concluding speech by Martin Luther King Jr., who arrived at the podium at the Lincoln Memorial around 3:30 P.M. There was no question that he had an eager audience. When Randolph presented King as the "moral leader of the nation," the applause and the enthusiasm were intense. A cheer went across the Mall; people who were sitting stood up. King was very aware that his position as the final major speaker meant that his words should try to pull together the effort. Working through the night, he had struggled to develop a speech that would speak to all the various audiences. He began with an analogy that the United States had given African Americans "a bad check" backed by "insufficient funds" to provide them the "unalienable rights of life, liberty and the pursuit of happiness." Speaking generally, he rejected suggestions that there was a need for "cooling off." Indeed, he warned, "there will be neither rest nor tranquility . . . until the Negro is guaranteed his citizenship rights." Addressing "my people," he cautioned them to practice nonviolence and to avoid a "distrust of all white people." Yet he rejected too conciliatory a tone, carefully listing the wide range of problems facing African Americans: police brutality, segregation, life in the ghetto, the denial of voting rights in the South, and the lack of political representation in the North. He asked all those present to return home, "knowing that this situation can and will be changed." These words, prepared for the march, conveyed the strength and the urgency of the civil rights movement.[59]

Yet King was neither finished nor satisfied with his statement. Energized by the enthusiasm of the crowd, he abandoned his written text and began to speak from memory. He returned to words he had used in speeches during that spring and summer.[60] Refined by practice, the opening phrases sounded like a poem:

> I say to you today, my friends, so even though we face the difficulties of today and tomorrow, I still have a dream. It is a dream deeply rooted in the American dream. I have a dream that one day this nation will rise up

and live out the true meaning of its creed: "We hold these truths to be self-evident, that all men are created equal."

With these words from the Declaration of Independence, King began an oral tour of a new South free of racism. The tour ended with his dream about Alabama, where he so recently had been imprisoned. Even there, he dreamed, "One day right there in Alabama, little black boys and black girls will be able to join hands with little white boys and white girls as sisters and brothers." He returned to his refrain, "I have a dream today."

King addressed the watching and listening world, declaring that his dream was "our faith," and that it could "transform the jangling discords of our nation into a beautiful symphony of brotherhood." Then, he predicted that the familiar words of "My Country 'Tis of Thee" would take on "new meaning." Using the closing words of the first stanza to work toward a vision of a country where freedom rang from every state, with sweat pouring down his face, King came to an inspiring and hopeful conclusion:

> When we allow freedom to ring, when we let it ring from every village, from every hamlet, from every state and every city, we will be able to speed up that day when all of God's children, black men and white men, Jews and Gentiles, Protestants and Catholics, will be able to join hands and sing in the words of the old Negro spiritual, "Free at last! free at last! Thank God almighty, we are free at last."[61]

The genius of King's decision to abandon his prepared remarks was that it allowed him to speak directly to the marchers. As he spoke, the interracial, peaceful march seemed to embody the dreams of which he spoke. Quoting from familiar American texts, he described a country—like the march—where people came together without regard to race. The crowd continued to applaud as King stepped back from the podium.

As the end of the program, Randolph and Rustin together asked those present to acknowledge the demands and make a pledge of "personal commitment." Rustin read the ten demands, raising his hand after each one for the marchers to cheer. Randolph followed with the pledge that asked the marchers to commit to using the full range of "actions" necessary to "the struggle for jobs and freedom for all Americans." Each marcher promised, "I will march and I will write letters," and "I will demonstrate and I will vote."[62] This moment reflected the original goal for the protest to be a method of broadening and strengthening the civil rights movement. Then the marchers began to file back to the buses and train station.

The Big Ten climbed into the limousines and drove to the White House to meet the president. Winning this meeting was an essential symbol of the cooperation behind the march, but its actual purpose was unclear. Kennedy greeted the leaders, particularly King, with congratulations. But the president did not allow their meeting simply to celebrate the day's event. Instead, he drew them into a discussion of the prospects for the civil rights bill, which he clearly considered the goal of the march. After about an hour of detailed discussion, reporters and photographers were allowed into the Cabinet Room to take pictures and ask questions (fig. 26). The president praised the march and soon released a statement that reiterated his support for programs that would ensure the economic and civil rights of African Americans.[63]

The style of the demonstration was dramatically different from that of earlier protests in Washington. First, the protest attracted at least five times more marchers than had been present for the Bonus March, yet there was much less attention paid to the behavior and role of individual marchers. And, participants spent less time in Washington than during previous protests because of the decisions about security and layout made by the organizers and authorities. Finally, though television meant that the demonstration was seen and the speeches heard by millions of viewers, in some ways, the visible form of the march received less attention than the speeches, in large part because of the newer technology of loudspeakers and television. Together—and in combination with changes in the larger political culture—these innovations made this march the most powerful march on Washington yet. Even before August 28, the support for the protest from a wide range of organizations, the agreement of the president to meet with the leaders, the attention paid by the media, and the commitment of thousands to participate helped legitimize the protest as an accepted part of American politics. Then, on August 28, the organizers demonstrated that enormous numbers of predominantly African American marchers could march peacefully on Washington. Though the highly visible police officers reminded both marchers and observers of the role of the government in the demonstration, the marchers and their leaders took possession of the Mall and Lincoln Memorial for the day and used them to assert their place in the nation. Finally, it was in this context that Martin Luther King's "I Have a Dream" speech was transformed into a national text articulating an inspiring vision of racial equality in America.

FIGURE 26. The leaders posing with the president and vice president, August 28, 1963. From left to right, Secretary of Labor W. Willard Wirtz, Floyd McKissick, Matthew Ahmann, Whitney Young, Reverend Martin Luther King Jr., John Lewis (partially obscured), Rabbi Joachim Prinz, Eugene Carson Blake, A. Philip Randolph, President John F. Kennedy, Vice President Lyndon B. Johnson (partially obscured), Walter Reuther, and Roy Wilkins. After all the cooperation between the organizers and the Kennedy administration before the march, this meeting publicly proclaimed Kennedy's endorsement of the principle of marching on Washington. Ironically, however, his message to the leaders during the meeting was that they needed to engage in traditional lobbying if they wanted to pass the civil rights bill. (Library of Congress, Prints and Photographs Division, *U.S. News and World Report* Magazine Collection, LC-U9–10380, no. 5)

LEGACIES

Signs of the powerful legacy of the March on Washington for Jobs and Freedom were the attempts to re-create the march in 1983, 1993, and 2000. Scheduling their protests for almost the same day, groups consciously modeled themselves after the 1963 march, with the issues of "Jobs and Freedom" recast to reflect the political climate of those moments. The first of these protests, the March on Washington for Jobs,

Peace, and Freedom, held on August 27, 1983, did appear to be successful. A broad coalition of groups that deplored the policies of President Ronald Reagan's administration came together behind the march. Though the organizing of the march and the event itself did not receive the extensive media coverage of its model, the enormous turnout of 300,000 surprised many observers and energized the groups behind the protest. The attempts in 1993 and 2000 seemed less significant since the turnouts were so much smaller than both the original and its first progeny.[64] These efforts to re-create the spirit of the 1963 demonstration and these assessments of success reflect the legacy of the original march. Once such national protests became part of the traditions of American politics, demonstrations could be judged by their predecessors and by their turnouts. And, for protests since 1963, the standard was high.

In the end, the legacy of the protest reflected the compromises that marked its organizing and the controversies and victories of the day itself. The march on August 28, 1963, is perceived as a success because it was massive, peaceful, and orderly, received official attention and extensive media coverage, and climaxed with King's effective speech. Yet, such simplistic assessments ignore the inevitable compromises of the organizers and the fact that its message became reduced to a single piece of legislation. Tellingly, in the decade after the march, for those most closely involved in its organizing, the 1963 March on Washington seemed less a model for influencing the United States people and politics than an example of what *not* to do.

Television reporters were the first to declare judgment: the demonstration was a success because of the turnout. Roger Mudd opened his CBS report with the earliest estimates of the number of marchers and returned to the figures repeatedly throughout the day. As NBC broke into its regular programming for brief reports from the march, its reporters also related the current crowd estimates.[65] Under pressure to provide instant evaluations of the march, television reports made turnout almost the exclusive criterion for success.

In general, the live footage dealt better than the reporters' commentary with the variety of meanings that such a large protest embodied. CBS interspersed its coverage of the restless crowd with interviews with senators, suggesting that elected officials had as much or more power than the thousands on the Mall. Juxtapositions used during the leaders' speeches suggested a different dynamic. While the voices of the leaders provided the soundtrack, the cameras switched constantly between leaders and shots of individuals and small groups in the crowd. The footage gave the marchers the role of barometer to the speeches of the leaders and implied that their reactions gave force to the leaders' words.[66]

Commentators and participants agreed that the television coverage could show the nation and the world people and ideas they had not seen before. To media-conscious participants like King, the television coverage spread the power of the march, since it allowed "millions of whites, for the first time," to have "a clear, long look at Negroes engaged in serious occupation." Likewise, Murray Kempton marveled that "every television camera at the disposal of the networks" broadcast as Rustin read the demands in his clear voice with "every sentence punctuated by his upraised hand." Kempton concluded, "No expression one-tenth so radical has ever been seen or heard by so many Americans."[67]

On television, the march took on a different shape when networks cut and edited their stories into shorter versions that evening. These editing choices reflected broader assumptions about the meaning of mass protest in America. In "framing" the demonstration, the reports focused on the leaders, particularly Martin Luther King Jr. NBC's roundup of the march, which ran from 11:00 to 11:45 P.M., eliminated both the direct calls for the civil rights bill in other speeches and King's own attack on the failure of the United States to protect the rights of African Americans. Instead, NBC broadcast short sections from the later part of King's speech. By focusing on the "I have a dream" portion, this kind of coverage obscured the balanced challenge of the protest behind a veil of optimism. In the footage, the massive crowd now served as a backdrop to King's words, rather than as responsible for the power of the speech.[68] By emphasizing King, this coverage narrowed the collective action of thousands to a single person.

Nevertheless, most observers immediately declared the march a historic success. Some cautioned that the refrain of "NOW" on the marchers' signs and in the leaders' speeches was unlikely to be fulfilled by immediate congressional action or social change. And, segregationists continued to fume about the march, the civil rights bill, and Kennedy's involvement. Nevertheless, the overwhelming impression was positive. Newspapers and magazines devoted column after column to the march and added laudatory editorials. Sympathetic senators and representatives made enthusiastic speeches in the House and Senate. The *Nation* said that the "march will go down in history as a superb example of orderly, democratic self-expression." The *New York Herald Tribune* titled its editorial "A Great Day in American History." Many comments verged on giving credit to the nation, sometimes at the expense of the organizers and protesters. Kennedy's statement on the march emphasized that it was part of the "workings of American Democracy." The *Washington Post* described the marchers as "representatives of every one of" America's "manifold aspects and estates."[69] This praise endorsed the particular style of the march and the day itself, but simultaneously blunted the march's broad political demands and the specific efforts of groups and individuals.

This blunting helps explain why most of the leaders involved in the March on Washington doubted the effectiveness of the protest that so many then and now considered a success. The compromises necessary to organize the march, the controversies on the day itself, and events in its aftermath divided the coalition and dampened enthusiasm for the tactic of mass protest in Washington. The bombing of an African American church in Birmingham that killed four young children on September 15 brought home that the people who gathered in Washington still faced terrible enemies. The successful delay of the civil rights bill by members of Congress meant that the march yielded no immediate legislative gains. Then, the assassination of President Kennedy changed the political atmosphere so dramatically that the moment of unity was difficult to sustain.[70] Within a few years, only Martin Luther King Jr. still saw protesting in Washington as a powerful tool for political change; even he wanted to change its form.

Wilkins and the NAACP and Lewis and SNCC came to reject the tactic for very different reasons; their attitudes reflected the increasingly apparent divide in the civil rights movement. For practical, conservative men like Wilkins, the lack of immediate results suggested that it was best to work at the national level with traditional tools. He supported extensive efforts to lobby for the civil rights bill. Eventually, on June 19, 1964, the bill passed. Throughout the 1960s, the NAACP continued such efforts, attempting to make "lobbying . . . a means of protest."[71] For SNCC activists, the march became the symbol of the limits both of mass demonstrations and of coalitions with whites. The last-minute editing of John Lewis's speech, according to one member, "produced a canker that never healed." After the violence directed at participants in Freedom Summer in 1964 and the riots in American cities in 1965, SNCC members adopted Black Power as their focus and used the incident at the march to argue that "whites diluted the strength and anger of the movement." Increasingly, SNCC members came to agree with Malcolm X, who described the march as "the Farce on Washington."[72]

Far more surprising was that both Rustin and Randolph grew doubt-ful about the power of marches on Washington. In 1964, Rustin wrote a much-discussed article arguing that African Americans needed to give up protest in favor of traditional political tactics. By 1965, shaken by the ri-ots in black neighborhoods, Randolph and Rustin publicly declared that the "days of demonstrations of tremendous dimensions . . . are practically over." Nevertheless, both Randolph and Rustin continued to remember the march in 1963 as a high point of the movement and their careers.[73]

Martin Luther King Jr. alone maintained faith in protests in Wash-ington, but even he thought the form of the 1963 march had serious weaknesses. The march and his speech had clearly improved his national and international reputation, paving the way for his Nobel Peace Prize. Yet, as the struggle to win equality and opportunity for African Ameri-cans continued to face severe obstacles, he grew doubtful about the mod-eration and lack of confrontation in 1963. As he designed a Poor Peo-ple's Campaign centered in Washington, he hoped to overcome what he saw as the weaknesses of the March on Washington. He rejected the no-tion of planning a protest with a coalition of leaders and instead put the SCLC staff in full control. Rather than bringing tens of thousands of marchers to Washington, he intended to begin in spring 1968 with just 3,000 carefully trained protesters who would explicitly echo the Bonus marchers by building shantytowns in the city. And the demonstration purposefully would not demand specific legislation so it would not be perceived as a failure if the bills did not pass. Instead, the point of the Poor People's Campaign was to illustrate the meaning of poverty to Washington and to the nation. Though the protest was to be nonviolent, this time King threatened to "tie up transportation in Washington, jam the hospitals, boycott schools and sit-in at Government offices."[74] King's hopes for the campaign indicated that he believed another—though very different—demonstration in the capital could provide a motivating sym-bol for the country. But this ambition was thwarted when King was as-sassinated on April 4, 1968.

King's aides in Atlanta decided to go ahead with the protest, but the logistics proved far more difficult than anyone had imagined. Setting up a shantytown on the Mall was a striking symbol, but weeks of rain, er-ratic supplies, squabbles, and even violence between the marchers soon proved the limits of the plan. Despite the confrontational tone of the demonstration, District and federal authorities—again echoing the early reactions to the Bonus Army—provided extensive support. Soon the or-ganizers backed away from the sustained direct action that King had proposed. As in 1963, the vision of an independent, confrontational protest faded under the pressure of making actual arrangements.[75]

Throughout the 1960s, Rustin, Wilkins, Lewis, and King grew disillusioned with the March on Washington for Jobs and Freedom. Their disillusionment arose from the compromises rooted in mass politics that had been necessary to organize the march. The cooperation of the organizers with federal and District officials had reduced fears of disorder, yet made the march less an independent effort by civil rights activists. The successful marketing of the protest familiarized thousands of Americans with the tactic and ensured the enormous turnout. By promoting the march as historic before it had even taken place, the organizers created higher stakes for the massive demonstration than it could possibly achieve in the contentious politics of the 1960s. In the next ten years, as the battle over America's military presence in Vietnam grew bitter, other protesters struggled to invent new forms of protesting in Washington.

CHAPTER SIX

THE "SPRING OFFENSIVE" OF 1971

Radicals and Marches on Washington

In the early 1990s, Bill Branson remembered his "first big action" with the Vietnam Veterans against the War (VVAW). An organizer for the group in California and a self-described "militant," in April 1971 he traveled to the capital. Nearly twenty years later, there was a tone of exultation as he described his and others' anticipation: "We figured if we were going all the way out there to Washington, to the belly of the beast, we were going to kick some ass." And he was sure he had. For a week, the VVAW activists camped on the Mall while they tried to show America the consequences of the war in Vietnam. Consciously intent on attracting media attention, the veterans re-created war scenes, testified about their experiences, and invited arrest at the Supreme Court. Branson celebrated that he and other veterans had taken "over everything— the Lincoln Memorial, the Rotunda—we walked in the streets." And, "Nobody stopped us."[1]

Branson was one of the hundreds of thousands of Americans who converged on Washington as part of the so-called Spring Offensive of 1971. The offensive was actually a loosely coordinated and tensely negotiated series of three demonstrations that sought, in radically different ways, to reenergize the idea of a march on Washington in the shadow of the increasingly revered March on Washington for Jobs and Freedom. The VVAW had come first, but they were soon followed by the National Peace Action Coalition's massive April 24 March against the War. Then, a few weeks later, the Mayday protests attempted to "shut down" the capital.

The protests of that spring evoked the entire eighty-year evolution of the march on Washington, from a tactic on the boundaries of American politics to a familiar and traditional part of political life. Demonstrations during the years since 1963, however, were not a smooth culmination of a long-developing tradition, but rather a series of tense, dramatic, and imaginative attempts to test the limits of that tradition. Struggles over the meaning of American citizenship and the legitimacy of criticizing the American state made protest in the capital as debated and as significant as it had been years earlier. Challenges to existing conventions about the uses of Washington's spaces again raised questions about the rights of Americans to use the public spaces of the capital for their political causes. The outcome of these struggles significantly shaped the subsequent options of organizers, officials, and the media.

Despite the conflicts among anti-war activists, the long battle for public support and political legitimacy of the march on Washington was winding down. Contemplating the coming set of protests, the editors of the *Washington Post* urged the city to "preserve its proud reputation of hospitality" so visible during the "Civil Rights March of 1963." King's widow, Coretta Scott King, declared that attending the April 24 march was part of her effort to fulfill her "husband's dream."[2] By 1971, the march on Washington had become familiar to all Americans and acceptable to most. In 1970, sociologist Amitai Etzioni declared that "demonstrations are becoming part of the daily routine of our democracy and its most distinctive mark." A year later, on the eve of the April 24 march, *Life* magazine writer Hugh Sidey also speculated that "it could be that protest is at last being recognized as part of the way of democratic life."[3]

Nevertheless, activists and observers were still divided and uneasy. In part, attitudes toward citizenship and the American nation had shifted. Since 1894, various "marginal" groups had developed, refined, and used the march on Washington to make dramatic claims for recognition of the citizenship of their members. But the use of the march on Washington as a forum to assert citizenship had less appeal in the later 1960s. Many participants in the social movements of the 1960s were certain of their *right* to speak and act as citizens of the United States of America, but doubted the value of their membership in that nation. For some observers, this view generated more unease. They argued that protesters who seemed to hate "their country" did not belong in the public spaces of the capital. In this atmosphere of transition and debate, many people asked, why march again in Washington? Would anything change?

For many, the answer was still yes and organizers in the major anti-war groups did make plans to return to Washington in the spring of 1971. Although full of doubts about Washington, about the Nixon administration, and about their place in the United States, the various groups called for demonstrations, organized their supporters, negotiated with authorities, and eventually staged their protests. And hundreds of thousands of protesters responded to the call. These groups used the public spaces of Washington in new ways, experimented with new performances of American citizenship, and challenged the prevailing traditions of marching on Washington. For the protesters and their observers, the Spring Offensive became a controversial series of tests of the political possibilities of the capital.

ORGANIZING THE SPRING OFFENSIVE

In May 1970, anti-war activists organized a massive protest against U.S. aggression in Cambodia with unprecedented speed. On the surface, the march was an unambiguous success: in just over a week, organizers filled the Mall with more than 200,000 marchers. The march represented the depth of hostility toward the Nixon administration and the growing power of the anti-war movement. Some activists even claimed credit when Nixon subsequently withdrew U.S. forces from Cambodia. One long-time leader of the anti-war movement hailed it as "an outstanding, albeit incomplete, victory." But the protest had also sparked long-simmering disagreements among anti-war activists. Some activists felt that the large, docile protest had accomplished nothing: even Nixon's withdrawal of troops seemed part of his overall strategy to continue limited U.S. involvement in Southeast Asia. These more radical activists were convinced that the very form of the "traditional" march on Washington was politically compromised. They had wanted to see massive civil disobedience in the capital, which they believed would have increased the awareness of the protests across the country and brought the business of the nation to a halt. The death of students at Kent State University just days before fueled these activists' conviction. More moderate activists argued against civil disobedience, fearing negative publicity and perhaps violence. In the end, the advocates of a large rally, reluctantly sanctioned by District and federal officials, triumphed. But their victory served to splinter the anti-war movement even more.[4]

The attractions and problems of the traditional march on Washington were accentuated by the physical and political transformation of the city during the previous decade. Since the 1963 march, the city had become increasingly monumental in its core and increasingly divided racially. Between the civil rights march of 1963 and the Spring Offensive, the divide between the federal ceremonial core and the rest of the capital city grew. New construction and development around Pennsylvania Avenue and the Mall separated the monumental icons of tourism and government from the shopping, business, and residential districts of the city. The massive new FBI building, the National Museum of American History and Technology, and the planning of the National Air and Space Museum showed that the triangular core of the city—bounded by the Lincoln Memorial, the White House, and the Capitol Building—was becoming a ceremonial space dedicated to remembering the past of the United States and honoring its heroes and achievements.[5] These physical changes in the capital city were certainly in the minds of protest organizers as they considered possible styles of demonstrating.

Organizers also had to consider their relationship to the District of Columbia as a whole. Residents and leaders of the District were adjusting to the social and political transitions of the last ten years. While Lyndon Johnson had granted District residents some increased autonomy, its residents were still virtually disenfranchised. In addition, the raw scars from the riots in 1968 still showed on the city. Most of the buildings damaged by fire had been torn down, but few of them had been replaced, despite million-dollar appropriations to pay for repairs. Meanwhile, new highways connecting suburbs in Virginia and Maryland to the District encouraged residents, especially white residents, to move out of the city and become commuters. The total population of the District dropped by 7,000 between 1960 and 1970 as the proportion of African American residents to white grew from 53 to 71 percent.[6] Such racial and political inequities made organizers uneasy as they contemplated another protest.

In the aftermath of the Cambodia protest in May, as activists regrouped, formed new organizations, and looked for new ways to cooperate and demonstrate, they shared a basic ambivalence about the nature of national political protest. On the one hand, they believed that they should demonstrate the public's disgust with the U.S. prosecution of war in Vietnam and that their protests should take advantage of the public spaces of Washington. On the other hand, they agreed their protests should also show the disgust they felt for the government itself. Many anti-war activists chafed at the nationalist symbolism of marches and searched for a way to make a march on Washington less patriotic, less bound to the state. Some organizers remained dedicated to "traditional" forms of marching; others were determined to forge new styles of protesting in the nation's capital. The visions of protest each group developed embraced different tactics, had different political strategies, and radically different goals.

During the summer of 1970, the first organization to regroup out of the splinters of the coalition that had organized the Cambodia protest was the National Peace Action Coalition (NPAC). They held a conventional view of the power politics of mass demonstrations and an optimistic view of the role of marches in building political movements and in raising the political consciousness of participants. They decided to call for two marches in April 1971: one in San Francisco; the other in Washington. These protests were to be peaceful, law abiding, and carefully organized. Like their predecessors, NPAC leaders believed that marches on Washington might shift the direction of federal policy. They saw vulnerability in the Nixon administration because of growing opposition to United States military involvement in Southeast Asia and claimed that "tremendous mass demonstrations . . . could convince the Nixon regime to throw in the towel on Indochina." Meanwhile, these two marches would help build a wide coalition of peace and labor activists who shared the demand for an immediate end to United States involvement in Indochina. Finally, and most radically, the organizers hoped these large, peaceful marches would transform the political consciousness of their participants. Many NPAC activists had strong ties to the Socialist Party. They hoped that even this rather traditional march on Washington could lead to new kinds of Americans, not bound by ideas of themselves as loyal citizens, but rather as revolutionaries.[7] People who came to protest might then begin to oppose the government in general and imagine a more complete political revolution. The coalition planned to take advantage of the newly improved space of Pennsylvania Avenue and the Mall to support their message. NPAC's combination of power politics with revolutionary ambition found wide support at a time when many Americans were either radical or deeply discontented with American foreign policy. Thousands of smaller peace groups across the country joined the coalition and endorsed this plan for a march on Washington. Nevertheless, NPAC's plan did not appeal to everyone.

Opponents of NPAC's proposed march advocated a more aggressive, disruptive, and insurgent style of protest. This alternative vision came from a group of activists who had been deeply disgruntled with the Cambodia protests, operating as the "People's Coalition for Peace and Justice." A traditional march on Washington, they complained, just "gave a platform to phony people in Congress," and was "a very liberal thing that had very little impact." At an August 1970 meeting of the coalition, they rejected a proposal for a "Long March" to Washington. The People's Coalition's leading theorist, David Dellinger, explained that "activists who were more radical, particularly those who were young, needed a different form of protest or else they would turn to destructiveness or withdrawal." Such "anti-marching sentiment," in Dellinger's words, led the People's Coalition supporters to embrace a plan that would attack the authorities and their power.[8] The plan came from Rennie Davis, a former member of Students for a Democratic Society and a founder of the Mayday Tribe, a cooperative that aligned itself with the People's Coalition. Davis called for a sustained demonstration that would "shut down" the capital. To achieve this goal, Davis planned that the protesters would block access to government buildings and stop traffic coming into the District during the first week of May. With commuters unable to reach their government jobs, federal offices would not be able to function. In his mind, the demonstration was a signal of distress, a Mayday cry, and an attempt to draw on the tradition of radical protests on May 1. As Davis explained in early February, part of the premise of the protest was political blackmail: "Unless Nixon commits himself to withdrawal by May 1—that is, if he won't stop the war—we intend to stop the government."[9] At another level, however, Davis was threatening a radical break with American political tradition. His rhetoric evoked the authorities' worst nightmare about marches on Washington: that a group of citizens would conquer the capital and rule on their own authority. In any case, the practical plan of shutting down the capital by blocking roads was a radical rejection of the capital's ceremonial power.

While the news media focused on plans for NPAC's peaceful April 24 assembly and the People's Coalition insurgent May Day action, other organizers were also planning new forms of protest for the spring of 1971. During the fall of 1970, the VVAW began planning their demonstration. Jan Crumb, a graduate of West Point, had founded the organization in 1967 to provide a forum for veterans who opposed the war.[10] They believed that their effort was special because they, unlike most of the politicians or protesters in Washington, had actually fought in Vietnam. Moreover, they asserted that their identity as veterans gave them special standing to speak to politicians and to the nation—like the unemployed men in Coxey's Army, the women suffragists, the veterans of World War I, and many of the civil rights marchers. Their experience of fighting, their emphasis on their special standing as veterans, and their yearning for redemption led them to develop a style of protest intended to dramatize the harrowing experience of battle. The veterans planned to co-opt the national public space by camping on part of the Mall and using it as a backdrop to bring their disillusionment into the national public view.

The three groups, as they became aware of each other, were far less inclined to compromise and come together under a unifying banner than protesters in previous decades had been. In 1963, when A. Philip Randolph and Martin Luther King Jr. independently called for protest in the capital, they felt obliged to consolidate their plans and create a single march. Moreover, they abandoned plans for civil disobedience in the interest of securing a wider coalition and more cooperation from federal officials. By 1971, in contrast, such cooperation and compromise was not possible within the deeply divided anti-war movement. Instead, each group—the National Peace Action Coalition, the People's Coalition for Peace and Justice and the Mayday Tribe, and the Vietnam Veterans against the War—would come to Washington with different supporters, different tactics, and different aims. The leaders of the National Coalition and the People's Coalition, including the Mayday Tribe, agreed to cooperate only after harsh criticism from yet other anti-war activists that the competing protests planned for spring 1971 were "intra-movement fratricide." Organizers responded by planning the "Spring Offensive," essentially a calendar for the protests.[11] All of these groups nominally united behind the mass demonstration being planned by the National Coalition for April 24. The People's Coalition and the Mayday Tribe would together sponsor civil disobedience in the following weeks. The VVAW's plans were also included on the calendar—without their explicit approval and to their eventual dismay.

"BUSINESS AS USUAL:"
OFFICIALS PREPARE FOR THE PROTESTS

Federal and District of Columbia authorities regarded plans for the Spring Offensive marches with studied indifference, echoing the display of unconcern adopted by President Cleveland and his aides in 1894 when Coxey's Army was heading toward Washington. Likewise, not since Browne was arrested for approaching the Capitol Building had there been so much uncertainty about control of—and access to—Washington's public spaces. However, President Nixon, his aides, other federal authorities and District leaders faced a very different situation. By this time, marches on Washington had become highly visible events in the nation's political struggles.

In the eight years since 1963, officials had grown accustomed to frequent demonstrations and increasingly tried to treat marches as problems of bureaucratic management. They had monitored everything from the quiet almost-daily pickets at the White House to the nightlong vigil during the March on the Pentagon in 1967 to the weeks long Resurrection City on the Mall in 1968. They focused on cooperation, with assigned staffers coordinating the responses of government agencies. Authorities across the capital established liaisons within departments for people planning to protest in Washington. The District's Office of Emergency Preparedness monitored all local agencies with responsibilities during natural disasters, civil emergencies, and political protests. By the late 1960s, federal authorities had also institutionalized special training for large demonstrations: the United States Army developed a five-day course, and the United States Park Police held regular "Crowd Control" seminars. Supplementing the FBI's efforts, by 1969 the army was devoting twenty full-time intelligence agents to monitoring protests in the District. By 1971, Metropolitan Police Chief Jerry Wilson could also report that his officers responded to protests with "standard operating procedures."[12]

Despite Richard Nixon's distaste for such protests, his administration recognized that they had become an intrinsic part of American political culture. This lesson did not come easily to the combative president or his aides. In contrast to Kennedy in 1963, Nixon and his aides deliberately limited their cooperation with the protesters. Staff members for both Presidents Johnson and Nixon had attempted to dissociate the president from public demonstrations in the District by exploring various ways to keep protesters away from the White House. Early in his administration, Nixon's aides had refused to grant permits to the Mobilization committee for its 1969 march up Pennsylvania Avenue and tried instead to confine the protest to the Mall, as had been done in 1963. An astute anti-war organizer saw this unconstitutional effort as a cynical attempt to turn the Mall into a "circus grounds" for protesters. But this attempt failed; the Mobilization did march on the avenue as did the anti-war protesters on April 24, 1971. Increasingly, Nixon's White House began to focus not on discouraging marches but on turning them to its own advantage. In 1969, President Nixon himself wondered to his advisor H. R.

Haldeman whether they might encourage "pro-administration rallies" to coincide with upcoming anti-war demonstrations. The following spring, administration officials tacitly supported Carl McIntire's pro-war March for Victory.[13]

Nixon appreciated keenly that the news media, particularly television, were becoming the final arbiter of the significance of national demonstrations. In the eight years since the March on Washington for Jobs and Freedom, more and more Americans turned to television as a primary source for news; nearly half considered it the most believable form of journalism. Network news broadcasts had increased to thirty minutes in the fall of 1963 and more vivid color footage appeared regularly after 1965. The result was an increasingly problematic balancing act for authorities as they faced unceasing protests against the Vietnam War and a broad range of other issues. Amitai Etzioni argued in 1971 that television was central to both the "evolution" and the "increasing frequency" of protests. And Nixon officials were convinced that the attention to protesters by television journalists was part of a conspiracy against the administration. Nixon and his allies routinely dismissed marching as a media-driven political tactic.[14]

The sense that the media exposure encouraged and empowered demonstrations created a strategic problem for all authorities in Washington, and especially for presidents. Since the first days of the anti-war movement, the media had turned to presidents for comments. At first, their criticisms often served to discredit anti-war protesters. But, over time, as the position of the protesters became more acceptable, reporters began to search for signs that protests bothered presidents. To avoid conceding protests the power to annoy them, presidents increasingly affected an air of public indifference. In response to the Spring Offensive of 1971, counsel to the president John Dean, who had special responsibility for monitoring protests for the president, let it be widely known that the policy toward the demonstrations was one of maintaining "business as usual."[15]

Nonetheless, officials had to negotiate with organizers over how protesters would use the city's public spaces. By 1971, requests to use the ceremonial center of the city for one-day protests—for large, "traditional" marches—were seen on all sides as routine. Experience with previous large anti-war demonstrations had made both organizers and officials familiar with the logistical realities of organizing large protests. Consequently, District and federal officials showed little concern about the National Peace Action Coalition's plans for a mass demonstration on

April 24, and their meetings were efficient, even cordial. Strikingly, Nixon officials felt no need to arrange for additional military troops to go to the District on April 24. The administration also made other surprising concessions. In an act that symbolized how much the attitudes of Washington authorities had changed since Jacob Coxey's arrest at the Capitol in 1894, Vice President Spiro Agnew gave permission to the organizers to use the west steps for speeches. President Nixon's statement that "people have a right to express themselves" suggested that a large, peaceful, one-day march in the capital's ceremonial spaces was a form of political participation that even he accepted.[16]

Authorities were more uncomfortable with the two other protests planned for the Spring Offensive—protests that challenged the parameters of the accepted "march on Washington." Authorities objected strenuously to the Vietnam Veterans against the War's plans to occupy part of the Mall for almost six days. Negotiations were protracted and characterized by official suspicion. When organizers reminded authorities of the precedent of Resurrection City during the Poor People's Campaign in 1968, their hostility only increased. The administration saw Resurrection City as a bad precedent that had resulted in "serious damage to park values." Accordingly, the Interior Department denied the veterans' request for permission to camp on the Mall and planned to demand an injunction to prevent this part of the demonstration.[17] Such preemptive moves symbolized how federal officials continued to worry about ceding too much public space to American citizens.

Officials, naturally, were even more disturbed by the Mayday protesters' plans for massive civil disobedience. This style of demonstration tested their basic beliefs about how citizens could legitimately protest in the nation's capital. As early as January 1971, FBI Director J. Edgar Hoover reported to Congress on the plans for the Mayday protests to justify his continued alarm about domestic unrest. As May drew nearer, official scrutiny increased. FBI agents interviewed people connected to the protest; administration officials like John Dean did their own research. Park Service representatives tried to discourage the People's Coalition and the Mayday Tribe by denying them any place to camp. Both federal and District officials repeatedly threatened that demonstrators who blocked streets would be arrested.[18]

The proliferation of protests between 1963 and 1971 significantly affected the reactions of federal and District officials. The increasing numbers of protests and participants required officials to refine their responses. Attempts to repress marches seemed unwise both because of the established tradition of the march on Washington and because such action was likely to generate even more media attention. Even the public threat of massive civil disobedience did not provoke, initially, officials into obviously repressive action. The authorities preferred careful behind-the-scenes preparation for the events to active denigration of the protests or their expected participants. As H. R. Haldeman expressed it later, they decided to let the Mayday protesters "hang themselves."[19]

OPERATION DEWEY CANYON THREE: APRIL 19–23, 1971

The first wave of the Spring Offensive hit Washington on Patriot's Day, the anniversary of the beginning of the American Revolution. Organized by the Vietnam Veterans against the War, men gathered in front of the national monuments to expose "the military myths of Viet-Nam."[20] The veterans aimed to show the American people how pointless the war was. And they wanted to show that their experience of fighting the war had forced them to rethink the meaning of their status in the nation.

VVAW organizers began recruiting veterans to come to Washington in late 1970. Announcements went out on FM rock stations and in underground newspapers; recruiters visited the halls of the Veterans of Foreign Wars and college campuses. In mid-April 1971, more than 2,000 veterans arrived in Washington and put up tents at the east end of the Mall.[21] In the shadow of the Capitol Building, they settled in for a week-long encampment, reviving the tactic used by Coxey's Army and the Bonus Army. From this base camp, they staged a series of theatrical actions dramatizing their beliefs and cause. Despite their deep doubts about American nationhood, the veterans presented themselves as legitimate citizens seeking a forum before political authorities. Many politicians and journalists accepted that claim and praised the protest. But their style of protest was anything but conventional.

The veterans' dramatic and original style of demonstrating had developed from a series of VVAW protests that creatively merged patriotic and anti-war images to express their deep doubts about the political legitimacy of the federal government. In 1970, they had staged a moving re-creation of the miserable Revolutionary War march from Morristown to Valley Forge. In 1971, they held "Winter Soldier" hearings to display their outrage.[22] Now, seeking even wider publicity, they turned to the monumental center of Washington, with its national visibility and historical associations.

The participants arrived in Washington on April 19 for what they called "a limited incursion" with the name Operation Dewey Canyon Three. Like the organizers of Coxey's Army and the Bonus Army, VVAW organizers associated their protest with a military maneuver—but rather than simply drawing on military metaphors to emphasize their masculine legitimacy, they used these metaphors to question the legitimacy of the military itself. They took the name from the military code word for the two covert invasions of Laos by United States and South Vietnamese forces, Dewey Canyon One and Two. Their title suggested they considered Washington, D.C., to be the equivalent of a foreign country, deserving of invasion. Though they pledged that the protest would be entirely nonviolent, they knowingly violated the prohibition on camping and at times used defiantly bellicose language.[23]

Federal officials did their best to repel the invasion. They disliked both the group's military rhetoric and its plans for an extended encampment on the Mall. Late in the day on April 19, an Interior Department attorney won an injunction from a federal judge prohibiting the camping. But the veterans, with the help of former attorney general Ramsey Clark, immediately appealed. The United States Court of Appeals reversed the ban—and pointedly reminded the Interior Department that it had, in previous years, permitted a Boy Scout jamboree on the Mall, as well as Resurrection City. Federal officials, convinced that this ruling would set a dangerous precedent, appealed successfully to the Supreme Court. Defiant, the veterans remained in their camp, awaiting arrest. In the end, on the morning of April 22, President Nixon backed off. Surprisingly, he advised the attorney general that the police should not "evict the veterans."[24]

The veterans were able to induce Nixon to back down in large part because of their special symbolic power as men who had fought for their country in wartime. The series of court injunctions inspired both the radical I. F. Stone and the editors of the *Christian Science Monitor* to remember that forty years earlier President Hoover and the Republican Party had paid dearly for the decision to evict the Bonus Army, which had also skillfully exploited its special status. During their week in the capital, the veterans emphasized their fraternal ties with each other and soldiers still in Vietnam; an oft-repeated slogan was "Bring my brothers home, bring 'em home." Such masculine rhetoric was effective. In the end, even the Nixon administration noted that they were "men who have served their country honorably."[25]

Emboldened by these acknowledgments and confident that they had earned respect, the veterans asserted their place in the capital. They took sacred national spaces that glorified military power and used them to show the brutal violence of war. In so doing, they broadened the ways in which protesters could use the public spaces of the capital. On the first day of the protest, they sought to hold a memorial service in Arlington Cemetery; when refused permission, they marched away, stepping in time to their chant, "One, two three four. We don't want your fucking war." On subsequent days, they took to the streets of the capital. Clothed in battle uniforms and fatigues, veterans performed mock search-and-destroy missions on Pennsylvania Avenue, firing toy M-16s at each other and dying in front of tourists. By the Capitol steps, they appeared to take a group of bystanders as prisoners; people who stopped to watch were asked belligerently, "You V.C.? You V.C.?" They went to the Supreme Court to seek a ruling that the war was illegal. Refused entry into the building, they in turn refused to leave and were arrested. That night, other veterans marched to the White House holding candles. In all these locations, the men's use of guerrilla theater visually brought the war home to Americans and emphasized their status as, quite literally, veterans of the conflict.[26] The effect of these performances was to connect Washington to the battlefields of Vietnam and symbolically to turn the tables on the imagery of the national capital (fig. 27).

Like many of their predecessors, the veterans supplemented their public performances with congressional lobbying. The veterans believed Congress could be "responsive to the will of the people," John Kerry told a Senate committee. To illustrate this hope, veterans went to the Capitol almost daily and invited sympathetic members of Congress to their camp. Less sympathetic members of Congress found their offices invaded by groups of angry veterans, who refused to leave until the representatives or senators personally explained their positions on the war. Back on the Mall, the veterans kept a running tally of the results of their "interviews" with members of Congress.[27]

The most spectacular and most televised lobbying came when Kerry appeared before the Senate Foreign Relations Committee on April 22, 1971. His presence at the hearing served as a critical moment to highlight the cause of the veterans and to make it more acceptable to most Americans. Twenty-seven years old, articulate, and clean-cut, Kerry was cordially greeted by sympathetic members of the committee when he testified about the experience of fighting in Vietnam and the lingering effect on the soldiers. Kerry justified the men's presence in the capital by noting their belief that they had to speak out against the war even though it

FIGURE 27. Members of the Vietnam Veterans against the War performing guerrilla street theater near the Capitol, April 21, 1971. By simulating their experiences of fighting in Vietnam, the veterans turned Washington into a battlefield. Though their performances did not always attract crowds of spectators, they made for vivid photographs and television coverage. (Library of Congress, Prints and Photographs Division, *U.S. News and World Report* Magazine Collection, LC-U9–24369, neg. 8A-9)

FIGURE 28. Members of the VVAW observing the Senate Foreign Relations Committee hearing where John Kerry is about to testify. The grim determination on their faces reflects the mixture of cynicism and hope that the veterans brought to Washington. (Library of Congress, Prints and Photographs Division, *U.S. News and World Report Magazine* Collection, LC-U9–24265B, no. 7A–8)

would have been easier to choose silence. He warned the committee that the United States "has created a monster in the form of millions of men . . . who have returned with a sense of anger and a sense of betrayal." He described how every day in Vietnam "someone has to die so that President Nixon won't be, and these are his words, 'the first President to lose a war.'" With his careful mixing of morality and practicality, Kerry came across as a proud American, deeply disappointed by United States policy in Vietnam, yet hopeful of the possibility for change (fig. 28).[28]

Kerry's testimony combined with the visual drama of the protest to create an ideal event for extended coverage on television. Every night for six days, the network news programs featured stories on the demonstration. In part, reporters focused on the legal back-and-forth over the encampment on the Mall, which provided something new to report each day. The veterans' journeys to different ceremonial sites in Washington offered particularly evocative visuals.[29] Although the stories and visuals occasionally revealed the radical postures of some VVAW members, for the most part the television coverage reinforced the dominant image of the protesters as loyal American men.

The skillful design of the week of protests and the extensive coverage resulted in considerable praise in a variety of forums. Leftist newspapers celebrated the demonstration. To a reporter for the *Guardian,* the protest signaled a shift from the traditional "reactionary political role" of veterans. In words echoing the praise that the March on Washington for Jobs and Freedom had received, I. F. Stone noted that the protest would be "remembered with pride in our history books." Editorials in the mainstream press and comments by some politicians agreed with Stone's assessment, but minimized the radical nature of the protest. Thomas Gannon, writing in the liberal Catholic magazine *America,* praised the veterans for giving the anti-war movement "its most poignant moral argument to date." Editors of the *Boston Globe* likened the veterans to Revolutionary War soldiers who had rebelled against an unjust government.[30]

Such praise horrified conservative critics of the anti-war movement, who stressed both the faults of the men and their politics. Representative John Rarick of Louisiana attacked the veterans for having beards, wearing shabby clothes, swearing, and using the "clenched fist salute," which he labeled the "Communist identification symbol." Connecting the demonstrators simultaneously to the detested civil rights movement, urban riots, and student protest, he condemned them as veterans not of the military but of "Selma, Watts, Newark, Chicago, Kent State, and other cities where the American people have encountered agitation, confusion, and violence." Smith Hempstone, a conservative columnist for the *Washington Star,* questioned whether most of the men present in Washington had actually served in Vietnam and alleged that they preferred "mobocracy" to democracy.[31]

President Nixon privately agreed with these critics but publicly limited his criticism. Some advisors arranged for a visit to the capital by Chief H. R. Rainwater, the national commander of the Veterans of Foreign Wars and a vehement critic of the VVAW. Rainwater tried to discredit the veterans by asserting that 40 percent of the people taking part in the demonstration "were either females, girl friends, or wives, or too young [to have served in Vietnam]." Yet Rainwater was frustrated by the praise and publicity lavished on Operation Dewey Canyon; he complained to the Senate Foreign Relations Committee that the networks gave the veterans more than an hour of prime time coverage. Likewise, Mary McGrory commented that footage of "three Gold Star mothers sobbing outside the locked gates of Arlington Cemetery" had resulted in a "public-relations catastrophe" for the administration and made the country appreciate the pleas of the veterans. She concluded, "The battle of the Mall has ended in total defeat for Richard Nixon." In a bitter postmortem, Nixon and Haldeman attributed the continued drop in presidential approval to the VVAW protest and concluded that the media's coverage of the veterans meant the administration was "getting pretty well chopped up."[32]

The success of Operation Dewey Canyon inspired some to hope that it might revive radical activism in the United States and usher in a whole new style of political protest. The widespread praise for the demonstration by both radical and mainstream newspaper reporters, the sympathetic and detailed coverage by network news programs, and the tolerance of the veterans' illegal acts suggested to some commentators that the anti-war movement might regain its strength. To some, the reception of Operation Dewey Canyon also suggested that new precedents had been set for protests. But the organizers themselves had been more astute when they described their plan as a "limited incursion" into national politics. For one thing, mainstream coverage of the demonstration muted the radical demands and anti-establishment nature of the protest. In addition, because of the veterans' status as exceptional citizens, the administration's tolerance of the camp amounted to a favor to a particular group, rather than a precedent that any citizen could use.

The veterans' final act in Washington vividly used patriotic symbols and public spaces to make themselves heard as concerned citizens. On the eve of the April 24 march, the veterans closed up their camp on the Mall and then marched to the west steps of the Capitol. In preparation for NPAC's April 24 march, a fence blocked off the top part of the steps. From a microphone, one by one, more than 750 veterans proceeded to describe what medals they had won in the war and to explain why these honors no longer had meaning. They then turned away from the microphone and threw the medals over the fence. "Citations for gallantry and exemplary service" had become for them "symbols of shame, dishonor, and inhumanity."[33] If television commentators missed some of the significance of this moment, the cameras still communicated the deep alienation these men felt from the country they had so recently served. Once again, the organizers of Operation Dewey Canyon had shown that sites that had seemed mainly useful for praising the American nation—from Arlington Cemetery to Pennsylvania Avenue—could become the locations for deeply moving criticisms of that nation.

"BE COUNTED THIS TIME": THE APRIL 24 MARCH AGAINST THE WAR

When the popular comic strip commentator Garry Trudeau decided to use *Doonesbury* to reflect on the Spring Offensive, he focused his sarcasm on the large, conventional April 24 march. In the first of a series on the march, the hippie Mark Slackmeyer enthuses about the "smell of revolution" in the spring air and urges the straight man Mike Doonesbury to travel with him to Washington to participate in the peace march. "Let us show the world we care!" he exclaims, "that we are still activists!" Mike snores. Nevertheless, the two do fly off to Washington. The earnest hippie argues that without the protests of the 1960s "this country would be a repressive police state haunted by pigs, fascists, gargoyles, and SSTs." Mike remains apathetic. The next strip suggests why: Trudeau focuses on the media's paradoxical ability to create excitement around a march and at the same time to diffuse its political meaning. The hippie Mark has a chance to speak before the rally but, stunned by the "three networks" that are filming him, his political coherence dissolves and he manages only a lame, "Hi, Mom." He later whines that the march was not covered by the *Washington Post*. Disaffected, Mike responds by reading from the paper's society column: "It was a smasho day of sunshine as masses of those delicious doves did their thing."[34]

The march certainly was popular. In the cool of the morning of April 24, participants began to gather in the Ellipse; as the sun rose higher, the space overflowed with protesters. By the end of the day, organizers proudly claimed that they had succeeded in attracting more than half a million people. They celebrated because they embraced the goal of a high turnout and did everything in their power to outdo earlier marches. In 1965, the first substantial anti-war march had been relatively small, attracting some 25,000 people; in 1967, the march against the Pentagon was joined by about 100,000 people; in 1969, the Mobilization against the Vietnam War surrounded the Washington Monument with at least half a million people, making it the largest march on record. Before the 1971 march, coordinator Fred Halstead bragged that organizers expected a million people.[35] In part, the large turnout confirmed for NPAC leaders that they had chosen the right tactic for opposing the war. They needed this assurance because they were painfully aware that even a large, peaceable, "classic" march on Washington might be dismissed as politically innocuous, even complacently establishmentarian.

For more than a year, the leaders of the National Peace Action Coalition had debated about the value of different styles of protest. To some, the planned march was dangerously radical because of its revolutionary rhetoric. To others, it was shamefully compromised by its liberal politics. As organizers made their plans and then held the event, they engaged this debate in ways that suggest the difficulty of their position. They attempted to balance competing—at times conflicting—visions of citizenship, one based on identity politics and one based on freedom and autonomy. This balancing act was endangered by the ability of many observers, particularly television reporters, to praise the protest as belonging to the tradition of marches on Washington. Such freedom to ignore the questions surrounding the protest highlights how much power the media had to legitimize certain kinds of protest, certain uses of the capital's public space, and, by implication, certain ideologies of citizenship. This power enraged both organizers and government officials; in fact, of course, the media also assisted one group in gaining credibility for its protest and the other's efforts to limit the demonstration's significance.

For NPAC organizers, the strategy of focusing on numbers, despite some real disadvantages, was a concrete way to calculate success. A focus solely on turnout versus strategic coalition building meant that the organizers welcomed all comers. This approach left the protest vulnerable to criticism by politicians seeking to discredit the entire march by associating it with its most radical participants. Yet, at the same time, radical activists complained that the obsession with a large turnout diminished the gravity and political significance of the march. Finally, there was always the risk that organizers might be embarrassed by low turnout, but they were confident they could meet this hurdle through careful planning. Defending the mass demonstration from its critics, Jerry Gordon justified the tactic as "the most effective way for involving the largest number of people." Characteristically, one poster urged all opponents of the war to attend on April 24 so that they would "Be Counted This Time."[36] Above all, at a time when there were many reservations about the effectiveness of protest, emphasizing the numbers gave organizers an easy way to gauge their success and to convince marchers that their participation had meaning.

Big numbers also masked the intense concern of organizers with building a diverse coalition to widen support for the protest. Organizers were careful to emphasize the presence of particular, symbolically important, groups of protesters. They gave pride of place to Vietnam veterans. At the head of the march, as it left the Ellipse and went by the White House on Pennsylvania Avenue, marched ex-soldiers dressed in battle fatigues, carrying a large sign supplied by NPAC. Many Americans considered the veterans' opposition particularly persuasive because they saw soldiers both as the ultimate citizens and as experts on the war. Even radical activists who rejected such views supported the anti-war vets because they believed both that soldiers were "oppressed" in military service and that, consequently, veterans had considerable revolutionary potential.

Organizers also welcomed union members. The socialist organizers in NPAC, in particular, saw the support of labor for the demonstration as an indicator of the growing revolutionary potential of the United States.[37] At the same time, organizers wanted to attract working-class participants to refute claims by President Nixon that only a young and privileged minority opposed the war, while a "silent majority" supported his position.

In their quest for "diversity" within the march, NPAC organizers were also responding to the contemporary popularity of identity politics, which was changing the meaning of citizenship. Frustrating conflicts over discrimination in the 1960s led to increasing acceptance of the notion that distinctive groups naturally held distinctive political views. As many activists had discovered, such notions could make it difficult to organize collective actions, unless each group received a distinctive place in the demonstration. One of the largest and most organized groups walking down Pennsylvania Avenue consisted of women. Of course, women had taken part in even the earliest protests against United States involvement in Vietnam. By the later 1960s, however, the nature of women's participation changed as the feminist movement grew more influential. Disgusted by sexism within the anti-war movement, some women turned to women-only demonstrations as early 1968; such demonstrations continued in the early 1970s. Wanting to include feminists in the protest, NPAC organizers made special buttons and signs for women and organized a separate marching contingent (fig. 29).[38]

The power of such appeals to identity politics was apparent in the planning of a "Third World" contingent. Charles Stephenson, one of the few African Americans among the leadership of the National Coalition, organized the group because he recognized that black participation in

FIGURE 29. Poster inviting women to take part in the April 24 demonstration. The specific targeting of women to participate in the march represented part of the organizers' attempt to negotiate the concern with diversity among participants that was increasingly important in the politics of citizenship. The slogan on the poster suggests both the high expectations surrounding the women's liberation movement and the need to rally supporters for yet another march on Washington. (United Women's Contingent, Yanker Collection, Library of Congress, Prints and Photographs Division, LC-USZ62–109802)

the anti-war movement had hitherto been limited and hoped that more would march if they were given a special group status. Stephenson strove to ensure that African American participants could emphasize concerns about the place of blacks in District of Columbia politics as well as their special reason to oppose the Vietnam War. Accordingly, the Third World group did not begin its march at the Ellipse but rather in the heart of the District's black community on Fourteenth Street, illustrating that their distinctive place as black citizens necessitated different political tactics.[39] For these groups, the large march became a setting for a portrayal of their particular causes.

As much as organizers strove to recognize and publicize the diversity of marchers, they also wanted to promote a vision of citizenship that depended on individuals' autonomy and self-expression. In a striking departure from previous capital protests, organizers abandoned dress codes, restrictions on signs, and the exclusion of controversial or disliked groups. Participants embraced "freedom" in politics during the march in their appearance and their behavior. Just as individual participants in 1963 departed early for Lincoln Memorial, people left early from the Ellipse despite the marshals' efforts to keep them there until the official starting time. For more than four hours, marchers proceeded down the Avenue in their own fashion. According to one observer, "few people bothered to look for a special group to march with," suggesting only a limited utility for identity politics on the day of the march itself. Neither did they march in ranks. Rather, many participants wandered on and off Pennsylvania Avenue, stopping to chat with friends, to climb on statues, or even, in some cases, to smoke marijuana.[40] By rejecting orderliness, the marchers dramatized their eroding confidence that discipline, such as the military discipline that had sent the troops to Vietnam, or respectability, which might involve passively accepting the decisions of the government, was politically valuable.

They projected a new political ethos about citizenship that was simultaneously cynical and humorous. One participant, conscious of restrictions on profanity by television producers, carried a sign that demanded "Eat Poop Nixon" (fig. 30). Another handwritten sign made vivid use of the president's nickname and a sexual innuendo: "Get that Dick Out of the White House."[41] If the use of drama in Washington reached back to Coxey's Army, the degree of irreverence of these performances was unprecedented.

The most dramatic change was that participants rejected traditional patriotism. Just two years before, during the Mobilization demonstra-

FIGURE 30. Marchers on Pennsylvania Avenue carrying homemade sign, April 24, 1971. Such humorous, often mocking, signs became a standard part of anti-war demonstrations and remain popular today. In contrast to the uniform signs supplied by organizers in 1963, the emphasis on freedom in the 1971 demonstration encouraged marchers to create such signs. The slogan of "Eat Poop" suggests the creator had media savvy since television broadcasters were unlikely to display signs with profanity. (Image from Putnam Barber film of April 24 march, in author's possession)

tion, thousands of demonstrators had carried the American flag to emphasize their patriotism. Most of the participants who displayed the flag on April 24 used it subversively. A small group carried a large flag, hung upside down, signaling distress at United States involvement in Indochina. Other protesters attacked United States flags; they tried and at times succeeded in removing them from poles near government buildings. Others just rejected the American flag entirely and carried the "enemy" flags: the red banner of North Vietnam and the blue and red banners of the National Liberation Front.[42]

The depth of political division that haunted the protesters and the nation came through also in the speeches given to the crowd on the Mall afterward. In contrast to previous demonstrations, there was little attempt to control the speakers to ensure a unified message. NPAC organizers felt the highest priority was to attract speakers representative of the political diversity of the anti-war movement. More than forty people assembled on the platform; each would have no more than six minutes to articulate his or her message.[43] The contrast with the 1963 March on Washington for Jobs and Freedom was obvious. There was no careful pacing of the speakers to ensure the maximum impact for the last speech and no formal or informal system to coordinate their messages. Rather, the speeches served mainly to expose the deep differences in opinion about the anti-war movement and the purpose of protesting. For liberals like union activist David Livingston, the movement had the potential to influence important political figures who would then solve the problem of the war in Vietnam by voting against it. He, like suffrage and civil rights activists before him, believed that a march on Washington could both teach about and rehabilitate the American political process. In contrast, radical speakers saw the war, the anti-war movement, and the march itself as antecedents to a revolutionary moment.

Such mixed messages hardly seemed to bother the participants. Many participants simply could not see the speakers; fewer could hear. Instead, the protesters ate lunch or played Frisbee; some napped or talked with friends. Such behavior confirmed for some observers that this kind of demonstration was at once acceptable and tame. To a reporter for a radical newspaper, however, such attitudes meant "the march and rally lacked any of the militant spirit that has marked earlier marches."[44]

Some participants tried to prove this assessment wrong on the day of the march. As the Mall began to empty around 4:00 P.M., a crowd of around 4,000 people that had collected near the Washington Monument grew restless. They were waiting for a rock concert to begin that was to continue through the evening. Someone began to climb one of the flagpoles surrounding the monument in an effort to remove yet another American flag from its pole. Soon others tried to remove the rest of the flags; some were successful. U.S. Park Police officers moved in to stop these efforts and arrested some participants. Demonstrators, however, resisted; some pelted the police van that arrived to take the arrested away "with a volley of rocks and bottles." Others sat in front and behind the van to prevent its removal. Without any backup available, the police retreated inside the monument. Outside, the protesters removed all the flags and then began to break up the park benches to fuel bonfires. As the demonstrators enjoyed the rock bands, these fires burned through the night.[45]

Television coverage, which largely defined the importance of the march, was relatively limited. Organizers were disappointed that all of the major networks had flatly refused to cover the march live.[46] Consequently, few Americans had the opportunity that viewers did in 1963 to judge the variety of the crowd and to hear all of the speakers. Instead, they were dependent on the short clips and brief commentaries that the networks chose to present. In the case of the April 24 march, such clips suggested a demonstration that fit within the conventions of the acceptable uses of national public spaces, and downplayed attempts by participants and speakers to argue for a new view of political legitimacy. This portrayal of the march did not satisfy anyone—organizers, radicals, the Nixon administration, or conservative observers.

Indeed, the reporting of the demonstration contained little hint that anything particularly controversial had taken place. Reflecting the widespread embrace of the politics of bigness, the report on the CBS news emphasized the organizers' claim that the demonstration was the "largest in D.C. history." The positive tone about the protest continued when reporters considered the speeches. They began with the words of heroic John Kerry and moved on to Senator Vance Hartke of Indiana. CBS's coverage ended with visuals of the large crowd, accompanied by an antiwar song sung by John Denver.[47] This coverage molded the image of the April 24 march into the familiar pattern of the March on Washington for Jobs and Freedom: an impressively huge number of citizens marching peacefully on Washington to gain reasonable political goals.

Such a portrayal seemed far from the mark in the eyes of many observers. To those who had radical aspirations, the stories disappointed because they did not acknowledge the racial diversity of the participants, the inclusion of separate contingents of women and Third World people, or the messages of the radical speakers. The Nixon administration complained about the portrayal of the protest also. Before it even took place, President Nixon told his aide H. R. Haldeman that he wanted it "downplayed as much as possible," and he tried to show his lack of concern by traveling to Camp David, the president's official retreat, on Friday, April 23.[48] Left behind in the capital, Haldeman sketched out how the White House should respond to the march. First, in his opinion, the Nixon administration could note that the march organizers had not achieved diversity. The crowd was "totally kids," he wrote, lacking both "hard hats"—the construction workers who symbolized Nixon's "silent majority" of supporters—and middle-aged people. Second, Haldeman stressed that the protest had little political meaning because the forty speakers included no candidates for political office. Such views show that Haldeman, like others in the country, continued to believe that one could judge a protest by the nature of its participants and the importance of the speakers. Despite the White House dismissal of the march as a failure, on Sunday morning disgruntled staff members still concluded that media coverage was "totally positive for demos [demonstrators]." What particularly outraged them, as well as other opponents of the anti-war movement, was that CBS and the other stations mostly ignored the destructive events at the Washington Memorial that had ended April 24.[49]

Such outrage could not change the dominant impression of the demonstration as a peaceful, indeed typical, march on Washington. The prevalence of that impression suggested the powerful claim citizens had won to Washington's public space in the wake of the 1963 civil rights march. Even people who closely observed the NPAC protest adopted the position that it was part of that tradition of marching on Washington. Despite the effort of the NPAC organizers to avoid replicating the format of a traditional march, despite the freewheeling and at times unpatriotic behavior of the participants, despite the revolutionary messages of some of the speakers, and despite the destruction near the Washington Monument, the April 24 march was packaged by the media as belonging to a now-acceptable political tradition.

Such a lasting impression suggests the emergence of a tacit bargain about freedom and citizenship during marches on Washington. The media, organizers, police, and participants all seemed to agree that as long as participants acted without explicit directions or endorsement from organizers, and as long as they confined their activities to the central core of Washington, they were free to express themselves—even to break some laws. This bargain did loosen the assumption that a controlled performance was essential to these national protests. It also left the impression—captured memorably by Trudeau's *Doonesbury* cartoons—that such large demonstrations were essentially about numbers of Americans who attended and the tone of the media coverage. Other aspects—the variety of political aspirations and identities, the lawbreaking, and the dismissive attitude of the Nixon administration—were barely consequential.

"SOCIAL CHAOS":
THE MAYDAY PROTESTS, MAY 3–5, 1971

Early on May 2, a cavalcade of buses arrived on the roads near West Potomac Park, south of the Mall. Out of the doors of the buses poured more than seven hundred District police officers. Their mission: to expel from the park the thousands of people who had arrived for a rock concert, the festive beginning of the Mayday protests. Over the course of the previous day, May 1, young people, ramshackle tents, cars, and vans had gradually covered the grounds of the park. The weather was warm.

Many people stripped off excess clothing. Into the evening, they listened to a diverse set of performers, including the Beach Boys, Country Joe and the Fish, and folksinger Phil Ochs. Speeches condemning American imperialism came right after announcements about lost children and bad acid. In the relative quiet before dawn, the police officers were probably edgy; intelligence agents warned them that "a lot of the people will no doubt be high on drugs so you will have to expect some odd behavior." Providing reconnaissance, an air force helicopter flew over their heads. Soon, armed with tear gas and dressed in riot gear, the officers moved into the park behind an armored sound truck. From the vehicle, an officer announced repeatedly: "This is the Metropolitan D.C. Police Department. Your permit for this encampment has been revoked. Anyone remaining will be arrested." The officers moved through the morning light encouraging everyone to leave the campsite and the city. To the officers' relief, the vast majority scattered. By midday, the campsite was empty. As police officials admitted and radio reporters concluded, this early-morning clearing of the camp was a preemptive strike designed to "break the back" of the protests scheduled to begin the following day.[50]

Despite this attempt to suppress the protest, the Mayday protests did take place over the following three days. Even when driven from their staging ground, at least 20,000 determined protesters remained in the city for the subsequent protests, which, they hoped, would create "a level of social chaos that America's leaders will be unable to accept." Organizers and participants were determined to make this protest more subversive than any previous demonstration in the capital, a place they saw as contemptible. To organizers, the most grotesque features of the capital were "the giant federal office buildings in downtown Washington." These buildings were visual evidence that the U.S. federal government did not embody a system of democratic decision making but rather was a bureaucratic machine that functioned of its own accord, with no concern for the protesters or their values. Indeed, organizers and most participants tended to want to reject the entire idea of national authority. One participant justified his intentional violation of law by explaining that it was "their law," not his.[51] Such belief in individual political authority was similar to that of Coxey and Browne in 1894, who had argued that the people had the right to use the capital as they deemed necessary.

For decades, officials had tried to prevent just this kind of march. But now, faced with the actuality of the protest, District and federal officials had jointly decided to focus publicly on condemning the protest and privately on ensuring they had sufficient security measures to suppress it. Their reaction was a mix of political theory about who ought to control the capital and strategic logic about how to discredit the anti-war movement generally. On the one hand, they believed firmly that the officials should and could authorize how people used the capital. On the other hand, they were confident that the protesters and their actions would appear so unacceptable that, as a practical matter, officials needed only to ensure that the protesters did not actually succeed in halting the government.

After a series of closeted meetings between Nixon aides, Chief Jerry Wilson, and several army generals, federal and District authorities assembled an impressive force of police officers, National Guardsmen, and soldiers in the capital on May 3. The authorities' intense response reflected the newness to the capital of the tactic of mass civil disobedience. In addition, they feared how the protest aimed to delegitimate the federal government and indeed to challenge the desirability of an American nation supported by loyal citizens. To make the protests seem local instead of national in scope, Nixon's press advisors decided that "all announcements Sunday and Monday should be made by city spokesmen, keeping Federal spokesmen in the background." President Nixon was in California—his trip carefully calculated to illustrate that the authorities did not fear the Mayday protests—and he merely commented that "the right to demonstrate for peace abroad does not include the right to disturb the peace at home."[52]

In the early morning of May 3, nearly 20,000 protesters gradually spread out around the District. Though some went near the targets of earlier protests—the Lincoln Memorial, the Capitol, and the White House—they had little interest in these central locations of national or political power. Rather than occupy the center of Washington, the protesters wanted to block it off. From January to April, organizers had analyzed the commuter traffic into the city and identified bottlenecks to target during the protest. By occupying these spots, they hoped the resulting traffic jams could send the capital into turmoil (see map 4). Many began their early-morning journey near Georgetown University, whose campus had become the temporary home for many of the people evicted from the campsite by the police the previous morning. Some blocked the end of the Key Bridge in order to prevent Virginia commuters from entering the District. Others went down M Street toward the White House. Some paused on the bridge over the Rock Creek Parkway and dropped benches and trashcans onto the roadway below. Near the Lincoln Memorial, people grabbed bicycle racks and wooden barricades and used them to block the traffic coming across Memorial Bridge. Near Dupont Circle, young people dashed in and out of the traffic, making the confusing intersections an even greater test of commuters' patience. As protesters blocked streets and stepped in front of cars, they reminded federal workers that the government "could not continue to carry on its business without your passive support."[53] For these protesters, local residents did not represent a potential audience or a logistical challenge; they were involuntary participants—as targets—in the demonstration itself.

The Mayday protesters rejected ties to the American nation and instead asserted their allegiances to the subordinated people of the world. In statements or printed materials, organizers rarely mentioned "citizens," but rather referred to participants as "the people." Supporters and participants repeatedly invoked heroes outside of the American pantheon. On their posters and other publicity appeared a stylized picture of Mahatma Gandhi, sitting cross-legged with his right fist in the air (fig. 31). The cover of the tactical manual featured a large profile of a generic Native American. Similarly, they called their camp in West Potomac Park Algonquian Peace City in honor of the Native Americans who had originally lived where the District was located. They even renamed the entire city for their protest: graffiti on the Tidal Basin Bridge proclaimed, "Welcome to Peace City—Mayday."[54]

At the same time, their tactics reflected a commitment to an alternative political culture. Rather than improve existing institutions or establish support for different leaders, Mayday protesters wanted to cultivate individual imagination and small-group initiative. Instead of targeting well-established organizations, the People's Coalition and the Mayday Tribe focused on the more informal networks that linked radicals, freaks, and hippies. The organizers spoke as if they shared the goals of earlier demonstrations when they claimed their demonstration would include "women, Gays, Blacks, Chicanos, Puerto Ricans, Indians, students, youth, families, clergymen, GIs." The reality, however, was different— around 85 percent of the people taking part in the protests were men and almost all appeared to be white.[55] Even before May 3, a Boston feminist group criticized the Mayday leadership as "racist and opportunistic" in appropriating Gandhi as a symbol for the protest and questioned whether the Mayday leaders understood how "the brutality of war is related to the racism and sexism of our society." In Peace City, two rapes occurred. Gay men encountered homophobia. A black man, noting how few African Americans showed up for the protest, questioned whether

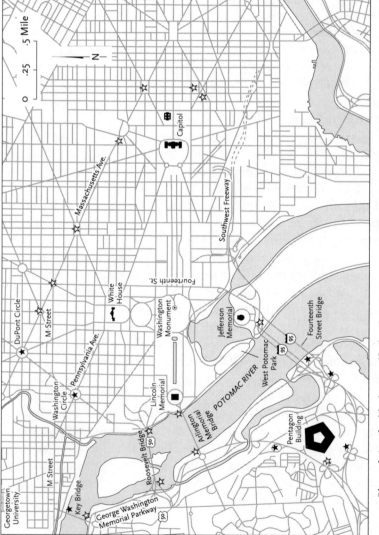

★ Locations on which protesters concentrated after preemptive clearing of West Potomac Park campsite.

☆ Planned locations for civil disobedience, mostly abandoned in order to concentrate on key targets.

MAP 4. Planned sites for blocking traffic for the Mayday protest, 1971. Source: Mayday Tactical Manual, Records of the People's Coalition for Peace and Justice (DG-84), box T-1, Swarthmore College Peace Collection.

FIGURE 31. Poster encouraging people to stay in Washington for the Mayday protests after the April 24 march. The emphasis on nonviolence reflected the concerns in the coalition behind the Mayday protests that "shutting down" Washington might cross over into destruction. At the same time, the appropriation of Gandhi as a visual symbol was part of a strategy of rejecting American traditions in favor of the "third world." (Mark Morris Design for People's Coalition for Peace and Justice, Yanker Collection, Library of Congress, Prints and Photographs Division, LC-USZC4–2878)

"anyone even bothered to talk to the people in the black community." Mayday organizers could claim that their political style was free of bias; arguably, though, their tactics resonated more with young white male activists, whose relatively privileged status in society made them less afraid of the police. During the protest, there was often an undercurrent of fraternalism—similar to that seen during the Vietnam veterans' protest in April—that excluded women and minorities even as it built solidarity.[56]

Ignoring these currents and emphasizing the autonomy of participants, organizers urged people to form "affinity groups," small groups of friends who would act in concert in the streets of Washington. During the actions on May 3, these groups of six or seven people stuck together, decided on their tactics, and protected each other from arrests. The goal for participants was to be "free, joyous, exciting, fun." One rambunctious group in Georgetown commandeered a truck, released its parking brake, and rode it down a hill to block an intersection; the people onboard laughed and waved to onlookers.[57]

John Dean observed these activities from an army helicopter; he remembered watching groups of demonstrators running from place to place; he noted the flashing blue lights of police cars combined with "pitched rock battles" to create a "general scene of chaos." Yet, the chaos did not pose much of a threat. Authorities clearly had the upper hand. Nearly all 5,000 members of the Metropolitan Police were on duty. Police Chief Wilson swore in 1,400 members of the D.C. National Guard as special police officers with authority to make arrests. Finally, 4,000 soldiers in the United States Army moved into the District early on Monday morning. Another 6,000 were on alert at nearby bases. As these forces assembled, the capital took on the appearance of military occupation (fig. 32). Chinook helicopters landed marines at the Washington Monument; troops and jeeps lined Memorial Bridge; police cars with sirens blaring and lights flashing zoomed across the city.[58] This mobilization was by far the largest response ever to a demonstration in Washington.

The authorities relied on their technological mastery of transportation and communications. One observer noted that "the group which possessed mobility . . . was not the demonstrators, but rather the police." Watching from helicopters hovering over the District, police officers noted the demonstrators' movements and relayed this information to their colleagues on the ground. Where traffic jams or debris blocked streets, police used motorcycles and scooters to reach the protesters. In addition, these officers could rely on an extensive and well-protected communication system that allowed them to relay their plans privately. Thanks to undercover infiltrators, they were able to monitor almost all of the demonstrators' communications. A *Washington Post* reporter concluded at the end of the day that "the [official] forces had demonstrators outnumbered and outmaneuvered."[59]

Fundamentally, however, the key to the authorities' success was a will-

FIGURE 32. Troops crossing bridge toward Virginia from the Lincoln Memorial on May 3, 1971. These men were just a small fraction of the mobilization of forces for the Mayday protests. Police officers, National Guardsmen, and soldiers spread around the city to ensure that they stopped the protesters before the capital was "shut down." They arrested 7,000 that day and 5,000 more over the next two days. (Library of Congress, Prints and Photographs Division, *U.S. News and World Report* Magazine Collection, LC-U9–24368, frame 21–21A)

ingness to arrest protesters en masse and without legal scruples. In their first contacts with the protesters around 5:00 A.M., the police attempted to disperse the protesters with direct charges or with tear gas; but the protesters were happy enough to evade capture and move on to new targets. Accordingly, the police began simply arresting them. The decision meant abandoning a procedure developed in 1968 to protect citizens from police abuse.[60] Around 6:30 A.M. on Monday morning, Chief Wilson ordered the officers on duty to skip completing the required forms and instead to bring protesters in and "lock 'em up." Police officers stopped trying to determine whether individuals were actively interfering with traffic or ignoring orders to move on and simply began grabbing anyone who looked young and longhaired. At Dupont Circle, some by-standers who showed sympathy toward a protester being clubbed by a police officer soon found themselves under arrest as well. By the end of the morning of May 3, police officers had arrested nearly 7,000 people.[61]

With the American Civil Liberties Union's help, fifteen people sued the District for illegal arrests on May 13; thousands more would soon join them. By September 1971, federal prosecutors had dropped charges against those protesters arrested at the Capitol on the last day of the demonstration. For participants on the first day of the Mayday protests, however, the legal issues would not be resolved until 1981. In that year, an appeals court finally settled the class action suit brought by more than a thousand protesters against the District and federal authorities. Protesters received compensation of between $750 and $2,500 for false arrest and violations of their freedom of speech.[62] Such rulings—though long in coming—legally confirmed what their lawyers had asserted from the start: that controlling protest in the capital had to occur with due regard to proper police procedures and constitutional rights.

In some ways, the major challenge to the authorities on May 3 was not suppressing the demonstration but rather transporting and housing the thousands of arrested people. More than once, officers found themselves holding crowds of arrested protesters with no way to transport them out of the area and not enough officers to guard them. Precinct cells filled quickly with the first wave of arrests. The police diverted the rest to two outdoor locations: the exercise yard of the main jail and a fenced yard at the Robert F. Kennedy Memorial Stadium. Inside and outside, there were inadequate toilet facilities and little water and food. In addition, the weather turned unseasonably chilly, and those outside were cold. Eventually, officials had to move thousands of protesters from the outside locations to the Uline Arena and the Washington Coliseum.[63]

The protests continued for two more days, and demonstrators continued to put significant pressure on the police forces in the city. There were few efforts to block streets after Monday. Instead, on May 4, protesters returned to conventional methods of civil disobedience. More than 4,000 people held a sit-in at the Justice Department, blocking the street in front until the police finally arrested them. By the end of the day, Chief Wilson felt that the demonstrators were "broken in spirit and strength." Still, on May 5, the remaining demonstrators—numbering around 2,000—marched to the United States Capitol. A few members of Congress met them to receive their demand for a definite date for the end of the war. The representatives were also present in an effort to keep the protest nominally legal. Protests on the Capitol grounds were still, under the 1872 law, illegal without a permit. Members of Congress, though, could always meet with groups of their constituents. Only a few demonstrators actually did talk to the representatives. The rest wandered up and down the stairs. One young man stripped off all of his clothes; others sang songs; occasionally, the crowd outside united on a single slogan and their voices carried inside the Capitol Building. Finally, police abandoned their attitude of tolerance and began to arrest them. It took more than thirteen buses to carry more than 1,400 people to jail. By the end of that day, the District had established a dubious record: more people had been arrested in the District in three days than had ever been arrested in the United States in one place during the same length of time.[64]

Meanwhile, those arrested continued to express their commitment to "freedom" and "joy." In the jails, participants sang and traded arrest stories. They shared food and rotated in and out of the beds. In the Coliseum, many weary protesters tried to sleep on the concrete floor wrapped in army blankets, as National Guardsmen surrounded them. Others, however, celebrated their arrests by dancing. At least a dozen men and women stripped; one wrote a slogan across his body: "Fuck Agnew."[65] Their actions showed that even if arrested and placed in a forbidding place, they could not be repressed.

Almost as soon as the first protesters were arrested, organizers and supportive attorneys questioned the legality of the arrests. They soon began to complain as well about the treatment of the prisoners. In cases of civil disobedience, when protesters cooperated with the police, the practice was for protesters to provide $10 in collateral for their appearance at a hearing and to be released quickly. In May 1971, however, authorities wanted higher amounts and delayed processing in order to prevent protesters from returning to the streets. Angry lawyers from the People's Coalition noted these changes, filed an appeal in a district court about the method of the arrests and the treatment of the prisoners. By midnight on May 3, they had won their first case when the judge ruled that the police had to release the prisoners by morning because of the improper arrest procedures.[66]

Even at the time, some protestors tried to claim that their tactics had worked. One declared the action "a heartening success." The irrepressible Rennie Davis, out on bail after being arrested on federal charges of conspiracy and interfering with federal employees, declared, "We are coming back again!" He threatened, "They are going to have to jail every young person in America before we can be stopped." David Dellinger celebrated the fact that the protests "ended the illusion that large national mobilizations" had to "be utterly predictable, ritualistic, one-day events."[67]

But most observers concluded that this protest had gone terribly wrong. Instead of a serious challenge to the continuation of the war, the Mayday protests led to an increased fear of the government's willingness to repress people's rights to protest in the capital. Many responded to a chilling set of images of the protest: those of the thousands of people held in what they called "detention camps." Noted writer and public moralist Jonathan Schell concluded, "The President seems to want to replace law enforcement with retaliation in kind—to deal with lawbreakers by suspending the law." Edward Kennedy told a college group in New York City that "lawlessness by the lawless does not justify lawlessness by the lawmen." The national executive director of the American Civil Liberties Union said that the government celebrated how it "kept our traffic system from a breakdown" when what it had really done was to cause a "breakdown in our system of justice."[68]

But criticism of the arrests (and the eventual legal vindication for those arrested) had little influence on public opinion about the Mayday protests. Television coverage of the protests portrayed them as a failure, criticized the demonstrators, and praised the police. Rarely did the protesters or anyone else attempt to explain the Mayday protesters' motives or their methods. For most Americans, the images that came to characterize the Mayday protests were of demonstrators running through the streets, police officers arresting them, and United States soldiers guarding bridges and monuments in the nation's capital. In print, Russell Baker described the protest as "The Peace Freak Follies of 1971." Even the editors of the *Washington Post,* generally sympathetic toward protesters and hostile to the Nixon administration, observed, "it was not so much a protest as a rampage."[69]

This coverage helped shape public opinion. A poll of nearly a thousand adults revealed that three-quarters of them approved of the police actions and about the same number disapproved of the demonstrations. Thousands of people reinforced the criticism of the protest and the praise of the authorities by sending telegrams to the Washington police force. They characterized the protesters as "bums," "culls," an "invasion of insects," and "wildmen who called themselves Americans." Obviously, these people did not see the protesters as citizens; they had no right to behave as they did in the capital. People across the country perceived that both the capital and the nation had been at risk of destruction. Two women from California wrote, "Keep up the good work. . . . We love our nation and are proud of our capital. They should not be permitted to make it a battlefield." This view that the capital was supposed to be a ceremonial place—not a political or public space for citizens to debate and protest—appeared in the telegrams repeatedly.[70]

President Nixon took full advantage of these criticisms. He and his staff also justified the authorities' action by defining the protesters as outside the norm of American citizens. When journalists at a press conference pointed out that many of the arrests appeared illegal, Nixon flashed anger. He insisted that the journalists did not appreciate the situation. "When people come in and slice tires, when they block traffic, when they make a trash bin out of Georgetown, and when they terrorize innocent bystanders," Nixon said, "they are not demonstrators, they are vandals and hoodlums and lawbreakers." Ever more extreme, Attorney General John Mitchell told a meeting of police officers that the Mayday demonstrators were like Hitler's Brownshirts, "who roamed the streets of Germany in the 1920s, . . . denying other citizens their civil rights."[71]

Charles Colson concluded that the protest "really turned out to be a great plus for us." Administration officials believed that people would increasingly identify all the parts of the Spring Offensive with the Mayday protests. Sensing a political opportunity, Haldeman asked Colson to create a system "to log all the quotes of the various Democratic candidates regarding the demonstrations of the last two weeks." Colson also saw the public reaction to the protest as an opportunity to "nail these guys . . . and nail them hard."[72]

For Nixon, his aides, and many concerned Americans, the Mayday protesters clarified how Washington could be used for protest. Demonstrators needed to respect the nation and the capital. If they did not, then they were not citizens and did not deserve the protections of the government. The Mayday protesters miscalculated not only their ability to disrupt the city but also the priorities of the public. Faced with the images from the Mayday protests, people cared less about civil liberties than about nationalism, patriotism, and getting to work on time. They feared not the government, but the protesters who violated the norms of citizenship. Ultimately, testing the boundaries of the conventional march only served to reinforce the strategic importance for protesters to stay within those boundaries.

LEGACIES

In the aftermath of the Spring Offensive, organizers, authorities, and journalists struggled to make sense of the weeks of protest in the capital. As in the case of many previous national demonstrations, the protests did not energize the movement or its cause. Instead, organizers, tired and still competitive, were divided over what to do next. Authorities, too, could not agree entirely on the meaning of either their accommodations of some protesters or the mass arrests during the Mayday protests. Meanwhile, journalists tried to explain to the American people the significance of the three weeks of political protest in the national public space. Their assessment was gloomy for the movement, but optimistic about the place of peaceful and orderly protest in the nation.

The enormous effort of organizing these events left many activists tired and dispirited. A wave of debates that in retrospect seem petty broke out in each of the organizations and led to splits and even fist-fights. The Mayday Tribe struggled with accusations of homophobia, the National Peace Action Coalition faced challenges of catering to liberals, and the Vietnam Veterans against the War divided over revolutionary versus more traditional politics.[73] None of these organizations or the activists involved in them survived the summer of 1971 with much of the confidence and spirit that had inspired them to go to Washington the previous spring. Once again, large protests marching on Washington had proved divisive, rather than unifying, to their organizers.

For members of the Nixon administration, the Spring Offensive served as a turning point. They were no longer very afraid of protest. The specter of the Mayday protests turned out to be useful for the Nixon administration as an example of disruptive protests that authorities should suppress. At the same time, the administration was able to use the Mayday protests politically by associating them with Democrats. As Patrick Buchanan began planning ways to attack Democratic presidential candidate George McGovern in the 1972 election, he chose the Mayday protests as a central motif. In a campaign plan, he compared Nixon's condemnation of the arrested demonstrators to McGovern's claim that if he were president, the Mayday protesters "would be having dinner in the White House instead of protesting outside." Buchanan envisioned a campaign commercial that juxtaposed these remarks with shots of "the mob trashing Georgetown."[74]

Despite this strategic thinking, the Spring Offensive had deeply unsettled the Nixon White House, increasing its sense of paranoia and its need for self-justification. In his memoirs, Jeb Magruder reported that the Mayday protests "intensified the pressures to find out what our 'enemies' were up to." Magruder did not provide an explanation for his conclusions, but his memories suggest that the Spring Offensive led the president and his aides to conclude that all opponents—not just Mayday protesters—might need firm, at times even illegal, control if Nixon wanted to protect his presidency and, by extension, the nation. Such pressures, in Magruder's account, led to events that included the break-in at the Watergate Apartments. Nixon himself would long remember the Mayday protests as part of a series of events that made the "first months of 1971 . . . the lowest point of my first term as president."[75]

For all—organizers, participants, authorities, and observers—the Spring Offensive required reassessment of the meaning of the public spaces of the capital. Those protesters who had brought to the capital deep doubts about the American system of government had discovered how difficult it was to use the public spaces of Washington to express such views. Many supporters of the Vietnam Veterans against the War and the National Peace Action Coalition were doubtful about the American political system, and some were doubtful about the value of their citizenship in the nation. The streets and monumental spaces of Washington celebrated a nationalistic definition of citizenship. Rather than break that association, the Spring Offensive seemed to reinforce it. In spite of their organizers' doubts, though, these two protests were assimilated into the "great tradition" of the march on Washington. Subsequent newspaper articles and commemorations have routinely cited both when recalling the past.

For participants in the Mayday protests, however, their tactics and their treatment of the capital were intentionally "un-American" and a challenge to that tradition. Politicians, and many American people, agreed with this assessment. And, they used it to excuse violating participants' rights. The reactions of the media, the Nixon administration, District officials, and the people who wrote to the police revealed that they wanted a firm boundary on the style of Washington protests. The willingness of the president to establish order at all costs and the popular support for his action sent a strong signal to activists in the United States.

The Spring Offensive also helped solidify the critical role of journalists and the media in creating the public meaning of marches on Washington. The idea of an immediate audience witnessing the events as they unfolded was no longer central to the organization of these events.

VVAW staged dramatizations, often with an acute sense of the effect they would have when transmitted by the media. For the half million or more people who participated in the April 24 march, participation seemed largely an end in itself, though reports of the size of the event were widely accepted as critical to its potential success in influencing policy. The organizers' attempts to sharpen the meaning of the event through the inclusion of a variety of messages and explicit inclusiveness had little impact on perceptions of the event as it occurred or in retrospect. The Mayday Tribe was even less tactical about developing a connection between their plans and any identified audience, though they clearly hoped to inspire a new militancy in the anti-war movement generally. As the events played out, mainstream journalists recast and judged these protests in ways that weakened protesters' radical political demands. Television and newspaper reports had done much to establish the popular and political legacy of the civil rights march in 1963. For the protests during the Spring Offensive, however, media—especially television— provided few details of the planning, limited coverage of the events themselves, and mostly ignored the political demands. An overview of the anti-war movement in the *New York Times Magazine* concluded that the protests left the cause at a new low point, even as the article focused its criticism of tactics on the Mayday protests.[76] The media's approach in 1971 oversimplified these complex protests and made them into events judged by the number and nature of their participants and their behavior in the capital.

The divisions among activists, the treatment by the authorities, and the coverage by the media combined to narrow the options for protesting in Washington after 1971. The result is that few protests in the capital would satisfy the expectations of people like the radical activists in 1971 or even like those who made up Coxey's Army in 1894. Nevertheless, the Spring Offensive did add new elements to the march on Washington. All three of the protests displayed a political style that emphasized personal commitment to politics and freedom in behavior. Such an emphasis broke with the concern for orderliness in earlier demonstrations and helped make the peaceful march on Washington a more flexible method to express political views and personal identities. In subsequent years, many more Americans would come to their capital and present their views in their national public space.

EPILOGUE

As I have worked on this book over the last several years, my friends have often joked that I would never finish because there will always be another march on Washington. Truly, the tactic is firmly established in the American political repertoire and if anything only gaining in popularity. For decades now, opponents of abortion have been marching to the Supreme Court annually; supporters of abortions have been rallying on the Mall with regularity. Gay rights activists have arranged a series of massive marches. Evangelical Christians have used the Mall for national prayer meetings. Probably the most memorable march in recent years was the enormous gathering of African American men who went to the Million Man March in 1995 for a "day of atonement." Meanwhile, a welter of other groups has turned to somber vigils or dramatic acts of civil disobedience to present their demands. As early as 1978, a journalist could write with confidence, "Washington has become, in season and out, the demonstration capital of the world." Protests, he concluded, "are a part of the landscape, the rule rather than the exception."[1]

Though marches today share much with their predecessors, the transformation of such demonstrations from anomalous to conventional has been significant. Some of the changes are rhetorical, but still important. No longer do organizers have to justify marching by linking their demonstrations symbolically with other political traditions. The organizers of Coxey's Army claimed they were just a "petition in boots," and the Bonus marchers said they were just doing a "new type of lobbying."

By 1941, organizers of the planned Negro March declared that mass demonstrations in the capital were a distinct and legitimate alternative to voting, lobbying, and petitioning for American citizens. Government officials and the media increasingly accepted this claim. By 1991, demonstrators in Washington against U.S. involvement in the Gulf War carried banners that declared, "To Protest is Patriotic."[2]

Where does this acceptance leave marching on Washington? In this new context, the meanings of the tactic have changed for organizers, participants, authorities, politicians, and journalists. Though legal citizenship in the United States is now much more inclusive than in 1894, there are still different understandings of who are full members of the political nation and how they should behave. In this atmosphere, how can protesters best use these marches to lay claim to American citizenship? How can protesters adapt to the ever-changing spaces of the capital? What political purposes do these protests serve now that they have become so pervasive? To what degree are they effective?

Today, many participants in marches on Washington still seek recognition as United States citizens—a status that continues to embrace both practical privileges and symbolic affirmation. The marches in support of the Equal Rights Amendment in the 1970s and early 1980s also continued to make the claim that women were full citizens of the nation, a claim made by the suffrage marchers at the beginning of the century. Nadine Smith, a director of the March on Washington for Lesbian, Gay, and Bi Equal Rights and Liberation in 1993, emphasized that the protest was to show that "we're on the outside and we want to be let in."[3] The stated purpose of limiting the Million Man March to black men was to present to the country an alternative view of black men from the criminals, deadbeats, or entertainers portrayed so often in the media. Instead, the men who gathered emphasized they had jobs, families, and a sense of responsibility, that they were respectable citizens.[4] For groups whose rights or status as citizens are slighted, the nation's capital has become the preeminent spot to reject such affronts and to claim full membership in the polity.

The success of previous groups making similar claims for recognition has changed the ways marchers typically represent American citizenship: early in the century, marchers represented citizenship against an idealized standard of respectable, white, masculine homogeneity, whereas many marchers today emphasize a new ideal of "diversity." The need for racial, ethnic, gender, religious, or other kinds of diversity had its origins in the need for coalition building, a need that A. Philip Randolph identified in 1941 as critical to staging influential protests. In addition, the growth of identity politics during the 1960s and 1970s made political inclusiveness a goal for most social movements. Organizers continue to seek wide coalitions so that marchers will appear to represent all kinds of Americans. The inclusion of numerous short speeches by representatives of every possible group during the National Peace Action Coalition's April 24 march against the Vietnam War recurred in many marches. As Donna Brazile, the chief coordinator for the Housing Now! march in 1989, frantically pulled together the speakers for the rally, she exulted when she found a Hispanic person willing to appear.[5] In the face of only gradual increases in the diversity of elected officials, who remain overwhelmingly white, wealthy, and male, such efforts suggest how marches on Washington often serve as ideal representations of American democracy.

This emphasis on inclusiveness and diversity in marches has meant trouble for groups representing particular interests or political identities. Groups ignored or excluded by organizers are liable to go on the attack. As soon as the Human Rights Campaign announced plans for the gay rights "Millennium March on Washington for Equality," other activists attacked the Campaign for excluding those who did not "fit into the corporate image of an 'American Family.'" On the other hand, because the marchers at a pro-choice demonstration in 1992 were disproportionately women, white, liberal, and affluent, the editors at the *Washington Times* concluded they did not represent the "run-of-the-mill American."[6] As much as the diversity of the United States is celebrated in most marches, defining the right amount of inclusiveness is difficult.

Public spaces and their symbolic meanings continue to play a crucial role in marching on Washington. Groups of citizens have continued to press the right to protest nearly everywhere in the capital, and court decisions have mainly ratified their claims. In 1972, the Supreme Court finally overturned the regulations of the 1882 Act Regulating the Use of the Capitol Grounds, paving the way for wider access to official spaces in the capital.[7] Individual protesters have held vigils in Lafayette Square for years, leading one judge to rule that sleeping in front of the White House is a legitimate expression of First Amendment rights. Despite the considerable disruption of traffic and commerce created by marches down Pennsylvania Avenue, the District of Columbia routinely issues permits so that groups can march near both the White House and the Capitol.

The Mall, in particular, has become a very useful space for people to convene mass demonstrations. A vast expanse of flat lawn, it allows large crowds to assemble, see each other, and experience themselves as protesting together. It is also removed from the daily operations of the city's commerce and governmental bureaucracy. Hundreds of thousands of people can assemble on the Mall and hardly affect traffic a few blocks away. Symbolically, it is a central location dominated by views of the Capitol Building and the White House. Such a space provides a common meeting ground for people to assemble, with hopes to shape public policy and shift public opinion.

Yet, none of these spaces in the capital should be taken for granted. Since Coxey and Browne led their supporters into the capital, critics have routinely complained that protests threaten the security of the capital. Now, security concerns threaten the right of protesters to public spaces. In 1995, the decision of federal officials to close off a portion of Pennsylvania Avenue to protect the White House from the risk of car bombs changed the nature of marching and protesting in Washington. As soon as the new security provisions were announced, protesters who had been using Lafayette Square for years faced more harassment and new court challenges.[8] After the terrorist attacks of September 11, 2001, federal officials in Washington naturally increased security at the White House, the Capitol, and the monuments on the Mall. Not long after, the Secret Service asked the National Park Service and the Metropolitan Police Department to deny permits for larger protests planned for areas near the White House, including Lafayette Square and the Ellipse. This policy was temporary; the restrictions on the use of the Ellipse were lifted by the end of November and all the limits were subject to review every thirty days. Nevertheless, the fears expressed by a Secret Service assistant director that "large groups . . . could unintentionally provide cover activity" for a terrorist attack on the White House suggest the ways in which authorities continue to see public protests as conflicting with the official uses of the capital.[9]

The availability of such public spaces is also threatened by efforts to improve the economic and ceremonial qualities of the capital. The continuing redevelopment effort along Pennsylvania Avenue has the potential to create powerful new constituencies that may argue against holding future marches in the most well established national public space. As commuters fill the new office buildings, their needs for easy traffic flow may trump the century-long tradition of allowing protests on the Avenue. Likewise, as more tourists flock to attractions, such as United

States Holocaust Memorial Museum and the planned National Museum of the American Indian, their preference for a peaceful visit to the capital may conflict with protesters' need for a location for their protests.[10] In simply spatial terms, the most serious threat is the World War II memorial, currently under construction between the Washington Monument and the Lincoln Memorial. When completed, it will change an open space often used for large demonstrations into an elaborate shrine. Protesters are often banned from similar areas—like the interior of the Lincoln Memorial or Arlington Cemetery—and a ban on large demonstrations in this part of the Mall could change the options for marchers on Washington.[11] As has been the case since Coxey's Army, the way that protesters can use the capital will continue to require complex negotiations between federal and District officials and organizers.

The triumph of marching on Washington—and the genre's adaptability—have raised new questions about the power of such demonstrations in the nation's capital. The tactic has been shaped by a series of negotiated compromises between marchers and authorities—compromises that have opened some opportunities and foreclosed others.

Years of experience with demonstrations in the capital by both organizers and authorities have made these demonstrations increasingly "business as usual," taking away from the excitement that surrounded them in earlier times. Following the path of Bayard Rustin, a cohort of experienced organizers have learned to negotiate the complexities of planning these demonstrations. Nellie Gray has organized a March for Life to the Supreme Court every year since 1973. Alice Cohan, who worked for the National Organization for Women, planned many pro-choice marches and consulted on the March on Washington for Lesbian, Gay and Bi Equal Rights and Liberation in 1993. These expert organizers have become increasingly sophisticated about making sure that participants can see and hear the speeches. They spend considerable sums on sound systems, often assembled by rock concert experts. They have also learned from inaugurations and sporting events to put huge video screens, called Jumbotrons, along the Mall so that participants can see and hear the speakers and entertainers (fig. 33). Frantic organizers for the Million Family March in 2000 admonished congressional representatives, "If we don't have the Jumbotrons, how are we going to get out our message."[12] Clearly, activists today struggle less than earlier organizers did with the problems of negotiating with authorities, recruiting participants, and struggling to articulate their position than they do with the practical logistics of video and sound technology.

District and federal procedures for responding to these protests have also evolved over time. When Coxey's Army marched on Washington in 1894, there were essentially no procedures for handling the situation. The Park Service has since developed detailed requirements for large demonstrations. Park Service officials hold regular meetings with organizers to ensure that protests proceed safely and without disrupting the daily business of the District. Cars and buses must park in suburban commuter lots, and participants take the subway into the center of the city. Such techniques reduce the disruption of traffic that can be caused by these large marches. An increasingly symbiotic relationship has developed between experienced organizers and authorities through the exchange of strategies for ensuring well-run marches on Washington. In the words of one of its officers, the Park Police now has "a world renowned reputation for effectively handling large-scale" demonstrations.[13]

The creation and enforcement of conventions about marching on Washington have foreclosed some options for American protesters. With the establishment of the large march as a legitimate form of political expression, other forms of protest have been dismissed and even ruthlessly suppressed. In a national public space where many different people attempt to carry on national debates, authorities will never approve of all styles of talk and behavior, and journalists will continue to consider only some events worthy of public notice. To meet these expectations, organizers often must compromise their more radical demands and conform to negotiated conventions about protesting. Most notably, since Nixon's effective suppression of the Mayday Tribe's protest in 1971, organizers have rarely called for such wide-scale disruptions of the capital.

Smaller groups of protesters have committed civil disobedience in Washington, but such actions have rarely attracted widespread attention; more often they have resulted in swift arrests by District or federal authorities. Some protesters have prevailed, like the farmers who drove their tractors around the capital and parked them on the Mall in 1978 in defiance of traffic regulations; they were seen as such exemplary citizens that President Carter felt he had little choice but to tolerate the disruption. During the protests against the World Bank and the International Monetary Fund, held in Washington from April 16 to April 18,

FIGURE 33. Million Man marchers filling the Mall and watching Louis Farrakhan on huge Jumbotrons. Though lacking the explicit policy purpose of most marches on Washington and controversial because of Farrakhan's leadership, this demonstration was typical of the accepted march on Washington, with its concern for a high turnout, its lack of any march through the capital in favor of a rally on the Mall, and its emphasis on personal affirmation. (Associated Press)

2000, however, federal and District authorities acted with determination to suppress these protests. They did everything they could to minimize the impact of the protests, from preemptive closing of the organizers' headquarters to sweep arrests. Again, activists objected to the draconian methods. Yet for the most part, as in 1971, journalists and the public accepted the suppression of the protest because its style violated the compromises that define the accepted march on Washington.[14]

The conventionality, familiarity, and predictability of marches have encouraged journalists to treat marches as unremarkable events, to pay less attention to their political demands, and to give them minimal coverage. Instead, organizers are lucky if their events receive a few seconds of mention on the networks' evening news and a well-placed article in major newspapers the next day.[15] Increasingly, the ways in which protests are covered are formulaic. There is almost always a reference to the 1963 March on Washington for Jobs and Freedom, used to gauge whether the present march is sufficiently orderly and inspirational. The resort of journalists to this easy reference not only tends to trivialize the memory of the 1963 march but also avoids dealing directly with the specific goals of contemporary marches.

In addition, journalists continue to use turnout as a key marker of success. Aware of the media's fixation on numbers, organizers, in turn, struggle to attract larger and larger numbers and to contest official estimates by the U.S. Park Police. Almost every group who has marched on Washington in the last three decades of the twentieth century has disputed the Park Service's figures as too low. Print media coverage routinely includes long discussions of the difference between "official" estimates and those of organizers. In 1995, the Million Man March organizers, after the Park Police reported only 400,000 participants, hired an expert who came up with a count of 837,000. They then sued the Park Service, charging the agency with racism. Convinced by this legal challenge that releasing these counts hurt its reputation, the Park Service now refuses to release its counts.[16]

These conflicts over "who counts" are so intense partly because organizers and the media still struggle for a standard by which to define the success of these huge efforts. In the beginning of protesting in the capital, simply gaining some level of tolerance and media attention was an accomplishment. Then, as toleration became routine, the hope for policy changes increased. Today, most people have come to recognize that marches on Washington are unlikely to win immediate policy changes. It is now unimaginable that Congress would pass conciliatory legislation as it did during the Bonus March, or that a president would issue an executive order to prevent a march, as Roosevelt did in response to the Negro March on Washington. Organizers in 1963 knew of this limit but still hoped that the March on Washington for Jobs and Freedom would speed the passage of the Civil Rights Act. By 1971, despite their deep disagreements about the purposes of protesting in the capital, all the organizers recognized that their efforts were not going to end the war. In 2000, Colbert King, a columnist for the *Washington Post,* observed the limits of the tactic with the comment, "No single march ever does the trick."[17]

Because of these limits, groups with national causes do not always go to Washington. In part, the nature of the contemporary media means that dramatic protests can be covered wherever they take place. More importantly, in the wake of the large protests of the 1960s and early 1970s, some activists grew disillusioned with the march on Washington. For example, activists against nuclear power and nuclear weapons frequently used civil disobedience against local symbols of the dangers— power plants, research laboratories, the Nevada test site. Similarly, the fight over abortion has taken place not just in Washington but also in front of clinics across the country, where opponents sought to shut them down and supporters sought to keep them open. These different styles of protest rejected, at times consciously, the orderly large march on Washington.

Given such criticism and limitations, the most effective use of the march on Washington has arguably become personal affirmation and movement building. A columnist wrote accurately—though somewhat contemptuously—of the Million Man March that it "was not so much a petitioning of the government as an exercise in group therapy."[18] When the Promisekeepers, a Christian evangelical group, went to Washington, they too were mainly interested in using the Mall as a place to confirm their commitment to be the best possible Christian men. Even at marches with more specifically political agendas, participants comment on how the actions serve to bring them together with other people. A participant in the 1993 March for Gay Rights—attended by 300,000 according to the Park Police and by more than a million according to organizers— claimed, "It's not the numbers. . . . It's the feeling . . . of being together." A college student who recruited participants for the Million Family March in October 2000 was not so much interested in any specific political change but rather said, "I just love anything that unifies a bunch of people."[19] Inevitably, at all marches, speakers refer to political causes and urge participants to take action, but for many participants the point of gathering in the capital is to make visible and confirm their personal identities.

Other protesters continue to press for more specific policy changes, but they usually couch their aspirations in the language of building momentum for political change. For some who have grown weary with marches, going on another march can restore faith. By 1986, Susan Dworkin, a veteran of the 1963 march and numerous protests for the women's liberation movement, had gradually "given up believing that marching in Washington served any practical political purpose." Nevertheless, she convinced herself to attend the March for Women's Lives in

1986. By the end of the day, inspired by the diversity of the crowd, especially the number of young people, she was convinced the pro-choice struggle would continue. Similarly, one of her political opponents, Reverend Frank A. Pavone, argued that the annual March for Life "gives encouragement to our friends in government" and "encourages us."[20]

Such personal, emotional goals may seem modest when compared with the blustering ambitions of earlier protesters, but they speak to the faith in marches on Washington that keeps Americans returning time after time to the capital. It is a faith rooted not so much in immediate change, but in the power of collective displays of citizenship, a kind of display that is impossible in voting booths or lobbying. These events make hard-won national public spaces into visible counterweights to the official spaces inhabited by elected representatives and appointed officials. Marches on Washington have been and continue to be occasions at which groups of citizens can project their plans and demands on national government, where they can build support for their causes, and act out their own visions of national politics and identity.

NOTES

ABBREVIATIONS

CNCR Records, SCPC: Records of the Center for Nonviolent Conflict Resolution, Haverford College; (RG CDG-A), Swarthmore College Peace Collection, Swarthmore, Pa.

CRDP, MSRC: Civil Rights Documentation Project, Moorland-Spingarn Research Center, Howard University

Davidson Collection, MSRC: Eugene C. Davidson Collection, Moorland-Spingarn Research Center, Howard University

LC: Library of Congress

Marshall Papers, JFKL: Papers of Burke Marshall, John F. Kennedy Presidential Library, National Archives

MPBRS Division, LC: Motion Picture, Broadcasting and Recorded Sound Division, Library of Congress

MPD Records, DCA: Records of the Metropolitan Police Department, District of Columbia (RG 16), District of Columbia Archives

MSRC: Moorland-Spingarn Research Center, Howard University

NA: National Archives

NAACP Records: Records of the National Association for the Advancement of Colored People, Manuscript Division, Library of Congress

NPS-NCP Records, WNRC: National Park Service, National Capital Parks Region Records, Washington National Record Center, Suitland, Md.

NUL Records: Records of the National Urban League, Manuscript Division, Library of Congress

NWP Records, II: Records of the National Woman's Party, Group II, Manuscript Division, Library of Congress

OEP Records, DCA: Records of the Office of Emergency Preparedness, District of Columbia (RG 23), District of Columbia Archives

PCPJ Records: Records of the People's Coalition for Peace and Justice (DG 84), Swarthmore College Peace Collection, Swarthmore, Pa.

Randolph Papers: Papers of A. Philip Randolph, Manuscript Division, Library of Congress

RG 79, NA: National Park Service, National Capital Parks, Subject Files, 1924–51 (RG 79), National Archives

RG 94, NA: Records of the Office of the Adjutant General (RG 94), National Archives

RG 165, NA: Records of the Military Intelligence Division (RG 165), National Archives

RG 351, NA: Records of the Government of the District of Columbia (RG 351), National Archives

Rustin Papers: Papers of Bayard Rustin, Manuscript Division, Library of Congress

Vertical Files, Washingtoniana Collection: Vertical Files, Washingtoniana Collection, Martin Luther King Library, District of Columbia

VVAW Records: Records of the Vietnam Veterans against the War (mss 370), Social Action Collection, State Historical Society of Wisconsin

WHSF, SMOF-Buchanan, NPM, NA: White House Special Files, Staff Members and Office Files: Patrick J. Buchanan, Nixon Presidential Materials, National Archives

WHSF, SMOF-Colson, NPM, NA: White House Special Files, Staff Members and Office Files: Charles Colson, Nixon Presidential Materials, National Archives

WHSF, SMOF-Dean, NPM, NA: White House Special Files, Staff Members and Office Files: John W. Dean III, Nixon Presidential Materials, National Archives

WHSF, SMOF-Haldeman, NPM, NA: White House Special Files, Staff Members and Office Files: H. R. Haldeman, Nixon Presidential Materials, National Archives

WHSF, SMOF-Krogh, NPM, NA: White House Special Files, Staff Members and Office Files: Egil Krogh, Nixon Presidential Materials, National Archives

WHSF-POF, NPM, NA: White House Special Files, President's Office Files, Nixon Presidential Materials, National Archives

INTRODUCTION

1. Randolph's speech is in "Speeches by the Leaders" (National Association for the Advancement of Colored People, 1963), "March on Washington—Speeches and Statements" folder, box A229, group IIIA, NAACP Records.

2. Joseph Hawley (Rep., Conn.), Senate, *Congressional Record,* 53rd Cong., 2nd sess., 20 April 1894, 26, pt. 4:3884.

3. E. P. Thompson, "The Moral Economy of the English Crowd," *Past and Present* 50 (February 1971), 76–136; Paul Gilje, *The Road to Mobocracy: Popular Disorder in New York City, 1763–1834* (Chapel Hill: University of North Carolina Press, 1987); and Peter Shaw, *American Patriots and the Rituals of Revolution* (Cambridge, Mass.: Harvard University Press, 1981).

4. Paul Gilje, *Road to Mobocracy.*

5. Kenneth R. Bowling, *The Creation of Washington, D.C.: The Idea and Location of the American Capital* (Fairfax, Va., and Lanham, Md.: George Mason University Press, 1992); see esp. 30–34, quote from 33. As many scholars have outlined, the motives for putting the capital along the Potomac were complex and varied; see Carl Abbott, *Political Terrain: Washington, D.C.: From Tidewater Town to Global Metropolis* (Chapel Hill: University of North Carolina Press, 1999).

6. On the changing meaning of assembly and petition, see Norman B. Smith, " 'Shall Make No Law Abridging . . .': An Analysis of the Neglected, but Nearly Absolute Right of Petition," *University of Cincinnati Law Review* 54.4 (1986); Colin Leys, "Petitioning in the Nineteenth and Twentieth Centuries," *Political Studies* 3.1 (1955); Thurston Greene, *The Language of the Constitution: A Sourcebook and Guide to the Ideas, Terms, and Vocabulary Used by the Framers of the United States Constitution* (Westport, Conn.: Greenwood Press, 1991), 53–57; and Akhil R. Amar, "The Bill of Rights as a Constitution," *Yale Law Journal* 100.5 (March 1991), esp. 1152–57. The Senate first banned petitioners in 1798; see George P. Furber and Committee on Privileges and Elections, 52nd Cong., 2d. Sess., *Precedents Relating to the Privileges of the Senate of the United States,* 1893, 20–44. A similar change occurred in England as petitioning in person became more common; see David Zaret, "Petitions and the 'Invention' of Public Opinion in the English Revolution," *American Journal of Sociology* 101.6 (1996), 1497–55.

7. See Elbert Peets, "Washington" [1937], chap. in Paul D. Spreiregen, ed., *On the Art of Designing Cities: Selected Essays of Elbert Peets* (Cambridge, Mass.: MIT Press, 1968); and John W. Reps, *Washington on View: The Nation's Capital since 1790* (Chapel Hill: University of North Carolina Press, 1991). On the importance of such ceremonies for creating nations, see Benedict Anderson, *Imagined Communities: Reflections on the Origins and Spread of Nationalism,* 2d ed. (London: Verso, 1991). On the importance of spectators, see Mary P. Ryan, *Women in Public: Between Banners and Ballots, 1825–1880* (Baltimore: Johns Hopkins University Press, 1990).

8. On the evolution of Washington, see Carl Abbott, *Political Terrain;* Alan Lessoff, *The Nation and Its City: Politics, "Corruption," and Progress in Washington, D.C., 1861–1902* (Baltimore: Johns Hopkins University Press, 1994); Constance M. Green, *Washington: Village and Capital, 1800–1878* (Princeton, N.J.: Princeton University Press, 1976 [1962]); and Constance M. Green, *Washington:*

Capital City, 1879–1950 (Princeton, N.J.: Princeton University Press, 1976 [1962]). On lobbying, see Margaret S. Thompson, *The "Spider Web": Congress and Lobbying in the Age of Grant* (Ithaca, N.Y.: Cornell University Press, 1985).

9. See Elbert Peets, "Washington"; and Norma Evenson, "Monumental Spaces," chap. in Richard W. Longstreth, ed., *The Mall in Washington, 1791–1991* (Washington, D.C.: National Gallery of Art, 1991).

10. Kenneth G. Alfers, *Law and Order in the Capital City: A History of the Washington Police, 1800–1886* (Washington, D.C.: George Washington University, 1976); and Richard Sylvester, *District of Columbia Police: A Retrospect of the Police Organizations of the Cities of Washington and Georgetown and the District of Columbia, with Biographical Sketches, Illustrations and Historic Cases* (Washington, D.C.: Gibson Bros., 1894). *An Act to Regulate the Use of the Capitol Grounds,* Senate 789, *Congressional Record,* 47th Cong., 1st sess., 26 June 1882, 13, pt. 6:5357. The Act appears to have been part of a campaign spearheaded by Senator Justin Morrill of Vermont to improve the atmosphere of the Capitol. According to Morrill's spoken comments, the problem in 1882 was not that of protest, but of vandalism. Justin Morrill (Rep., Vt.), Senate, *Congressional Record,* 47th Cong., 1st sess., 16 March 1882, 13, pt. 2:1949. This Act had a lasting effect on demonstrations in Washington. Not until the 1970s were its restrictions on public speaking and parading determined to be violations of the First Amendment. The law was overturned in *Jeannette Rankin Brigade v. Chief of Capitol Police,* 342 F. Supp. 575 (1972), and the Supreme Court upheld the decision in *Chief of Capitol Police v. Jeannette Rankin Brigade,* 409 U.S. 972 (1972).

11. On the encampment, see Stuart C. McConnell, *Glorious Contentment: The Grand Army of the Republic, 1865–1900* (Chapel Hill: University of North Carolina Press, 1992), 14–15; and Alan Lessoff, *The Nation and Its City,* 157.

12. Susan G. Davis, *Parades and Power: Street Theatre in Nineteenth-Century Philadelphia* (Philadelphia: Temple University Press, 1986).

13. On mainstream parties, see Michael E. McGerr, *The Decline of Popular Politics: The American North, 1865–1928* (New York: Oxford University Press, 1986). On third parties, Lawrence Goodwyn, *The Populist Moment: A Short History of the Agrarian Revolution in America* (New York: Oxford University Press, 1978); and Robert C. McMath Jr., *American Populism: A Social History, 1877–1898* (New York: Hill and Wang, 1993).

14. See Iver Bernstein, *The New York City Draft Riots: Their Significance for American Society and Politics in the Age of the Civil War* (New York: Oxford University Press, 1990).

15. Henry Watterson, "The Political Situation, *Louisville Courier-Journal* [January 5, 1877]," reprinted in Arthur Krock, ed., *The Editorials of Henry Watterson* (New York: George H. Doran, 1923), 55. For Tilden's objections, see Abram S. Hewitt, "Secret History of the Disputed Election, 1876–77," chap. in Allan Nevins, ed., *Selected Writings of Abram S. Hewitt* (New York: Columbia University Press, 1937), 163. For Grant's reaction, see William S. McFeely, *Grant: A Biography* (New York: Norton, 1981), 447; and Roy Morris Jr., " 'Master Fraud of the Century': The Disputed Election of 1876," *American His-*

tory Illustrated 23.7 (November 1988). For the announcements of plans, see "Dennis Kearney, the Agitator," *Washington Evening Star,* 29 July 1878, 1. For reports of the actual speech, see "Kearney at the Capitol," *Washington Evening Star,* 30 August 1878, 4; "Kearney at the Capital," *New York Times,* 30 August 1878, 5; and "Kearney on a Rampage in Washington," *San Francisco Chronicle,* 30 August 1878, 3. The only complete coverage of the events at the Capitol came in the *Chronicle,* for which Browne was an occasional contributor and most likely the author of these stories.

16. In addition, it helps to illustrate how much observers and participants at the time of these protests saw the events in light of their other political experiences. For more on this view, see Doug McAdam, *Political Process and the Development of Black Insurgency, 1930–1970* (Chicago: University of Chicago Press, 1982).

17. My preference for the term "public space" rather than "public sphere" has come out of conversations with the historical sociologist David Zaret and historian Ari Kelman, and reading their work. See David Zaret, "Petitions and the 'Invention' of Public Opinion, 1497–1555," and Ari Kelman, *A River and Its City: An Environmental History of New Orleans* (Berkeley: University of California Press, 2003). The most useful overview of the discussion about the public sphere appears in Craig Calhoun, "Introduction: Habermas and the Public Sphere," chap. in Craig Calhoun, ed., *Habermas and the Public Sphere* (Cambridge, Mass.: MIT Press, 1992).

At times, protesters, casual users, and scholars have claimed that there are no rules governing the use of such areas. For example, M. Christine Boyer presents an idealized, but unidentified, vision of public space that is open to "the entire populace, all groups, all neighborhoods, all regions of the country." See M. C. Boyer, "The City of Illusion: New York's Public Places," chap. in Paul L. Knox, ed., *The Restless Urban Landscape* (Englewood Cliffs, N.J.: Prentice-Hall, 1993). For the evolution of constraints, see Roy Rosenzweig and Elizabeth Blackmar, *The Park and the People: A History of Central Park* (Ithaca, N.Y.: Cornell University Press, 1992), introduction; Don Mitchell, "The End of Public Space? People's Park, Definitions of the Public, and Democracy," *Annals of the Association of American Geographers* 85.1 (1995), 108–33; and Murray Edelman, "Space and the Social Order," *Journal of Architectural Education* 32 (November 1978), 1–9. For Tiananmen Square, see David Strand, "Protest in Beijing: Civil Society and the Public Sphere in China," *Problems of Communism* 39 (May/June 1990), 1–9.

18. Thomas B. Edsall and Mary D. Edsall, *Chain Reaction: The Impact of Race, Rights, and Taxes on American Politics* (New York: Norton, 1991); and James A. Morone, *The Democratic Wish: Popular Participation and the Limits of American Government* (New York: Basic Books, 1990).

1. "WITHOUT PRECEDENT"

1. Carlos A. Schwantes, *Coxey's Army: An American Odyssey* (Lincoln: University of Nebraska Press, 1985), 259. The speech was printed in remarks by

William Allen (Pop., Neb.), Senate, *Congressional Record,* 53rd Cong., 2d sess., 9 May 1894, 26, pt. 5:4512.

2. *An Act to Regulate the Use of the Capitol Grounds,* Senate 789, *Congressional Record,* 47th Cong., 1st sess., 26 June 1882, 13, pt. 6:5357. The terms of this law affected the way marchers approached the Capitol Building for ninety years; it was overturned by judicial action in 1972. The details are discussed in the introduction in note 10.

3. *Telegram,* 3 April 1894, quoted in Herman C. Voeltz, "Coxey's Army in Oregon, 1894," *Oregon Historical Quarterly* 65 (September 1964), 168; Joseph Hawley (Rep., Conn.), Senate, *Congressional Record,* 53rd Cong., 2d sess., 20 April 1894, 26, pt. 4:3884.

4. On Coxey's biography, see Donald L. McMurry, *Coxey's Army: A Study of the Industrial Army Movement of 1894* (Seattle: University of Washington Press, 1968 [1929]), 21–26; Carlos A. Schwantes, *Coxey's Army,* 34–36; Henry Vincent, *The Story of the Commonweal* (New York: Arno, 1969 [1894]), 49–50; Shirley P. Austin, "The Downfall of Coxeyism," *Chautauquan* 18 (July 1894), 452; and Bernard Howson, "Jacob Sechler Coxey: A Biography of a Monetary Reformer, 1854–1951" (Ph.D. diss., Ohio State University, 1973). For other labor radicals and businessmen of the time, see Herbert G. Gutman, *Work, Culture, and Society in Industrializing America: Essays in American Working-Class and Social History* (New York: Knopf, 1977), esp. "Protestantism and the American Labor Movement" chap.; Paul Krause, *The Battle for Homestead, 1880–1892: Politics, Culture, and Steel* (Pittsburgh: University of Pittsburgh Press, 1992), esp. "The Life and Times of 'Beeswax' Taylor: Exemplary Paradoxes of American Labor" chap.

5. On the course of the depression, Samuel T. McSeveney, *The Politics of Depression: Political Behavior in the Northeast, 1893–1896* (New York: Oxford University Press, 1972), 33–35; rates of unemployment from Charles Hoffman, *The Depression of the Nineties: An Economic History* (Westport, Conn.: Greenwood, 1970), 106; see also Samuel Rezneck, "Unemployment, Unrest and Relief in the United States during the Depression of 1893–1897," *Journal of Political Economy* 61 (August 1953), 324–45.

6. On labor in this period, see David Montgomery, *The Fall of the House of Labor: The Workplace, the State, and American Labor Activism, 1865–1925* (New York: Cambridge University Press, 1987). On Populists, see Lawrence Goodwyn, *The Populist Moment: A Short History of the Agrarian Revolution in America* (New York: Oxford University Press, 1978), and Robert C. McMath, *American Populism: A Social History, 1877–1898* (New York: Hill and Wang, 1993). On changes in political culture and the responsibilities of the national government, see Morton Keller, *Affairs of State: Public Life in Late Nineteenth Century America* (Cambridge, Mass.: Harvard University Press, 1977); and Michael E. McGerr, *The Decline of Popular Politics: The American North, 1865–1928* (New York: Oxford University Press, 1986).

7. On the "good roads" movement, see Howard L. Preston, *Dirt Roads to Dixie: Accessibility and Modernization in the South, 1885–1935* (Knoxville: University of Tennessee Press, 1991), 12, 26. This description is taken from the bill as it was announced in 1894, but according to Coxey, this was the same bill

he had drawn up in 1891; Henry Vincent, *Story of the Commonweal,* 52–53. Estimates of federal spending and hourly wages from Charles Hoffman, *The Depression of the Nineties,* 219, 257.

8. See numerous examples of such claims in Franklin Folsom, *Impatient Armies of the Poor: The Story of Collective Action of the Unemployed, 1808–1942* (Niwot: University Press of Colorado, 1991). For efforts in the 1870s that were mostly unsuccessful, see Herbert G. Gutman, "The Failure of the Movement by the Unemployed for Public Works in 1873," *Political Science Quarterly* 80 (June 1965), 254–76. For specific programs that were adopted, see Leah H. Feder, *Unemployment Relief in Periods of Depression: A Study of Measures Adopted in Certain American Cities, 1857 through 1922* (New York: Russell Sage Foundation, 1936), esp. 72–97.

9. See Robert H. Wiebe, *The Search for Order, 1877–1920* (New York: Hill and Wang, 1967), 111–27.

10. This account of Browne's life draws on Henry Vincent, *Story of the Commonweal,* 109–13; and Browne's memoirs, Carl S. Browne, *When Coxey's Army Marcht on Washington* (San Francisco: n.p., 1944) (the unusual spelling, "marcht," is Browne's). See also Donald L. McMurry, *Coxey's Army,* 30–32.

11. On the Chinese Exclusion movement, see Elmer Sandmeyer, *The Anti-Chinese Movement in California* (Urbana: University of Illinois Press, 1973); Alexander Saxton, *The Indispensable Enemy: Labor and the Anti-Chinese Movement in California* (Berkeley: University of California Press, 1971); and Neil L. Shumsky, *The Evolution of Political Protest and the Workingmen's Party of California* (Columbus: Ohio State University Press, 1992). For Browne's dramatic account, greatly exaggerating the importance of the event at the Capitol, see Henry Vincent, *Story of the Commonweal,* 110. For newspaper coverage, see "Kearney at the Capitol," *Washington Evening Star,* 30 August 1878, 4; "Kearney at the Capital," *New York Times,* 30 August 1878, 5; and "Kearney on a Rampage in Washington," *San Francisco Chronicle,* 30 August 1878, 3.

12. Henry Vincent, *Story of the Commonweal,* 110–11. On theosophy generally, see S. F. Hecht, "Essence of Theosophy," *Current Literature* 15 (March 1894), 269.

13. On the importance of the networks forged at such events to social movements and political protest, see Sidney G. Tarrow, *Power in Movement: Social Movements, Collective Action, and Politics* (New York: Cambridge University Press, 1994), 54–57; Henry Vincent, *Story of the Commonweal,* 112; on the Bimetallic Convention, see Carlos A. Schwantes, *Coxey's Army,* 24–25; on Browne's visit to Ohio, ibid., 28–32.

14. Coxey details these steps in Jacob S. Coxey, "To the Members of the Public," Bulletin No. 6 of the J. S. Coxey Good Roads Association of U.S., 25 January 1895, Papers of Jacob Sechler Coxey Sr., 1874–1976, at Massillon Museum (Columbus: Ohio Historical Society, 1977[?]), reel 2 (cited hereafter as Coxey Papers).

15. Carl S. Browne, *When Coxey's Army Marcht,* 5; Carlos A. Schwantes, *Coxey's Army,* 32–33.

16. Carl S. Browne, *When Coxey's Army Marcht,* 5; Henry Vincent, *Story of the Commonweal,* 50, 112. Carl S. Browne, "On to Washington," Bulletin No.

2 of the J. S. Coxey Good Roads Association, 31 January 1894, Coxey Papers, reel 1; Jacob S. Coxey, "To the Members," Coxey Papers, reel 2.

17. Osman C. Hooper, "The Coxey Movement in Ohio," *Ohio State Archeological and Historical Society* 9 (1901), 162–64. In associating their cause with Christ so directly, Browne showed the influence of working-class notions that Christians should work to change the industrial system rather than passively await salvation; see Clark Halker, "Jesus Was a Carpenter: Labor Song-Poets, Labor Protest, and True Religion in Gilded Age America," *Labor History* 32.2 (Spring 1991), 273–90.

18. Jacob S. Coxey, "To the Members," Coxey Papers; Henry Vincent, *Story of the Commonweal,* 52–53.

19. "The Coxey Crusade," *Review of Reviews* 10 (July 1894), 64. Regarding May 1, see Michael Kazin and Steven J. Ross, "America's Labor Day: The Dilemma of a Workers' Celebration," *Journal of American History* 78.4 (March 1992), 1304–5; and Eric J. Hobsbawm, *Workers: Worlds of Labor* (New York: Pantheon Books, 1984), 74–79.

20. Coxey's May 1 speech quoted in William Allen, Senate, 4512. Demands quoted in Donald L. McMurry, *Coxey's Army,* 305. Fry may have taken the term "Industrial Army" from Edward Bellamy, *Looking Backward, 2000–1887* (Boston: Houghton Mifflin, 1966 [1888]). On Fry, Carlos A. Schwantes, *Coxey's Army,* 86–87; on Redstone's background, 143. For Redstone's activities, "A Fizzle at the Start," *Washington Post,* 15 March 1894, 1.

21. William Peffer (Pop., Kans.), Senate, *Congressional Record,* 53rd Cong., 2d sess., 19 March 1894, 26, pt. 4:3076.

22. "Army of Tramps" from "The March of Tramps to Washington," *Independent* 46 (26 April 1894), 10–11. On the development of the wire services, see the detailed and authoritative account in Richard A. Schwarzlose, *The Nation's Newsbrokers, Volume 2: The Rush to Institution from 1865 to 1920* (Evanston, Ill.: Northwestern University Press, 1990); and Menahem Blondheim, *News over the Wires: The Telegraph and the Flow of Public Information in America, 1844–1897* (Cambridge, Mass.: Harvard University Press, 1994). On the power of these new forms of media to spread stories across the country, see Carl S. Smith, *Urban Disorder and the Shape of Belief: The Great Chicago Fire, the Haymarket Bomb, and the Model Town of Pullman* (Chicago: University of Chicago Press, 1995), esp. 28.

23. Browne claimed responsibility for these reports; Carl S. Browne, *When Coxey's Army Marcht,* 7. Schwantes gives credit to the reporter; Carlos A. Schwantes, *Coxey's Army,* 40.

24. Baker's experience comes from Ray S. Baker, *American Chronicle* (New York: Charles Scribner's Sons, 1945), 6–15; the number of reporters and Western Union operators is noted in W. T. Stead, " 'Coxeyism': A Character Sketch," *American Review of Reviews* 10 (July 1894), 52. Schwantes found information in "142 runs of newspapers from 31 states and territories and the District of Columbia"; Carlos A. Schwantes, *Coxey's Army,* 281.

25. Carlos A. Schwantes, *Coxey's Army,* 83–97; Carl S. Browne, *When Coxey's Army Marcht,* 8; Henry Vincent, *Story of the Commonweal,* 105; "In Dreams He Sees an Army," *New York Times,* 25 March 1894, 5. "Coxey's Army Start," *Washington Post,* 26 March 1894, 2. That the source of this story is the

wire services is indicated by the fact that the story in the *New York Times* on the same day used identical language in several places, see "Coxey's Army on the Move," *New York Times,* 26 March 1894, 1.

26. W. T. Stead, "Coxeyism," 48. Each day, newspapers carried stories detailing where the marchers had camped, the reaction of the local people, the weather, and their numbers. On the phenomenon of the serial story, see Thomas J. Schlereth, *Victorian America: Transformations in Everyday Life, 1876–1915* (New York: HarperCollins, 1991), 182–87.

27. Quote from "Traveling All Night," *Washington Post,* 19 April 1894, 2. On Haymarket, see Paul Avrich, *The Haymarket Tragedy* (Princeton, N.J.: Princeton University Press, 1984); David R. Roediger and Franklin Rosemont, *Haymarket Scrapbook* (Chicago: C. H. Kerr Pub. Co., 1986); and Carl S. Smith, *Urban Disorder.*

28. Carlos A. Schwantes, *Coxey's Army,* 149–65; *Times* quoted 161. The use of the federal troops was authorized by Attorney General Richard Olney and was considered appropriate since the economic depression had driven the Northern Pacific into receivership supervised by a federal bankruptcy court. Consequently, an attack on the Northern Pacific was considered an attack on the federal government. This policy and precedents for it are described in Gerald G. Eggert, *Railroad Labor Disputes: The Beginnings of Federal Strike Policy* (Ann Arbor: University of Michigan Press, 1967), 136–52.

29. *Independent* 46 (29 March 1894), 11.

30. The prevalence of veterans' organizations, like the Grand Army of the Republic, also heightened the association of "army" with organized groups; see Stuart C. McConnell, *Glorious Contentment: The Grand Army of the Republic, 1865–1900* (Chapel Hill: University of North Carolina Press, 1992). While naturally the term implied a kind of armed militancy, this association was not always present. The Salvation Army's entry into the United States in 1879 gave the term a Christian tinge; Thomas J. Schlereth, *Victorian America,* 268.

31. "Coxey's Army on the Move," 1; *Gazette* and *Ledger* quoted in *Public Opinion* 17 (12 April 1894), 43–44. John McCook, "Tramps," *Charities Review* 3 (December 1893), 59. On tramps, see Michael B. Katz, *Poverty and Policy in American History* (New York: Academic Press, 1983), 151–81; Michael Davis, "Forced to Tramp: The Perspective of the Labor Press, 1877–1900," chap. in Eric H. Monkkonen, ed., *Walking to Work: Tramps in America, 1790–1935* (Lincoln: University of Nebraska Press, 1984). The most thorough treatment of tramps is Paul T. Ringenbach, *Tramps and Reformers, 1873–1916: The Discovery of Unemployment in New York* (Westport, Conn.: Greenwood, 1973).

32. "The March of Tramps to Washington," 10–11.

33. For broader discussions of citizenship during this period, see Linda K. Kerber, *No Constitutional Right to Be Ladies: Women and the Obligations of Citizenship* (New York: Hill and Wang, 1998); Michael Schudson, *The Good Citizen: A History of American Civic Life* (New York: Martin Kessler Books, 1998); and Rogers M. Smith, *Civic Ideals: Conflicting Visions of Citizenship in U.S. History* (New Haven, Conn.: Yale University Press, 1997). For early plans of the authorities, "Laws to Squelch Him," *Washington Post,* 24 March 1894, 1. On Cleveland's intercession, see "In Advance of Coxey," *Washington Post,* 24 April 1894, 2.

34. For descriptions of the reception given the marchers, see Henry Vincent, *Story of the Commonweal,* 55–56; and "Coxey's Army on the Move," 1. On the symbolic importance of marching in ranks, see William H. McNeill, *Keeping Together in Time: Dance and Drill in Human History* (Cambridge, Mass.: Harvard University Press, 1995), esp. 101–52. On a resurgence of interest in the American flag during this period, see Michael G. Kammen, *Mystic Chords of Memory: The Transformation of Tradition in American Culture* (New York: Knopf, 1991), 181–205. On the close relationship between family and citizenship, see Linda K. Kerber, *No Constitutional Right to Be Ladies,* and Michael Schudson, *Good Citizen.*

35. Carol Pateman and Nancy Fraser have shown how gendered assumptions and values shaped the eighteenth-century notion of citizens: see Carol Pateman, *The Disorder of Women: Democracy, Feminism, and Political Theory* (Stanford, Calif.: Stanford University Press, 1989); Nancy Fraser, "Struggle over Needs: Outline of a Socialist-Feminist Critical Theory of Late Capitalist Political Culture," chap. in *Unruly Practices: Power, Discourse, and Gender in Contemporary Social Theory* (Minneapolis: University of Minnesota Press, 1989); and Nancy Fraser, "Rethinking the Public Sphere: A Contribution to the Critique of Actually Existing Democracy," chap. in Craig Calhoun, ed., *Habermas and the Public Sphere* (Cambridge, Mass.: MIT Press, 1992). My thanks to Ruth Feldstein for her insights into the relationship of citizenship to the march. The marchers' trip is described in detail in Carlos A. Schwantes, *Coxey's Army,* 49–82, 168–72.

36. "Straightforward" from Stanley Waterloo, "Introduction" to Henry Vincent, *Story of the Commonweal,* 12. "Coxey in New York," *Washington Post,* 22 April 1894, 1.

37. Carl S. Browne, *When Coxey's Army Marcht,* 16. Women in Los Angeles sang for a group of men as they departed; Henry W. Splitter, "Concerning Vinette's Los Angeles Regiment of Coxey's Army," *Pacific Historical Review* 17 (February 1948), 31. Diggs quoted in "Lauding Coxey's Band," *Washington Post,* 22 April 1894, 3.

38. These arguments generated their own problems, as journalists uncovered accusations from Coxey's first wife that he had not paid her alimony on time; see "Mrs. Caroline Coxey's Wrath," *Washington Post,* 8 May 1894.

39. "Lauding Coxey's Band," 3; "Agitation among the Women," *Washington Post,* 25 April 1894, 1; Carl S. Browne, "On to Washington," Coxey Papers, reel 1. Reports of rejection of women: "Coxey's Clever Move," *Washington Post,* 21 March 1894, 2; and Henry Vincent, *Story of the Commonweal,* 123, 143.

40. Coxey quoted in Henry Vincent, *Story of the Commonweal,* 51; Henry Frank, "The Crusade of the Unemployed," *Arena* 10 (July 1894), 242.

41. Coxey and Browne, like the Populists and other working-class groups, were trying to create on the national level a sense of the moral economy that was critical to local demonstrations. See E. P. Thompson, "The Moral Economy of the English Crowd," *Past and Present* 50 (February 1971), 76–136; Norman Pollack, *The Just Polity: Populism, Law and Human Welfare* (Urbana: University of Illinois Press, 1987).

42. Coxey quoted in Henry Vincent, *Story of the Commonweal,* 51, 61; "favored few," H. L. Stetson, "The Industrial Army," *Independent* 46 (31 May

1894), 5. Norman Pollack argues that the Populist movement as a whole tended to share the Commonwealers' faith in the power of national government to solve the country's problems if run properly. Norman Pollack, *Just Polity.*

43. See reports in *Independent* 46 (5 April 1894), 9; and "Traveling All Night," 2.

44. Vincent's official history often used the framework of conversion when he described the Commonwealers' encounters with communities. Hostile towns and fearful townspeople had only to see the men and they embraced them and their cause. See Henry Vincent, *Story of the Commonweal,* 58–75. In Jack London's account of his days with Fry's Army in the West, he also pointed to the support of neighboring communities; Jack London, *Jack London on the Road: The Tramp Diary, and Other Hobo Writings,* Richard W. Etulain, ed. (Logan: Utah State University Press, 1979), 49–54. By the end of April, police plans to manage Coxey's Army no longer included simply arresting them as tramps; see "Police Precautions," *Washington Post,* 30 April 1894, 2.

45. Guard in the Capitol, "Fizzle at the Start," 1. On militia, "Preparing for Coxey," *Washington Post,* 23 March 1894, 1. On Secret Service, Matthew F. Griffin, "Secret Service Memories [Part 1]," *Flynn's* 13 (13 March 1926), 906–27; and Matthew F. Griffin, "Secret Service Memories [Part 2]," *Flynn's* 14 (20 March 1926), 86–98. Some of their reports were sent to the White House; William P. Hazen to John G. Carlisle, 20 April 1894, *Grover Cleveland Papers, 1828–1945* (Washington, D.C.: Presidential Papers Microfilm, Library of Congress, 1958), reel 84; William P. Hazen to John G. Carlisle, 24 April 1894, *Cleveland Papers,* reel 84; and William P. Hazen to John G. Carlisle, 26 April 1894, *Cleveland Papers,* reel 84. Moore's plans in "Two Now in Coxey's Army," *New York Times,* 24 March 1894, 3. On April 14, District Commissioner George Truesdell met with Henry Thurber, Cleveland's personal secretary, to discuss methods of controlling the army; letter enclosing the relevant regulations, George Truesdell to Henry Thurber, 15 April 1894, *Cleveland Papers,* reel 84.

46. William Peffer (Pop., Kans.), Senate, *Congressional Record,* 53rd Cong., 2d sess., 19 April 1894, 26, pt. 4:3842–43. William Allen (Pop., Neb.), Senate, *Congressional Record,* 53rd Cong., 2d sess., 19 April 1894, 26, pt. 4:3843–44. Others echoed Allen's complaints about the different treatment of lobbyists than that planned for the Commonwealers. Stetson compared the Commonweal to the "Chamber of Commerce of New York City," which "sent its members by carload to Washington to influence Congress"; H. L. Stetson, "Industrial Army," 5. For background on lobbyists during this period, see James Bryce, whose temperate view of lobbyists attributes the prevalence of such people on Capitol Hill to the committee system in Congress; James B. Bryce, *The American Commonwealth: Vol. 1, the National Government, the State Governments* (London: Macmillan, 1891), 647–52.

47. William Allen (Pop., Neb.), Senate, *Congressional Record,* 53rd Cong., 2d sess., 26 April 1894, 26, pt. 5:4106. While the attacks on the Commonweal shared a common interpretation of the threat posed by the demonstration, partisan politics did shape the explanations for the cause of the protest. Republicans tended to argue that Democrats' attempts to reduce the tariff—being debated at the same time—had caused the economic crisis and thus given the marchers their

cause. Democrats preferred to argue that the "followers of Coxey learned their lesson from the Republicans," whose protectionist stance encouraged people to ask for help from the national government; *Louisville Courier-Journal* quoted in *Public Opinion* 17 (26 April 1894), 95. The Republican *Boston Advertiser* predicted that if Congress were to "defeat the Wilson bill and then adjourn promptly, there would be little heard of Coxey or his Army thereafter"; quoted in *Public Opinion* 17 (26 April 1894), 95.

48. Grover Cleveland, "Inaugural Address, March 4, 1893," in *Inaugural Addresses of the Presidents of the United States from George Washington, 1789, to Richard Milhous Nixon, 1969* (Washington, D.C.: U.S. GPO, 1969), 165.

49. Edward Wolcott (Rep., Colo.), Senate, *Congressional Record,* 53rd Cong., 2d sess., 26 April 1894, 26, pt. 5:4107.

50. Joseph Hawley, Senate, 3884; "Bourke Cockran's Idea of Coxeyism," *New York Times,* 1 May 1894, 2.

51. On the investigation of strikes, Mary O. Furner, "The Republican Tradition and the New Liberalism," chap. in Michael J. Lacey and Mary O. Furner, eds., *The State and Social Investigation in Britain and the United States* (Washington, D.C.: Woodrow Wilson Center Press, 1993), 171–241. Lauros G. McConachie, *Congressional Committees: A Study of the Origin and Development of Our National and Local Legislative Methods* (New York: Crowell, 1898), 56, 63.

52. Joseph Dolph (Rep., Conn.), Senate, *Congressional Record,* 53rd Cong., 2d sess., 26 April 1894, 26, pt. 5:4107.

53. When asked subsequently if anyone had ever been arrested under this statute, Police Superintendent Moore said "No"; "Coxey before a Jury," *Washington Post,* 5 May 1894, 1. "Odd Fellows in Line," *Washington Post,* 27 April 1894, 5. Vincent thought this event was staged to set the precedent for the Coxey Army; Henry Vincent, *Story of the Commonweal,* 329. See also testimony about the failure to enforce this provision in William Allen, Senate, 3844.

54. Quote from B. R. Keim, *Keim's Illustrated Hand-Book: Washington and Its Environs: A Descriptive and Historical Hand-Book of the Capital of the United States of America* (Washington, D.C., 1884), 20. See also George G. Evans, *Visitors' Companion at Our Nation's Capital: A Complete Guide for Washington and Its Environs* (Philadelphia: G. G. Evans, 1892). On improvements to the capital, see Alan Lessoff, *The Nation and Its City: Politics, "Corruption," and Progress in Washington, D.C., 1861–1902* (Baltimore: Johns Hopkins University Press, 1994); and Carl Abbott, *Political Terrain: Washington, D.C., From Tidewater Town to Global Metropolis* (Chapel Hill: University of North Carolina Press, 1999).

55. John Tracey, "Emergency Relief at Washington," *American Review of Reviews* 19 (March 1894), 295–96; "$30,000 for the Poor," *Washington Post,* 9 December 1893, 2. "Relief Work Closed," *Washington Post,* 4 April 1894, 5. On visits to the camp, "Coxey and His 300," *Washington Post,* 30 April 1894, 1; Carlos A. Schwantes, *Coxey's Army,* 173.

56. "Coxey and his 300," 1; "Police Precautions," 2; "600 Policemen on Duty," *Washington Post,* 1 May 1894, 2; *New York Times,* 1 May 1894, 4; "The Attenuation of Coxey," *Washington Post,* 30 April 1894, 4.

57. "On the Capitol Steps," *Washington Post,* 1 May 1894, 1; "Coxey Will Defy the Law," *New York Times,* 1 May 1894, 1.

58. In the 1890s, courts still interpreted the rights established by the First Amendment in relatively narrow terms; they routinely allowed authorities to prevent protests in public streets and parks. Still, District authorities recognized that Coxey's Army's plans for a protest directed at Congress clearly came within the scope of the Amendment. On the right to assemble, see Samuel Walker, *In Defense of American Liberties: A History of the ACLU* (New York: Oxford University Press, 1990), 28, 55, 108–11; M. G. Abernathy, *The Right of Assembly and Association* (Columbia: University of South Carolina Press, 1981); and Robin Handley, "Public Order, Petitioning and Freedom of Assembly," *Journal of Legal History* 7 (1986), 136–38.

59. "Property of people" from Coxey's speech, reprinted in William Allen, Senate, 4512. Accounts of the march, "Climax of Folly," *Washington Post,* 2 May 1894, 1; Carl S. Browne, *When Coxey's Army Marcht,* 18–22.

60. This fact was reflected in the title of Woodrow Wilson's influential book on Congress; Woodrow Wilson, *Congressional Government: A Study in American Politics* (Boston: Houghton, Mifflin, 1885); Margaret S. Thompson, *The "Spider Web": Congress and Lobbying in the Age of Grant* (Ithaca, N.Y.: Cornell University Press, 1985), 28.

61. On importance of crowds, see Susan Herbst, *Numbered Voices: How Opinion Polling Has Shaped American Politics* (Chicago: University of Chicago Press, 1993). On makeup of crowd, see "Climax of Folly," 1.

62. Carl S. Browne, *When Coxey's Army Marcht,* 21; "600 Policemen," 2.

63. See photograph in Mary Cable, *The Avenue of the Presidents* (Boston: Houghton Mifflin, 1969), 172. A member of Congress noted that the several congressmen were "within sight" of the police beating the crowd back; Tom Johnson (Dem., Ohio), House, *Congressional Record,* 53rd Cong., 2d sess., 2 May 1894, 26, pt. 5:4335.

64. Carl S. Browne, *When Coxey's Army Marcht,* 23; [Anonymous], Telegram, 1 May 1894, *Cleveland Papers,* reel 84; A. C. Hall, "An Observer in Coxey's Camp," *Independent* 46 (17 May 1894), 4.

65. [Anonymous], Telegram, on police actions; *Washington Evening Star* quoted in A. C. Hall, "Observer in Coxey's Camp," 4; for Coxey's view of Capitol, see the speech he had planned to give, reprinted in William Allen, Senate, 4512.

66. Kate Foote, "Our Washington Letter," *Independent* (10 May 1894), 6.

67. "Coxey Had His Day," *Washington Post,* 2 May 1894, 4.

68. "Browne's Special Order," *Washington Post,* 2 May 1894, 2.

69. William Allen, Senate, 4512–14.

70. "Coxey on the Stand," *Washington Post,* 8 May 1894. See "[Trial Coverage]," *Washington Post,* 4 May 1894–22 May 1894.

71. William Allen, Senate, 4511–16.

72. John Sherman (Rep., Ohio), Senate, *Congressional Record,* 53rd Cong., 2d sess., 9 May 1894, 26, pt. 5:4517; John Gordon (Dem., Ga.), Senate, *Congressional Record,* 53rd Cong., 2d sess., 10 May 1894, 26, pt. 5:4564, 4565; George Hoar (Rep., Mass.), Senate, *Congressional Record,* 53rd Cong., 2d sess., 10 May 1894, 26, pt. 5:4570.

73. Crisp quoted in *Public Opinion* 17 (26 April 1894), 136; "Coxey before a Committee," *Washington Post,* 10 May 1894, 7.

74. Carlos A. Schwantes, *Coxey's Army,* 224–26; "War on the Tramps," *Washington Post,* 2.

75. "Prison Doors Opened," *Washington Post,* 11 June 1894, 1.

76. The sympathetic *Review of Reviews* saw the July Fourth plans as an attempt to restore the "prestige of the movement" by expressing "a most excellent patriotic feeling." *American Review of Reviews* 10 (July 1894), 5; this report notes that Browne planned to include in the parade "a good many thousands of the colored people of the District of Columbia." Description of the event, "A Bit of Buffoonery," *Washington Post,* 5 July 1894, 1.

77. On Browne's departure, see "Oklahoma Sam in Command," *Washington Post,* 8 July 1894, 3; Jacob S. Coxey, "To the Members," Coxey Papers, reel 2. "Record of Political Events," *Political Science Quarterly* 9 (December 1894), 769–71; *Washington Post,* July 5–August 10, 1894. For the details on the bitter strike in the summer of 1894, see Stanley Buder, *Pullman: An Experiment in Industrial Order and Community Planning, 1880–1930* (New York: Oxford University Press, 1967).

78. Joseph V. Tracy, "A Mission to Coxey's Army," *Catholic World* 59 (August 1894), 666–80; account of their last days based on Carlos A. Schwantes, *Coxey's Army,* 246–60; and miscellaneous articles on Coxey's Army, *Washington Post,* 10–15 August 1894.

79. Michael Parrish, *Anxious Decades: America in Prosperity and Depression, 1920–1941* (New York: Norton, 1992); Howard L. Preston, *Dirt Roads to Dixie.*

80. *Old C. Collier, On to Washington; or, Old Cap. Collier With the Coxey Army,* Norman L. Munro, pseud. (New York: Munro's Publishing House, 1894).

81. Arthur Young, "Carl Browne: The Labor Knight," *Masses* 5 (April 1914), 16. See also Donald L. McMurry, *Coxey's Army,* 291; and Carlos A. Schwantes, *Coxey's Army,* 258–59. For Coxey's activities until 1928, see Donald L. McMurry, *Coxey's Army,* 286–91; on activities in 1930s and 1940s, Carlos A. Schwantes, *Coxey's Army,* 259.

82. See reference to "Coxey's Army" as "the entourage of interns, nurses and medical students which follows a chief of staff on his rounds," in H. L. Mencken, *The American Language: An Inquiry into the Development of English in the United States, Supplement II* (New York: Knopf, 1948), 755. "Unorganized gang" from Lester V. Berrey and Melvin Van den Bark, *The American Thesaurus of Slang: A Complete Reference Book of Colloquial Speech* (New York: Thomas Y. Crowell, 1942), 789.

83. "No Monopoly for Coxey," *Washington Post,* 29 March 1894, 4; Joseph Hawley, Senate, 3884.

2. A "NATIONAL" DEMONSTRATION

1. Robert S. Gallagher, " 'I Was Arrested, of Course': An Interview with Alice Paul," *American Heritage* 25 (February 1974), 16–24, 92–94. For another set of memories of the march, see Alice Paul and Amelia R. Fry, *Conversations with Alice Paul: Woman Suffrage and the Equal Rights Amendment; an Interview*

(Berkeley: Regional Oral History Office, University of California, Berkeley, 1976), esp. 68–81.

2. The standard account of the procession is Sidney R. Bland, "New Life in an Old Movement: Alice Paul and the Great Suffrage Parade of 1913 in Washington, D.C.," *Records of the Columbia Historical Society* 48 (1971), 657–78. See also Christine Lunardini, *From Equal Suffrage to Equal Rights: Alice Paul and the National Women's Party, 1910–1928* (New York: New York University Press, 1986), esp. the chap. "Pageant and Politics." Two historians have considered the use of demonstrations by woman suffragists in extremely useful articles: Ellen C. DuBois, "Marching Towards Power: Woman Suffrage Parades, 1910–1915," chap. in William Graebner, ed., *True Stories from the American Past* (New York: McGraw-Hill, 1993), 88–106; and Michael E. McGerr, "Political Style and Women's Power, 1830–1930," *Journal of American History* 77.3 (December 1990), 864–85.

3. Accounts of the victory of the federal amendment inevitably highlight the 1913 procession. See, for example, Penelope P. B. Huse, "Appeals to Congress," chap. in *National American Woman Suffrage Association, Victory, How Women Won It: A Centennial Symposium, 1840–1940* (New York: H. W. Wilson, 1940), 102.

4. The debate about the significance of the Progressive Era and its coherence is a vital one for historians. My focus on visibility developed from the work of a number of scholars, including Richard L. McCormick, *The Party Period and Public Policy: American Politics from the Age of Jackson to the Progressive Era* (New York: Oxford University Press, 1986); Alan Dawley, *Struggles for Justice: Social Responsibility and the Liberal State* (Cambridge, Mass.: Harvard University Press, 1991); and Daniel T. Rodgers, *Atlantic Crossings: Social Politics in a Progressive Age* (Cambridge, Mass.: Belknap Press of Harvard University Press, 1998). My focus has also been influenced by the work of cultural and media historians who have noted changes in the way people saw and learned about each other during this period; see William Leach, *Land of Desire: Merchants, Power, and the Rise of a New American Culture* (New York: Pantheon, 1993); and Carl S. Smith, *Urban Disorder and the Shape of Belief: The Great Chicago Fire, the Haymarket Bomb, and the Model Town of Pullman* (Chicago: University of Chicago Press, 1995). Theorists of political culture and the public sphere have also drawn attention to how visibility works in different periods for different purposes: Murray Edelman, *Constructing the Political Spectacle* (Chicago: University of Chicago Press, 1988); and Nicholas Garnham, "The Media and the Public Sphere," chap. in Craig Calhoun, ed., *Habermas and the Public Sphere* (Cambridge, Mass.: MIT Press, 1992).

5. Within the British suffrage movement, "militant" referred to those "suffragettes" willing to perform illegal acts and risk arrests for the cause of suffrage, in contrast to the moderate suffragists, who preferred education and legal means. The militants in England pioneered the public parades and demonstrations, but the moderates soon adopted these techniques when they became legal. In the United States, where most of the suffrage movement condemned the actions of the "militants" in England, some suffragists and newspapers characterized legal street protests as "militant" actions.

6. Midge Mackenzie, *Shoulder to Shoulder: A Documentary* (New York: Knopf, 1975), 20, 34, 42. Caroline Katzenstein, *Lifting the Curtain: The State and National Woman Suffrage Campaigns in Pennsylvania as I Saw Them* (Philadelphia: Dorrance, 1955), 41–42.

7. On Paul's return, see Ida H. Harper, *The History of Woman Suffrage*, vol. 5 (New York: National American Woman Suffrage Association, 1922), 280–81. Sara H. Graham, *Woman Suffrage and the New Democracy* (New Haven, Conn.: Yale University Press, 1996), esp. 33–98.

8. The first English language edition was Gustave Le Bon, *The Crowd: A Study of the Popular Mind* (London: E. Benn, 1896). Macmillan published the first American edition in 1897. This paragraph relies on Erika King's excellent short essay on the issue: "Democracy and the 'Sovereign Crowd' in Pre–World War I American Magazines," *Journal of American Culture* 15 (Winter 1992), 27–32.

9. See, for one example of the academic consideration, George E. Howard, "Social Psychology of the Spectator," *American Journal of Sociology* 18 (March 1913), 613–21. For a very positive view of crowds, see Gerald S. Lee, *Crowds: A Moving-Picture of Democracy* (Garden City, N.Y.: Doubleday, Page, 1913). For a comment on this work, see Gregory W. Bush, *Lord of Attention: Gerald Stanley Lee and the Crowd Metaphor in Industrializing America* (Amherst: University of Massachusetts Press, 1991). For a general discussion, see Eugene Leach, " 'Mental Epidemics': Crowd Psychology and American Culture, 1890–1940," *American Studies* 33 (Spring 1992), 5–29.

10. Quote from Paul S. Reinsch, *American Legislatures and Legislative Methods* (New York: Century, 1907), 291. On reforms, see Margaret A. Schaffner, *Lobbying* (Madison, Wisc.: Free Library Commission, Legislative Reference Department, 1906). See also "Regulation of the Lobby," *Nation* 71 (13 September 1900), 206; "A New Way of Treating Lobbyists," *Chautauquan* 41 (March 1905), 12; Joseph Lee, "A People's Lobbyist," *Independent* 62 (May 1907), 1203–6; and "Among the World's Workers: A Lobbyist for the People," *World's Work* 15 (November 1907–April 1908), 9599–9601. For a defense of lobbying by industrial interests, see the review of debates over lobbying on the tariff in "The President's War on the Tariff Lobby," *Literary Digest* 46.23 (7 June 1913), 1257–58. Anti-lobbying sentiment increased, however, as the tariff debate continued; see John C. O'Laughlin, "The Invisible Government under Searchlight," *American Review of Reviews* 48 (13 September 1913), 334–38.

11. On the association of vice with being seen in public and women's struggles to change it, see Mary P. Ryan, *Women in Public: Between Banners and Ballots, 1825–1880* (Baltimore: Johns Hopkins University Press, 1990); Robyn Muncy, *Creating a Female Dominion in American Reform, 1890–1935* (New York: Oxford University Press, 1991); and Paula Baker, *The Moral Framework of Public Life: Gender, Politics and the State in Rural New York, 1870–1930* (Oxford: Oxford University Press, 1991). Ellen C. DuBois, "Working Women, Class Relations, and Suffrage Militance: Harriot Stanton Blatch and the New York Woman Suffrage Movement, 1894–1909," *Journal of American History* 74 (June 1987), 53; Harriot S. Blatch and Alma Lutz, *Challenging Years: The Memoirs of Harriot Stanton Blatch* (New York: G. P. Putnam's Sons, 1940), 129–55; Ida H. Harper, *Woman Suffrage*, vol. 5, 286; and Caroline Katzenstein, *Lifting the Curtain*, 41–53. Shaw

quoted in "Wants Suffragist Gusto," *Public Ledger,* 11 November 1909, "Newspaper Clippings, October 1907–December 28, 1912" folder, box 265, NWP Records, II. On the open-air meetings, see *National American Woman Suffrage Association, Forty-Second Annual Report of the National American Woman Suffrage Association, Given at the Convention, Held at Washington, D.C., April 14 to 19, Inclusive* (New York: National American Woman Suffrage Association [NAWSA], 1910), 52; and Ida H. Harper, *Woman Suffrage,* vol. 5, 280–81.

12. Caroline Katzenstein, *Lifting the Curtain,* 33, 40–53, 74.

13. Ida H. Harper, *Woman Suffrage,* vol. 5, 339. On Paul's maneuverings, see Ellen C. DuBois, *Harriot Stanton Blatch and the Winning of Woman Suffrage* (New Haven, Conn.: Yale University Press, 1997), 184–85. On the lack of action by Congress, see Eleanor Flexner, *Century of Struggle: The Woman's Rights Movement in the United States* (New York: Atheneum, 1974 [1959]), 172–75.

14. See Alice Paul to the Official Board of the NAWSA, 16 December 1912, *National Woman's Party Papers: The Suffrage Years* (Sanford, N.C.: Microfilming Corporation of America, 1981), reel 1 (cited hereafter as *NWP, Suffrage);* and Mary W. Dennett, Telegram to Alice Paul, 18 December 1912, *NWP, Suffrage,* reel 1.

15. For these activities see Alice Paul to the Official Board of the NAWSA, *NWP, Suffrage,* reel 1. See also Alice Paul and Amelia R. Fry, *Conversations with Alice Paul,* 70.

16. Dora Lewis to Alice Paul, 17 December 1912, *NWP, Suffrage,* reel 1. Alice Paul to the Official Board of the NAWSA. "The Suffrage Parade," *Washington Post,* 7 January 1913, 6.

17. *Davis v. Commonwealth of Massachusetts,* 167 U.S. 43 (1897), 733. See Shawn F. Peters, *Judging Jehovah's Witnesses: Religious Persecution and the Dawn of the Rights Revolution* (Lawrence: University Press of Kansas, 2000); Diane H. Winston, *Red-Hot and Righteous: The Urban Religion of the Salvation Army* (Cambridge, Mass.: Harvard University Press, 1999); Melvyn Dubofsky, *We Shall Be All: A History of the Industrial Workers of the World* (Chicago: Quadrangle Books, 1969); and William Preston, *Aliens and Dissenters: Federal Suppression of Radicals, 1903–1933* (Urbana: University of Illinois Press, 1994). On tolerance of respectable protests, C. E. Baker, "Unreasoned Reasonableness: Mandatory Parade Permits and Time, Place, and Manner Regulations," *Northwestern Law Review* (December 1983), gives an overview of the evolution of permitting methods and court rulings; see also A. L. H. Street, "Prohibiting Parades in Streets," *American City* 27 (December 1922), who reviews state rulings on city regulations and concludes that cities should use caution in denying permits.

18. On inaugurations during this period, see Glenn D. Kittler, *Hail to the Chief! The Inauguration Days of Our Presidents* (Philadelphia: Chilton, 1965); and Carol M. Highsmith and Ted Landphair, *Pennsylvania Avenue: America's Main Street* (Washington, D.C.: American Institute of Architects Press, 1988), 86–91. On exclusion of women, see "Women Are Barred," *Washington Evening Star,* 12 February 1913, 2. On Paul's strategy, see Alice Paul to the Official Board of the NAWSA.

19. Carol M. Highsmith and Ted Landphair, *Pennsylvania Avenue,* 68–69; Constance M. Green, *Washington: Capital City, 1879–1950* (Princeton, N.J.: Princeton University Press, 1976), 138–40, picture facing 143.

20. On permissions generally, see Alice Paul to the Official Board of the NAWSA. "First time" in Alice Paul to Mary Ware Dennett, 6 January 1913, *NWP, Suffrage,* reel 1; Franklin MacVeagh to Mrs. William Kent, 2 January 1913, *NWP, Suffrage,* reel 1. The suffragists also received authorization to use the plaza surrounding the Peace Memorial from the president pro-tem of the Senate, Jacob Gallinger, and the Speaker of the House, Champ Clark. Unlike the leaders of Coxey's Army, the suffragists would not violate the regulations against assembling at the Capitol; Alice Paul to Champ Clark, 8 January 1913, *NWP, Suffrage,* reel 1. This letter contains Clark's notation that "permission as asked above granted as far as I am concerned." The suffragists received permission as well from Colonel Spencer Cosby of the U.S. Army to use the driveways behind the White House for the end of the procession and for the pageant to set up on; Alice Paul to Col. Spencer Cosby, 28 December 1912, *NWP, Suffrage,* reel 1, frame 50.

21. Richard Sylvester, *District of Columbia Police: A Retrospect of the Police Organizations of the Cities of Washington and Georgetown and the District of Columbia, with Biographical Sketches, Illustrations and Historic Cases* (Washington, D.C.: Gibson Bros., 1894); and John R. Young and Edwin C.R. Humphries, *The Metropolitan Police Department, Washington, D.C.: Official Illustrated History* (Washington, D.C.: Lawrence Publishing, 1908).

22. Testimony of Richard Sylvester, Senate Committee on the District of Columbia, Senate Report 53, *Suffrage Parade by a Subcommittee Under S. Res. 499,* 63rd Cong., 1st sess., 1913; "dignified" on 137; "bowery" on 196. Description of Sixteenth Street as "Executive Avenue," Rand, McNally and Company, *Pictorial Guide to Washington* (Chicago: Rand, McNally and Company, 1914), 152–53.

23. "Side street" from Helen Gardener to Hon. Cuno Rudolph, 5 January 1913, in Testimony of Helen Gardener, Senate Committee on the District of Columbia, Senate Report 53, 441; "present" from Florence Etheridge to [District commissioners], 4 January 1913, *NWP, Suffrage,* reel 1.

24. "Delegations" from Alice Paul to Crystal Eastman Benedict, 31 December 1912, *NWP, Suffrage,* reel 1. "All" and quote from *Washington Times* from Alice Paul to Mary Ware Dennett. *Post* editorial: "Suffrage Parade," 6. "Taft Backs Women," *Washington Post,* 7 January 1913, 1. On Sylvester's assent, see Alice Paul to Mary Ware Dennett, 9 January 1913, *NWP, Suffrage,* reel 1.

25. Estimates of the number of marchers ranged from 5,000 to 10,000. "Doors" from Alice Paul to Suffrage Section of the Philanthropic Committee, Philadelphia Yearly Meeting, 7 January 1913, *NWP, Suffrage,* reel 1. Description of the start comes from Mary U. F. Baughman, *The Day "Those Creatures" Shook a City: Recollections of the Woman's Suffrage Procession, March 3, 1913* (Hyattsville, Md.: 1963) in NWP Records, II, folder 3, box 254. Because of the pageant on the south steps of the Treasury Building, the route of the march was slightly unusual, going behind the Treasury Building to the south, then turning north up the pathway between the Treasury Building and the White House, and turning west again on Pennsylvania Avenue to pass in front of the White House. See Alice Paul to Richard Sylvester, 6 January 1913, *NWP, Suffrage,* reel 1, for details. Continental Hall was later renamed Constitution Hall. Suffragists' accounts of the parade all mention this exchange with Wilson, though the news-

papers only note that the crowds were smaller than was normal for the arrival of the new president. See Inez H. Irwin, *The Story of the Woman's Party* (New York: Harcourt, Brace, 1921), 30. For newspaper accounts of Wilson's arrival, see "Suffragists Draw 225,000 Persons to Parade for Ballot," *New York Herald,* 4 March 1913, 3; the second headline read: "Few See Advertised Arrival of Mr. Wilson"; "Wilson Takes Office Today as 28th President," *New York Times,* 4 March 1913, 1, notes that Wilson "got his first glimpse of Washington as a deserted village," because everyone was on the Avenue.

26. Testimony of Helen Gardener, Senate Committee on the District of Columbia, Senate Report 53, 450.

27. Alice Paul to Anna Farrell, 28 December 1912, *NWP, Suffrage,* reel 1. See also "Suffragists Plan Brilliant Pageant before Inaugural," *Washington Times,* 28 December 1912, "Newspaper Clippings" folder, box 265, NWP Records, II, for similar language that also mentions that the procession will be "much more beautiful" than the New York Suffrage Parade of 1912.

28. Testimony of Hannah Cassel Mills, Senate Committee on the District of Columbia, Senate Report 53, 115; Anna H. Shaw to Alice Paul, 22 January 1913, *NWP, Suffrage,* reel 1. On criticisms of suffragists and their attempts to counter them, see Kay Sloan, "Sexual Warfare in the Silent Cinema: Comedies and Melodramas of Woman Suffragism," *American Quarterly* 33 (Fall 1981), 418–20. A historian of the "suffragette" movement in England also pointed out the importance of dignity to even the most militant of suffragists; Rosamund Billington, "Ideology and Feminism: Why the Suffragettes Were 'Wild Women,'" *Women's Studies International Forum* 5.6 (1982), 672.

29. "Barefooted Women in Gauze, Despite Cold, Pose in Tableaux on the Treasury Plaza," *Washington Post,* 4 March 1913, 10; and *Official Program,* Woman Suffrage Procession, 3 March 1913, "Miscellany, 1913" file, *Records of the National American Woman Suffrage Association, 1850–1960* (Washington, D.C.: Library of Congress, 1981), reel 58.

30. *Official Program.* For the most part, descriptions of the pageant in newspaper accounts echo or quote verbatim from the program, which raises questions about how the pageant actually appeared to the spectators; for example, see the following headline: "Woman's Beauty, Grace and Art Bewilder the Capital," *Washington Post,* 4 March 1913, 1.

31. Percy MacKaye, "Art and the Woman's Movement: A Comment on the National Suffrage Pageant," *Forum* 49 (June 1913), 684.

32. For example, the *Washington Evening Star* called her "one of the most beautiful women in all the land"; "Beauty and Dignity of Great Parade Impress Throngs," *Washington Evening Star,* 3 March 1913, 4. Ecstasy quote from "Mobs at Capital Defy Police; Block Suffrage Parade," *Chicago Tribune,* 4 March 1913, 2. On the tradition of the beautiful woman, see Mary P. Ryan, *Women in Public,* 19–57.

33. See Chairman, Pageant Committee to Alice Bower, 16 January 1913, *NWP, Suffrage,* reel 1. The suffragists' use of color for political purposes coincided with the commercial proliferation of brightly colored products made with colorfast chemical dyes; see Thomas J. Schlereth, *Victorian America: Transformations in Everyday Life, 1876–1915* (New York: HarperCollins, 1991), 148.

34. Catherine D. Bowen, *Miracle at Philadelphia: The Story of the Constitutional Convention, May to September, 1787* (Boston: Little, Brown, 1966).

35. Picture in "Suffragists Draw 225,000 Persons," 3; "Washington Waiting for the New President," Cartoon 196, *NWP, Suffrage,* reel 96. On drilling, see Testimony of Harriet Taylor Upton, Senate Committee on the District of Columbia, Senate Report 53, 22–24; and repeated reports on the Chicago delegations' practicing in *Chicago Tribune,* 1–5 March 1913.

36. For a detailed exploration of pageantry, see David Glassberg, *American Historical Pageantry: The Uses of Tradition in the Early Twentieth Century* (Chapel Hill: University of North Carolina Press, 1990). His account makes clear that pageants were rarely used for such explicitly political purposes. Besides the suffrage pageant, the other notable exceptions were an enormous pageant to benefit Industrial Workers of the World strikers in Paterson, N.J., held in New York City three months after the woman suffrage pageant, and "The Star of Ethiopia," by W. E. B. Du Bois, produced in 1914; David Glassberg, *American Historical Pageantry,* 128–35.

37. Elizabeth A. Hyde to "Ladies," 1 February 1913, *NWP, Suffrage,* reel 1. While the organizers refused to give up the costumes entirely, they did create an awkwardly titled fifth section for "Un-Uniformed Marchers" to allow marchers like Hyde to avoid the dangers of costumes. Acknowledging that fashion trends limited the reality of this freedom, Richard Sennett has identified clothing as central to the idea of freedom for the "public man" and woman in the late nineteenth century; Richard Sennett, *The Fall of Public Man* (New York: W. W. Norton, 1992 [1976]), 147, 183–94. "A plain walk" from Dora Lewis to Alice Paul, 1 January 1913, *NWP, Suffrage,* reel 1. "We want" from Chairman, Pageant Committee, to Jeannette Rankin, 18 January 1913, *NWP, Suffrage,* reel 1.

38. "Female Sense of Color Beauty Will Charm Inaugural Crowds," *Milwaukee Leader,* 18 February 1913, folder 2, box 265, NWP Records, II. "Pretty Girls Are Offered $2 to Parade, $3 Not to Parade," *Washington Post,* 28 February 1913, 3. *New York Herald,* 4 March 1913, 8. See also "Barefooted Women in Gauze," 10. On limits of beauty as a political tool, see Barbara Sichtermann, *Femininity, the Politics of the Personal,* Helga Geyer-Ryan, trans. (Minneapolis: University of Minnesota Press, 1986), 48–49.

39. Concerns about participating in interracial parades were not limited to the woman suffragists in the early spring of 1913. The inaugural parade was marked by its own controversy over whites and blacks marching together. In February, at the same time as women were barred from the "men's" parade, the governor of South Carolina declared he would not let his National Guard march in the inaugural parade because they would have marched after a group of black guardsmen from the District of Columbia. "Women Are Barred," 2.

40. Paul's concern in Alice Paul to Alice Stone Blackwell, 15 January 1913, *NWP, Suffrage,* reel 1. Paul's stilted response to request from Howard students in Alice Paul to Miss C. L. Hunt, 9 January 1913, *NWP, Suffrage,* reel 1. "Color question" and "Southern city" from a letter by another organizer [unsigned] to Alice Stone Blackwell, 14 January 1913, *NWP, Suffrage,* reel 1. "We are not making" and "scattered" from Alice Paul to Alice Stone Blackwell.

41. Carrie W. Clifford, *Crisis* 5 (April 1913), 296. Carrie Clifford was a founder of the D.C. branch and served as chair and vice president of the branch's executive committee. See Lewis N. Walker Jr., "The Struggles and Attempts to Establish Branch Autonomy and Hegemony: A History of the District of Columbia Branch National Association for the Advancement of Colored People, 1912–1942" (Ph.D. diss., University of Delaware, 1979), 61–62.

42. W. E. B. Du Bois, *Crisis* 5 (April 1913), 267. Du Bois's remarks on the importance of keeping white supremacy out of the woman suffrage movement are summarized in "Women Suffrage Delegates Welcome Dr. W. E. B. Du Bois," *Philadelphia Tribune,* 30 November 1912, 1. In late April 1913, Paul passionately defended the demonstration against Du Bois's charges, but much of the spirit, if not all the substance, of his report was accurate. Alice Paul to W. E. B. Du Bois, 25 April 1913, *NWP, Suffrage,* reel 2.

43. Quote from "Illinois Women Feature Parade," *Chicago Tribune,* 4 March 1913, 3. Picture: "Virginia Brooks, 'Mrs' Belle Squire, Mrs Ida Wells Barnett," *Chicago Tribune,* 5 March 1913, 5. More details on the conflict in "Marches in Parade Despite Protests," *Chicago Defender,* 8 March 1913, 8; and "Women in Big Pageant Unprotected, Battle through Avenue Mobs," *Washington Herald,* 4 March 1913, 4. Aileen Kraditor uses this incident as an example of the "persistence of white supremacy as an issue within the suffrage movement until its final victory in 1920"; Aileen S. Kraditor, *The Ideas of the Woman Suffrage Movement, 1890–1920* (New York: Norton, 1981 [1965]), 212. See also Rosalyn Terborg-Penn, *African American Women in the Struggle for the Vote, 1850–1920* (Bloomington: Indiana University Press, 1998).

44. Mary W. Dennett to Alice Paul, 14 January 1913, *NWP, Suffrage,* reel 1.

45. Testimony of Admiral K. Van Reysen, Senate Committee on the District of Columbia, Senate Report 53, 11.

46. Testimony of Elizabeth V. Brown, Senate Committee on the District of Columbia, Senate Report 53, 45. For physical assaults, see Testimony of Vernat Hatfield, Senate Committee on the District of Columbia, Senate Report 53, 52; and Testimony of Maud Cecil Gunther, Senate Committee on the District of Columbia, Senate Report 53, 56–57.

47. For retreat of pageant performers, see "Woman's Beauty," 1. For arrests, see Testimony of Richard Sylvester, Senate Committee on the District of Columbia, Senate Report 53, 172, 185. For injuries, see "Score the Police for Inefficiency," *Washington Evening Star,* 4 March 1913, 1. "Crowd came closer" from Testimony of Harriet Taylor Upton, Senate Committee on the District of Columbia, Senate Report 53, 22–23. "The crowd" from Testimony of Abby Scott Baker, Senate Committee on the District of Columbia, Senate Report 53, 36.

48. According to Sylvester, 729 men were on the Avenue for the whole procession, and another 221 helped at the Capitol and then reassembled at the end of the procession; Testimony of Richard Sylvester, Senate Committee on the District of Columbia, Senate Report 53, 160–63. On the experience of the force with inaugurals, see John R. Young and Edwin C. R. Humphries, *Metropolitan Police Department,* 225–27. On decision to call cavalry, Testimony of Richard Sylvester, Senate Committee on the District of Columbia, Senate Report 53, 156.

On their efforts, Testimony of Hon. Henry L. Stimson, Former Secretary of War, Senate Committee on the District of Columbia, Senate Report 53, 121.

49. On meetings, see "Are to Help Pageant," *Washington Post,* 11 January 1913, "Newspaper Clippings, Jan. 3–Dec 9, 1913" folder, box 265, NWP Records, II. On publicity, see Alice Paul to Mrs. Lawrence Lewis, 31 January 1913, *NWP, Suffrage,* reel 1. On turnout, see Testimony of Richard Boyle, Inspector Metropolitan Police, Senate Committee on the District of Columbia, Senate Report 53, 365. Many D.C. residents who were spectators testified at the hearings; see, for example, Testimony of Jeannette King Gallinger; Testimony of Reverend J. Henning Nelms; and Testimony of David R. Carll, in Senate Committee on the District of Columbia, Senate Report 53. "Suffragists Draw 225,000 Persons," 3. On the importance of such reports of crowds to political campaigns, see Susan Herbst, *Numbered Voices: How Opinion Polling Has Shaped American Politics* (Chicago: University of Chicago Press, 1993).

50. During a parade in New York City in 1912, the spectators "swarm[ed] all over Fifth Avenue," and the suffragists complained afterward to the city government; "Suffrage Leaders Face Waldo to Show Police Failed Them," *New York Globe,* 10 May 1912, in *Scrapbooks of Harriot Stanton Blatch* (microfilm) (Washington, D.C.: Library of Congress, n.d.), reel 1. See also Ellen Carol DuBois, "Marching towards Power," 96–97. Crowds were enough of a problem at suffrage parades to warrant a report by Lawrence F. Fuld, "Police News," *National Municipal Review* 2 (July 1913), 483. Sylvester's cautions in Testimony of Miss. Elsie M. Hill, in Senate Committee on the District of Columbia, Senate Report 53, 128.

51. On requests, see Helen Gardener to Hon. Cuno Rudolph, in Senate Committee on the District of Columbia, Senate Report 53, 441; and "Ask Military Guard," *Washington Evening Star,* February 1913, folder 2, box 265, NWP Records, II. On meetings, see Testimony of Commissioner John A. Johnston, Senate Committee on the District of Columbia, Senate Report 53, 225–28; and Testimony of Hon. Henry L. Stimson, Senate Committee on the District of Columbia, Senate Report 53, 117–20. On decision to put troops "on call," see Henry L. Stimson, Statement, 7 March 1913, file 2012341, box 7145, Records of the Office of the Adjutant General (RG 94), NA. This authorization violated the normal procedure of using the U.S. Army to control domestic troubles. Normally, local officials would first call up the local National Guard and then only after they could not restore peace would the army be mobilized. The suffragists' conception of their demonstration as national led them to think of the army as the appropriate police force, and they repeatedly pleaded for this form of protection.

52. "Sum Up Day's Work," *Washington Post,* 4 March 1913, 6.

53. New Hampshire suffragist, Testimony of Agnes M. Jenks, Senate Committee on the District of Columbia, Senate Report 53, 27. Testimony of Patricia Street, ibid., 70.

54. Harriot S. Blatch and Alma Lutz, *Challenging Years,* 197. For an account of how harassment of suffragists in England inspired similar complaints, see Martha Vicinus, "Male Space and Women's Bodies: The English Suffragette Movement," chap. in Judith Friedlander and New Family and New Woman Research Planning Group, eds., *Stratégies des Femmes: Women in Culture and Pol-*

itics, a Century of Change (Bloomington: Indiana University Press, 1986), esp. 213, 217.

55. Testimony of Mrs. Sara T. Moller, Senate Committee on the District of Columbia, Senate Report 53, 126. Paul's comment, "Suffragists Draw 225,000 Persons," 3.

56. For affidavits, see Testimony of Richard Sylvester, Senate Committee on the District of Columbia, Senate Report 53, 199–202. For illustrative photographs, see exhibit 39 in Senate Committee on the District of Columbia, Senate Report 53. John Daley, police officer, letter to Richard Sylvester, quoted in Testimony of Richard Sylvester, Senate Committee on the District of Columbia, Senate Report 53, 186. Schneider's letter quoted in Testimony of Richard Sylvester, Senate Committee on the District of Columbia, Senate Report 53, 192. See similar reasoning by another officer, John Muhall, in his letter to Sylvester, quoted in Testimony of Richard Sylvester, Senate Committee on the District of Columbia, Senate Report 53, 170. Prominent Washingtonian quoted in Testimony of Richard Sylvester, Senate Committee on the District of Columbia, Senate Report 53, 727. The notion of women and woman suffrage resulting in unmanageable crowds of women had a long history. Senator Vest of Missouri objected virulently to passage of the Suffrage Amendment in 1887, concluding his speech with descriptions of women during the French Revolution: "Who led those bloodthirsty mobs? Who shrieked loudest in that hurricane of passions? Women"; Vest quoted in Eleanor Flexner, *Century of Struggle,* 175.

57. "Derby Hats" from Testimony of Helen Gardener, Senate Committee on the District of Columbia, Senate Report 53, 448. Gardener based her comment on exhibit 16. "Spring styles" from Testimony of Helena Hill Weed, Senate Committee on the District of Columbia, Senate Report 53, 455.

58. Senate Committee on the District of Columbia, Senate Report 53, xiii–xvi.

59. "Anti-Suffragism Gets a Hard Blow," *New York Times,* 5 March 1913, 16.

60. About meeting, see Memorandum for the President, 13 March 1913, "89: Suffrage, 1913, March–April" folder, series 4, Case Files, *Woodrow Wilson Papers* (Washington, D.C.: Presidential Papers Microfilming Project, Library of Congress, n.d.), reel 207; about disappointing results, see Inez H. Irwin, *Story of the Woman's Party,* 33–38.

61. Ida H. Harper, *Woman Suffrage,* vol. 5, 378–81.

62. Inez H. Irwin, *Story of the Woman's Party,* 193–291.

63. Alice Paul to Mrs. Robert Adamson, 29 January 1917, *NWP, Suffrage,* reel 38.

64. A number of supporters of Paul's organization withdrew their support; Inez H. Irwin, *Story of the Woman's Party,* 257–58. For NAWSA's position, see Carrie C. Catt, "Why We Did Not Picket the White House," *Good Housekeeping* 66 (March 1918), 32. This view prevailed at the time. On the basis of a detailed study of Wilson's private papers, Sara H. Graham, "Woodrow Wilson, Alice Paul, and the Woman Suffrage Movement," *Political Science Quarterly* 98 (Winter 1983–84), 645–79, concludes that Wilson did take action because of the picketing. For more details on the association's reaction, see Sara H. Graham, *Woman Suffrage and the New Democracy.*

65. Quote from " 'Dry' Army to March," *Washington Post,* 2 December 1913, 11; details in "WCTU Leaders Plan for Visit to Capitol," *Washington Evening Star,* 8 December 1913, 2; "Liquor's Enemies, Men and Women, Besiege Capital," *Washington Evening Star,* 10 December 1913, 1; and "Rum Foes at Capitol," *Washington Post,* 11 December 1913, 2.

66. Dixon Merrit, "The Klan on Parade," *Outlook* 140 (19 August 1925); "The Klan Walks in Washington," *Literary Digest* 86 (22 August 1925); and Constance M. Green, *Washington: Capital City,* 327.

67. "The Washington Riots," *Independent* 99 (2 August 1919), 147.

68. Robert H. Wiebe, *The Search for Order, 1877–1920* (New York: Hill and Wang, 1967), 295; and Nancy F. Cott, *The Grounding of Modern Feminism* (New Haven, Conn.: Yale University Press, 1987), 121.

3. "A NEW TYPE OF LOBBYING"

1. Sheila Graves, "Reflecting on Desperate Times," *Wenatchee World,* 20 February 1992, 9. My thanks to Wilfred Woods, publisher of the *Wenatchee World,* for providing me with a copy of this article. Walter W. Waters as told to William C. White, *B.E.F.: The Whole Story of the Bonus Army* (New York: John Day, 1933). Two historians have investigated the Bonus March in detail. Roger Daniels provides a comprehensive look at the background to the bonus, the legislative battles, the role of the police chief, the legacy of the march on future battles for veterans' benefits, and a final chapter entitled "The Bonus March as Myth"; Roger Daniels, *The Bonus March: An Episode of the Great Depression* (Westport, Conn.: Greenwood, 1971). Published three years later, Donald Lisio's study of the response of officials to the protest is particularly effective at showing Hoover's tolerance toward political demonstrations in Washington, the preparations of the Army for suppressing the Bonus March, and the tendency of protesters and authorities to accuse each other of conspiracy during the protest; Donald J. Lisio, *The President and Protest: Hoover, Conspiracy and the Bonus Riot* (Columbia: University of Missouri Press, 1974). Lisio revised his book slightly and republished it in 1994 to reflect the confirmation of his thesis in newly available sources: Donald J. Lisio, *The President and Protest: Hoover, MacArthur, and the Bonus Riot* (New York: Fordham University Press, 1994). Subsequent references are to the 1974 book.

2. Sheila Graves, "Reflecting on Desperate Times," 9. A search on electronic library catalogs revealed more copies of the book, including the original edition, than could easily be counted.

3. Walter W. Waters, *B.E.F.,* 13–15; veteran, 32–33.

4. Ibid., 19–26.

5. Ibid.

6. Roger Daniels, *Bonus March,* 14–40; Katherine Mayo, *Soldiers What Next* (Boston: Houghton Mifflin, 1934), 41–51; and Donald J. Lisio, "Bread and Butter Politics," chap. in Stephen Ward, ed., *The War Generation: Veterans of the First World War* (Port Washington, N.Y.: Kennikat Press, 1975), 42–43. On the popularity of old-age pensions and insurance, see Theda Skocpol, *Protecting Soldiers and Mothers: The Political Origins of Social Policy in the United States*

(Cambridge, Mass.: Harvard University Press, 1992), 234–35. On claims, Donald J. Lisio, *President and Protest,* 46–47. Coxey's testimony in House Committee on Ways and Means, Payment of Adjusted-Compensation Certificates, 72nd Cong., 1st sess., 191–203. Hoover quoted in "Presidential Vetoes of Bonus Bills," *Congressional Digest* 11 (November 1932), 269. Number of applications, House Committee on Ways and Means, Payment of Adjusted-Compensation Certificates, 309, 556. Donald J. Lisio, *President and Protest,* 35–39; and Roger Daniels, *Bonus March,* 42–45.

7. House, *Transportation Issued to Veterans Who Were Temporarily Resident in the District of Columbia,* 72nd Cong., 2d sess., 1932, H. Doc. 488, serial 9681, 7. The idea that with hard work and a little luck or money one could get ahead was a dominant theme in advice columns, advertising, and popular movies of the 1930s; see Lawrence W. Levine, "American Culture and the Great Depression," chap. in *The Unpredictable Past: Explorations in American Cultural History* (New York: Oxford University Press, 1993), 217–21. On extent of unemployment, see Irving Bernstein, *The Lean Years: A History of the American Worker, 1920–1933* (Boston: Houghton Mifflin, 1960), 312–17. On Portland economic situation, see Roger Daniels, *Bonus March,* 74. On "self-blame," see Lawrence W. Levine, "American Culture and the Great Depression," 211–17. On organized efforts by the unemployed and their tendency to concentrate on local issues until the New Deal, see Daniel J. Leab, "United We Eat: The Creation and Organization of Unemployed Councils in 1930," *Labor History* 8 (Fall 1967), 300–315; Annelise Orleck, " 'We Are That Mythical Thing Called the Public': Militant Housewives during the Great Depression," *Feminist Studies* 19 (Spring 1993), 147–72; Roy Rosenzweig, "Radicals and the Jobless: The Museteities and the Unemployed Leagues, 1932–1936," *Labor History* 16 (Winter 1975), 52–60; and Roy Rosenzweig, " 'Socialism in Our Time': The Socialist Party and the Unemployed, 1929–1936," *Labor History* 20 (Fall 1979), 485–509. The most important exception was the Communist Party's National Hunger March of 1931, described below, which focused on Washington, D.C.

8. Hoover quoted in "Pro Bono Politico," *Time* 19 (11 April 1932), 19; La Guardia in House Committee on Ways and Means, Payment of Adjusted-Compensation Certificates, 317; on La Guardia's leadership on these issues, see Jordan Schwarz, *The Interregnum of Despair: Hoover, Congress and the Depression* (Urbana: University of Illinois Press, 1970), 41, 146, 163. On Patman's activities, Roger Daniels, *Bonus March,* 63–64; and Walter W. Waters, *B.E.F.,* 62. For summary of the reasons, House Committee on Ways and Means, "Majority and Minority Reports," *Congressional Digest* 11 (November 1932), 274–79.

9. Walter W. Waters, *B.E.F.,* 16–17, 26–29; and Roger Daniels, *Bonus March,* 76–77.

10. Waters's background in J. H. Lewis (Dem., Ill.), Senate, *Congressional Record,* 72nd Cong., 1st sess., 28 June 1932, 75, pt. 13:14106; Walter W. Waters, *B.E.F.,* 4–7; "Youthful Leader Arouses Nation," *B.E.F. News* 1 (25 June 1932), 2; and interview with Wilma Waters by author, 26 August 1994. On need for discipline, Walter W. Waters, *B.E.F.,* 13–17, 27–31; Donald J. Lisio, *President and Protest,* 64–67; and Roger Daniels, *Bonus March,* 76.

11. "Police stem effort by Bonus marchers to blockade railroad," Universal Newsreels (May 1932), reel UN-4-47-1, RG 200, NA; Walter W. Waters, *B.E.F.,* 39–56; and Roger Daniels, *Bonus March,* 80–82.

12. On transport, Walter W. Waters, *B.E.F.,* 56–61; "Heroes," *Time* 19 (6 June 1932), 15.

13. "Bonus Vote to Halt Invasion Not Likely," *Washington Post,* 27 May 1932, 4; "Dramatic Story of B.E.F. Told from Beginning," *B.E.F. News* 1 (2 July 1932), 2; and Walter W. Waters, *B.E.F.,* 63–64. Waters quoted in Roger Daniels, *Bonus March,* 80.

14. On arrival time, see Alfred T. Smith, Daily Report on "Bonus March" to Chief of Staff [General Douglas MacArthur], 31 May 1932, file 10110–2452/292A, box 2832, RG 165, NA (hereafter cited as Alfred T. Smith, Daily Report). Bennett quoted in "Bonus Marchers Reach Capital to Demand Payment," *Washington Post,* 30 May 1932, 1; on Bennett's background, see Roger Daniels, *Bonus March,* 99. "Forceful courtesy" from "Tactics of Police in March Praised," *Washington Evening Star,* 8 December 1931, 2.

15. Movements of veterans toward the city drawn from "Heroes: B.E.F.," *Time* 19 (13 June 1932), 14; and Summary of Latest Press and Other Reports of Numbers of "Bonus Marchers" Coming to Washington, 4 June 1932, file 10110–2452/294b, box 2832, RG 165, NA. On counts in city, "Plot to Cause Riots in Bonus Parade Is Seen," *Washington Post,* 7 June 1932, 1; and Alfred T. Smith, Daily Report, 7 June 1932, file 10110–2452/297, box 2833, RG 165, NA. On camp life, "Dramatic Story of B.E.F.," 8; and "Dispatches as Bonus Army Mobilizes on Wide Front," *Washington Post,* 8 June 1932, 1. On headquarters, Alfred T. Smith, Daily Report, 1 June 1932, file 10110–2452/293e, box 2832, RG 165, NA.

16. Details on Glassford from Donald J. Lisio, *President and Protest,* 51–53; and Roger Daniels, *Bonus March,* 89–90. On Glassford's appointment and military officers as police chiefs in general, see "Major-General to Mop Up Washington," *Literary Digest* 104 (22 February 1930), 14–15.

17. On March 6, 1930, protest, see " 'Red Thursday' Riots Fizzle in U.S.," *Washington Herald,* 7 March 1930, 1–2; "Tear Gas Routs Reds before White House," *New York Times,* 7 March 1930, 1–2; and Franklin Folsom, *Impatient Armies of the Poor: The Story of Collective Action of the Unemployed, 1808–1942* (Niwot: University Press of Colorado, 1991), 245–60. On the Hunger March generally, see "Was the Hunger March a Flop?" *Literary Digest* 111 (19 December 1931), 9; and "Stop the Communists," *Washington Post,* 30 November 1931, 6. See also Franklin Folsom, *Impatient Armies of the Poor,* 284–300; and Harvey Klehr, *The Heyday of American Communism: The Depression Decade* (New York: 1984), 56–58. On Glassford's behavior, see John Dos Passos, "Red Day on Capitol Hill: Hunger March," *New Republic* 69 (23 December 1931), 154; and "Law and Order Preserved," *Washington Post,* 9 December 1931, 6. "Forceful courtesy" from "Tactics of Police," 2.

18. On Hoover's assistance with Hunger March, Donald J. Lisio, *President and Protest,* 59–60. On Hoover's greeting of the group known as Cox's Army,

see "14,000 Idle Petition for U.S. Work," *Washington Times,* 7 January 1932, 1; "Cox's Army," *Time* 19 (18 January 1932), 10; and Donald J. Lisio, *President and Protest,* 62.

19. On Glassford's "campaign of discouragement," see his testimony to Senate Committee on the District of Columbia, *Emergency Unemployment Relief and Care of Persons in Distress,* 72nd Cong., 1st sess., 1932, 1, 4, 6, 11–14. On Glassford's simultaneous efforts to help, "Glassford Moves to Limit Veterans' Stay to 48 Hours," *Washington Post,* 26 May 1932, 1; and Roger Daniels, *Bonus March,* 88–92.

20. Glassford quoted in Owen P. White, "General Glassford's Story: An Interview," *Collier's* 90 (29 October 1932), 10; see also Roger Daniels, *Bonus March,* 91–94, 96–97.

21. Pelham Glassford to the Secretary of War, 28 May 1932, File "240 Bonus (5–28–32)," box 1181, Central Files, 1926–39, RG 94, NA; "Bonus Army to Erect Own Camp Near City," *Washington Post,* 28 May 1932, 1, 7; Donald J. Lisio, *President and Protest,* 73; and Roger Daniels, *Bonus March,* 98. Walter W. Waters, *B.E.F.,* 62–64.

22. On the League plans, see Testimony of J. A. Lazar to House Committee on Ways and Means, *Payment of Adjusted-Compensation Certificates,* 277; "Duped by the Reds," *Washington Post,* 3 June 1932, 6; see also "Order at All Costs," *Washington Post,* 5 June 1932, 6. Pelham Glassford to District Commissioners, 3 June 1932, file 4–641, "District-Military Relations—The Bonus Marchers," box 233, RG 351, NA; and Edward J. Brophy, "Fighting Crime with Tear Gas," *American City* 33 (July 1925), 60.

23. Pelham Glassford to District Commissioners. On the "White Plan," see Roy Talbert, *Negative Intelligence: The Army and the American Left, 1917–1941* (Jackson: University Press of Mississippi, 1991), 212–13.

24. Military Intelligence Division (MID). Roy Talbert, *Negative Intelligence,* 221–22, 235–36. R. C. Foy, Daily Report, 3 June 1932, file 10110–2452/294a, box 2832, RG 165, NA. "U.S. Develops Special Gun for Possible Use in Riots," *Washington Post,* 25 May 1932, 7. John W. Killigrew, "The Army and the Bonus Incident," *Military Affairs* 26 (Summer 1962), 60–61.

25. On House vote, "Heroes: B.E.F.," 15; and Donald J. Lisio, *President and Protest,* 99. For 4,800 (MID's number) and 8,000 (the *Post* and Waters's estimate), Alfred T. Smith, Bonus Marchers Parade, 8 June 1932, file 10110–2452/298h, box 2833, RG 165, NA. "100,000 View Parade of Bonus Army," *Washington Post,* 8 June 1932, 1; and Walter W. Waters, *B.E.F.,* 84. On the scheduling of parade, see Roger Daniels, *Bonus March,* 112.

26. Baltimore and Ohio Railroad Company, Passenger Traffic Department, *Washington: The Place of Pilgrimage for Patriotic Americans* (n.p.: Baltimore and Ohio Railroad Company, 1925). Changes in Washington tourist attractions and federal building from Federal Writers' Project, *Washington, City and Capital* (Washington, D.C.: U.S. GPO, 1937). See also Constance M. Green, *Washington: Capital City, 1879–1950* (Princeton, N.J.: Princeton University Press, 1976), 291. "A visual symbol" in R. L. Duffus, "A New National Symbol," *New York Times Magazine* (15 May 1932), 10–11.

27. Walter W. Waters, *B.E.F.,* 83; and "The 'Ghost Parade' of the Bonus Seekers," *Literary Digest* 113 (18 June 1932), 6. "100,000 View," 1, 2. The prominent display of those injured was a response to the criticism of the march by the Disabled American Veterans of the World War, who opposed the bonus payment because they believed that only veterans injured during the war deserved special assistance; see comments by E. C. Babcock, leader of the Disabled American Veterans of the World War; "Babcock Urges 'Army' to Leave Washington," *Washington Post,* 7 June 1932, 4.

28. "The Bonus Army," *Commonweal* 16 (15 June 1932), 173–74. On events in Italy and Germany, and American reactions, see John P. Diggins, *Mussolini and Fascism: The View from America* (Princeton, N.J.: Princeton University Press, 1972); and James Diehl, "Germany: Veterans' Politics under Three Flags," chap. in Stephen Ward, ed., *The War Generation: Veterans of the First World War* (Port Washington, N.Y.: Kennikat Press, 1975), 135–86. Borah quoted in "Veteran Forces Defy Request to Leave Thursday," *Washington Post,* 5 June 1932, 1.

29. On parade, "100,000 View," 2; Alfred T. Smith, Bonus Marchers Parade, RG 165, NA. Gibbons quoted in "Ghost Parade," 6. On black veterans' presence, Roy Wilkins, "The Bonuseers Ban Jim Crow," *Crisis* 39 (October 1932), 316–17; and Testimony of Roy Wilkins, Senate Committee on Manufactures, *Federal Emergency Measures to Relieve Unemployment,* 72nd Cong. 1st sess., 1932, 20–21. Cartoon in *B.E.F. News,* 9 July 1932, 1.

30. George Creel, "Four Million Citizen Defenders," *Everybody's Magazine,* 1917, quoted in David M. Kennedy, *Over Here: The First World War and American Society* (New York: Oxford University Press, 1980), 145. For a general overview of this period and these issues, see Philip Gleason, "Americans All: World War II and the Shaping of American Identity," *Review of Politics* 43.4 (October 1981), 483–518. On "cultural pluralism," see Horace Kallen, *Culture and Democracy in the United States: Studies in the Group Psychology of the American Peoples* (New York: Arno, 1970 [1924]); and Philip Gleason, "Americans All," 504–5. "Polyglot" from Gardner Jackson, "Unknown Soldiers," *Survey* 68 (1 August 1932), 344.

31. "Order at All Costs," 6; "Send Veterans Home," *Washington Post,* 9 June 1932, 6; "The Week," *New Republic* 71 (15 June 1932), 110; "B.E.F. (Cont'd)," *Time* 19 (20 June 1932), 11; John Blaine (Rep., Wisc.), Senate, *Congressional Record,* 72nd Cong., 1st sess., 11 June 1932, 75, pt. 11:12673. On response by citizens, see "2 Railroads Agree to BEF Cut Rates," *Washington Post,* 23 June 1932, 1; and "The Ragged Army," *Nation* 16 (20 July 1932), 299. Walter W. Waters, *B.E.F.,* 85.

32. Walter W. Waters, *B.E.F.,* 146.

33. On appointment, "Bill in Senate Seeks $75,000 for Marchers," *Washington Post,* 31 May 1932, 1; MID report, "List of Leaders in Bonus March Camp," n.d. [1932], file 10110–2452/388, box 2833, RG 165, NA. In April, the Philadelphia police had arrested Foulkrod "on charges of unlawful assembly, inciting to riot, and making and using slanderous comments against the Government"; see Senate Committee on the District of Columbia, *Emergency Unemployment Relief,* 19. Pictures of marchers on steps of Capitol, "How Veterans Keep Busy as They Campaign for Bonus Bill," *Washington Post,* 7 June 1932, 18;

for example of references to Bonus marchers in galleries, Burton Wheeler (Dem., Mont.), Senate, *Congressional Record*, 72nd Cong., 1st sess., 9 June 1932, 75, pt. 11:12433. A member noted that some veterans talked to members of Congress, others waited around the Capitol, and others tried to get into the galleries; Henry O. Meisel, *Bonus Expeditionary Forces: The True Facts* (New London, Wisc.: Press-Republican, 1932), 4. Walter W. Waters, *B.E.F.*, 81.

34. Willard Cooper, "The Soldier Vote," *Atlantic Monthly* 134 (September 1924), 391, 387; "The Veteran's Bloc," *Commonweal* 13 (4 March 1931), 479–80. On American Legion and its ambivalence about the bonus campaign, see William Pencak, *For God and Country: The American Legion, 1919–1941* (Boston: Northeastern University Press, 1989), 74–75, 197–205. E. Pendleton Herring attributes the growth of these methods to new rules that changed the governance of the House of Representatives, the enthusiasm for "open committee hearings," the change to direct election of senators, a "keener and more intelligent public scrutiny of affairs," the declining power of the political parties, and finally the war, which both expanded the scope of the national policy and gave the groups new techniques of propaganda; E. Pendleton Herring, *Group Representation before Congress* (Baltimore: John Hopkins University Press, 1929), 41–52. He notes advantages of these groups in his concluding section, 240–68.

35. Debate on the bill in the House took place over three days; see House, *Congressional Record*, 72nd Cong., 1st. sess., 13 June 1932, 75, pt. 12:12844–55; ibid., 14 June 1932, 12911–39; ibid., 15 June 1932, 13015–54.

36. On the ambivalence with which Americans embraced increased government action during this period, see Barry D. Karl, *The Uneasy State: The United States from 1915 to 1945* (Chicago: University of Chicago Press, 1983), especially the epilogue. On the multiple attitudes of Americans, see Lawrence W. Levine, "American Culture and the Great Depression," 207–30; and Lawrence W. Levine, "Hollywood's Washington: Film Images of National Politics during the Great Depression," both chaps. in *The Unpredictable Past*, 232–55. Noting the various views of the American people, Robert S. McElvaine argues that over time support for "moral economics" grew stronger than that of "acquisitive individualism," but would agree, I think, that this balance was hardly established in 1932; see Robert S. McElvaine, *The Great Depression: America, 1929–1941* (New York: Times Books, 1993), esp. chap. "American Values and Culture in the Great Depression." The phrase "rugged individualism" came from Herbert Hoover, *American Individualism* (Garden City, N.Y.: Doubleday, 1922), and was often quoted in 1932.

37. Walter W. Waters, *B.E.F.*, 146–52; for Waters's statement, see Elsie Robinson, "Grim, Staunch, They Bear It Manfully," *Washington Times*, 18 June 1932, reprinted in Senate, *Congressional Record*, 72nd Cong., 1st sess., 18 June 1932, 75, pt. 12:13385–86.

38. Walter W. Waters, *B.E.F.*, 146–52; for marchers' reaction to defeat, Alfred T. Smith, Daily Report, 18 June 1932, file 10110–2452/343, box 2833, RG 165, NA; and "Bonus Beaten by Senate Vote of 62 to 18, Leader Urges Marchers to Remain Here," *Washington Post*, 18 June 1932, 1.

39. Alfred T. Smith, Daily Report, 13 June 1932, file 10110–2452/316, box 2833, RG 165, NA. Distribution of Bonus marchers: Police Figures on June 21, file 10110–2452/352, box 2833, RG 165, NA.

40. On dysentery reports, Alfred T. Smith, Daily Report, 5 July 1932, file 10110–2452/397, box 2833, RG 165, NA; " 'Swat the Fly' Week," *B.E.F. News,* 9 July 1932, 2; and "Heroes: Break Up," *Time* 20 (18 July 1932), 11. On decline in Washingtonians' support, John H. Bartlett, *The Bonus March and the New Deal* (Chicago: M. A. Donohue, 1937), 25; and "Veterans Face Starvation; Waters' Plea Results in Speedy Results," *B.E.F. News,* 9 July 1932, 2.

41. "Factional Strife Hits Bonus Forces," *Washington Post,* 25 June 1932, 1–2. "Complete dictatorial," from Alfred T. Smith, Daily Report, 27 June 1932, file 10110–2452/374, box 2833, RG 165, NA; "Waters Gets 12,000 Votes as B.E.F. Head," *Washington Post,* 30 June 1932, 1; and Walter W. Waters, *B.E.F.,* 156–57.

42. Mauritz Hallgren, in "The Bonus Army Scares Mr. Hoover," *Nation* 135 (27 July 1932), 73, praised the newspaper as "well-edited and ably written."

43. On radio, Walter W. Waters, *B.E.F.,* 163; the *Post* reported Glassford lifted the ban in "Marines Called, Leave Capitol, March Goes On," *Washington Post,* 15 July 1932, 3; "The B.E.F. and the Movies," *B.E.F. News,* 25 June 1932, 4; a representative from the American Federation of Labor reported that marchers at a rally at the Capitol went wild when a speaker made the claim that the White House was ordering theaters not to show newsreel pictures; Budd McKillips, "Unbiased Report of B.E.F. March from Representative of Labor," *B.E.F. News,* 16 July 1932, 7. On movie attendance, Robert S. McElvaine, *Great Depression,* 208. On radio news, Malcolm M. Willey and Stuart A. Rice, "The Agencies of Communication," chap. in President's Research Committee on Social Trends and Wesley C. Mitchell, eds., *Recent Social Trends in the United States Report* (New York: McGraw-Hill, 1933), 211. Raymond Fielding, *The American Newsreel, 1911–1967* (Norman: University of Oklahoma Press, 1972), provides a detailed account of the development of the newsreel. On styles of reporting, see Edward Bliss, *Now the News: The Story of Broadcast Journalism* (New York: Columbia University Press, 1991), 10–34.

44. On purges by Waters, see Harry Bacrach, Testimony, 30 August 1932, correspondence: 95–16–26, sec. 7, classified Subject Files, box 13991, Central Files, Records of the Justice Department (RG 60), NA. "Bonus Army to Stage Demonstration Today," *Washington Post,* 2 July 1932, 1; and "Bonus Veterans Will Stage Mute Parade along Avenue," *Washington Post,* 3 July 1932, 1.

45. John Dos Passos, "Washington and Chicago: The Veterans Come Home to Roost," *New Republic* 71 (29 June 1932), 178; and "New Influence of B.E.F. Arouses National Interest," *B.E.F. News,* 16 July 1932, 1.

46. Walter W. Waters, *B.E.F.,* 109. Although accurate counts of the number of women and children in Washington are difficult to obtain, still it is clear that they made up only a small proportion of the total marchers. The administrator of the Department of Veterans' Affairs reported that of 5,751 people transported out of the city by July 26, 221 were women and 247 were children. See Frank T. Hines, Memorandum for the President, 26 July 1932, correspondence: 95–16–26, classified Subject Files, box 13991, Central Files, RG 94, NA; and House, Supplemental Estimate for Veterans' Administration, 72nd Cong., 1st. sess., 1932, H. Doc. 362, serial 9549.

47. On Wilma Waters, "House Body Favors $100,000 for B.E.F.," *Washington Post,* 7 July 1932, 8; and Sheila Graves, "Reflecting on Desperate Times,"

9. On children, "Stork Visits Bonus Forces and Baby Boy Joins Heroes," *Washington Post*, 1 July 1932, 5; and "Milk for Children Provided," *Washington Post*, 9 July 1932, 8.

48. Editorials challenged the veterans to protect their families; see "Are You Curs and Cowards?" *B.E.F. News*, 16 July 1932, 4. On the specific context of the 1930s, see Alice Kessler-Harris, "In the Nation's Image: The Gendered Limits of Social Citizenship in the Depression Era," *Journal of American History* 86 (December 1999), 1251–79.

49. On Glassford's resignation, "B.E.F. Faces Hunger as Funds Give Out; Bakers' Aid Sought," *Washington Post*, 28 June 1932, 1. On transportation offer, see House, *Transportation Issued to Veterans*, 1; and Walter W. Waters, *B.E.F.*, 159–60. Reflecting the concern with departures, Smith's memo to the chief of staff now featured the number of departing veterans in addition to the census of veterans in the city; see Alfred T. Smith, Daily Report, 9 July–24 July 1932, RG 165, NA. Estimates of number of marchers, Walter W. Waters, *B.E.F.*, 179; and [untitled graph of number of Bonus marchers in District], 2 August 1932, file 10110–2452/446, box 2833, RG 165, NA.

50. "Most intransigent" in "The Week," *New Republic* 71 (3 August 1932), 300. Other criticisms of the remaining veterans are in Alfred T. Smith, Daily Report, 9 July 1932, file 10110–2452/408, box 2833, RG 165, NA; and H. W. Blakeley, "When the Army Was Smeared," *Combat Forces Journal* 2 (February 1952), 28.

51. Alfred T. Smith, Daily Report, 12 July 1932, file 10110–2452/414, box 2833, RG 165, NA; and Donald J. Lisio, *President and Protest*, 126–31. "Bonus Seekers in Night March around Capitol," *Washington Post*, 14 July 1932, 1–2; Alfred T. Smith, Daily Report, 14 July 1932, file 10110–2452/416, box 2833, RG 165, NA; Alfred T. Smith, Daily Report, 15 July 1932, file 10110–2452/419, box 2833, RG 165, NA; and Roger Daniels, *Bonus March*, 129–33.

52. "Trouble at Capitol," *New York Times*, 17 July 1932, 16; "No Man's Land," *Time* 20 (25 July 1932), 8–9; Walter W. Waters, *B.E.F.*, 168–71; and Roger Daniels, *Bonus March*, 133–34.

53. Workers Ex-Servicemen's League, "Program for the Successful Struggle for the Bonus," Bulletin No. 3, 30 June 1932, file 10110–2452/392, box 2833, RG 165, NA. As was often the case in Communist literature, the word "fight" did not necessarily mean violence. The paragraph below simply called for "organized and disciplined" parades to present demands and petitions, but to outsiders the rhetoric implied much more. On limited effect of WESL group, see Alfred T. Smith, Daily Report, 1 July 1932, file 10110–2452/390, box 2833, RG 165, NA.

54. "Picketing Is Averted by Big Force," *Washington Post*, 17 July 1932, 1, 3; Paul Anderson, "Some Sweet-Smelling Politics," *Nation* 135 (3 August 1932), 102; Roger Daniels, *Bonus March*, 134–36; and Donald J. Lisio, *President and Protest*, 134–38.

55. Dwight D. Eisenhower, *At Ease: Stories I Tell to Friends* (Garden City, N.Y.: Doubleday, 1967), 217; Donald J. Lisio, *President and Protest*, 209–14.

56. U. S. Grant to Luther Reichfelder, 21 July 1932, file 4–632, "District-Military Relations, The Bonus Marchers," box 233, RG 351, NA; Daniel Garges

to Major and Superintendent of Police, 21 July 1932, file 4–632, ibid. On Glass-ford's fears, Pelham Glassford to District Commissioners, 22 July 1932, ibid. Donald J. Lisio provides a detailed account of this stage of demonstration in *President and Protest,* 143–65. Adding another layer of confusion to the process was the fact that two businesses located near the Pennsylvania Avenue camps had received injunctions preventing the demolition of their buildings, which meant that the work was unlikely to proceed; Walter W. Waters, *B.E.F.,* 187.

57. H. W. Blakeley, "When the Army," 27–28.

58. Walter W. Waters, *B.E.F.,* quote on 183, 185–206; "Bonus Heads Indi-cate Resistance to Ouster," *Washington Post,* 24 July 1932, 18; and Donald J. Lisio, *President and Protest,* 150–65.

59. Statement of Lewis I. H. Edwards, inspector, executive officer, and assis-tant superintendent, Metropolitan Police Force, 3 August 1932, file 4–631, "Dis-trict Military Relations—The Bonus Marchers," box 253, RG 351, NA; "Battle of Washington," *Time* 20 (8 August 1932), 5–6; and Roger Daniels, *Bonus March,* 149–56.

60. Statement of Lewis I. H. Edwards, RG 351, NA; and Roger Daniels, *Bonus March,* 149–56.

61. On debate, see Luther Reichfelder to Attorney General, 2 August 1932, file 4–632, "District Military Relations—The Bonus Marchers," box 253, RG 351, NA. Roger Daniels, *Bonus March,* 150–55; and Donald J. Lisio, *President and Protest,* 181–84.

62. Reflecting his view that the evictions were unnecessary, Daniels argues forcefully that the commissioners overreacted to this initial riot and issued the orders before the killings; Lisio suggests that the evidence is obscure on this mat-ter; see Roger Daniels, *Bonus March,* 163–66; and Donald J. Lisio, *President and Protest,* 186–88, 204.

63. On chronology of orders, see Luther Reichfelder to Attorney General, RG 351, NA; phone call to army noted in G-2 Log, 28 July 1932, file 10110–2452/443a, box 2833, RG 165, NA; Hoover's statement and commis-sioner's request in "Herbert Hoover, "Statement of President on Ordering Out Troops," *Washington Post,* 29 July 1932, 1; and Donald J. Lisio, *President and Protest,* 196–97.

64. On MacArthur's insistence on leading, Dwight D. Eisenhower, *At Ease,* 213–16. On atmosphere, "The Week," *New Republic* 71 (10 August 1932), 326. On number of troops, John W. Killigrew, "Army and the Bonus Incident," 62.

65. H. W. Blakeley, "When the Army," 29; G-2 Log; Donald J. Lisio, *Presi-dent and Protest,* 204–7.

66. Donald J. Lisio, *President and Protest,* 207–8; Walter W. Waters, *B.E.F.,* 99.

67. Dwight D. Eisenhower, *At Ease,* 217; Donald J. Lisio, *President and Protest,* 209–14; Roger Daniels, *Bonus March,* 169–71; and Walter W. Waters, *B.E.F.,* 232–37. On the soldiers setting fire to the camps, see George V. H. Mose-ley, *Memorandum for the Secretary of War,* 17 December 1932, "240 Bonus 6–12–32" file, box 1180, RG 94, NA. On announcements, see "Masterbooks," reel 69, Red Network, NBC Radio Collection, Recorded Sound Reference Center, LC. On MacArthur's treatment of press, see Roger Daniels, *Bonus March,* 306–7.

68. MacArthur quoted in "One Slain, 60 Hurt as Troops Rout B.E.F. with Gas Bombs and Flames," *Washington Post*, 29 July 1932, 4.

69. Herbert Hoover, "Text of Hoover's Letter to District Commissioners," *Washington Post*, 30 July 1932, 1. On Hoover's general reaction, Donald J. Lisio, *President and Protest*, 229–33.

70. On efforts to find Communist Bonus marchers, see "50 Seized as Reds Face Deportation," *Washington Post*, 30 July 1932, 1. On attorney general's meeting, Donald J. Lisio, *President and Protest*, 240–41; and David Williams, " 'They Never Stopped Watching Us': FBI Political Surveillance, 1924–1936," *UCLA Historical Journal* 2 (1981), 15–16. Sec. Hurley quoted in "Finis for the B.E.F.," *Washington Post*, 4 August 1932, 6.

71. *Times* quoted in "Swords or Charity," *Commonweal* 16 (10 August 1932). General Van Horn Moseley, who participated in the evacuation, collected related materials into a scrapbook that tended to praise the evictions; see "The Bonus Army" Scrapbook, n.d., cont. 8, Papers of General G. Van Horn Moseley, Manuscript Division, LC. For review of press coverage of the evacuation, see Louis Leibovich, "Press Reaction to the Bonus March of 1932," *Journalism Monographs* 122 (1990), 17–24; and Donald J. Lisio, *President and Protest*, 231.

72. Reflecting their close contact with the march, editorials in the Washington papers did make these points; see "Disperse the Bonus Army," *Washington Post*, 30 July 1932, 6.

73. VA report, *Nation* 135 (7 September 1932), 201–2. For general accounts of the failure of efforts to discredit marchers, see David Williams, "They Never Stopped," 16; and Donald J. Lisio, *President and Protest*, 241–53. Glassford's rebuttal began on July 29 and continued through the fall; see "Glassford Denies He Plans to Resign," *Washington Post*, 30 July 1932, 3; and "The Bonus Bomb Bursts into the Campaign," *Literary Digest* 114 (24 September 1932), 12. On further reactions, "Again, Bonuseers," *Time* 20 (12 September 1932), 10; "The Week," *New Republic* 72 (7 September 1932), 84; American Civil Liberties Union, *"Land of the Pilgrims' Pride": 1932–1933* (ACLU Annual Report), 1933, *American Civil Liberties Union Records and Publications, 1917–75* (Glen Rock, N.J.: Microfilming Corp. of America, 1976), reel 87. For other criticisms, see Paul Anderson, "Tear-Gas, Bayonets, and Votes: The President Opens His Reelection Campaign," *Nation* 135 (17 August 1932), 138–40; William F. Sands, "How Revolution May Be Caused," *Commonweal* 16 (17 August 1932), 382–84; "The Folly of Hatred," *Collier's* 90 (10 September 1932), 50; and "The Way It Was Done," *Survey* 68 (15 September 1932), 418. Because of the criticism, Hoover quickly became defensive about the evacuation. By the 1940s, he considered "the misrepresentation of the bonus incident for political purposes surpassed any similar action in American history"; Herbert Hoover, *The Memoirs of Herbert Hoover; Vol. 3, The Great Depression, 1929–1941* (New York: Macmillan, 1951), 218–32; Donald J. Lisio, *President and Protest*, 277–78; and Roger Daniels, *Bonus March*, 270–72. [Editorial cartoon], "Chicago Herald and Examiner," *Chicago Herald and Examiner*, "240 Bonus 5–28–32" file, box 1181, RG 94, NA.

74. Song quoted in Harold Meyerson and Ernest Harburg, *Who Put the Rainbow in the Wizard of Oz? Yip Harburg, Lyricist* (Ann Arbor: University of Michigan Press, 1993), 49; for the background on the song and its reception, see 43–55 and the interview with Harburg in Studs Terkel, *Hard Times: An Oral History of the Great Depression* (New York: Avon, 1970), 34–36. On the presence of the Bonus marchers in these movies, see Lawrence W. Levine, "Hollywood's Washington," 241–42. Other quickly published accounts of the Bonus marchers include a Communist-sponsored publication, *Ballads of the B.E.F.* (New York: Coventry House, 1932); John H. Bartlett, *Bonus March and the New Deal;* and Henry O. Meisel, *Bonus Expeditionary Forces and an Interview with Glassford;* Owen P. White, "General Glassford's Story," 10–12.

75. On Glassford's resignation, "Glassford Denies," 3; and Owen P. White, "General Glassford's Story," 10–12. On Brown, Donald J. Lisio, *President and Protest,* 188; "Meeting the Marchers," *Washington Post,* 25 November 1932, 6; "Spectators," in Edward Dahlberg, "Hunger on the March," *Nation* 135 (28 December 1932), 644; and "Excellent Police Work," *Washington Times,* 9 December 1932, 24. MID reports on the calls for the Hunger March were numerous, but had none of the personal involvement of reports on the Bonus Army; see file 10110–2452/490a, /497, /500, /501, /504, /507–/513, box 2833; file 10110–2662/20, /24, /25, box 2842; file 10110–2674/1–2, box 2856, RG 165, NA.

76. On revival of Bonus agitation, "Where Roosevelt Stands on the Bonus," *Literary Digest* 114 (29 October 1932), 5; and Roger Daniels, *Bonus March,* 211–41.

77. "Killed" from *Nation* 136 (31 May 1933), 600. On eventual victory, Roger Daniels, *Bonus March,* 211–41; and Gary D. Best, *FDR and the Bonus Marchers, 1933–1935* (Westport, Conn.: Praeger, 1992). Arthur Schlesinger Jr. uses Roosevelt's approach to the second Bonus Army as an one of his several vignettes to illustrate the "new spirit" of Washington in 1933; see Arthur Schlesinger Jr., *The Age of Roosevelt: The Coming of the New Deal* (Boston: Houghton Mifflin, 1958), 14–15.

78. "This Week," *New Republic* 71 (28 July 1932), 273. "Vets Suspicious of Loan Proffers," *B.E.F. News,* 9 July 1932, 1. *Nation* 136 (3 May 1933), 487. Although some Americans viewed Gandhi's resistance efforts with alarm, there was also considerable positive response; on views toward Gandhi's activities in the 1930s, see Manoranjan Jha, *Civil Disobedience and After: American Reaction to Political Developments in India During 1930–1935* (Meerut: Meenakshi Prakashan, 1973).

79. David R. Barber, "Hunger Army March Reminds Capital of Coxey's Invasion," *Washington Post,* 6 December 1931, 17; "Was the Hunger March," 9. "Bonus Groups Ignore Police Plea to Leave," *Washington Post,* 9 June 1932, 3.

80. George Sokolsky, "Will Revolution Come?" *Atlantic Monthly* 150 (August 1932), 190; and F. Anderson to Secretary of War Hurley, 9 September 1932, "240 Bonus (5–28–32)" file, box 1181, RG 94, NA.

4. "PRESSURE, MORE PRESSURE, AND STILL MORE PRESSURE"

1. Eugene Davidson, Transcript of Eugene Davidson, oral history interview, Robert Martin, interviewer (28 June 1968), CRDP, MSRC. Eugene Davidson, The Birth of Executive Order 8802, n.d., folder 43: "Other Organizational Affiliations," box 91–2, Davidson Collection, MSRC.

2. For signs of how influential it was in the short run, see Roi Ottley, *New World a-Coming: Inside Black America* (Boston: Houghton Mifflin, 1943), 248–53, 289–305; the numerous references to the threatened protest in Rayford W. Logan, *What the Negro Wants* (Chapel Hill: University of North Carolina Press, 1942); Gunnar Myrdal, Richard M. E. Sterner, and Arnold M. Rose, *An American Dilemma: The Negro Problem and Modern Democracy* (New York: Harper and Brothers, 1944), vol. 2, 850–52; and Adam C. Powell Jr., *Marching Blacks: An Interpretive History of the Rise of the Black Common Man* (New York: Dial Press, 1945), 148–62. The first detailed account, written during the 1950s, examines the march as both a tactic of "pressure group" politics and a mass movement; however, the original march receives only limited attention; see Herbert Garfinkel, *When Negroes March: The March on Washington Movement in the Organizational Politics for FEPC* (Glencoe, Ill.: Free Press, 1959). Accounts written since the 1960s emphasize Randolph as a "pioneer" and the march as a precedent for the more recent civil rights movement; Jervis Anderson, *A. Philip Randolph: A Biographical Portrait* (New York: Harcourt Brace Jovanovich, 1973), esp. "Let the Negro Masses Speak" chap; Gary J. Hunter, "'Don't Buy from Where You Can't Work': Black Urban Boycott Movements during the Depression, 1929–1941" (Ph.D. diss., University of Michigan, 1977), esp. chap. "Getting It All Together: The March on Washington Movement," 283–302; Paula F. Pfeffer, *A. Philip Randolph: Pioneer of the Civil Rights Movement* (Baton Rouge: Louisiana State University Press, 1990); and John H. Bracey Jr. and August Meier, "Allies or Adversaries? The NAACP, A. Philip Randolph and the 1941 March on Washington," *Georgia Historical Quarterly* 75 (Spring 1991), 1–17. For accounts that emphasize the Roosevelt administration's role, see Joseph Lash, *Eleanor and Franklin: The Story of Their Relationship, Based on Eleanor Roosevelt's Private Papers* (New York: Norton, 1971), 512–35; Daniel Kryder, "The American State and the Management of Race Conflict in the Workplace and in the Army, 1941–1945," *Polity* 26 (Summer 1994), 602–34; Daniel Kryder, *Divided Arsenal: Race and the American State during World War II* (New York: Cambridge University Press, 2000), 53–67; and Doris Kearns Goodwin, *No Ordinary Time: Franklin and Eleanor Roosevelt: The Home Front in World War II* (New York: Simon and Schuster, 1994), 246–53.

3. "Roosevelt's Executive Order," *Chicago Defender*, 12 July 1941, 14.

4. A. Philip Randolph, How to Blast the Bottlenecks of Race Prejudice in National Defense, Press Release, 15 January 1941, Scrapbook, vol. 2, box 55, Randolph Papers.

5. On Negro Congress and Randolph, see John B. Kirby, *Black Americans in the Roosevelt Era: Liberalism and Race* (Knoxville: University of Tennessee

Press, 1980), 164–70; Paula F. Pfeffer, *A. Philip Randolph,* 32–43; Jervis Anderson, *A. Philip Randolph,* 229–40; and Edwin R. Embree, *13 against the Odds* (New York: Viking Press, 1944), 212.

6. A. Philip Randolph, "Call to Negro America," flyer, 1 May 1941, "March on Washington Movement, Printed Matter" folder, box 27, Randolph Papers. Of regular soldiers, blacks represented only 2 percent of the total; the proportion of black officers was even smaller: there were only 5 black officers in comparison to 1,359 white officers. Richard Dalfiume observes, "If one could not participate fully in the defense of his country, he could not lay claim to the rights of a full-fledged citizen"; Richard Dalfiume, "The 'Forgotten Years' of the Negro Revolution," chap. in Bernard Sternsher, ed., *The Negro in Depression and War: Prelude to Revolution, 1930–1945* (Chicago: Quadrangle Books, 1969), 300. See also Lee Finkle, *Forum for Protest: The Black Press during World War II* (Rutherford, N.J.: Fairleigh Dickinson University Press, 1975), 131; and Frank Crosswaith and Alfred B. Lewis, "Discrimination, Incorporated," *Social Action* 8.1 (1942), 16.

7. Contracts, figure cited in David G. McCullough, *Truman* (New York: Simon and Schuster, 1992), 254. Walter White, " 'It's Our Country Too': The Negro Demands the Right to Be Allowed to Fight for It," *Saturday Evening Post* 213 (14 December 1940), 27, 61–70; and A. Philip Randolph, "Call to Negro America," Randolph Papers. See also John H. Bracey Jr. and August Meier, "Allies or Adversaries," 3–6.

8. "Executive Order Bans Civil Service Jim Crow," *Crisis* 47 (December 1940), 390. Congressional action, quote from Harvard Sitkoff, *A New Deal for Blacks: The Emergence of Civil Rights as a National Issue* (New York: Oxford University Press, 1978), 69; and Nancy J. Weiss, *Farewell to the Party of Lincoln: Black Politics in the Age of FDR* (Princeton, N.J.: Princeton University Press, 1983), 51–55. On implementation of these and similar clauses, W. J. Trent Jr., "Federal Sanctions Directed against Racial Discrimination," *Phylon* 3 (1942), 171–82; and Charles S. Johnson, "Negro Labor in Public Housing," *Crisis* 48 (February 1941), 45. Outside of work programs, the Roosevelt administration was reluctant to act; see John T. Eliff, "Aspects of Federal Civil Rights Enforcement: The Justice Department and the FBI, 1939–1964," *Perspectives in American History* 5 (1971), 605–17. For NAACP activities, "How You Can Help Expose Jim Crow in National Defense," *Crisis* 48 (March 1941), 84. On comparable activities by the National Urban League, see Lester Granger, "The President, the Negro, and Defense," *Opportunity* 19 (July 1941), 205. On conferences, see "Chronicle of Race Relations," *Phylon* 2 (1941), 89. On letter-writing campaigns, see "White House Blesses Jim Crow," *Crisis* 47 (November 1940), 357. On gradual changes, see Lester Granger, "President, the Negro, and Defense," 207; Campbell C. Johnson, "The Mobilization of Negro Manpower for the Armed Forces," *Journal of Negro Education* 12 (Summer 1943), 298–306; George Q. Flynn, "Selective Service and American Blacks during World War II," *Journal of Negro History* 69 (Winter 1984), 14–25; Lee Finkle, *Forum for Protest,* 129–62; and Merl Reed, *Seedtime for the Modern Civil Rights Movement: The President's Committee on Fair Employment Practice, 1941–1946* (Baton Rouge: Louisiana State University Press, 1991), 16.

9. For articles criticizing treatment, see "Second World War," *Phylon* 1

(1940), 371; and Anonymous [identified as a "Negro enlisted man"], "Jim Crow in the Army Camps," *Crisis* 47 (December 1940), 385. Logan quoted in Lee Finkle, *Forum for Protest*, 92.

10. For accounts of September 1940 meeting, see Walter White, *A Man Called White: The Autobiography of Walter White* (New York: Viking, 1948), 186–88; Joseph Lash, *Eleanor and Franklin*, 529–33; and "White House Blesses Jim Crow," 350–51, 357. For the controversy over the press release, see "NAACP Charges Roosevelt with Trickery," *Washington Tribune*, 29 October 1940, 1; and Nancy J. Weiss, *Farewell to the Party of Lincoln*, 274–78. Jervis Anderson, *A. Philip Randolph*, 247–48. Lester Granger claimed that Randolph was inspired to call for a march on Washington by a woman who spoke out at a mass meeting in Chicago; on the basis of his other remarks, however, it seems likely that Granger was remembering a meeting that took place after Randolph's decision and press release. Granger's story is recounted in Guichard Parris and Lester Brooks, *Blacks in the City: A History of the National Urban League* (Boston: Little, Brown, 1971), 290, and was repeated by Harvard Sitkoff, *New Deal for Blacks*, 314.

11. "Era of the pioneer" phrase from speech by Eleanor Roosevelt, quoted in John B. Kirby, *Black Americans*, 80. Roosevelt quoted in Doris Kearns Goodwin, *No Ordinary Time*, 201. A. Philip Randolph, "Call to Negro America," Randolph Papers.

12. A. Philip Randolph, "Call to Negro America," Randolph Papers. V. O. Key, *Politics, Parties and Pressure Groups* (New York: Thomas Y. Crowell, 1942). On the move away from belief in ideal values toward relativism, see Edward A. Purcell, *The Crisis of Democratic Theory: Scientific Naturalism and the Problem of Value* (Lexington: University Press of Kentucky, 1973), 197–217. Another prominent scholar who asserted this view was E. Pendleton Herring, *The Politics of Democracy: American Parties in Action* (New York: W. W. Norton, 1940). On Herring's place in political science in the 1940s, see Edward A. Purcell, *Crisis of Democratic Theory*, 213–17. The practice of businessmen lobbying government officials for special favors still drew attacks; see Kenneth G. Crawford, *The Pressure Boys: The Inside Story of Lobbying in America* (New York: J. Messner, 1939).

13. A. Philip Randolph, "Call to Negro America," Randolph Papers; and A. Philip Randolph to Lester Granger, 26 March 1941, "March on Washington Committee, 1941" folder, box 13, series 6, NUL Records. Biographical information on Randolph drawn from Jervis Anderson, *A. Philip Randolph*, 1–229; Paula F. Pfeffer, *A. Philip Randolph*, 6–44; and FBI, Memorandum Re: A. Philip Randolph [1942], file 100–55616–6, *FBI File on A. Philip Randolph* (microfilm) (New York: Scholarly Resources, 1990), reel 1. On demonstrations in 1930s, see FBI, Memorandum; and "Brotherhood of Sleeping Car Porters Plan Huge Patriotic Demonstration," *New York Age*, 7 September 1940, Scrapbook, vol. 1, box 54, Randolph Papers. On labor protests, Lizabeth Cohen, *Making a New Deal: Industrial Workers in Chicago, 1919–1939* (New York: Cambridge University Press, 1990), 251–321; and Cheryl L. Greenberg, *"Or Does It Explode?" Black Harlem in the Great Depression* (New York: Oxford University Press, 1991), 93–139.

14. On jobs campaigns, see Gary J. Hunter, "Don't Buy," passim; Cheryl L. Greenberg, *"Or Does It Explode?"* 113–39; August Meier and Elliott M. Rud-

wick, "The Origins of Nonviolent Direct Action in Afro-American Protest: A Note on Historical Discontinuities," chap. in August Meier and Elliott M. Rudwick, eds., *Along the Color Line: Explorations in the Black Experience* (Urbana: University of Illinois Press, 1976), 314–32. On legal cases, see *New Negro Alliance v. Sanitary Grocery Co.,* 303 U.S. 552 (1938), and "public forum" in *Hague v. Committee for Industrial Organization,* 307 U.S. 496 (1939); Adam C. Powell Jr., *Marching Blacks,* 113; and M. G. Abernathy, *The Right of Assembly and Association* (Columbia: University of South Carolina Press, 1981).

15. On protests in Washington between 1932 and 1946, see Robert Cohen, *When the Old Left Was Young: Student Radicals and America's First Mass Student Movement, 1929–1941* (New York: Oxford University Press, 1993), 50, 188–237, 315; "Jewish GIs Hit Britain's Stand on Palestine," *Washington Post,* 16 July 1946, "Parades and Picketing, 1946–1949" folder, Vertical Files, Washingtoniana Collection; demonstrations by "Friends of Spanish Democracy," "Veterans of the Lincoln Brigade," "Workers Alliance of America," see Miscellaneous Reports, file 1115–40: "Field Days, Parades, Etc.," box 9, RG 79, NA; on housewives, Annelise Orleck, " 'We Are That Mythical Thing Called the Public': Militant Housewives during the Great Depression," *Feminist Studies* 19 (Spring 1993), 147–72; on pacifists, see Robert Cooney and Helen Michalowski (based on the work of Marty Jezer), *The Power of the People: Active Nonviolence in the United States* (Philadelphia: New Society Publishers, 1987), 74–123. Randolph remembered that some people brought up concerns about the Bonus March; see A. Philip Randolph, Transcript of A. Philip Randolph, oral history interview, Robert Martin, interviewer (14 January 1969), 59, CRDP, MSRC. On references to Coxey's Army, see Charley Cherokee, "National Grapevine," *Chicago Defender,* 31 May 1941, 5; and "Let the New Coxey's Army March," *Baltimore Afro-American,* 21 June 1941, 4.

16. On Scottsboro efforts and demonstrations, see James E. Goodman, *Stories of Scottsboro* (New York: Pantheon Books, 1994). On Anderson concert, see Scott Sandage, "A Marble House Divided: The Lincoln Memorial, the Civil Rights Movement, and the Politics of Memory," *Journal of American History* 80 (June 1993), 135–67. "Effectiveness" from "Sweet Reasonableness—No March on Washington," *Baltimore Afro-American,* 5 July 1941, 4.

17. Randolph's policy was officially adopted by the committee organizing the march; Minutes of Subcommittee Meeting on "March to Washington," 10 April 1941, "March on Washington Committee, General, 1940–1941" folder, box A416, group II, NAACP Records. Gunnar Myrdal pointed to this disjunction between the American creed and American practice in terms of African Americans; see Gunnar Myrdal, Richard M. E. Sterner, and Arnold M. Rose, *American Dilemma,* 1, 3–82.

18. A. Philip Randolph, How to Blast, Randolph Papers.

19. A. Philip Randolph to Walter White, 11 May 1941, "March on Washington Committee—A. Philip Randolph, 1941" folder, box A417, group II, NAACP Records.

20. Claude MacKay quoted in Jervis Anderson, *A. Philip Randolph,* 230–31. A. Philip Randolph, "Why I Refused Reelection as President of the NNC," *Washington Tribune,* 11 May 1940, 1.

21. Jervis Anderson, *A. Philip Randolph,* 248–49. A. Philip Randolph to

Walter White, 18 March 1941, "March on Washington Committee—A. Philip Randolph, 1941" folder, box A417, group II, NAACP Records; Walter White to A. Philip Randolph, 20 March 1941, ibid. See also John H. Bracey Jr. and August Meier, "Allies or Adversaries," 8–9.

22. The committee is listed in A. Philip Randolph, "Call to Negro America," Randolph Papers. On occupation of leaders, see "To All Branches," 12 May 1941, "March on Washington Committee, General, 1940–41" folder, box A416, group II, NAACP Records; and "Roosevelt Opposed to March on Washington," *Pittsburgh Courier,* 28 June 1941, 4. On political activities and organizing experience: on Crosswaith, see Cheryl L. Greenberg, *"Or Does It Explode?"* 109–13; and Surdarshan Kapur, *Raising Up a Prophet: The African-American Encounter with Gandhi* (Boston: Beacon Press, 1992), 42. On Powell, see Adam C. Powell Jr., *Marching Black* and "Smashing the Color Line," *Opportunity* 19 (May 1941), 130–31. On meetings with federal officials, Lester Granger, "President, the Negro, and Defense," 205. On coalitions and common political goals in the 1930s, see Harvard Sitkoff, *New Deal for Blacks,* 245–49; and Nancy J. Weiss, *Farewell to the Party of Lincoln,* 67–68, 146. Even the Elks had spoken out against discrimination in New Deal and defense programs; see Charles H. Wesley, *History of the Improved Benevolent and Protective Order of Elks of the World, 1898–1954* (Washington, D.C.: Association for the Study of Negro Life and History, 1955), 227–315. On Wilson and Coxey's Army, see Rayford W. Logan, "James Finley Wilson," in Rayford W. Logan and Michael R. Winston, eds., *Dictionary of American Negro Biography* (New York: Norton, 1982), 663. On name and date, Minutes of Subcommittee Meeting, 10 April 1941, NAACP Records.

23. Even Randolph traveled for two weeks in May for the porters' union. See "Minutes of Meeting of Subcommittee to Draft Program for "MARCH ON WASHINGTON, 23 April 1941, "March on Washington, 1941" folder, box 13, series 6, NUL Records. On Randolph's departure, see the hurried note to Lester Granger, in which he explains, "Will return May 19 and shall plan to put all my time on March for 30 days"; A. Philip Randolph to Lester Granger, 6 May 1941, "March on Washington Committee, 1941" file, box 13, series 6, NUL Records. On his appointment, see A. Philip Randolph to Lester Granger, NUL Records; and "South Rallies to Job March on Washington," *Pittsburgh Courier,* 24 May 1941, 23. On Davidson's biography, see Eugene Davidson, Transcript of Eugene Davidson, CRDP, MSRC; materials in the Davidson Collection, MSRC; "Eugene Davidson," Vertical File, MSRC, which includes obituaries from the *Washington Post,* 7 March 1979, B6, and the *Washington Evening Star,* 7 March 1976, B7; and Gary J. Hunter, "Don't Buy," 131–47. On role of Washington office, Minutes of Meeting of Subcommittee, 23 April 1941, NUL Records.

24. A. Philip Randolph, Transcript of A. Philip Randolph, 58, CRDP, MSRC. NUL and NAACP memberships from Roscoe E. Lewis, "The Role of Pressure Groups in Maintaining Morale among Negroes," *Journal of Negro Education* 12 (Summer 1943), 468. Letters to members: "To All Branches," NAACP Records; and Lester Granger, Memorandum to the Executive Secretaries, 20 May 1941, "March on Washington Committee, 1941" file, box 13, series 6, NUL Records. On emphasis put on local committees, see Plan to Mobilize 10,000 Negroes to March on Washington, D.C. (undated; before 3 April

1941), "March on Washington Committee—A. Philip Randolph, 1941" folder, box A417, group II, NAACP Records; and "To All Branches," NAACP Records. Locations: Negro March-on-Washington Committee, Bulletin, 22 May 1941, "March on Washington Movement, Miscellaneous Items" folder, box 26, Randolph Papers.

25. Penn Kimball, "Negroes to March to Capital to Protest Discrimination," *PM,* 18 June 1941, 8; A. Philip Randolph, Why and How the March Was Postponed [n.d., July 1941?], "March on Washington, General, 1942" folder, box A416, group II, NAACP Records. Although they did not report on the march efforts, some white-controlled dailies did criticize the discrimination against African Americans when endorsing administration statements condemning such treatment; see "Dailies Urge Halt to Defense Jim Crow," *Baltimore Afro-American,* 21 June 1941, 7. On black press in 1940 and 1941, see Lee Finkle, *Forum for Protest,* 51–62. Associated Negro Press was founded in 1919; see Gunnar Myrdal, Richard M. E. Sterner, and Arnold M. Rose, *American Dilemma,* vol. 2, 923.

26. On conservatism of editors, see Lee Finkle, "The Conservative Aims of Militant Rhetoric: Black Protest during World War II," *Journal of American History* 60 (December 1973), 693–713; and "Slightly Effective Embarrassment," *Pittsburgh Courier,* 24 May 1941, 8. J. A. Rogers, "Rogers Says: March on Washington an Effective Means of Forcing Democracy," *Pittsburgh Courier,* 28 June 1941, 24. "Let the New Coxey's Army March," 4. Kate Smith's song "We Are Americans, All" was a hit in 1941. "The Crusade for Democracy," *Chicago Defender,* 28 June 1941, 14.

27. On NAACP schedule, Charley Cherokee, "National Grapevine [31 May 1941]," 5. On organizational support, see "Jobs Parade under Fire by White House," *Chicago Defender,* 21 June 1941, 2; "Roosevelt Opposed," 1; and A. Philip Randolph, Why and How, NAACP Records. On contributions, Financial Report, [August 5, 1941], "March on Washington Committee—A. Philip Randolph, 1941" folder, box A417, group II, NAACP Records.

28. Joe Louis's contribution, Financial Report, NAACP Records. Sidney R. Redmond to Walter White, 14 May 1941, "March on Washington Committee, General, 1940–1941" folder, box A416, group II, NAACP Records. "Scores of letters" from "Randolph Won't Halt Job March," *Baltimore Afro American,* 21 June 1941, 2. Slogan on button quoted in Minutes of Meeting of Subcommittee, 23 April 1941, NUL Records; number of buttons bought calculated from Financial Report, NAACP Records. The report says that $900 was received from the sale of buttons by the national committee, but notes that local committees were allowed to keep half the receipts from the sale of buttons. Initial calls, A. Philip Randolph, How to Blast, Randolph Papers; Davidson's claim, "50,000 to Hit at U.S. Defense Discrimination," *Chicago Defender,* 17 May 1941, 3; 100,000 figure from A. Philip Randolph, Negroes Out to Shake America for Jobs and Justice in National Defense, Press Release, 29 May 1941, Scrapbook, vol. 2, box 55, Randolph Papers.

29. On growth of Washington, see Oliver McKee Jr., "Washington as Boom Town," *North American Review* 239 (February 1935), 177–83; Elbert Peets, "Washington" [1937], chap. in Paul D. Spreiregen, ed., *On the Art of Designing Cities: Selected Essays of Elbert Peets* (Cambridge, Mass.: MIT Press, 1968),

67–78; William B. Rhoads, "Franklin D. Roosevelt and Washington Architecture," *Records of the Columbia Historical Society* 52 (1989), 104–62. On the mall specifically, see Elbert Peets, "New Plans for the Uncompleted Mall" [1935], chap. in Paul D. Spreiregen, ed., *On the Art of Designing Cities;* "Marred Mall," *Newsweek* 18 (1 December 1941), 22; and Norma Evenson, "Monumental Spaces," chap. in Richard W. Longstreth, ed., *The Mall in Washington, 1791–1991* (Washington, D.C.: National Gallery of Art, 1991), 19–34. On growth and tourists in 1941, "Golden Flood," *Newsweek* 17 (4 May 1941), 18. On atmosphere in Washington during the 1940s, see Willard M. Kiplinger, *Washington Is Like That* (New York: Harper's, 1942). Frederick Barkley, "Axis of Democracy," *New York Times Magazine* (16 November 1941), 16. On educative possibilities of places, see J. B. Jackson, "American Public Space," *Public Interest* 74 (Winter 1984), 52–65.

30. For statistics and customs of segregation in general, see Louis Lautier, "Jim Crow in the Nation's Capitol," *Crisis* 47 (April 1940), 107; George Goodman, "Behind the Scenes in Washington," *Opportunity* 18 (August 1940), 243; and especially, National Committee on Segregation in the Nation's Capital, *Segregation in Washington* (Chicago: 1948). Some challenges to federally segregated facilities succeeded during the 1930s, but not all; see Constance M. Green, *The Secret City: A History of Race Relations in the Nation's Capital* (Princeton, N.J.: Princeton University Press, 1967), 230, 260–61.

31. "Arthur Mitchell Brands Randolph 'Most Dangerous,'" *Houston Defender*, 28 June 1941, Scrapbook, vol. 2, box 55, Randolph Papers. Robert Westbrook argues that the "family" became the major justification for fighting World War II, which suggests the centrality of the family to conceptions of the nation during this period; see Robert Westbrook, "Fighting for the American Family: Private Interests and Political Obligation in World War II," chap. in Richard W. Fox and T. J. J. Lears, eds., *The Power of Culture: Critical Essays in American History* (Chicago: University of Chicago Press, 1993), 195–221. Minutes of Subcommittee Meeting, 10 April 1941, NAACP Records.

32. A. Philip Randolph, "Call to Negro America," Randolph Papers; "'March of Mourning' Set for Nation's Capitol," *Chicago Defender*, 17 May 1941, 3.

33. Davidson quoted in "50,000 to Hit," 3. They also planned to invite Marian Anderson; see Plan to Mobilize, NAACP Records, and Minutes of Meeting of Subcommittee, 23 April 1941, NUL Records.

34. Plan to Mobilize, NAACP Records; Davidson quoted in "50,000 to Hit," 3. On date of letters, see Jervis Anderson, *A. Philip Randolph*, 374.

35. Charley Cherokee, "National Grapevine [31 May 1941]," 5. On D.C. branch decision, see John Lovell Jr. to Thurman Dodson, 8 May 1941, "March on Washington Committee—A. Philip Randolph, 1941" folder, box A417, group II, NAACP Records. On interracial organizing generally, see John B. Kirby, *Black Americans*, 48–96; and, in the District specifically, Constance M. Green, *Secret City*, 215–49.

36. Mitchell's speech: "Jobs Parade," 1; "'Most Dangerous Negro in America' to Blast Charges by Rep. Mitchell," *Chicago Defender*, 28 June 1941, 6; and "Administration Pressure Brought on March to D.C.," *Crisis* 48 (July 1941), 230–31. On Mitchell's political career, see Christopher R. Reed, "Black Chicago

Political Realignment during the Great Depression and New Deal," chap. in Kenneth L. Kusmer, ed., *Depression, War, and the New Migration, 1930–1960* (New York: Garland, 1991). "That March on Washington," *Pittsburgh Courier,* 14 June 1941, 6.

37. A. Philip Randolph, "Call to Negro America," Randolph Papers.

38. On invitations, see A. Philip Randolph, Employment in the Defense Industry, 25 June 1941, "March on Washington 1941" file, box 34, Randolph Papers; and Jervis Anderson, *A. Philip Randolph,* 304. On surveillance of Randolph, see FBI, Memorandum, FBI file on Randolph. Intelligence reports from May and early June, J. E. Hoover to Captain Alan Goodrich Kirk, director, Naval Intelligence, 24 May 1941, file 10218–461/1; W. T. Bals to Asst. Chief of Staff, G-2, 27 May 1941, file 10218–461/1; and Allan G. Kirk to J. Edgar Hoover, 31 May 1941, file 10218–463/2, all in RG 165, NA, microfilm 1440, reel 6. Roosevelt's feelings in Memorandum, F.D.R. to Marvin McIntyre, 7 June 1941, quoted in Daniel Kryder, "American State," 611.

39. On events confronting the Roosevelt administration, see Doris Kearns Goodwin, *No Ordinary Time,* 201–46; on investigations of contractors and strikes, see David G. McCullough, *Truman,* 253–69; Bennett M. Rich, *The Presidents and Civil Disorder* (Washington, D.C.: Brookings Institution, 1941), 177–88; and Nelson Lichtenstein, *Labor's War at Home: The CIO in World War II* (New York: Cambridge University Press, 1982). March leader Channing Tobias, quoted in Minutes of Local Unit of Negro March-on-Washington Committee, 14 June 1941, "March on Washington Committee, General, 1940–41" folder, box A416, group II, NAACP Records. ANP report, "March Perturbs D.C. Police Officials," *Chicago Defender,* 21 June 1941, 2.

40. Roosevelt's tolerance of protest extended to assistance in the case of the Bonus March and again in 1937 when he arranged tents and food to be sent to striking sharecroppers in Missouri when they were evicted from their homes; see John A. Salmond, *A Southern Rebel: The Life and Times of Aubrey Willis Williams, 1890–1965* (Chapel Hill: University of North Carolina Press, 1983), 171–72. Roosevelt had even advised organizers for a previous march by the American Youth Congress in 1937 and greeted a delegation; see Joseph Lash, *Eleanor and Franklin,* 546–48. His treatment of youth marchers in 1940 is described in Joseph Lash, *Eleanor and Franklin,* 601–7. Roosevelt also refused to send army troops when asked by governors faced with social or labor unrest; see Bennett M. Rich, *Presidents and Civil Disorder,* 177. Groups of pacifists had been going to protest in Washington since February; see "March to White House," *New York Times,* 2 February 1941, 6; and "Peace Vigil Ends Today, APM Plans New Campaign," *Daily Worker,* 21 June 1941, 2. On presidential intervention, see "White House Pickets Attacked by Marine," *New York Times,* 15 May 1941, 16; and Jervis Anderson, *A. Philip Randolph,* 374.

41. Eleanor Roosevelt to A. Philip Randolph, 5 June 1941, reprinted in numerous black newspapers; see "Mrs. Roosevelt Opposes Washington March," *Pittsburgh Courier,* 21 June 1941, 4. On political situation facing Roosevelt, see Daniel Kryder, "American State," 607.

42. "Mrs. Roosevelt Opposes Washington March," 4. On scheduling, see "Jobs Parade," 2; and A. Philip Randolph, Employment in the Defense Industry,

Randolph Papers. The president's directive to Williams quoted in Joseph Lash, *Eleanor and Franklin,* 534; see also the slightly different and more formal description of this conversation based on a later oral history in John A. Salmond, *Southern Rebel,* 174. "Thresh it out" from Edwin Watson, "Memorandum for the President," 14 June 1941, quoted in Jervis Anderson, *A. Philip Randolph,* 256. Roosevelt's decision to meet with leaders, Joseph Lash, *Eleanor and Franklin,* 534. In this section, I have reconstructed a number of meetings. As noted, the descriptions of the events have been drawn from the newspaper reports, minutes for the June 15 meeting, Randolph's speeches, and oral histories; as a result, participants' quotes are paraphrases by observers of the meetings either at the time or later. They should not be considered the actual words; in cases where conflicting accounts of the meetings occur, I have tried to rely on the accounts published in 1941 or soon after.

43. On debate, see Minutes of Local Unit, NAACP Records, and discussion of this meeting in John H. Bracey Jr. and August Meier, "Allies or Adversaries," 12.

44. A. Philip Randolph, Telegram to Franklin D. Roosevelt, 16 June 1941, quoted in Jervis Anderson, *A. Philip Randolph,* 256; "Let the New Coxey's Army March," 4.

45. The order of these proposals changed between June 14 and June 18, when they were presented to the president; for the proposed version, see Minutes of Local Unit, NAACP; for final version, see Proposals of the Negro March-On-Washington Committee, 18 June 1941, "March on Washington Movement: Principles and Structures" folder, box 26, Randolph Papers.

46. On the restriction to Randolph and White, see Jervis Anderson, *A. Philip Randolph,* 256. "Roosevelt Opposed," 1; "FD Names Body to Study Defense Bias," *Chicago Defender,* 28 June 1941, 1. Leaders' characterization in A. Philip Randolph, Employment in the Defense Industry, Randolph Papers. With the exception of the openings to their stories, the two accounts of this meeting were virtually identical and clearly based on the detailed comments of someone who was present at the meeting. For clarity, I will cite the *Chicago Defender* account below as "FD Names Body."

47. Jervis Anderson, *A. Philip Randolph,* 256. Newspaper accounts in the black newspapers did not mention this beginning, most likely because they did not want to mar the glory of this conference with the president's avoidance tactics. "FD Names Body," 2.

48. La Guardia quoted in A. Philip Randolph, Transcript of A. Philip Randolph, 63, CRDP, MSRC. Local army officer in Statement of Captain Walker, P.I.O., Fort Myer, Va., to G-3 at 11:15 A.M., 24 June 1941, file 10218–463/5, RG 165, NA, microfilm 1440, reel 6. For accusations of police brutality against blacks, see "3,000 March in Capital against Police Terror," *Daily Worker,* 20 September 1941, "Washington, D.C., general" folder, *Schomburg Center Clipping File, 1925–74* (microfiche) (New York: Schomburg Center for Research in Black Culture, New York Public Library, 1975), fiche 005,667–1; and "March Perturbs," 2. On race relations during this period generally, see Constance M. Green, *Secret City,* 215–73.

49. Roosevelt's comment in Jervis Anderson, *A. Philip Randolph,* 257–58. Exchange about the president and "groups" in "FD Names Body," 2.

50. Account of this conversation based on Jervis Anderson, *A. Philip Randolph,* 257–58, and Walter White, *Man Called White,* 192. The question about the turnout did not appear in the newspaper accounts. It has become part of the mythology surrounding this confrontation that Randolph and White were bluffing. For one account that stresses this claim was a bluff, see Rayford W. Logan, Transcript of Dr. Rayford W. Logan, oral history interview, Vincent J. Brown, interviewer (26 June 1967), 28–31, CRDP, MSRC.

51. "FD Names Body," 2; Walter White, *Man Called White,* 192; and Jervis Anderson, *A. Philip Randolph,* 258. On leaders' attitudes, *Amsterdam News,* 21 June 1941, quoted in Louis Ruchames, *Race, Jobs and Politics: The Story of FEPC* (New York: Columbia University Press, 1953), 20.

52. On continued negotiations, see John A. Salmond, *Southern Rebel,* 175. Telegram, Walter White to Roy Wilkins, 19 June 1941, quoted in John H. Bracey Jr. and August Meier, "Allies or Adversaries," 15. On Rauh's amazement, see Joseph L. Rauh, Transcript of Joseph L. Rauh Jr., oral history interview, Katherine Shannon, interviewer (28 August 1967), 28–30, CRDP, MSRC. On Eleanor Roosevelt's call, Doris Kearns Goodwin, *No Ordinary Time,* 252.

53. Statement of Captain Walker, RG 165, NA, microfilm 1440, reel 6; Theodore Arter to Assistant Chief of Staff, G-2, Washington, D.C., 26 June 1941, file 10218–463/7, ibid. The White Plans had been revised in 1936 on the orders of one of MacArthur's successors, General Malin Craig, who was very concerned about domestic insurrection; the war colleges also developed new training programs in riot control. See Joan M. Jensen, *Army Surveillance in America, 1775–1980* (New Haven, Conn.: Yale University Press, 1991), 204–18, 301. Joseph L. Rauh, Transcript, 31–32, CRDP, MSRC.

54. Agreement: Doris Kearns Goodwin, *No Ordinary Time,* 252; and Franklin D. Roosevelt, "Executive Order 8802," June 25, 1941, in Franklin D. Roosevelt and Samuel I. Rosenman, *The Public Papers and Addresses of Franklin D. Roosevelt; Vol. 10, 1941: The Call to Battle Stations* (New York: Random House, 1950), 233–35.

55. Eugene Davidson, Birth of Executive Order 8802, Davidson Collection, MSRC; A. Philip Randolph, Employment in the Defense Industry, Randolph Papers. Neither Davidson nor Randolph referred explicitly to the problem of discrimination by the military in descriptions of this stage of the negotiations, but a subsequent article about the executive order suggested that this was their aim; "F.D. Order Kills Defense Bias," *Chicago Defender,* 5 July 1941, 1. Eugene Davidson, Birth of Executive Order 8802, 2–4, Davidson Collection, MSRC.

56. On trip to White House, see John A. Salmond, *Southern Rebel,* 176; and Eugene Davidson, Birth of Executive Order 8802, Davidson Collection, MSRC. President quoted in Joseph Lash, *Eleanor and Franklin,* 535.

57. Mary M. Bethune to Eleanor Roosevelt, 10 July 1941, in Susan Ware, William Henry Chafe, and Franklin D. Roosevelt Library, eds., *Papers of Eleanor Roosevelt, 1933–1945* (microfilm) (Frederick, Md.: University Publications of America, 1986), reel 1; "Roosevelt's Executive Order," 14; and A. Philip Randolph, Employment in the Defense Industry, Randolph Papers.

58. "Discrimination Barred by FDR," *PM,* 26 June 1941, 19; and "President Orders an Even Break for Minorities in Defense Jobs," *New York Times,* 26 June

1941, 12. Mark Ethridge to Stephen Early, 23 December 1941, quoted in Daniel Kryder, "American State," 612. The compromises in Executive Order 8802 reappeared during the war. Kryder concludes, "The forceful pursuit of the war simultaneously intensified social conflict and provided strong imperative for the postponement of the conflict's clear resolution"; Daniel Kryder, "American State," 634.

59. "The Negro's War," *Fortune* 25 (June 1942), 80. On the presence of a sympathetic editor at *Fortune*, see Kenneth R. Janken, *Rayford W. Logan and the Dilemma of the African-American Intellectual* (Amherst: University of Massachusetts Press, 1993), 133.

60. A. Philip Randolph, Negroes Will Not March on Washington [n.d.; probably June 25], folder 42: "Press Releases," box 91–2; delegates quoted in "Conference Resolutions," *Crisis* (September 1941), 296; "Laud FDR at March Victory Meeting," *Pittsburgh Courier*, 12 July 1941, 7. On lack of enforcement mechanisms, see Lester Granger, "President, the Negro, and Defense," 470; "Richmond Group Calls FDR's Edict Useless," *Baltimore Afro-American*, 5 July 1941, 8; and Lee Finkle, *Forum for Protest*, 97–99.

61. On limited effect of order, see "American Negroes," *Phylon* 3 (1942), 328; on the committee's operation, see Louis Ruchames, *Race, Jobs and Politics*, 28–56, and Herbert Garfinkel, *When Negroes March*, 73–82.

62. J. A. Rogers, "Rogers Says: Agitation against Hitler Has Little Effect on Negroes," *Pittsburgh Courier*, 12 July 1941, 24. New York Youth Division to the National Executive Committee for March on Washington for Jobs and Equal Participation in National Defense, 28 June 1941, "March on Washington Movement, Correspondence B-W 1941" folder, box 24, Randolph Papers. Richard Parrish, a member of the Negro March committee, was not contacted on the night of June 24 when the other leaders agreed to cancel.

63. "An end in itself . . ." from A. Philip Randolph, Why and How, NAACP Records; metaphor of strike from A. Philip Randolph to Hope Williams, Everett Thomas, and Richard Parrish, 18 July 1941, "March on Washington Movement, Correspondence B-W 1941" folder, box 24, Randolph Papers. In this reply to the letter of the New York Youth Division, Randolph blamed the nature of the complaints on what he called "a fraction that religiously follow the Communist Party line as a bible of unerring salvation."

64. Plan of National Organization—March on Washington, 3 August 1942, "March on Washington Movement, Principles and Structures" folder, box 26, Randolph Papers; and A. Philip Randolph, "Keynote Address," March on Washington Movement, *March on Washington Movement: Proceedings of Conference Held in Detroit, September 26–27, 1942*, 6. On methods of organizing supporters locally, see March on Washington Movement, ibid., 8, 10, 22, 30. On nonviolent direct action and civil disobedience, see "We Are Americans! Conference Program," "MOWM, 1941–1945: Chronology, 1942" folder, *Schomburg Clipping File*, fiches 002,968–3 and 002,968–4; and Report of the Special Committee, 19 October 1946, "March on Washington Movement, 1941–1945: Chronology, 1943–1965; misc." folder, *Schomburg Clipping File*, fiche 002,968–4.

65. *New York Times*, 13 June 1942, quoted in Herbert Garfinkel, *When Negroes March*, 90; Report on the MARCH ON WASHINGTON Policy Conference, 26

September 1942–27 September 1942, "March on Washington Committee—A. Philip Randolph, 1942" folder, box A417, group II, NAACP Records; A. Philip Randolph, "Keynote Address," 9. For a report on criticism of the failure to march, see Ernest Johnson, Memorandum to Lawrence Irvine, President, New York Division of MOWM, 23 September 1942, "March on Washington, 1942" folder, series 1, box 28, NUL Records; and an editorial in the *Pittsburgh Courier,* 2 January 1943, quoted in Herbert Garfinkel, *When Negroes March,* 134.

66. John E. Rankin (Dem., Miss.), House, *Congressional Record,* 77th Cong., 2d sess., 22 June 1942, 88, pt. 9, appendix: A2354. Virginus Dabney, "Nearer and Nearer the Precipice," *Atlantic* 171 (January 1943), 94. See also John T. Graves, "The Southern Negro and the War Crisis," *Virginia Quarterly Review* 18 (Autumn 1942), 500–517.

67. "Women Picket the White House," *New York Times,* 6 November 1941, 14. On pickets generally, see Robert Cooney and Helen Michalowski, *Power of the People,* 94–111; and Jo Ann Robinson, *Abraham Went Out: A Biography of A. J. Muste* (Philadelphia: Temple University Press, 1981), 87. On housewives, see Cabell B. H. Phillips, *The 1940s: Decades of Triumph* (New York: Macmillan, 1975), 277. On other protests, see "Parades and Picketing folder, 1946–1949" folder, Vertical Files, Washingtoniana Collection.

68. Randolph's actions in L. D. Reddick, "The Negro Policy of the American Army since World War II," *Journal of Negro History* 38 (April 1953), 198–206; and Paula F. Pfeffer, *A. Philip Randolph,* 104–5, 146–47. Bayard Rustin served as executive secretary of this committee; Jo Ann Robinson, *Abraham Went Out,* 115. Grant Reynolds, "A Triumph for Civil Disobedience," *Nation* 167 (28 August 1948), 228–29. See FBI, Various Reports, 1948, file 100–55616, *FBI File on A. Philip Randolph,* reel 1. Once again, Randolph probably canceled too soon; it took another year for the army to even design a plan for decreasing segregation, and it was not until 1951 that Jim Crow was ended for troops in Korea; L. D. Reddick, "Negro Policy of the American Army," 197–215.

69. On convention, Walter White, *Man Called White,* 348–49.

70. Robert L. Harris Jr., "Racial Equality and the United Nations Charter," chap. in Armstead L. Robinson and Patricia Sullivan, eds., *New Directions in Civil Rights Studies* (Charlottesville: University Press of Virginia, 1991), 126–48; and Mary L. Dudziak, "Desegregation as a Cold War Imperative," *Stanford Law Review* 61.1 (1988), 61–120.

5. "IN THE GREAT TRADITION"

1. Tom Kahn, "The Power of the March—and After," *Dissent* 10 (Autumn 1963), 315–20.

2. During the fall and winter of 1994–95, Harvard Community Health Plan used such clips in commercials promoting its health management organization in the Massachusetts and Rhode Island area. I saw the textbooks at Classical High School, Providence, Rhode Island, in spring 1995.

3. The most comprehensive study of the demonstration is Thomas Gentile, *March on Washington, August 28, 1963* (Washington, D.C.: New Day Publica-

tions, 1983), but this account needs to be supplemented by the accounts in David J. Garrow, *Bearing the Cross: Martin Luther King, Jr. and the Southern Christian Leadership Conference* (New York: Vintage, 1986), 264–305, and Taylor Branch, *Parting the Waters: America in the King Years, 1954–1963* (New York: Simon and Schuster, 1988), 816–87.

4. Harvard Sitkoff, *The Struggle for Black Equality, 1954–1965* (New York: Hill and Wang, 1981), 68–96; number of protesters, Allen J. Matusow, *The Unraveling of America: A History of Liberalism in the 1960s* (New York: Harper and Row, 1984), 89.

5. See Allen J. Matusow, *Unraveling of America,* 3–122, and Michael Barone, *Our Country: The Shaping of America from Roosevelt to Reagan* (New York: Free Press, 1990), 319–64.

6. Other scholars have connected the rise of the civil rights movement to "mass culture." See Adolph L. Reed, *Race, Politics, and Culture: Critical Essays on the Radicalism of the 1960's* (Westport, Conn.: Greenwood, 1986), 61–95. Elias Canetti observes that the "modern treasure is the million"; and it is the most common word for crowds; Elias Canetti, *Crowds and Power* (New York: Continuum, 1981 [1973]), 185. On the use of numbers in politics generally, see Susan Herbst, *Numbered Voices: How Opinion Polling Has Shaped American Politics* (Chicago: University of Chicago Press, 1993).

7. A. Philip Randolph, Why the Emancipation March on Washington for Jobs? 13 May 1963, "Speeches and Writings, 1963" folder, box 36, Randolph Papers. Jervis Anderson, *A. Philip Randolph: A Biographical Portrait* (New York: Harcourt Brace Jovanovich, 1973), 321–24. On initial plans, A. Philip Randolph to Roy Wilkins, 25 March 1963, "March on Washington—Correspondence—General (March–June)" folder, box 27, Rustin Papers, and Minutes, Meeting on Emancipation March on Washington, 10 April 1963. In 1959, frustrated by the lack of support for African Americans in the AFL-CIO, Randolph had formed the Negro American Labor Council to bring together African American labor activists; Paula F. Pfeffer, *A. Philip Randolph: Pioneer of the Civil Rights Movement* (Baton Rouge: Louisiana State University Press, 1990), 206–39; and Jervis Anderson, *A. Philip Randolph,* 305–15.

8. For a comprehensive account of these marches, see Paula F. Pfeffer, *A. Philip Randolph,* "The Preliminary Civil Rights Marches" chap.

9. Jervis Anderson, *A. Philip Randolph,* 319–20; Taylor Branch, *Parting the Waters,* 846–47; and Thomas R. Brooks, "A Strategist without a Movement," *New York Times Magazine,* 16 February 1969, reprinted in August Meier, John H. Bracey, Jr., and Elliott M. Rudwick, eds., *Black Protest in the Sixties* (New York: M. Wiener, 1991). On Rustin's belief in Gandhi's methods and his influence on Randolph, see Susanna McBee, "Organiser of D.C. March Is Devoted to Non-Violence," *Washington Post,* 11 August 1963, A6; and Paula F. Pfeffer, *A. Philip Randolph,* 62.

10. On King's role in the Prayer Pilgrimage and the youth marches, see David J. Garrow, *Bearing the Cross,* 91–94, 109, 111, 112, 117. *Ebony* labeled King "No. 1," David J. Garrow, *Bearing the Cross,* 94. After 1959, King and his advisors considered protesting in Washington again; in 1962, they discussed holding

some sort of "march on Washington" to protest Kennedy's failure to forbid segregation in federally funded housing. See discussion of planned protest by Stanley Levison, recorded by FBI wiretaps, 27 March 1962, *The Martin Luther King, Jr., FBI File, Part II: The King-Levison FBI File* (microfilm), ed. David J. Garrow (Frederick, Md.: University Publications of America, 1987), reel 1; 30 March 1962, ibid.; 11 April 1962, ibid. (hereafter cited as *King-Levison FBI File*). Another planned demonstration in Washington, to have been led by King on 1 January 1963, is discussed in a memo from J. Edgar Hoover, Memorandum to Attorney General [Robert F. Kennedy], 3 June 1963, file 100–106670,128, *The Martin Luther King, Jr., FBI File* (microfilm), ed. David J. Garrow (Frederick, Md.: University Publications of America, 1984), reel 21 (hereafter cited as *King FBI File*). Neither of these protests occurred.

11. On his philosophy and attitude toward protests, see Roy Wilkins, *Standing Fast: The Autobiography of Roy Wilkins,* Tom Mathews, collab. (New York: Viking Press, 1982), esp. 133–36, 209–10, 220, 237–38; Roy Wilkins, Memorandum to Board of Directors, 5 June 1957, "Prayer Pilgrimage, 1957" folder, box G2, group III, NAACP Records; and Roy Wilkins to Dr. C. B. Powell, publisher, *Amsterdam News,* June 4, 1957, ibid. These letters are in response to article by James L. Hicks, "King Emerges as Top Negro Leader," *Amsterdam News,* June 1, 1957, clipping in "Prayer Pilgrimage, June 1957" folder, box A245, group III, NAACP Records. Wilkins's ill feelings about the Prayer Pilgrimage increased when the NAACP found itself responsible for unexpected bills for the event. See also Roy Wilkins to Henry Moon, 5 June 1957, "General Correspondence, 1957, M-Z" folder, box 5, the Papers of Roy Wilkins, Manuscript Division, LC. Roy Wilkins to A. Philip Randolph, 22 September 1958, "Youth March on Washington, 1958" folder, box A334, group III, NAACP Records. On the NAACP political strategy, see Denton L. Watson, *Lion in the Lobby: Clarence Mitchell, Jr.'s Struggle for the Passage of Civil Rights Laws* (New York: William Morrow, 1990), 182, 332–33, 348–49, 463–64. Whereas NAACP efforts sometimes involved mass lobbying delegations, Wilkins and his legislative advisors tended to focus on targeting "individual members of Congress"; Denton L. Watson, *Lion in the Lobby,* 332–33.

12. A. Philip Randolph to Roy Wilkins, Rustin Papers. On attendance at meeting, see Minutes, 10 April 1963, Rustin Papers. For CORE's support, see August Meier and Elliott M. Rudwick, *CORE: A Study in the Civil Rights Movement, 1942–1968* (New York: Oxford University Press, 1973), 224.

13. On King's activities in Birmingham, see Taylor Branch, *Parting the Waters,* 673–806; and Harvard Sitkoff, *Struggle for Black Equality,* 128–45. King's trip to Los Angeles is described in Arthur Schlesinger Jr., *Robert Kennedy and His Times* (New York: Ballantine Books, 1978), 354–55. For a view of the "supercity" not long after King visited, John L. Chapman, *Incredible Los Angeles* (New York: Harper and Row, 1967). Transcript of Conversation between Levison, King, and Jones, 1 June 1963; *King-Levison FBI File,* reel 4; and David J. Garrow, *Bearing the Cross,* 265–67. The FBI recorded his conversations because the agency believed Levison was an active member of the Communist Party trying to subvert the civil rights movement by advising King. Levison had supported the Party earlier, but by the mid-1950s he had ended his support. Allen J. Matusow, *Unraveling of America,* 80.

14. King's comment reported in Fred Halstead, "Capital March to Win Rights Urged by Martin Luther King," *Militant* 27 (17 June 1963), 1, 8. SCLC's representative, "Massive Protest Seen if Congress Fails to Aid Negroes," *New York Times,* 12 June 1963, 23. On Randolph's reaction, Transcript of Conversation between King and Levison, 6 June 1963, *King-Levison FBI File,* reel 4. Decision to combine, Michael E. J. Ledden to Captain Thomas I. Herlihy, Washington Metropolitan Police, 17 June 1963, "File 2–111A District Public Relations. Civil Rights Demonstrations—Policy (Folder No. 1)," box 101, RG 351, NA.

15. Transcript of Conversation between Levison, Jones, King, Ralph Abernathy, Andrew Young, and Wyatt Walker, 10 June 1963; *King-Levison FBI File,* reel 4; Transcript of Conversation between King and Levison, 12 June 1963, ibid.; David J. Garrow, *Bearing the Cross,* 267. For background on Kennedy's decision, Carl M. Brauer, *John F. Kennedy and the Second Reconstruction* (New York: Columbia University Press, 1977), 230–71. "Spontaneous" comes from Transcript of Conversation between Jones and Levison, 2 June 1963 ; *King-Levison FBI File,* reel 4. See also David J. Garrow, *Bearing the Cross,* 270; and "Negro March on Capitol Is Scheduled for August," *New York Times,* 22 June 1963, 9.

16. On arrest, see Roy Wilkins, *Standing Fast,* 288. On refusal to call off protests, Richard J. H. Johnston, "Integrationists Bar Truce; Say Protests Will Go On," *New York Times,* 20 June 1963, 1.

17. Details of this meeting drawn from Taylor Branch, *Parting the Waters,* 839–41, and David J. Garrow, *Bearing the Cross,* 271.

18. Roy Wilkins, *Standing Fast,* 291–92; Marjorie Hunter, "Negroes Inform Kennedy of Plan for New Protests," *New York Times,* 23 June 1963, 63; Dan Day, "Capital Spotlight," *Baltimore Afro-American,* 6 July 1963, 4.

19. On SNCC's support for the march, see Emily Stoper, *The Student Nonviolent Coordinating Committee: The Growth of Radicalism in a Civil Rights Organization* (Brooklyn: Carlson Pub., 1989), 41–42; Howard Zinn, *SNCC, the New Abolitionists* (Boston: Beacon Press, 1964), 174–80; and Clayborne Carson, *In Struggle: SNCC and the Black Awakening* (Cambridge: Harvard University Press, 1981), 90–95. On the disappointment with the decision to forgo direct action, see James Forman, *The Making of Black Revolutionaries: A Personal Account* (New York: Macmillan, 1972), 332; Thomas Gentile, *March on Washington,* 49. King and Wilkins quoted in Richard L. Worsnop, "Mass Demonstrations," *Editorial Research Reports* 2 (14 August 1963), 586.

20. The Time Is Now, 12 July 1963, "March on Washington, Fliers and Leaflets" folder, box 29, Rustin Papers.

21. M. S. Handler, "Chicago Negroes Boo Mayor Daley," *New York Times,* 5 July 1963, 1; and M. S. Handler, "N.A.A.C.P. Leader Scores Meredith," *New York Times,* 6 July 1963, 1, 5; convention debate and Wilkins's quote in "Angry at Everybody," *Time* (12 July 1963), 18–19.

22. John F. Kennedy, "Transcript of the President's News Conference on Foreign and Domestic Matters," *New York Times,* 18 July 1963, 8. On the tendency of democratic governments to take on these multiple roles, see Susan Herbst, *Politics at the Margin: Historical Studies of Public Expression outside the Mainstream* (New York: Cambridge University Press, 1994), 24–26.

23. On pervasiveness of protests, see Joseph L. Rauh, Transcript of Joseph L. Rauh, Jr., oral history interview, Katherine Shannon, interviewer (28 August 1967), 24, CRDP, MSRC. For Rosenberg protests, Walter Schneir and Miriam Schneir, *Invitation to an Inquest* (Garden City, N.Y.: Doubleday, 1965), 237, 244–46, 250–51. For evidence of Eisenhower's reluctant support, see E. T. Scoyen to Clarence Mitchell, 16 April 1957, "Prayer Pilgrimage for Freedom, 1957" folder, box G2, group IIIG; NAACP Records; Clarence Mitchell, Memorandum, 18 April 1957, ibid. Aides to Eisenhower had told the organizers of the Youth March that the president was unavailable, but the delegation called, nevertheless, irritating the administration; see Rocco Siciliano to A. Philip Randolph, 29 October 1958, "Subject File: White House Conference, Eisenhower, Correspondence," box 31, Randolph Papers; and subsequent exchanges dated 12 and 19 November in same folder. The next year, aides made sure there were people to meet with representatives: Thomas E. Stephens to A. Philip Randolph, 17 March 1959, "Youth March for Integrated Schools, Correspondence, 1959" folder, box 31, Randolph Papers. On White House protests and quote from officer, see Eugene Roberts Jr. and Douglas Ward, "The Press, Protesters, and Presidents," chap. in Frank B. Freidel and William Pencak, eds., *The White House: The First Two Hundred Years* (Boston: Northeastern University Press, 1994), 134–35.

24. "Massive Protest," 23; Haley quoted in "Riot Is Feared," *New York Times*, 15 July 1963, 11. "Race Trouble in the Nation's Capital," *U.S. News and World Report* (21 January 1963), 72–75. Martha Derthick, *City Politics in Washington, D.C.* (Cambridge: Joint Center for Urban Studies of the Massachusetts Institute of Technology and Harvard University, 1962).

25. Minutes of Meeting, 11 July 1963, file 2–111a: "District Public Relations, Civil Rights Demonstrations—Policy (Folder No. 1)," box 101, RG 351, NA; Robert Murray, Statement by Chief of Police Robert Murray, 21 August 1963, "March on Washington, Speeches and Statements, 1963" folder, box A229, group IIIA, NAACP Records; Warren Young and William Lambert, "Marchers' Master Plan," *Life* (23 August 1963), 70; and Thomas Gentile, *March on Washington*, 148–50.

26. On assistance generally, see Arthur Schlesinger Jr., *Robert Kennedy*, 376–77; Denton L. Watson, *Lion in the Lobby*, 558; and Thomas Gentile, *March on Washington*, 62–68, 125–29. "Kennedy to Meet Leaders of Rally," *New York Times*, 20 August 1963, 16.

27. Ben Franklin, "Rights Marchers to Strain Capital," *New York Times*, 12 August 1963, 12. Kennedy quoted in Carl M. Brauer, *Kennedy and the Second Reconstruction*, 77; on Rustin's presentation, see E. G. Wiener to Bayard Rustin, 19 August 1963, "March on Washington—Correspondence—General (August 22–23)" folder, box 28, Rustin Papers. On USIA film, Gerald Grady, "*The March* by James Blue," 30 April 1993, presentation at "Towards a History of the 1960s" conference, Madison, Wisc.; Nicholas Cull, "Auteurs of Ideology: USIA Documentary Film Propaganda in the Kennedy Era as Seen in Bruce Herschensohn's *The Five Cities of June* (1963) and James Blue's *The March* (1964)," *Film History* 10 (1998), 298–310; and James Blue, *The March*, 1964, item 765, Records of the United States Information Agency (RIS 306), NA. On VOA, Ben-

jamin Muse, *The American Negro Revolution: From Nonviolence to Black Power, 1963–1967* (Bloomington: Indiana University Press, 1968), 3. Peter Grose, "Americans Abroad Give Support to Rights March," *New York Times,* 22 August 1963, 18. On more about these efforts to express sympathy for the march abroad, see Mary L. Dudziak, *Cold War Civil Rights: Race and the Image of American Democracy* (Princeton, N.J.: Princeton University Press, 2000), 190–91.

28. On these negotiations, see Minutes, 11 July 1963, RG 351, NA; Rachelle Horowitz, interview, Scott Sandage, interviewer (20 December 1989), transcript in author's possession; and Thomas Gentile, *March on Washington,* 67–70.

29. On decline of Pennsylvania Avenue, see Wolf Von Eckart, "The Architects and the Bureaucrats," *New Republic* 146 (18 June 1962), 28; "Washington, D.C.," *Architectural Forum* 118 (January 1963), 97; and Mary Cable, *The Avenue of the Presidents* (Boston: Houghton Mifflin, 1969), 197–203. On administration's goal, see Carol M. Highsmith and Ted Landphair, *Pennsylvania Avenue: America's Main Street* (Washington, D.C.: American Institute of Architects Press, 1988), 121. Organizing Manual No. 2, "March on Washington—Logistics" folder, box 29, Rustin Papers.

30. W. J. Bryan Dorn (Dem., S. C.), House, *Congressional Record,* 88th Cong., 1st sess., 26 August 1963, 109, pt. 12:15818. Malcolm X quoted in "Church to Enlist Catholics Here for Capital Civil Rights Rally," *New York Times,* 11 August 1963, 61.

31. [Untitled count of publicity materials], 2 August 1963, "March on Washington—Financial Papers—Expenditures" folder, box 29, Rustin Papers.

32. Transcript of Conversation, 10 June 1963, *King-Levison FBI File,* reel 4. Arthur Schlesinger Jr., *Robert Kennedy,* 377. Tom Kahn, "Power of the March," 317.

33. For background on Rustin, see Jacqueline Trescott, "Bayard Rustin: Contradictions of a Legendary Leader," *Washington Post,* 21 August 1982, 1, 7; and Robert Cooney and Helen Michalowski (based on the work of Marty Jezer), *The Power of the People: Active Nonviolence in the United States* (Philadelphia: New Society Publishers, 1987), 73, 118, 124, 133, 137, 156. Comments on Rustin's ability from "On the March," *Newsweek* 62 (2 September 1963), 18. For details on his methods, see Harvey Swados, "Revolution on the March," *Nation* 197 (7 September 1963), 104. Two biographers of Rustin provide more details on his phenomenal organizing abilities; Jervis Anderson, *Bayard Rustin: Troubles I've Seen: A Biography* (New York: HarperCollins, 1997); and Daniel Levine, *Bayard Rustin and the Civil Rights Movement* (New Brunswick, N.J.: Rutgers University Press, 2000).

34. For contributions, see Contribution List, "March on Washington, Financial Papers and Expenditures" folder, box 29, Rustin Papers. For totals, see Balance Sheet, 26 February 1964, "March on Washington, Financial Papers and Expenditures" folder, box 29, ibid.; and Thomas Gentile, *March on Washington,* 133. Louis Calta, " 'Freedom' Shows in South Planned," *New York Times,* 11 July 1963, 22; "Rally at Birmingham," *New York Times,* 7 August 1963, 20; "Performance to Aid March on Capital," *New York Times,* 9 August 1963, 10; and Murray Schumach, "Hollywood Cause," *New York Times,* 25 August

1963, 2:7. Charlton Heston appeared on the *Today Show* on 26 August 1963, summarized on National Broadcasting Company, Subject Cards, folder 8: "Poor People's Campaign, NBC Special Reports," box 11, CRDP, MSRC.

35. Organizing Manual No. 1, "March on Washington—Logistics" folder, box 29. "Wagner Back; Favors Leave for Rights Marchers," *New York Times,* 13 August 1963, 1.

36. Ralph Mathews, "The Cast Has Changed But the Play's the Same," *Baltimore Afro-American,* 7 September 1963, 8; Aubrey Williams to Martin Luther King Jr., n.d., "March on Washington Correspondence—General, July 1–29" folder, box 27, Rustin Papers; and Organizing Manual No. 1, Rustin Papers. See Eric J. Hobsbawm and Terence O. Ranger, *The Invention of Tradition* (New York: Cambridge University Press, 1983). Robert Nix (Dem., Pa.), House, *Congressional Record,* 88th Cong., 1st sess., 22 August 1963, 109, pt. 12:15616–18. A *New York Times* article echoed his remarks; Nan Robertson, "Protest Marchers Are Nothing New to Nation's Capital," *New York Times,* 25 August 1963, 80.

37. For an early endorsement by a black newspaper, see "Come on Down, Marchers," *Baltimore Afro-American,* 6 July 1963, 5. On declining power of black newspapers, "A Victim of Negro Progress," *Time* 62 (26 August 1963), 50. On appointment of public relations person, see Bayard Rustin to Walter Fauntroy et al., 8 August 1962, "March on Washington, Correspondence, General, August 8–11, 1963" folder, box 28, Rustin Papers; and Thomas Gentile, *March on Washington,* 54. For mention of Rustin's appearance on the TV news, see Francis Hall to Bayard Rustin, 20 August 1963, "March on Washington—Correspondence—Rustin, Bayard" folder, box 29, Rustin Papers.

38. Organizing Manual No. 2, Rustin Papers. On changes in citizenship, Ronald T. Takaki, *Strangers from a Different Shore: A History of Asian Americans* (Boston: Little, Brown, 1989), 413–18. On how the movement changed participants' vision of citizenship, see Charles M. Payne, *I've Got the Light of Freedom: The Organizing Tradition and the Mississippi Freedom Struggle* (Berkeley: University of California Press, 1995).

39. Randolph quoted in Martin Arnold, "Rights March on Washington Reported Growing," *New York Times,* 4 August 1963, 57. On Nation of Islam during this period, see Taylor Branch, *Pillar of Fire: America in the King Years, 1963–65* (New York: Simon and Schuster, 1998), 1–20.

40. For endorsements and other efforts see "2 Catholic Leaders Back Clergy on Plans to Join March," *New York Times,* 11 July 1963, 19; "On the March," 20; "Performance to Aid," 10; and "Episcopal Bishops Support Kennedy on Rights," *New York Times,* 13 August 1963, 7. For the full range of groups that considered or chose to support or participate in the protest, see letters in the folders "March on Washington—Correspondence—General" of various dates, Rustin Papers, and Contribution List, ibid.

41. Anna A. Hedgeman, Memorandum to A. Philip Randolph, 16 August 1963, "March on Washington, August 14–26, 1963" folder, box 25, part 2, NUL Records.

42. Organizing Manual No. 2. Joseph Loftus, "Faubus Declares G.O.P. 'Good,'" *New York Times,* 19 August 1963, 15; Strom Thurmond (Dem., S.C.), Senate, *Congressional Record,* 88th Cong., 1st sess, 13 August 1963, 109, pt.

11:14836–44. On Kennedy's pressure about Levison, Taylor Branch, *Parting the Waters,* 834–38. On FBI's persistence, see Thomas Gentile, *March on Washington,* 73–75; for examples, Denis E. Dillon, Memorandum to Burke Marshall, 19 April 1963, "Subject File: Demonstrations: Memoranda Based on FBI Reports, Aug. 1963," box 32, Marshall Papers, JFKL; and David Marlin to Burke Marshall, 20 and 21 August 1963, ibid.

43. Organizing Manual No. 1, Rustin Papers; repeated in Organizing Manual No. 2, ibid.

44. Bayard Rustin to Sidney Hertzberg, 5 August 1963, "March on Washington—Correspondence—General, August 5" folder, box 28; Organizing Manual No. 2. Complaints about minimum wage demands, Barbara Moffett to A. Philip Randolph, 2 August 1963, "March on Washington—Correspondence—General, August 1–2, 1963" folder, box 28, Rustin Papers. Final list of demands, Organizing Manual No. 2, Rustin Papers.

45. Minutes of Special Meeting of the Commissioners, 27 August 1963, file 2–111a, "District Public Relations, Civil Rights Demonstrations—Policy (Folder No. 1)," box 101, RG 351, NA. See an early request for this policy from a Virginia member of Congress, Henry Edgerton to Walter Tobriner, 16 July 1963, file 2–111a, "District Public Relations, Civil Rights Demonstrations—Policy (Folder No. 1)," box 101, RG 351, NA.

46. On enthusiasm, see M. S. Handler, "40,000 From New York Are to Take Part in Capital March," *New York Times,* 23 August 1963, 81.

47. Ruth B. Mordecai, "If Not Now, When," *Our Age* 5 (6 October 1963), 4. Buses in Tunnel, see "NBC News Presents 'March on Washington' " on NBC, Subject Cards, CRDP, MSRC. On trains, see "We Shall Overcome," *Baltimore Afro-American,* 31 August 1963, 2; on atmosphere in station, see "The March's Meaning," *Time* 82 (6 September 1963), 14. James Blue's movie for the USIA gives an excellent impression of this excitement; see James Blue, *The March.* For estimates of marchers, Metropolitan Police Department, Press Releases, Nos. 4 and 5, 28 August 1963, file 2–111A, folder no. 2, box 101, RG 351, NA. For Randolph's announcement, see CBS News, "March on Washington for Jobs and Freedom," 28 August 1963, FCA 4854–4859, MPBRS Division, LC, reel 3 (hereafter cited as CBS News, "March on Washington").

48. Joseph Loftus, "Traffic Control Works Smoothly in Capital although Volume Exceeds Predictions," *New York Times,* 29 August 1963, 19.

49. Number of passes, "News From the NAACP," Press Release, 31 August 1963, "March on Washington Press Releases" folder, box 31, Rustin Papers. Social scientists have observed that social movements that engage in conscious efforts to work with the media are rewarded by more coverage; William A. Gamson and Gadi Wolfsfeld, "Movements and Media as Interacting Systems," *Annals of the American Academy of Political and Social Science* 528 (July 1993), 121. "TV and Radio Slate Rights March Show," *New York Times,* 28 August 1963, 21; Val Adams, "TV: Coverage of March," *New York Times,* 29 August 1963, 59; "Europeans View the March on TV," *New York Times,* 29 August 1963, 59. On Telstar, "Meeting in Space," *Time* 82:3 (19 July 1963), 55. For details on arrangements with journalists and the locations of cameras, see correspondence between staff at the National Capital Parks and various press and television companies

and the detailed maps in "August 28th March on Washington" file, Jett's files, box 68, acc: 72A-6215; and "A-8219 Marches and Demonstrations—1/1/63 to 1/1/66" file, box 8, acc: 79–7524, NPS-NCP Records, WNRC.

50. Nan Robertson, "For 200,000 Who Were There It Was a Date to Live Forever," *New York Times,* 29 August 1963, 20; E. W. Kenworthy, "200,000 March for Civil Rights in Orderly Washington Rally; President Sees Gain for Negro," *New York Times,* 29 August 1963, 16. Richard Starnes, "Many an Ancient Hurt Was Eased," *Washington Daily News,* 29 August 1963, 37. On desire of crowds to move, see Elias Canetti, *Crowds and Power,* 29–30.

51. NBC reporter quoted on summary card on "NBC News Special, August 28, 1963," NBC, Subject Cards, CRDP, MSRC; *Time* report: "March's Meaning," 13. For statements suggesting people stay away from "downtown Washington," see WMAL, "An Editorial," 18 August 1963, "March on Washington—Press Release" folder, box 31, Rustin Papers. For deserted feeling, see comments by German reporter noted by Edward Morgan, "Edward Morgan and the News," 28 August 1963, "MOW—General Correspondence, Sept 1–25, 1963" folder, box A228, group III, NAACP Records; and Edwin Dale, "Most of Capital Deserted for Day," *New York Times,* 29 August 1963, 17.

52. A reporter recounted at least one incident where a marshal tried to prevent an activist from carrying his own sign, but the marshal backed down; Inez Robb, " 'For God's Sake Leave the Kid Alone,' " *Washington Daily News,* 29 August 1963, 10. For a list of the slogans, see Bayard Rustin to Religious, Labor, Fraternal, and Civil Rights Organizations, 21 August 1963, "March on Washington—Correspondence—General, August 21, 1963" folder, box 28, Rustin Papers. Some of the unions prepared their own signs with the permission of the march organizers; see Bayard Rustin to Jack Conway and William Oliver, 20 August 1963, "March on Washington—Correspondence—General, August 20, 1963" folder, box 28, ibid.

53. On behavior of crowd, "News from the NAACP," Press Release, 30 August 1963, "March on Washington Press Releases" folder, box 31, Rustin Papers.

54. Leaders' itinerary for August 28 march, "March on Washington, 1963" folder, *Schomburg Center Clipping File, 1925–1974* (microfiche) (New York: Schomburg Center for Research in Black Culture, New York Public Library, 1975), fiche 005,966–1. On legislation's status, see "Move to Speed Bill Rejected," *New York Times,* 20 August 1963, 16. On interruption of meeting, Denton L. Watson, *Lion in the Lobby,* 559. A newsreel shows the aides setting up this picture most clearly; see "The March on Washington," Universal Newsreels, 200 UN 36–71–1, Motion Picture, Sound and Video Branch, NA.

55. On international actions and coverage, see Mary L. Dudziak, *Cold War Civil Rights,* 192–98.

56. All quotes from the events at the Lincoln Memorial in the next several paragraphs, "Speeches by the Leaders" (National Association for the Advancement of Colored People, 1963), "March on Washington—Speeches and Statements" folder, box A229, group IIIA, NAACP Records. For the enthusiasm, see CBS News, "March on Washington," reel 5. For the importance of music to the civil rights movement, particularly for building community within the movement, see Vincent Harding, "Community as a Liberating Theme in Civil Rights

History," in Armstead L. Robinson and Patricia Sullivan, eds., *New Directions in Civil Rights Studies* (Charlottesville: University Press of Virginia, 1991), 21.

57. There are many accounts of this controversy. In the following, I have depended for the original wording and the negotiations over the changes on Nicolaus Mills, "Heard and Unheard Speeches: What Really Happened at the March on Washington," *Dissent* 35 (Summer 1988), 288–91; Garth E. Pauley, "John Lewis's 'Serious Revolution': Rhetoric, Resistance, and Revision at the March on Washington," *Quarterly Journal of Speech* 84 (1998), 320–40. See also David J. Garrow, *Bearing the Cross*, 281–83; and Taylor Branch, *Parting the Waters*, 873–74, 878–80. The press reported on the changes in some detail; see Susanna McBee, "Restrained Militancy Marks Rally Speeches," *Washington Post*, 29 August 1963, file 2–111a: "District Public Relations, Civil Rights Demonstrations—Policy (Folder No. 1)," box 101, RG 351, NA. CBS News, "March on Washington," reel 3.

58. CBS News, "March on Washington," reel 3.

59. "Speeches by the Leaders," NAACP Records; CBS News, "March on Washington," reels 5 and 6. On writing of the speech, Taylor Branch, *Parting the Waters*, 875–76.

60. On switch from text, see David J. Garrow, *Bearing the Cross*, 283; and Taylor Branch, *Parting the Waters*, 882. According to Branch, King had delivered versions of the "Dream" speech three times before; Taylor Branch, *Parting the Waters*, 689, 882–83. For one recording at a previous meeting, see Martin Luther King Jr., "The Great March to Freedom, Rev. Martin Luther King Speaks, Detroit, June 23, 1963," LP recording 906, Gordy, 1963. The refrain in the earlier speech was "I have a dream this afternoon," rather than the more powerful "I have a dream today" in August.

61. "Speeches by the Leaders," NAACP Records. For another analysis of the speech, see Keith D. Miller, *Voice of Deliverance: The Language of Martin Luther King, Jr. and Its Sources* (New York: Free Press, 1992), 142–50.

62. "Rights Marchers' Pledge," *New York Times*, 29 August 1963, 16.

63. Taylor Branch, *Parting the Waters*, 883–87; E. W. Kenworthy, "200,000 March," 1, 16; and John F. Kennedy, "Texts of the President's Statements on Rights and on Labor Day," *New York Times*, 29 August 1963, 16.

64. For details on the March on Washington for Jobs, Peace, and Freedom held on August 27, 1983, see Mark Perry and Ken Cummins, "The Dream Divided: The Dilemma of the New Coalition," Washington, D.C., City Paper, 2 September 1983, 1, 6–7. For march held on August 28, 1993, see DeNeen L. Brown, "Thousands March to Mark a Dream," *Washington Post*, 29 August 1993, A1, A18. For "Redeem the Dream" rally in 2000, see Cindy Loose and Chris L. Jenkins, "Rallying to 'Redeem the Dream': Rights Leaders Target Racial Profiling," *Washington Post*, 27 August 2000, C1.

65. Val Adams, "TV: Coverage of March," 59. Mudd's first serious commentary was on the size of the crowd, and he summed up his reporting as the marchers filed away by mentioning that the final estimate was that about 210,000 marchers had gathered at the Memorial; CBS News, "March on Washington," reels 1 and 6. NBC, Summary, August 28, 1983, NBC, Subject Cards, CRDP, MSRC.

66. CBS News, "March on Washington," reel 1. Murray Edelman argues

that it is important to recognize that leaders depend on supporters for their positions; Murray Edelman, *Constructing the Political Spectacle* (Chicago: University of Chicago Press, 1988), "The Construction and Use of Political Leaders" chap.

67. Martin Luther King Jr., "Why We Can't Wait," quoted in Robert J. Norrell, "One Thing We Did Right: Reflections on the Movement," in Armstead L. Robinson and Patricia Sullivan, eds., *New Directions*, 73; Murray Kempton, "The March on Washington," *New Republic* 149 (14 September 1963), 19. Scholars have also praised the coverage; J. F. MacDonald, *Blacks and White TV: Afro-Americans in Television since 1948* (Chicago: Nelson-Hall, 1983), 99.

68. A number of scholars have discussed how the media present certain issues in terms of recognizable conventions and standards; for an overview, see Murray Edelman, *Constructing the Political Spectacle;* for demonstrations specifically, see Todd Gitlin, *The Whole World Is Watching: Mass Media in the Making and Unmaking of the New Left* (Berkeley: University of California Press, 1980); Melvin Small, *Covering Dissent: The Media and the Anti-Vietnam War Movement* (New Brunswick, N.J.: Rutgers University Press, 1994); and Sidney G. Tarrow, *Power in Movement: Social Movements, Collective Action, and Politics* (New York: Cambridge University Press, 1994), 126–29. James Reston, " 'I Have a Dream' " *New York Times,* 29 August 1963, 1, 17; " 'A Dream . . . I Have a Dream,' " *Newsweek* 62 (9 September 1963); and NBC News, "March on Washington, NBC News Special," 28 August 1963, FDA 0209, MPBRS Division, LC.

69. On cautions and critiques, see Warren Weaver, "Congress Cordial but Not Swayed," *New York Times,* 29 August 1963, 1; "March's Meaning," 1. "The March," *Nation* 197 (14 September 1963), 121. "A Great Day in American History," *New York Herald Tribune,* 29 August 1963, reprinted as part of remarks by Paul Douglas (Dem., Ill.), Senate, *Congressional Record,* 88th Cong., 1st sess., 3 September 1963, 109, pt. 12:16232. John F. Kennedy, "President's Statements on Rights," 16. "Living Petition," *Washington Post,* 29 August 1963, reprinted as part of remarks by Paul Douglas, Senate, 16230–31.

70. On events after the march, see Taylor Branch, *Parting the Waters,* 888–992.

71. Denton L. Watson, *Lion in the Lobby,* 590–619; Gilbert Ware, "Lobbying as a Means of Protest: The NAACP as an Agent of Equality," *Journal of Negro Education* (Spring 1964), 103–9.

72. Mary King, *Freedom Song: A Personal Story of the 1960s Civil Rights Movement* (New York: Morrow, 1987), 182; Gene Roberts, "The Story of Snick: From 'Freedom High' to Black Power," *New York Times Magazine,* 25 September 1966, reprinted in August Meier, John H. Bracey Jr., and Elliott M. Rudwick, *Black Protest,* 147; and Malcolm X, *The Autobiography of Malcolm X* (New York: Grove Press, 1965), 278–81.

73. Bayard Rustin, "From Protest to Politics," *Commentary* 39 (February 1965), 111–22; and A. Philip Randolph, "Opening Remarks," at Conference of Negro Leaders, National Council of Churches, New York, January 30–31, 1965, reprinted as "Foreword" in Lerone Bennett, *Confrontation: Black and White* (Chicago: Johnson Pub., 1965), viii.

74. Jose Yglesias, "Dr. King's March on Washington, Part II," *New York Times Magazine* (31 March 1968), 277–93.

75. Tom Kahn, Why the Poor People's Campaign Failed, "Mobilization in Support of the Poor People's Campaign, Articles and Newspaper Clippings" folder, box 33, Rustin Papers; Steve Fayer, Sarah Flynn, and Henry Hampton, *Voices of Freedom: An Oral History of the Civil Rights Movement from the 1950s through the 1980s* (New York: Bantam Books, 1990), 473–83; and Southern Christian Leadership Conference, *The Poor People's Campaign* (Atlanta: Southern Christian Leadership Conference, 1968).

6. THE "SPRING OFFENSIVE" OF 1971

1. Bill Branson's memories in Richard Stacewicz, *Winter Soldiers: An Oral History of the Vietnam Veterans against the War* (New York: Twayne Publishers, 1997), 243–46. For a broad understanding of veterans who opposed the war, see Richard Moser, *The New Winter Soldier: GI and Veteran Dissent during the Vietnam Era* (New Brunswick, N.J.: Rutgers University Press, 1995).

2. "The Demonstrations," *Washington Post,* 19 April 1971, A20. Coretta Scott King to Ruth Gabe-Colby, 26 March 1971, "Correspondence: Other Organizations, 1968–1971" file, box 7, VVAW Records.

3. Amitai Etzioni, *Demonstration Democracy* (New York: Gordan and Breach, 1970), 1. Hugh Sidey, "Something Different This Spring," *Life* 70 (23 April 1971), 2B.

4. These disagreements began well before the Cambodia Rally, but that rally served as the final straw for people in both camps. The conflicts surrounding the demonstration are described in Tom Wells, *The War Within: America's Battle over Vietnam* (Berkeley: University of California Press, 1994), 403–77. An eventual NPAC supporter provides a more passionate account in Fred Halstead, *Out Now! A Participant's Account of the American Movement against the Vietnam War* (New York: Monad Press, 1978). Arthur Waskow, "The Mobe in Washington: What Happened," *WIN* 6 (1 June 1970), 6–10, explains why he and others believed that the decision to avoid civil disobedience was a mistake.

5. On changes along Pennsylvania Avenue, see Benjamin Forgey, "Along the Avenue Made for a Parade," *Washington Post,* 16 January 1993, G1, G4.

6. On conditions in the city, see Sam Smith, *Captive Capital: Colonial Life in Modern Washington* (Bloomington: Indiana University Press, 1974); on riots, see D.C. History Curriculum Project, *City of Magnificent Intentions: A History of the District of Columbia* (Washington, D.C.: Intac, 1983), 497–99. Population figures from Donald B. Dodd, comp., *Historical Statistics of the United States: Two Centuries of the Census, 1790–1990* (1993).

7. The details of the decision to hold the marches can be found in the minutes of various meetings held during the summer and fall of 1970; see Steering Committee Meeting, 18 July 1970 and 19 September 1970, *National Peace Action Coalition Microfilm* (Madison: State Historical Society of Wisconsin, n.d.), reel 1 (hereafter cited as *NPAC Microfilm*); and Jerry Gordon's long explanation to Kay Camp of the Women's International League for Peace and Freedom, 9 December 1970, ibid.

8. "Phony people" by Sid Peck, a leading member of PCPJ, quoted in Nancy Zaroulis and Gerald Sullivan, *Who Spoke Up? American Protest against the War*

in Vietnam (Garden City, N.Y.: Doubleday, 1984), 297. "Long March" in Jerry Coffin, "Movement Mish-Mash in Milwaukee," *WIN* 6 (August 1970), 25. Dellinger quoted in Charles C. Walker, Chicago Conference Plans 1971 Spring Peace Actions, "Coordinating Committee" file, box 3, PCPJ Records.

9. On term and threats, "Midwest Regional Newsletter of the National Coalition against War, Racism, and Repression," 22 September 1970, in House Committee on Internal Security, National Peace Action Coalition (NPAC) and *People's Coalition for Peace and Justice (PCPJ) Hearings,* 92nd Cong., 1st sess., 1971, pt. 1:1671; and Seattle Caucus, "We Are Going to Stop It," in House Committee on Internal Security, *NPAC and PCPJ Hearings,* pt. 3:3465. Davis quoted in Doug Jenness, "Mass Action versus Calculated Confrontation: An Answer to the May Day Tribe," *Militant,* 30 April 1971, 9. For a profile of Davis's trajectory through movements in the 1960s, see Todd Gitlin, *The Whole World Is Watching: Mass Media in the Making and Unmaking of the New Left* (Berkeley: University of California Press, 1980), 167–70.

10. For background on the organization, see History, "Historical Information, n.d." file, box 1, VVAW Records.

11. Norma Becker, "Letter," *Guardian,* 20 February 1971, 8.

12. On the general shift, see Howard V. Covell, "Detailed Police Planning Key to Orderly Rally," *FBI Law Enforcement Bulletin* 32 (November 1963), 3–6, 17; and Eugene Roberts Jr. and Douglas Ward, "The Press, Protesters, and Presidents," chap. in Frank B. Freidel and William Pencak, *The White House: The First Two Hundred Years* (Boston: Northeastern University Press, 1994), 135–37. The development of the District's agency is in the Guide to Collection, OEP Records, DCA. On army, see Alfred Beye to John Dean, 21 October 1969, "Demonstration—November, 1969: Washington, D.C. (folder 2)" file, Subject Files: Demonstrations and Domestic Intelligence, box 82, WHSF, SMOF-Dean, NPM, NA. On monitoring of protests, Christopher Pyle, *Military Surveillance of Civilian Politics, 1967–1970* (New York: Garland, 1986), 192. Jerry Wilson, testimony in Senate Committee on the Judiciary, *Federal Handling of Demonstrations,* 91st Cong., 2d sess., 1970, 30.

13. On exploration of limiting protests, see Gene Knorr to Bud Krogh, 13 October 1969, "White House Picketing [1969–1970]" file, box 21, Subject Files, WHSF, SMOF-Krogh, NPM, NA. After the protest against the Cambodia invasion, officials in the Secret Service revived the idea of banning demonstrations near the White House, but again it was shelved; Thomas Kelley to Richard Kleindienst, 28 May 1970, "Demonstration—5/9/70" file, Subject Files: Demonstrations and Domestic Intelligence, box 82, WHSF, SMOF-Dean, NPM, NA. On stalling, see Ron Young, Testimony, Senate Committee on the Judiciary, *Federal Handling of Demonstrations,* 15. Anti-war organizer Dick Fernandez quoted in New Mobilization Committee Meeting, 23 October 1969, "Demonstration—November, 1969: Washington, D.C. (folder 1)" file, Subject File: "Demonstrations and Domestic Intelligence," box 82, WHSF, SMOF-Dean, NPM, NA. Memorandum, Richard Nixon to H. R. Haldeman, 22 September 1969, quoted in Jeb S. Magruder, *An American Life: One Man's Road to Watergate* (New York: Atheneum, 1974), 75; Charles DeBenedetti, *An American Ordeal: The Antiwar Movement of the Vietnam Era,* Charles Chatfield, collab. (Syracuse, N.Y.:

Syracuse University Press, 1990), 271; and Charles Colson to H. R. Haldeman, 28 April 1971, "April 1971" file, box 128, WHSF, SMOF-Haldeman, NPM, NA.

14. Harold W. Stanley and Richard G. Niemi, *Vital Statistics on American Politics* (Washington, D.C.: C.Q. Press, 1988), 58; Erik Barnouw, *Tube of Plenty: The Evolution of American Television* (New York: Oxford University Press, 1990 [1975]), 401; and Amitai Etzioni, *Demonstration Democracy,* 13. The spring 1971 protests coincided with some of the Nixon administration's most virulent attacks on the networks; Marilyn A. Lashner, *The Chilling Effect in TV News: Intimidation by the Nixon White House* (New York: Praeger, 1984), 107.

15. On media's attention to president, see Todd Gitlin, *The Whole World Is Watching,* 80. John Dean to H. R. Haldeman and John Ehrlichman, 16 April 1971, "Demonstration May 1971, 1 of 3 files (confidential)" file, Subject Files: Demonstration and Domestic Intelligence, box 83, WHSF, SMOF-Dean, NPM, NA.

16. Paul W. Valentine, "U.S., Antiwar Group in Accord on Protest," *Washington Post,* 17 April 1971, B1. President quoted in James M. Naughton, "White House Sets a Quiet Tone for Today's Antiwar Protest," *New York Times,* 24 April 1971, 12.

17. Check List for Notice Forms: "Vietnam Veterans against the War, April 19–23, 1971" file, box 2, acc: 79–770002, NPS-NCP Records, WNRC; Mitchell Melish to Michael Phelan, 15 April 1971, ibid.; and Mitchell Melish to Attorney General, 12 April 1971, "National Peace Action Coalition" file, box 2, acc: 79–770002, NPS-NCP Records, WNRC.

18. Richard Starnes, "Hoover Fears D.C. Trouble," *Washington Daily News,* 6 January 1971, "People's Coalition for Peace and Justice, May Day 1971" file, box 32, OEP Records, DCA. American Civil Liberties Union of the National Capital Area, *Mayday 1971: Order without Law: An ACLU Study of the Largest Sweep Arrests in American History* (Washington, D.C.: ACLU, 1972), 52. John Dean to Jack Caulfield, 7 April 1971, "JWD Chron File April 1971" file, box 2, WHSF, SMOF-Dean, NPM, NA.

19. Haldeman Notes, Staff Meeting, 25 April 1971, "H Notes April–June '71 [April 1 to May 19, 1971] part I" file, box 43, WHSF, SMOF-Haldeman, NPM, NA.

20. Jan Crumb to Allard Lowenstein, 30 January 1970, "Correspondence: Political Campaigns, A-Z, '69–71" file, box 7, VVAW Records.

21. On recruiting efforts, Carl Bernstein, "Viet Veterans Camped on Mall Resemble Basic Training Outfit," *Washington Post,* 22 April 1971, A14.

22. "History," "Historical Information, n.d." file, box 1; VVAW Records; Operation RAW: Interim Report no. 2, 31 July 1970, "Correspondence, Memorandum to Coordinators, 1968–1972" file, box 6, VVAW Records. On Winter Soldier Hearings, see Richard Moser, *New Winter Soldier,* 110–11. See the accounts of both events in Richard Stacewicz, *Winter Soldiers,* 229–241.

23. Poster, "Operation Dewey Canyon III," "Vietnam Veterans against the War" file, box 20, Contemporary Issues Collection, Special Collections, University of California, Davis.

24. Sanford Ungar, "Vets Camping Plea Refused," *Washington Post,* 17 April 1971, B3; Sanford Ungar, "Vets Can Use Mall, Court Quickly Rules," *Washington Post,* 20 April 1971, A12; and Sanford Ungar and William Claiborne, "Vets' Camp on Mall Banned by Burger," *Washington Post,* 21 April 1971, A1. Nixon's

advice in H.R. Haldeman, *The Haldeman Diaries: Inside the Nixon White House* (Santa Monica, Calif.: Sony Imagesoft, 1994), Entry, 22 April 1971.

25. On cautions about Bonus Army, see "Beware of Veterans," *Christian Science Monitor,* 22 April 1971, in "Dewey Canyon III" flyer, "Programs: Dewey Canyon III, 1971 April, General Information" file, box 13, VVAW Records; and Stone's remarks to the veterans on the Mall, John Kerry and Vietnam Veterans against the War, *The New Soldier* (New York: Macmillan, 1971), 76. On slogans, see Paul W. Valentine, "Vets March on Hill, Protest Their War," *Washington Post,* 20 April 1971, A12. Nixon aide quoted in Sanford Ungar and William Claiborne, "Judge Lift Ban on Vets, Scolds U.S.," *Washington Post,* 23 April 1971, A6.

26. Coverage by ABC, CBS, NBC, April 19–23, 1971, Vanderbilt Television News Abstracts Website, http://tvnews.vanderbilt.edu/abstracts.html; Sanford Ungar and Carl Bernstein, "Veterans Turn Minor Prelude into a Major Antiwar Event," *Washington Post,* 24 April 1971, A4. Art Goldberg, "Vietnam Vets: The Anti-War Army," *Ramparts* 10 (July 1971), 11–12. Guerrilla theater as a political tool exploded in the 1960s; see Henry Lesnick, "Some Introductory Notes to Guerrilla/Street Theater," chap. in *Guerrilla-Street Theater* (New York: Avon Books, 1973).

27. Testimony of John Kerry, Senate Committee on Foreign Relations, *Legislative Proposals Relating to the War in Southeast Asia,* Hearings, 92nd Cong., 1st sess., 1920–1971, 184, 188. For photos documenting visits on Capitol Hill and to the camp itself, see John Kerry and Vietnam Veterans against the War, *New Soldier,* 59, 69–71, 89, 91.

28. On Kerry's background and appearance, "Angry War Veteran," *New York Times,* 23 April 1971, 4; and J.F. Ter Horst, "Detroit News," *Detroit News,* 1 May 1971, "Chuck [Charles J.] Colson, May 1971, part 1 of 2" file, box 78, WHSF, SMOF-Haldeman, NPM, NA. On testimony, "Fulbright Panel Hears Antiwar Vet," *Washington Post,* 23 April 1971, A4. Praise from Mary McGrory, "Peace Offensive Crushes Nixon," reprinted in Donald M. Fraser (Dem., Minn.), House, *Congressional Record,* 92nd Cong., 1st. Sess., 23 April 1971, 117, pt. 9:11805; praise from Senator Pell, Senate Committee on Foreign Relations, *Legislative Proposals,* 191.

29. Description of television coverage based on Abstracts, 19–24 April 1971, Vanderbilt Television News Abstracts Website, http://tvnews.vanderbilt.edu/abstracts.html.

30. Irwin Silber, "3000 Vets March," *Guardian,* 5 May 1971, 1, 6–7; and I.F. Stone, "Peace Is Still a Long, Long March Away," *I.F. Stone's Bi-Weekly,* 3 May 1971, 1. Thomas Gannon, "Warriors Oppose the War," *America* 124 (15 May 1971), 516; and quote from *Boston Globe* in "Dewey Canyon III" flyer, VVAW Records.

31. John R. Rarick (Dem., La.), House, *Congressional Record,* 92nd Cong., 1st sess., 23 April 1971, 177, pt. 9:11794; Smith Hempstone, "Our Times," *Washington Evening Star,* 29 April 1971, "April 16–April 30, 1971" file, "President's Handwriting," box 30, WHSF-POF, NPM, NA.

32. On Rainwater, see his Statement to Senate Committee on Foreign Relations, *Legislative Proposals;* Sanford Ungar and William Claiborne, "Vets' Camp

on Mall," A12; and Charles Colson, Telephone Call Recommendation, 23 April 1971, "President's Handwriting, April 16 thru 30, 1971" file, box 10, WHSF-POF, NPM, NA. On the president and Haldeman's conclusions, see H. R. Haldeman, *Haldeman Diaries,* 23 April 1971. Mary McGrory, "Peace Offensive Crushes Nixon," reprinted in Donald M. Fraser, House, 11805.

33. Art Goldberg, "Vietnam Vets," 14. Sanford Ungar and Carl Bernstein, "Veterans Turn Minor Prelude," A7. For general description, see John Kerry and Vietnam Veterans against the War, *New Soldier;* and Richard Moser, *New Winter Soldier,* 112–17.

34. Gary Trudeau, Doonesbury Comic Strips, *San Francisco Chronicle,* 1–5 May 1971.

35. "April 24th Can't Be Ignored," Press Release, 27 March 1971, *NPAC Microfilm,* reel 4; Rod Such, "Mass Turnout Expected April 24," *Guardian,* 17 April 1971, 4. Sanford Ungar and William Claiborne, "Vets' Camp on Mall," A6.

36. Jerry Gordon to Rose Daitsman, 2 January 1970, *NPAC Microfilm,* reel 4. Westchester Peace Council, "Be Counted This Time," Poster, 1971, Yanker Poster Collection, POS 6 U.S., no 818 (C size), Prints and Photographs Division, LC.

37. Howard Wallace, "Mounting Labor Support for April 24," *Intercontinental Press,* 22 March 1971, 251.

38. NPAC to Dear Friend, 18 March 1971, *NPAC Microfilm,* reel 1; "Join the Women's Contingent," in House Committee on Internal Security, *NPAC and PCPJ Hearings,* pt. 4:3613.

39. On plans for contingent, see form letter from Charles Stephenson, [1971, ca. 13 February], *NPAC Microfilm,* reel 1; and "Antiwar Activities Backed by Blacks," *Washington Post,* 30 March 1971, clipping in *NPAC Microfilm,* reel 3.

40. Rod Such, "Protest Demands 'Out Now,'" *Guardian,* 5 May 1971, 3; "Progress Report for Special Events or Emergencies: National Peace Action Coalition," 24 April 1971, in "Mayday Report," book 3, box 2, MPD Records, DCA; and "Washington: Half a Million March on April 24," *Liberation News Service,* 28 April 1971, 8.

41. Putnam Barber, Super 8 film footage (24 April 1971), in author's possession.

42. Putnam Barber, Super 8 film footage; "Washington: Half a Million," 8; and Kay van Deurs, "how we happened to paint pennsylvania avenue with the theatre of the 6 dragons," *WIN* 7 (June 1971), 11–12.

43. On diversity as goal, see Doug Jenness, "April 24: Class Collaboration or Independent Struggle," *Militant,* 28 May 1971, 15. On number and schedule for speakers, D.C. Office of Civil Defense, Plan of Operation for National Peace Action Coalition March and Rally, 21 April 1971, "NPAC March & Rally 24 Apr 1971" file, box 27, OEP Records, DCA.

44. On audibility, see G. Vijayam, "The Mass Rally in Washington, April 24, 1971, Field Notes No. 33," June 1971, "Field Notes, 27–45" file, box 3, CNCR Records, SCPC. See also UPI report copied onto "Information Source Data," 024165, box 27, OEP Records, DCA. On attitude toward speeches, see Jim Mann, "Protest: They Came, But the Anger Has Softened," *Washington Post,* 25 April 1971, A19; and Paul W. Valentine and Richard M. Cohen, "End War Now, Throng Demands: Over 175,000 Rally at Capitol," *Washington Post,* 25 April

1971, A1. Criticism of lack of "militant spirit," "April 24," *Fifth Estate* 6 (12 April 1929–12 May 1971), 1.

45. On events at the Monument, see Department of Interior, Demonstration Report, Spring 1971, "National Peace Action Coalition" file, box 2, acc: 79–770002, NPS-NCP Records, WNRC; Estimate of Costs Incurred—NPAC Demonstration, n.d., "National Peace Action Coalition" file, box 2, acc: 79–770002, NPS-NCP Records, WNRC; and testimony by Russell E. Dickenson, director of National Capital Parks, and Alfred D. Beye, deputy chief, United States Park Police, House Committee on Internal Security, *NPAC and PCPJ Hearings,* 1449–52.

46. Harry Ring, "NPAC Asks for Live TV Coverage," *Militant,* 9 April 1971, 4; and Steering Committee Minutes, 27 March 1971, NPAC *Microfilm,* reel 1. Some local stations in the District did carry some of the march live; "Information Source Data," 024095, 24 April 1971, box 27, OEP Records, DCA.

47. *CBS Evening News,* April 24, 1971, Vanderbilt Television News Abstracts Website, http://tvnews.vanderbilt.edu/abstracts.html.

48. H. R. Haldeman, *Haldeman Diaries,* 24 April 1971. This trip drew criticism from the editors of the *New York Times,* who argued he should have stayed in the capital and listened to the demonstrators' "reasonable expression of public opinion"; "Demonstration in Washington," *New York Times,* 26 April 1971, 34.

49. "Totally kids" from Haldeman Notes, 24 April 1971, "H Notes April–June '71 [1 April–19 May 1971] part I" file, box 43, 24 April [1971], "H Notes April–June '71 [1 April–19 May 1971], Part I" file, box 43, WHSF, SMOF-Haldeman, NPM, NA; and "totally positive" from Haldeman Notes, 25 April 1971, WHSF, SMOF-Haldeman, NPM, NA. On outrage over ignoring Washington Monument events, see opening remarks by Richard Chord, House Committee on Internal Security, *NPAC and PCPJ Hearings,* 1445–46.

50. On concert and atmosphere, see "Troops Mass Near Capital and Protesters Assemble," *New York Times,* 2 May 1971, 69. William H. Kuenning, *Free to Go: The Story of a Family's Involvement in the 1971 Mayday Activities in Washington* (Lombard, Ill.: Unicorn Publications, 1971), 9; and "Mayday: 12,000 Busts Can't Stop the People's Peace," *Liberation News Service,* 8 May 1971, 1. On warnings, see "Briefing Session, 1200 hours," 1 May 1971, and "Briefing Session, 2000 hours," 1 May 1971, "Mayday Report," book 3, MPD Records, DCA. The sense of nervous anticipation also comes through in an interview by the author with Detective Kenny Green, U.S. Park Police, 28 March 1997. Detective Green was a young officer in 1971, and the Mayday protests were one of his first experiences with anti-war protesters. On preemptive nature, see Richard Hollaran, "30,000 Protesters Routed in Capital," *New York Times,* 3 May 1971; Unlabeled Minutes of Meeting on Mayday Protests, 6 May 1971, WHSF, SMOF-Dean, NPM, NA. "Break the back" from "Information Source Data," 024748 and 024833, "People's Coalition for Peace and Justice, May Day, 1971" file, box 31, OEP Records, DCA.

51. "The Latest Word on Mayday," *Liberation News Service,* 24 April 1971, 13. Participant quoted in "Controversy Mounts over Arrests Here," *Washington Post,* 6 May 1971, A14.

52. Public Information Suggestions from Ziegler/Scali, 1 May 1971, "Demonstration—May 1971, 2 of 3 files (secret)" file, box 83, WHSF, SMOF-Dean, NPM, NA. Nixon quoted in John Dean, *Blind Ambition: The White House Years* (New York: Pocket Books, 1977), 42.

53. See Herbert M. Kritzer, "Mobile Tactics at Dupont Circle, Field Notes 25," May 1971, "Field Notes 1–26" file, box 3, CNCR Records, SCPC; "Information Source Data" reports, 024857–025001, "PCPJ-Mayday-NPAC et al., Feb/71–June 30/71" file 2 of 4, box 29, OEP Records, DCA; "Mayday: 12,000 Busts," 1, and "Mayday Tactics: Stay Together and Keep Moving," *Liberation News Service*, 8 May 1971, 13. "Mayday: What Does It Mean for Federal Employees," pamphlet, "Material from Refile Box (1992)" file, refile box, PCPJ Records.

54. Poster in House Committee on Internal Security, *NPAC and PCPJ Hearings*, pt. 3:3422–23; Mayday Tactical Manual, folder 2 "PCPJ," temporary box 1, PCPJ Records; graffiti shown in Exhibit 1, House Committee on Internal Security, *NPAC and PCPJ Hearings*, 1595–98. "May Flowers," pamphlet, "Mayday May 1970" *[sic]* file, box 1, acc: 81 A-3, PCPJ Records.

55. On goals of diversity, "May Flowers," PCPJ Records. Male participation based on the percentage of men among the total arrested. There were no reports that the police avoided arresting women; reports on arrests to John Dean, 3 May 1971, "May 3, 1971, PCPJ, Traffic Blockade" file, box 31, OEP Records, DCA. For particularly good pictures of those arrested, see "Mayday Report," book 3, MPD Records, DCA.

56. "Racist" from "Additional RMBB from Boston Committee of Women to Defend the Right to Live," *Liberation News Service*, April 1924, 10. On rapes and quote from black man, "Getting It Together in West Patomac *[sic]* Park," *Liberation News Service*, 1 May 1971, 7. David Dellinger had celebrated the "fraternal solidarity" of the protesters in Chicago in 1968; David Dellinger, *Revolutionary Nonviolence: Essays by Dave Dellinger* (Indianapolis: Bobbs-Merrill, 1970), 319.

57. Mayday Tactical Manual; Michael P. Lerner, "May Day: Anatomy of the Movement," *Ramparts* 10 (July 1971), 19; Bill Wingell, "Mayday Protest Activity in Washington, D.C.—May 1971, Field Notes 30," June 1971, "Field Notes 27–45" file, box 3, CNCR Records, SCPC; "Mayday Tactics," 13.

58. John Dean, *Blind Ambition*, 43; Paul W. Valentine, "7,000 Arrested in Disruptions," *Washington Post*, 4 May 1971, A1; "The Biggest Bust," *Newsweek* 77.5 (17 May 1971), 24. On National Guard call-up, see "Order of the Commissioner No. 71–121," 29 April 1971, in "Mayday Report," book 3, MPD Records, DCA. Number of troops from R. S. Townsend to John Dean, n.d., "Cost of Demonstrations, May 1971 (confidential)" file, box 81, WHSF, SMOF-Dean, NPM, NA.

59. "The group" from Herbert M. Kritzer, "Mobile Tactics at Dupont Circle," CNCR Records, SCPC; Richard E. Tilley to Assistant Chief of Police, 23 April 1971, in "Mayday Report," book 2, box 2, MPD Records, DCA; and Donald Graham, "Communications, Luck Keep Forces One Up on Protesters," *Washington Post*, 4 May 1971, A13.

60. For development of arrest procedures, see District of Columbia Human Relations Commission, *Mayday 1971: Challenge to Civil Liberty* (Washington, D.C.: District of Columbia Government, 1971), 3. Jerry Wilson, Memorandum:

Arrests in Connection with Demonstrations, 16 April 1971, "People's Coalition for Peace and Justice, May Day" file, box 31, OEP Records, DCA.

61. District of Columbia Human Relations Commission, *Mayday 1971*, 9–11; "Biggest Bust," 25–26; Herbert M. Kritzer, "Mobile Tactics at Dupont Circle," CNCR Records, SCPC; American Civil Liberties Union of the National Capital Area, *Mayday 1971*, 7–9; "Day's Drama: Protesters, Police, Commuters Converge," *Washington Post*, 4 May 1971, A14; Paul W. Valentine, "7,000 Arrested," A1.

62. Initial suits: Stephen Torgoff, "Antiwar Forces Prepare for Legal Battles," *Guardian*, 26 May 1971, 3. Capitol protesters cleared: "800 Mayday Demonstrators Cleared," *Intercontinental Press* 9 (13 September 1971), 756. Laura Kieran, "D.C. to Pay $2.2 Million to Antiwar Demonstrators," *Washington Post*, 2 May 1981, B8.

63. District of Columbia Human Relations Commission, *Mayday 1971*, 13.

64. Wilson's opinion in John Dean to the President, 4 May 1971, "Demonstration—May 1971, 2 of 3 files (Secret)" file, box 83, WHSF, SMOF-Dean, NPM, NA. On protests, see Michael P. Lerner, "May Day," 40–41; and "Biggest Bust," 25–26. For 1872 law, see discussion in Introduction and in chapter 1.

65. See account in William H. Kuenning, *Free to Go*, and pictures in "Mayday Report," book 3, MPD Records, DCA.

66. For details on changes in procedure and successful lawsuits, see American Civil Liberties Union of the National Capital Area, *Mayday 1971*.

67. "Heartening success" from Sidney Lens to People's Coalition, n.d. [June 1971?], "PCPJ: Materials, 1971–1973" file, temporary box 1, PCPJ Records. Davis quoted in Robert M. Smith, "2 War Foes Face U.S. Jury Inquiry," *New York Times*, 7 May 1971, 45. David Dellinger, "A New Stage of Struggle: Mayday and the Fall Offensive," *Liberation* 16 (September 1971), 12.

68. Jonathan Schell, *Observing the Nixon Years* (New York: Pantheon Books, 1989), 94. Excerpts from Address of Senator Edward Kennedy, 5 May 1971, attached to John Dean to Dick Howard, 25 May 1971, "Demonstration—May 1971, 3 of 3 files (Secret)" file, box 84, WHSF, SMOF-Dean, NPM, NA. American Civil Liberties Union of the National Capital Area, *Mayday 1971*.

69. Russell Baker, "Is Street Theater on Its Way Out?" *Washington Evening Star*, 6 May 1971, "Vietnam War, Mayday Protests, May 2–4, 1971, #1," file, Vertical Files, Washingtoniana Collection. "The Movement, the Medium and the Message," *Washington Post*, 4 May 1971, A16.

70. Poll results in Charles Colson to H.R. Haldeman, 20 May 1971, "Chuck [Charles Colson] May 1971, part 2 of 2" file, box 78, WHSF, SMOF-Haldeman, NPM, NA. Telegrams collected in "Mayday Report," book 3, MPD Records, DCA.

71. Nixon quoted in Stephen E. Ambrose, *Nixon: The Triumph of a Politician, 1962–1972* (New York: Simon and Schuster, 1989), 438. Mitchell in "Antiwar Group Defies Witch Hunt," *Intercontinental Press* 9 (31 May 1971), 493.

72. Charles Colson to H.R. Haldeman, 5 May 1971, "May 1971" file, box 129, WHSF, SMOF-Haldeman, NPM, NA; and H.R. Haldeman to Chuck Colson, 4 May 1971, "H.R. Haldeman—Chron May [1971]" file, box 196, WHSF,

SMOF-Haldeman, NPM, NA. "Nail" from Charles Colson to Clark MacGregor, 4 May 1971, "May 1971" file, box 129, WHSF, SMOF-Haldeman, NPM, NA.

73. On NPAC problems, see Harry Ring, "PL-SDS Fails to Break Up NPAC Gathering," *Militant,* 16 July 1971, 13. On VVAW divisions, see Jan Crumb, Letter of Resignation, 17 May 1971, "Correspondence: Resignations" file, box 7, VVAW Records; and National Coordinating Committee to All Coordinators, 10 December 1971, "Correspondence, Memorandum to Coordinators, 1968–1972" file, box 6, VVAW Records.

74. Excerpt on "May Day Demonstrators," " 'The Book' [folder 3 of 3]" file, box 11, WHSF, SMOF-Buchanan, NPM, NA.

75. Jeb S. Magruder, *American Life,* 165. Richard M. Nixon, *RN: The Memoirs of Richard Nixon* (New York: Grosset & Dunlap, 1978), 497.

76. Joseph Lelyveld, "Status of the Movement: The 'Energy Levels' Are Low," *New York Times Magazine,* 7 November 1971, 37.

EPILOGUE

1. Haynes Johnson, "Washington Remains Demonstration Capital of the World," *Washington Post,* 19 July 1978, 3. In 1996, for example, the Park Service received about 2,000 applications to use the Mall, Lafayette Square in front of the White House, or other federal areas for protests. For 1996 figures, see Larry Van Dyne, "Trouble Makers," *Washingtonian* 31.5 (February 1996), 56.

2. Vicky Hutchings, "Regular People," *New Statesmen and Society* 4 (22 February 1991), 16.

3. Gary Lee and Linda Wheeler, "Gay-Rights March Organizers Say 1 Million May Participate," *Washington Post,* 19 March 1993, A41.

4. Karen De Witt, "Black Men Say the March in Washington Is about Them, Not Farrakhan," *New York Times,* 15 October 1995, national edition, 22.

5. Donna Britt, "The Organizer, in Control and Back in Action," *Washington Post,* 7 October 1989, C1

6. Shawn Zeller, "Backward March: Why Are Gays Protesting a Gay Rights March?" *New Republic* 222 (17 April 2000), 24. Editorial, "Marching Out of Step," *Washington Times,* 7 April 1992, F2.

7. *Chief of Capitol Police v. Jeannette Rankin Brigade,* 409 U.S. 972 (1972).

8. Todd S. Purdum, "Clinton Bans Traffic in Front of the White House," *New York Times,* 21 May 1995, 1, 28. On increased scrutiny, see website by protesters in Lafayette Square, "1601 Pennsylvania Avenue," http://prop1.org/ (accessed February 2000).

9. National Capital Region, National Park Service, "Records of Determination for a partial and temporary public use limitation at certain Federal parks," 25 September 2001, and ibid., "Records of Determination to extend a partial and temporary public use limitation at certain Federal parks," 25 October 2001, 23 November 2001, and 20 December 2001. For concerns of Secret Service, see C. Danny Spriggs, Assistant Director, Office of Protective Operations, United States Secret Service to Terry Carlstrom, Regional Director, National Capital Region, National Park Service, 21 November 2001. This letter and the "Records

of Determination" were supplied to me by Randolph Myers, attorney-advisor for the National Capital Region, Department of the Interior.

10. For such conflicts, see the debate about federal regulations banning T-shirt sales on the Mall in 1994 and 1995. Tourist and other supporters of the ban testified about the necessity of preserving "the beauty of the Mall," while defenders of the sales spoke of the need to preserve the freedom of speech and expression. See discussion in National Park Service, "National Capital Region Parks: Special Regulations: 36 CFR Part 7," *Federal Register* 60.67 (7 April 1995), 17639–48. See also request for advice on how to avoid demonstrations in Washington, "Travel Questions," *New York Times,* 16 June 1991, Travel section, 4.

11. For criticisms of the siting of the World War II memorial, see Paul Goldberger, "Not in Our Front Yard," *New Yorker* (7 August 2000), 27–28; Jon Wiener, "Save the Mall," *Nation* 271 (13 November 2000), 8; Judy S. Feldman, Memories and Memorial Mishaps: The Case of the Proposed World War II Memorial, May 2000, Save the Mall website, www.savethemall.org/memories.html (accessed on 7 December 2000). On the static nature of memorials, see Sanford Levinson, *Written in Stone: Public Monuments in Changing Societies* (Durham, N.C.: Duke University Press, 1998), 7.

12. On experienced organizers, parking arrangements, and sound, see Larry Van Dyne, "Trouble Makers," 107. On Alice Cohan's involvement in planning marches, see also Russell Cate, "As Calls Come Pouring in, Organizers Face Off with the National Park Service," *Washington Blade,* 12 February 1993, 23. Million Family organizers quoted in Darryl Fears and Serge F. Kovaleski, "From Chaos to Cohesion," *Washington Post,* 20 October 2000, A1.

13. Larry Van Dyne, "Trouble Makers," 107; "world-renowned" from Joseph R. Cox, "Strategies for Effective Crowd Control," *Police Chief* 65.6 (June 1998), 29. Author's interviews with Detective Kenny Green and Sergeant Joseph R. Cox, U.S. Park Police, 25 March 1997; author's interview with Gary Scott, chief historian, National Capital Park Region, National Park Service, 24 March 1997; author's interview with Sandra Ally, Public Relations, National Capital Park Region, National Park Service, and Randolph Myers, attorney-advisor, National Capital Parks, Office of the Solicitor, Department of the Interior, 26 March 1998.

14. Arthur Santana, "Nice Cop-Tough Cop Tactic Paid Off for District Police," *Washington Post,* 20 April 2000, B1; David Montgomery, "Suit Says Police Violated Protesters' Rights," *Washington Post,* 28 July 2000, A4.

15. For complaints by protesters about the limited coverage of their efforts, see Vicky Hutchings, "Regular People," 16; and "The Talk of the Town: Notes and Comments," *New Yorker* 66 (11 February 1991), 26—where the participant writes of how one channel gave "the demonstration about thirty seconds. CBS, I am told, disposed of it in something closer to twenty seconds, and the *Times* put it on page 17."

16. Larry Van Dyne, "Trouble Makers," 109; and Sari Horwitz and Hamil R. Harris, "Farrakhan Threatens to Sue Park Police over March Count," *Washington Post,* 18 October 1995, A8.

17. Colbert I. King, "More Important Than Marches," *Washington Post,* 21 October 2000, A23.

18. Pete Dexter, "Too Early to Congratulate Men Who Gathered in D.C.," *Sacramento Bee,* 23 October 1995, A2.

19. Jeffrey Schmalz, "Gay Americans Throng Capital in Appeal for Rights," *New York Times,* 26 April 1993, B8. College student quoted in Manny Fernandez, Million Man March, 16 October 2000, Washington Post Online, www.washingtonpost.com (accessed on 25 October 2000).

20. Susan Dworkin, "Marching on Washington," *Ms.* 14.12 (June 1986), 86. Frank Pavone, 25 Years of Roe V. Wade, Priests for Life, www.priestforlife.org (accessed on 12 May 1998).

BIBLIOGRAPHICAL ESSAY

Writing this book took me into many libraries, through the pages of countless books, and into areas of scholarship I had never explored. My working bibliography contains more than 2,000 references and does not even include everything in my file drawers. There is no reason to list them all here. Rather, in this essay, I have chosen to highlight the scholarship most influential on my work and the resources most necessary for those who might want to look at these marches in more detail. The notes to the chapters can lead readers to specific sources.

INFLUENCES

Though a historian, I was inspired by this project to explore the work of political scientists and sociologists on protests and social movements. A comprehensive review of this scholarship is found in Sidney G. Tarrow, *Power in Movement: Social Movements, Collective Action, and Politics* (New York: Cambridge University Press, 1994; second edition 1998). Though drawing on a full range of scholars, Tarrow is particularly persuaded by resource mobilization theory, which holds that material and financial resources, organizational skills, and experienced organizers are key to successful social movements. Some of the best scholarship influenced by this theory is collected in Mayer N. Zald and John D. McCarthy, eds., *Social Movements in an Organizational Society: Collected Essays* (New Brunswick, N.J.: Transaction Books, 1987). I have found this emphasis useful for understanding the skills necessary for organizers to plan these demonstrations. At the same time, some of this work suffers from either too narrow a focus on the internal dynamics of movements or too broad a definition of "resources."

To avoid these faults, it is essential to understand the dynamic relationships between protesters, authorities, and the media. In his work, Tarrow also emphasizes the importance of "political opportunities" for social movements. Such

BIBLIOGRPAHICAL ESSAY

moments of upheaval—whether caused by economic depression, war, or significant political transition—clearly influenced the marches I studied. Scholarship on nonviolent direct action helps focus attention on the dynamics between authorities and protesters at specific moments; see Ronald McCarthy and Christopher Kruegler, *Toward Research and Theory Building in the Study of Nonviolent Action* (Cambridge, Mass.: The Albert Einstein Institution, 1993) for a useful overview. In many ways, the most influential work came from Charles Tilly, a historically oriented sociologist. A good summary of his thinking can be found in "Speaking Your Mind without Elections, Surveys, or Social Movements," *Public Opinion Quarterly* 47 (Winter 1983), 461–78. For a more detailed approach see *Popular Contention in Great Britain, 1758–1834* (Cambridge, Mass.: Harvard University Press, 1995). Naturally, close studies of individual movements are necessary to understand these dynamics; they often reveal specific challenges and opportunities facing groups trying to change policy and their political situations. Some are mentioned below in the sections on individual chapters.

Over the course of my research, I began to appreciate marches on Washington as a kind of performance, which became an increasingly ritualized part of the American political tradition. For this perspective, the work of anthropologist Victor Turner is suggestive; see his *Blazing the Trail: Way Marks in the Exploration of Symbols* (Tucson: University of Arizona Press, 1992). Also useful is Murray Edelman's body of work on symbolic politics, *The Symbolic Uses of Politics* (1964; Urbana: University of Illinois Press, 1985) and *Constructing the Political Spectacle* (Chicago: University of Chicago Press, 1988). On the invention of political traditions, I, like so many others, am influenced by Eric Hobsbawm and Terence Ranger, *The Invention of Tradition* (1983; Cambridge, U.K.: Canto, 1992). For understanding the design and response to these events, I find provocative Elias Canetti, *Crowds and Power,* trans. Carol Stewart (1962; New York: Continuum Publishing, 1981).

This study argues that protest in Washington drew on and modified earlier and local traditions of public protest and rituals. E. P. Thompson's "The Moral Economy of the English Crowd," *Past and Present* 50 (February 1971), 76–136, remains the most elegant interpretation of protest in traditional British culture. To understand how these traditions developed and changed in the United States before 1894, I found valuable Mary Blewett, *Men, Women and Work: Class, Gender, and Protest in the New England Shoe Industry, 1780–1910* (Urbana: University of Illinois Press, 1988); Susan G. Davis, *Parades and Power: Street Theatre in Nineteenth-Century Philadelphia* (Philadelphia: Temple University Press, 1986); Paul Gilje, *The Road to Mobocracy: Popular Disorder in New York City, 1763–1834* (Chapel Hill: University of North Carolina Press, 1987); and Neil Larry Shumsky, *The Evolution of Political Protest and the Workingmen's Party of California* (Columbus: Ohio State University Press, 1991). A celebratory account, based on work by Marty Jezer, of public protest in the United States since the Revolutionary War can be found in Robert Cooney and Helen Michalowski, *The Power of the People: Active Nonviolence in the United States* (Philadelphia: New Society Publishers, 1987).

I have tried throughout this study to understand the negotiations and relationships among organizers, authorities, and journalists. Organizers' methods and motives are well explored in the literature on social movements discussed above. In contrast, the treatment of political protest by the courts in the United States deserves more attention. Robin Handley, "Public Order, Petitioning, and Freedom of Assembly," *Journal of Legal History* 7 (September 1986), 123–55, is particularly suggestive, though most of the discussion focuses on practices in Britain. Overviews are provided in M. Glenn Abernathy, *The Right of Assembly and Association,* 2d rev. ed. (Columbia: University of South Carolina Press, 1981), and C. E. Baker, "Unreasoned Reasonableness: Mandatory Parade Permits and Time, Place, and Manner Regulations," *Northwestern Law Review* (December 1983), 937–1024. For a careful look at the meaning of the First Amendment to its drafters, see Akhil R. Amar, "The Bill of Rights as a Constitution," *Yale Law Journal* 100 (March 1991), 1131–210.

There is no comprehensive look at authorities in the United States and their response to demonstrations. For an examination of dynamics during recent protests, see Clark McPhail, David Schweingruber, and John McCarthy, "Policing Protest in the United States: 1960–1995," in *Policing Protest: The Control of Mass Demonstrations in Western Democracies,* Donatella Della Porta and Herbert Reiter, eds. (Minneapolis: University of Minnesota Press, 1998), 49–69. There are, however, useful works on federal agencies and their response to political unrest. On the army, see Roy Talbert Jr., *Negative Intelligence: The Army and the American Left, 1917–1941* (Jackson: University Press of Mississippi, 1991); Gerald G. Eggert, *Railroad Labor Disputes: The Beginnings of Federal Strike Policy* (Ann Arbor: University of Michigan Press, 1967); Joan M. Jensen, *Army Surveillance in America, 1775–1980* (New Haven, Conn.: Yale University Press, 1991). On the Federal Bureau of Investigation, see Athan G. Theoharis and John Stuart Cox, *The Boss: J. Edgar Hoover and the Great American Inquisition* (Philadelphia: Temple University Press, 1988). In most of these works, the focus is so broad that the specific responses to marches receive scant attention.

I also seek to explain how changes in the forms of journalism over this period have shaped the nature of the protests. Overviews of the press are useful, such as Edwin Emery and Michael C. Emery, *The Press and America: An Interpretive History of the Mass Media* (Englewood Cliffs, N.J.: Prentice-Hall, 1984). Among communication scholars, the notion of how journalists "frame" events in conventional ways has proven influential in studies of movements. The term originated with Erving Goffman's *Frame Analysis: An Essay on the Organization of Experience* (New York: Harper and Row, 1974). Such insights help me understand the efforts of journalists covering the first demonstrations in Washington to transform them into events they understood better. Over time, as marches on Washington became more familiar, journalists developed specific conventions for them. The introduction of television changed much. For understanding its influences, I suggest Erik Barnouw's classic, *Tube of Plenty: The Evolution of American Television,* 2d rev. ed. (New York: Oxford University Press, 1990), and Michael Schudson, *The Power of News* (Cambridge, Mass.: Harvard University Press, 1995).

All of these studies of movements, authorities, and the media helped me to ask broad questions about the history of nationalism and citizenship. Since the first march, organizers needed to arrange their protests in Washington in ways that spoke to national beliefs and took advantage of views of political legitimacy. Benedict Anderson's *Imagined Communities: Reflections on the Origin and*

Spread of Nationalism, 2d ed. (London: Verso Press, 1991) provides a provocative look at how nation-states develop rhetorically. On citizenship generally, feminist theorists have explored the assumptions that underlie citizenship in the
Western world: see especially Carol Pateman, *The Disorder of Women: Democracy, Feminism, and Political Theory* (Stanford: Stanford University Press, 1989),
and Nancy Fraser, *Unruly Practices: Power, Discourse, and Gender in Contemporary Social Theory* (Minneapolis: University of Minnesota Press, 1989). Historians interested in the cultural construction of politics have used their theories
in a number of studies: see Lynn Hunt, *Politics, Culture, and Class in the French
Revolution* (Berkeley: University of California Press, 1984); Mary P. Ryan,
Women in Public: Between Banners and Ballots, 1825–1880 (Baltimore: Johns
Hopkins University Press, 1990); and Carroll Smith-Rosenberg, "Dis-Covering
the Subject of the 'Great Constitutional Discussion,' 1786–1789," *Journal of
American History* 79 (December 1992), 841–73. Recent overviews of citizenship
in the United States show the influence of these studies. I saw much resonance
with my own conclusions in Rogers M. Smith, *Civic Ideals: Conflicting Visions
of Citizenship in U.S. History* (New Haven, Conn.: Yale University Press, 1997),
and Michael Schudson, *The Good Citizen: A History of American Civic Life*
(New York: Martin Kessler Books, 1998).

Thinking about citizenship and the nation in the context of these political activities that took place outside of official political channels led me to look at recent
debates about the nature of the public sphere. Jurgen Habermas used the term
"public sphere" in 1969 to refer to the space between the state and society where
citizens think and perform their vision of politics, a space that he saw as critical to
the functioning of democratic states. While Habermas has backed away from some
of his earlier historical and ideological statements about the public sphere, recent
scholars have found it a useful concept to discuss how people can and do influence
politics. For a compilation of Habermas's current views and the renewed debate
over the concept, see Craig Calhoun, ed., *Habermas and the Public Sphere* (Cambridge, Mass.: MIT Press, 1992). This collection, particularly the contributions by
Nancy Fraser, Michael Schudson, Geoff Eley, and Mary Ryan, helped me clarify
the importance of looking at the contemporary historical context of the media, citizenship, and politics in the United States in each era of my study. Such attention,
these scholars emphasized, helps ground the abstraction of the public sphere in the
varieties of ways that different people engage in politics and public life. The potential of this grounding can be seen clearly in the exemplary work of David Zaret,
"Petitions and the 'Invention' of Public Opinion in the English Revolution," *American Journal of Sociology* 101.6 (1996), 1497–555. Susan Herbst has written two
provocative books that influenced my thinking on political practices: *Numbered
Voices: How Opinion Polling Has Shaped American Politics* (Chicago: University
of Chicago Press, 1993) and *Politics at the Margin: Historical Studies of Public Expression outside the Mainstream* (New York: Cambridge University Press, 1994).

Over the course of engaging in this literature, I became increasingly convinced
that the term "public space" was more useful for my purposes. Some critiques of
Habermas have pointed to his lack of focus on the actual places that people used
for political actions; see, for example, Iris Marion Young, "Impartiality and the
Civic Public: Some Implications of Feminist Critiques of Moral and Political

Theory," in *Feminism as Critique: Essays on the Politics of Gender in Late-Capitalist Societies*, Seyla Benhabib and Drucilla Cornell, eds. (Cambridge, U.K.: Polity Press, 1987), 56–76. As I shifted to this term, I began to look at the work of urban geographers. J. B. Jackson's elegant essay, "American Public Space," *Public Interest* 74 (1984), 52–65, was an early inspiration. Later I encountered Murray Edelman, "Space and the Social Order," *Journal of Architectural Education* 32 (1978), 1–9; Charles T. Goodsell, *The Social Meaning of Civic Space: Studying Political Authority through Architecture* (Lawrence: University Press of Kansas, 1988); and Don Mitchell, "The End of Public Space? People's Park, Definitions of the Public, and Democracy," *Annals of the Association of American Geographers* 85.1 (1995), 108–33. Conversations with Ari Kelman, as well as his study of the Mississippi River and the City of New Orleans, provided immense help in navigating this literature; see his *A River and a City: An Environmental History of New Orleans* (Berkeley: University of California Press, 2003).

As I studied this literature and pursued my own archival work, the spatial and political evolution of the District of Columbia remained a subject of continuing interest. Constance Green's two volumes—*Washington: Village and Capital, 1800–1878* (1962) and *Washington: Capital City, 1879–1950* (1962), reprinted as *Washington: A History of the Capital, 1800–1950* (Princeton, N.J.: Princeton University Press, 1976)—still provide much of the necessary background, especially when supplemented with her more detailed *The Secret City: A History of Race Relations in the Nation's Capital* (Princeton, N.J.: Princeton University Press, 1967). Works that build on and expand her work include Alan Lessoff, *The Nation and Its City: Politics, "Corruption," and Progress in Washington, D.C., 1861–1902* (Baltimore: Johns Hopkins University Press, 1994), and Carl Abbott, *Political Terrain: Washington, D.C.: From Tidewater Town to Global Metropolis* (Chapel Hill: University of North Carolina Press, 1999). Reading in the *Records of the Columbia History Society* and its successor, *Washington History*, also brought the changes in the city alive to me.

Since I wanted to understand the changes in the capital's appearance, I also turned to scholars concerned with its landscape and particular locations. Two more informal histories of Pennsylvania Avenue are particularly useful, Carol M. Highsmith and Ted Landphair, *Pennsylvania Avenue: America's Main Street* (Washington, D.C.: American Institute of Architects Press, 1988), and Mary Cable, *The Avenue of Presidents* (Boston: Houghton Mifflin, 1969). I also recommend the volume prepared by the Federal Writers' Project of the Works Progress Administration: *Washington: City and Capital* (Washington, D.C.: Government Printing Office, 1937). Early on, I discovered the marvelous essays in Richard W. Longstreth, ed., *The Mall in Washington, 1791–1991* (Washington, D.C.: National Gallery of Art, 1991). Later I became intrigued by the idiosyncratic but provocative work of Elbert Peets, whose essays on Washington, written from the 1920s to the 1950s, are included in *On the Art of Designing Cities: Selected Essays of Elbert Peets*, Paul D. Spreiregen, ed. (Cambridge, Mass.: MIT Press, 1968). And, walking the city itself and participating in marches are excellent ways to appreciate how these protests relate to the capital's landscape.

SPECIFIC SOURCES

For the history specifically of marches on Washington, there are a wide variety of primary and secondary sources. The only other study to attempt a comprehensive approach is Norman Gilbert's "The Mass Protest Phenomenon: An Examination of Marches on Washington" (Ph.D. dissertation, Northern Illinois University, 1971), based almost exclusively on secondary, published sources. In addition, some scholars have examined how protesters used specific locations in Washington. Eugene Roberts Jr. and Douglas B. Ward looked at the area near the White House in "The Press, Protestors, and Presidents," in *The White House: The First Two Hundred Years,* Frank Freidel and William Pencak, eds. (Boston: Northeastern University Press, 1994), 125–40. In an excellent article, Scott Sandage considers the history of using the Lincoln Memorial by protesters; see "A Marble House Divided: The Lincoln Memorial, the Civil Rights Movement, and the Politics of Memory," *Journal of American History* 80 (June 1993), 135–67. Still lacking is a sustained look at protests near the Capitol.

While there is no single archival source for materials on all demonstrations in Washington, a few collections are useful for sources on specific demonstrations. Several collections at the National Archives deserve notice. To understand the reaction of the District of Columbia government to protests, there are valuable materials in Record Group 351, which contains papers and reports from the government of the District of Columbia, even though it is by no means complete. Also useful is Record Group 165: Military Intelligence Division, Correspondence 1917–1941, which contains reports on the Bonus marchers and the Negro March. In addition, the newsreel collection in the Motion Picture and Sound Division of the Archives has footage of several demonstrations in the capital, including the Bonus March and the March on Washington for Jobs and Freedom. Under such categories as "Parades," "Picketing," and specific names of protests, the vertical files at the Washingtoniana Division, Martin Luther King Library of the District of Columbia, provide both specific and general background.

The first chapter, on Coxey's Army, drew on a range of published and unpublished sources. My path was guided by Carlos A. Schwantes's authoritative and exhaustively researched *Coxey's Army: An American Odyssey* (Lincoln: University of Nebraska Press, 1985), which emphasizes the story of the various groups that assembled throughout the country and the importance of local causes for the protest. Donald L. McMurry's earlier account, *Coxey's Army: A Study of the Industrial Army Movement of 1894* (1929; Seattle: University of Washington, 1968), effectively puts the movement in the context of the economic depression. In addition, I read the accounts of the protest in the *Washington Post* and the *New York Times* as well as drawing on the extensive coverage in periodicals. The account by the historian of the demonstration is also essential; see Henry Vincent, *The Story of the Commonweal: Complete and Graphic Narrative of the Origin and Growth of the Movement* (Chicago: W. B. Conkey, 1894; reprint, New York: Arno Press, 1969). Carl Browne's memoirs, *When Coxey's "Army" Marcht* [sic] *on Washington, 1894,* Wm. McDevitt, ed. (San Francisco, 1944), may not be completely reliable but it provides biographical and colorful details necessary for understanding his role in the protest. The response of Congress, the District government, and the Cleveland administration to the protest appears in newspapers and magazines, the *Congressional Record*, and in some scattered references in *The Papers of Grover Cleveland*, available on microfilm. To understand the political culture of this moment, I found useful Morton Keller, *Affairs of State: Public Life in Late Nineteenth Century America* (Cambridge, Mass.: Harvard University Press, 1977); Richard L. McCormick, *The Party Period and Public Policy: American Politics from the Age of Jackson to the Progressive Era* (New York: Oxford University Press, 1986); and Michael E. McGerr, *The Decline of Popular Politics: The American North, 1865–1928* (New York: Oxford University Press, 1986). On the Populist movement, which influenced the leaders and supporters of the protest, see the succinct overview of the movement and its significance by Robert C. McMath Jr., *American Populism: A Social History, 1877–1898* (New York: Hill and Wang, 1993).

The Woman's Suffrage Procession and Pageant, the focus of chapter 2, has both more organized and more plentiful sources than exist for the march by Coxey's Army. I was able to draw on Sidney Bland's article, "New Life in an Old Movement: Alice Paul and the Great Suffrage Parade of 1913 in Washington, D.C.," *Records of the Columbian Historical Society* 48 (1971–72), 657–78, and the chapter "Pageant and Politics," in Christine Lunardini's *From Equal Suffrage to Equal Rights: Alice Paul and the National Woman's Party, 1910–1928* (New York: New York University Press, 1986). Nevertheless, most of my interpretation developed from probing the collections at the Library of Congress of the records of the National Woman's Party and the National American Woman Suffrage Association. Other information is found in the report on the parade by the Senate Committee on the District of Columbia: *Senate Report 53 Suffrage Parade*, 63rd Cong., 1st sess. (1913). In addition, some memoirs and oral histories discuss the parade; particularly useful are Inez Haynes Irwin, *The Story of the Woman's Party* (New York: Harcourt, Brace, 1921); the interview with Alice Paul by Robert S. Gallagher, "I was arrested, of course," *American Heritage* 25 (February 1974), 16–24, 92–94; and the longer oral history in Alice Paul, *Conversations with Alice Paul: Woman Suffrage and the Equal Rights Amendment*, interview by Amelia R. Fry (Berkeley: University of California, Berkeley, 1976). In addition to the books by Michael E. McGerr and Richard L. McCormick mentioned above, the political culture of this moment is well described by Alan Dawley, *Struggles for Justice: Social Responsibility and the Liberal State* (Cambridge, Mass.: Harvard University Press, 1991). On the woman suffrage movement during this period, besides Christine Lunardini, see Linda G. Ford, *Iron-Jawed Angels: The Suffrage Militancy of the National Woman's Party, 1912–1920* (Lanham, Md.: University Press of America, 1991); Ellen DuBois, "Marching toward Power: Woman Suffrage Parades, 1910–1915," in *True Stories from the American Past*, ed. William Graebner (New York: McGraw-Hill, 1993), 88–106, and her *Harriot Stanton Blatch and the Winning of Woman Suffrage* (New Haven, Conn.: Yale University Press, 1997); Sara Hunter Graham, *Woman Suffrage and the New Democracy* (New Haven, Conn.: Yale University Press, 1996); and Rosalyn Terborg-Penn, *African American Women in the Struggle for the Vote, 1850–1920* (Bloomington: Indiana University Press, 1998).

The sources on the Bonus March, the focus of chapter 3, are extremely rich.

I developed my own approach after reviewing the two essential histories of the protest, Roger Daniels, *The Bonus March: An Episode of the Great Depression* (Westport, Conn.: Greenwood, 1971), and Donald J. Lisio, *The President and Protest: Hoover, Conspiracy and the Bonus Riot* (Columbia: University of Missouri Press, 1974). (Lisio updated this book in *The President and Protest: Hoover, MacArthur, and the Bonus Riot* [New York: Fordham University Press, 1994]; however, I relied on the earlier volume.) Besides stories in newspapers and periodicals, I also relied on the account by march leader William Waters as told to William C. White, *B.E.F.: The Whole Story of the Bonus Army* (New York: John Day Company, 1933). In addition to the numerous reports included in both the records of the District of Columbia and the Military Intelligence Division at the National Archives, Record Group 94, Office of the Adjutant General, Central Files, 1926–1939 includes numerous files on the Bonus controversy. Clearly, dramatic changes took place in American life and politics during the early 1930s. My view of the moment surrounding the Bonus Army was shaped by Alan Brinkley, *Voices of Protest: Huey Long, Father Coughlin, and the Great Depression* (New York: Alfred A. Knopf, 1982); Barry Karl, *The Uneasy State: The United States from 1915 to 1945* (Chicago: University of Chicago Press, 1983); Lawrence Levine, "American Culture and the Great Depression," in *The Unpredictable Past: Explorations in American Cultural History* (New York: Oxford University Press, 1993); and Robert McElvaine, *The Great Depression: America, 1929–1941* (New York: Times Books, 1993). Both Daniels and Lisio provide essential information on the treatment of veterans; also useful are Theda Skocpol, *Protecting Soldiers and Mothers: The Political Origins of Social Policy in the United States* (Cambridge, Mass.: Harvard University Press, 1992), and William Pencak, *For God and Country: The American Legion, 1919–1941* (Boston: Northeastern University Press, 1989).

The Negro March on Washington (chapter 4) is the least well known of the five demonstrations I studied. While brief accounts of the planning and cancellation of the march occur in histories of the civil rights movement, the proposed protest lacks the kind of in-depth review available for the other marches. Herbert Garfinkel provides an overview of the impetus for the march in *When Negroes March: The March on Washington Movement in the Organizational Politics for FEPC* (Glencoe, Ill.: Free Press, 1959), but he is more interested in the later March on Washington Movement rather than the Negro March itself. More useful are the accounts in Paula F. Pfeffer, *A. Philip Randolph, Pioneer of the Civil Rights Movement* (Baton Rouge: Louisiana State University Press, 1990), and John H. Bracey Jr. and August Meier, "Allies or Adversaries? The NAACP, A. Philip Randolph and the 1941 March on Washington," *Georgia Historical Quarterly* 75 (Spring 1991), 1–17. The planning of the march and the response of the Roosevelt administration can be traced in the records of the National Association for the Advancement of Colored People and the National Urban League, as well as the papers of A. Philip Randolph, all available in the Manuscript Division of the Library of Congress. The papers of Eugene Davidson and oral histories of some participants are available at the Moorland-Spingarn Research Center at Howard University. Also essential is the coverage given the march in various black newspapers; I reviewed the *Pittsburgh Courier*, the *Bal-*

timore Afro-American, and the *Chicago Defender.* To understand the political tensions raised by the demonstrations, I found essential Daniel Kryder, "The American State and the Management of Race Conflict in the Workplace and in the Army, 1941–1945," *Polity* 26 (Summer 1994), 602–34, and Doris Kearns Goodwin, *No Ordinary Time: Franklin and Eleanor Roosevelt: The Home Front in World War II* (New York: Simon and Schuster, 1994). For specific background on African Americans, I relied on Harvard Sitkoff, *A New Deal for Blacks: The Emergence of Civil Rights as a National Issue, vol. I, The Depression Decade* (New York: Oxford University Press, 1978), and Nancy Weiss, *Farewell to the Party of Lincoln: Black Politics in the Age of FDR* (Princeton, N.J.: Princeton University Press, 1983).

The sources on the March on Washington for Jobs and Freedom (chapter 5) are extensive. A comprehensive but somewhat incoherent overview is provided by Thomas Gentile, *March on Washington: August 28, 1963* (Washington, D.C.: New Day Publications, 1983). This account needs to be supplemented by the briefer but better researched versions in David Garrow, *Bearing the Cross: Martin Luther King, Jr., and the Southern Christian Leadership Conference* (New York: Vintage Books, 1986), and Taylor Branch, *Parting the Waters: America in the King Years, 1954–63* (New York: Simon and Schuster, 1988). The papers of A. Philip Randolph contain some references to the 1963 march; much more useful are those of Bayard Rustin, also available at the Library of Congress. Extremely valuable for tracing the decision to hold the march are the FBI files on Martin Luther King Jr.; they are available in two microfilm collections edited by David Garrow, *The Martin Luther King, Jr., FBI File* (Frederick, Md.: University Publications of America, 1984), and *The Martin Luther King, Jr., FBI File, Part II: The King-Levison File* (Frederick, Md.: University Publications of America, 1987). There are also useful records in the Presidential Office Files as well as the papers of Burke Marshall and Charles Horsky at the John F. Kennedy Library. The Motion Picture, Broadcasting and Recorded Sound Division of the Library of Congress has film of the live coverage of the march by CBS as well as the shorter reports by ABC. To understand changes in American politics between 1945 and 1963, I found comprehensive Michael Barone's *Our Country: The Shaping of America from Roosevelt to Reagan* (New York: Free Press, 1990). Also suggestive were a number of essays in the collection edited by Steve Fraser and Gary Gerstle, *The Rise and Fall of the New Deal Order, 1930–1980* (Princeton, N.J.: Princeton University Press, 1989). The literature on the civil rights movement is voluminous; Garrow's and Branch's studies are based on the best research but can be usefully supplemented with Charles M. Payne, *I've Got the Light of Freedom: The Organizing Tradition and the Mississippi Freedom Struggle* (Berkeley: University of California Press, 1995), to see the dynamics outside of the purview of more well known organizers. Carl M. Brauer, *John F. Kennedy and the Second Reconstruction* (New York: Columbia University Press, 1977), is useful for Kennedy's actions and inactions.

The studies of the anti–Vietnam War movement (chapter 6) inevitably contain some mention of the Spring Offensive, mostly as a symbol of the divisiveness of the movement by the early 1970s. The most comprehensive and balanced account is now Tom Wells, *The War Within: America's Battle over Vietnam* (Berkeley:

University of California Press, 1994). Of the three sponsoring organizations, the Vietnam Veterans against the War has received the most scholarly attention; see Richard Moser, *The New Winter Soldier: GI and Veteran Dissent during the Vietnam Era* (New Brunswick, N.J.: Rutgers University Press, 1995); Richard Stacewicz, *Winter Soldiers: An Oral History of the Vietnam Veterans against the War* (New York: Twayne Publishers, 1997). Fred Haltstead's *Out Now! A Participant's Account of the American Movement against the Vietnam War* (New York: Monad Press, 1978) can serve as informal account of the faction that ended up as the National Peace Action Coalition. Because I wanted to look at the series of demonstrations more in terms of how they reflected the debates surrounding marches on Washington rather than the debates within the movement, I depended less on these accounts than on the archival sources. The Records of the Vietnam Veterans against the War are in the Social Action Collection, State Historical Society of Wisconsin. The State Historical Society of Wisconsin has released on microfilm the records of the National Peace Action Coalition. Those of the People's Coalition for Peace and Justice (DG-84) are at the Swarthmore College Peace Collection. Both the Wisconsin and Swarthmore libraries also have smaller collections that contained some useful information; these appear in the notes. For the response of authorities to this protest, there is much information available in the Nixon Presidential Materials at the National Archives. Two further collections at the District of Columbia Archives are particularly useful: the records of the Office of Emergency Preparedness and the Metropolitan Police Department's Mayday Reports. In addition, thanks to the help of Thaddeus McCory, I was able to look at records from the National Capital Division of the National Park Service, stored at the Washington National Records Center. On the broader context of the period, Wells's book on the anti-war movement provides essential details, as does Todd Gitlin's *The Whole World Is Watching: Mass Media in the Making and Unmaking of the New Left* (Berkeley: University of California Press, 1980). James T. Patterson captures the mixture of hopes and disappointments bedeviling the country in 1971 in *Grand Expectations: The United States, 1945–1974* (New York: Oxford University Press, 1996).

For the study of marches on Washington since the 1970s (Epilogue), I relied on my own observations, the reading of newspapers and publications, and some scholarly studies. Barbara Epstein's *Political Protest and Cultural Revolution: Nonviolent Direct Action in the 1970s and 1980s* (Berkeley: University of California Press, 1991) analyzes the return to local, community-based protests. My final observation is that the paucity of in-depth studies of individual protests during this period may indicate just how familiar a part of American politics such protests have become.

ACKNOWLEDGMENTS

In the largest sense, I owe this project to my connections to the city of Washington. I first lived there in the home of my great-grandmother, Lucy Lombardi Barber. With my father, I explored the city with a child's wonder. I returned as an adult and relearned the city, its public spaces, and its research halls. And since then, though living far away, I have often felt as though I was present in the city as I wrote.

This book had its more explicit beginnings while I was a graduate student in the Department of History at Brown University. A student, whose name I've now forgotten, wrote a paper on the March on Washington for Jobs and Freedom that pricked my latent interest in the tactic. As I shaped that interest into a dissertation topic, I had the support of three generous professors. Mari Jo Buhle read overly long chapters and provided astute suggestions. John L. Thomas was my mentor in teaching and writing. Finally, as the director of the dissertation, James T. Patterson allowed me the freedom to define the project as I wished, as well as giving needed criticism and essential support. In subsequent years, his comments on revisions and papers helped me imagine this book as something akin to his own accessible and insightful political histories.

I was the recipient of much kindness and guidance from librarians and archivists across the country. In Washington, the knowledgeable staff of the Manuscript, Motion Picture, and Prints and Photograph Divisions of the Library of Congress were among the first to have to deal with my wide-ranging requests. Numerous people at the National Archives, both in the original building and in the new College Park facility, helped me negotiate those rich collections. Roxanna Dean and other members of the staff at the Washingtoniana Room of the District of Columbia Public Library provided helpful hints and ready access to useful materials. Dorothy Provine, the archivist at the poorly funded District of Columbia Archives, helped me as I gathered key materials from their collections. In addition, with the extraordinary help of Thaddeus McCory of the National

Capital Division of the National Park Service, I was able to look at key records stored at the Washington National Records Center when it appeared that bureaucratic snafus might prevent my access. Esme Bhan and Avril Madison guided me to various resources in the Manuscript and Oral History Collection at the Moorland-Spingarn Research Center at Howard University. Joellen ElBashir, the present curator, granted me permission to quote and cite from oral history transcripts.

Further afield, I benefited from the help of the efficient staff at the Swarthmore College Peace Collection and the State Historical Society of Wisconsin. A trip to the special collections of the University of California, Los Angeles, allowed me to examine Pelham Glassford's personal papers. At the Rockefeller Library of Brown University and the Shields Library of the University of California, Davis, the staffs of the Interlibrary Loan Offices handled numerous requests with efficiency and kindness. Jane Kimball generously shared her expertise in navigating the University of California library system.

Conversations with several experts also informed this project. Scott Sandage, who also explored many of these same archives as part of his research on political protests at the Lincoln Memorial, generously shared his materials and ideas. I also want to thank Wilma Waters of Wenatchee, Washington, who spent a long morning with me sharing memories of the Bonus March, led by her late husband, Walter Waters. Wilfred Woods and Joan Peterson made this meeting possible and I owe them my gratitude. I also benefited from the insights of Sandra Ally, public relations officer for the National Capital Park Region; Detective Kenny Green and Sergeant Joseph Cox, U.S. Park Police; Gary Scott, chief historian, National Capital Park Region; and Randolph Myers, attorney-advisor, National Capital Parks, Office of the Solicitor, Department of the Interior.

A number of audiences and readers have shared their reactions to the results of this writing and research. The names of the different conferences are less important than the people who accompanied me on panels or made astute comments. In particular, I'd like to thank Jane Levey and Kathryn Smith, who welcomed me into the D.C. History Roundtable. Sharing ideas with my co-panelists, David Witwer, Padraic Kennedy, Ari Kelman, John Fairfield, Mary Dudziak, Nicholas Cull, Lary May, and Belinda Davis, was extremely helpful. Commentators and organizers, including Mary Ryan, Ron Walters, Roger Lane, Andreas Daum, and Christof Mauch, were uniformly supportive. In each place, the comments and discussions were constructive and inspirational, reflecting the best of scholarly interchange. In addition, readers for the University of California Press, including an anonymous reader, Mary Dudziak, and Joyce Appleby, made helpful comments on the entire manuscript.

I am also indebted to several institutional sources for the financial support that made completion of this project possible. Since 1994, as a Truman Scholar, I have benefited immensely from the support of the Harry S. Truman Foundation, which funded portions of my undergraduate and graduate education. Brown University's Department of History both arranged for teaching assistantships and provided funds to travel to conferences. I am also thankful for the Roland G. Richardson Fellowship from the Graduate School of Brown University, which allowed me to continue my research in Washington. As I completed the dissertation, my life was immeasurably improved by two fellowships. A dissertation fellowship from the National Endowment for the Humanities (FD-21920–94) allowed me to concentrate on the project from 1994 to 1995. During the same period, the John Nicholas Brown Center for the Study of American Civilization in Providence provided me with a beautiful office and contact with a wonderful group of scholars and staff members.

The dissertation became a book while I was an assistant professor in the Department of History at the University of California, Davis. Financial support from the Academic Senate, the Davis Humanities Institute, the Institute for Governmental Affairs, the UC-Davis Washington Center, the Dean's Office, and the Provost's Office was critical. This support funded research trips and, most importantly, research assistance. The help of the following UC, Davis, undergraduates was essential: Christian Farr, Erin Nantell, Laurel Welch, Sean MacNeil, Amy Whitlatch, and Heather Heckler. Graduate students in the history department provided interpretive help and performed exceptionally tedious tasks; thanks to Andrew Wood, Samantha Yates, Tobias Green, Jill Hough, and especially George Jarrett. My colleagues at the California State Archives made the final stages of this project stress free.

A wide community of colleagues talked about, read, and commented on my work. They forced me to consider the broader implications of the stories I had encountered in my research and supported me when I did not think I could complete this work. My fellow graduate students in the history department at Brown provided me with models of intellectual achievement. In particular, I want to thank the following people for discussing my ideas and commenting on drafts: Gabrielle Friedman, Ari Kelman, Chris Mauriello, Lyde Sizer, David Witwer, and Bernard Yamron. No sentence can fully express my appreciation for what I called the "diss group." This group of Brown University graduate students read my rough drafts and shared their own awe-inspiring scholarship. The membership varied over the years, and I thank all the women who participated, especially Gail Bederman, Ruth Feldstein, Jane Gerhard, Melani McAllister, Donna Penn, Uta Poiger, and Jessica Shubow.

Other friendships also combined emotional support and challenging intellectual exchange. Beginning in 1994 and continuing to a phone conversation just a few minutes ago, John W. Sweet read and commented on every piece of this book. Despite living on the opposite coast and studying a different period of American history, he made this book better than it would have been without his help. Marcia Shia listened to my stories and housed me in the District of Columbia. At the University of California, Davis, my colleague and friend Lorena Oropeza read much of the manuscript and helped during some of the most difficult periods of its writing. Other members of the department also read pieces of the manuscript; in particular I want to thank the late Roland Marchand, Ruth Rosen, and Alan Taylor. Because of a chance phone call, Laura Santigian became my writing partner in 1999, and stunned me with her dedication and insights. Monica McCormick, my editor at the University of California Press, has both shared great lunches and offered constant encouragement. Her dedication has been matched by that of other members of the Press's staff, especially Sue Carter and Suzanne Knott.

As a single person without children who transplanted herself to the West Coast in the midst of this project, I turned to groups and friends for support. I thank the staff and friends of the McClatchy Library in Sacramento, Sacramento's Women's Mt. Bike Group, and the Sierra 2 Dogixiliary for keeping me connected to other pursuits. For cheering me on, I am grateful to Emily Albu, Misha Anthony, Patty Aune, Liz Belyea, Tim Bustos, Joan Cadden, Kim Carr, Steve Deyle, Erin Galvez, Jolene Hood, Jane Kimball, George Knott, Cathy Kudlick, Susan Mann, Ted Margadant, Pam Martell, Chris and Kirsten Reberg-Horton, Paul Turner, Krystyna Von Henneberg, and Clarence Walker.

Finally, I can honestly say that without my family this book would not have happened. My whole extended family remained remarkably interested, even as they kept wondering when it would be done. For housing, vacations, parking spaces, and other sundries, I turned to my aunt Lucy Stroock, my great-aunt Kristi Hay, my great-uncles Jeff Barber and Mervyn Holland, and my second cousins, Lucy Lapidus, Charlie Hay, and Joanne Crerand. My grandfather, William L. Holland, himself a scholar, read and admired. My stepfather, Robert Winne, provided advice and books. My stepmother, Valerie Lynch, finished her own dissertation as I began my own, and always assured me the book would be done. My brother, Jon Barber, helped me mark accomplishments by jumping in icy rivers, biking up Mt. Tam, and walking on California beaches.

My parents' support for my work has been unflinching. As a historical editor, my mother, Patricia G. Holland, introduced me to the study of history when I was a child; as an active member of the feminist movement, she taught me about politics and took me to demonstrations; as a mother, she provided me with both financial and emotional support. During one desperate moment, she spent her vacation reading files at the National Archives with me. Besides taking me to anti–Vietnam war protests in Washington, my father, Putnam Barber, read every word of this book, sometimes three or four times. He brought to the project his training as a sociologist, his enthusiasm for history, and his ear for good writing. He helped me see and say what was both interesting and needed. For a long, backbreaking week in December 2000, he figured out such important matters as where the semicolons went in the endnotes. I dedicate this work to both of them in appreciation and with the earnest hope that they will continue to take such an active role in my life.

INDEX

Text: 10/13 Sabon
Display: Sabon, Scala Sans
Compositor: Binghamton Valley Composition, LLC
Printer: Malloy Lithographing, Inc.